YOUR GUIDE TO THE BEST SEATS AT THE BEST PRICES:

SEATS

150 SEATING PLANS
to New York Metro Area Theatres, Concert Halls, & Sport Stadiums

WITH RESTAURANT COUPONS
valued up to $200

SANDY MILLMAN

Member, New York City Convention and Visitors Bureau

An Applause Original

SEATS:
Your Guide to the Best Seats at the Best Prices

By Sandy Millman

Library of Congress Cataloging-In-Publication Data
Millman, Sandy
Seats : the insider's guide to the performing arts and sports in New York / by Sandy Millman
p. cm.
Includes index.

ISBN 1-55783-301-X (pbk.)
1. Theaters--New York (State)--New York--Charts, diagrams, etc. 2.Sports facilities--New York (State)--New York--Charts, diagrams, etc. I. Title
.
PN227.N5M46 1997
792'.097471--dc21 97-28481
CIP

British Library Catalogue in Publication Data
A catalogue record for this book is available from the British Library

APPLAUSE BOOKS

211 West 71st Street
New York, NY 10023
Phone (212) 496-7511
Fax: (212) 721-2856

HOW TO USE SEATS

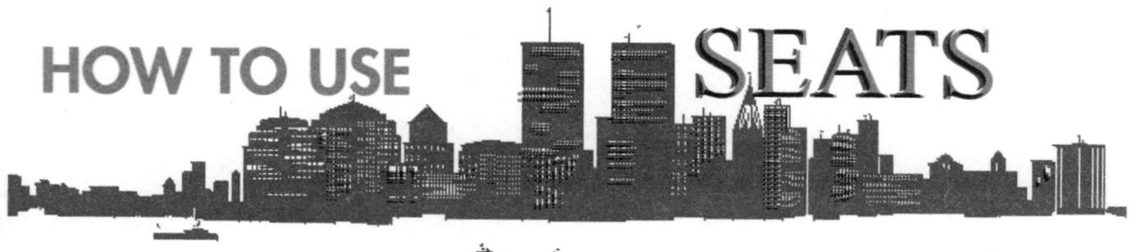

Seats is dedicated to keeping theatre aficionados up-to-date on all theatre changes and improvements. It has been created to take the guess work out of ordering tickets on the phone or by mail to spare you from any unpleasant surprises once you find your seat at a performance.

SEATS was formulated to teach you the inside secrets favored by Savvy New Yorkers when they order theatre seats, attend sporting events at area stadiums and order concert hall tickets.

SEATS has three main goals:

1. To let you know exactly what seats you are paying for.

2. To show you the various price breaks between rows. You save money by ordering your seats in rows just behind, or next to, the highest price seats and enjoy virtually the same view.

3. To give you the same hot tips to saving money on a night out in New York that veteran bargain hunters rely on for their recreation.

When ordering tickets by phone, have your copy of SEATS opened to the page of the theater offering the production you want. Based on your budget and the layout of the theatre, strategically choose the best seats in the house for you. Confirm that the prices haven't changed and that your seats are within the price range you want.

Seat configurations may change slightly from show to show. These changes are generally confined to the orchestra if the stage extends out into the audience; two more rows might be added if the stage contracts. Occasionally the last row in the orchestra may be taken up with sound equipment.

SEATS helps you plan your visit to the theatre by giving you detailed subway and bus directions to the theatres, convenient parking garages, and taxi directions. We also recommend nearby restaurants.

Wheelchair locations are shown where they exist as well as theatres with assisted listening devices.

Telecharge has a hotline especially for wheelchair information, (212) 239-6200. For the hearing impaired, Sound Associates will reserve a device at all Broadway theaters, (212) 582-7678.

Detailed driving directions are given on each page for out-of-town theatres. These theatres are within an easy drive from New York and regularly advertise their productions in the various metropolitan newspapers. These venues have proven popular with New Yorkers since they offer a day-trip or a weekend out of the city for sightseeing, dining and a show. Visitors to New York have also begun to learn about this "secret theatre" and are now taking advantage of the relatively low prices and the fringe benefits of " off, off, off, off Broadway."

Coupons at the rear of SEATS for restaurant savings and other discounts offer a further bonus to the reader. The first time you use any of the coupons for three or more people you will have earned back your entire purchase price of this book. Since space is limited we included only those restaurants which we considered "fun" and distinctive. Savings of $200 or more are possible.

SEATS has over three times as many seating plans as any other such diredtory ever. But there are still a few holdouts, a handful of theatres who ignored our repeated pleas for information. We trust you'll see them in our next edition.

THE SAVVY NEW YORKER'S GUIDE TO TICKET BARGAINS

TKTS

The best-known discount in town is the famous TKTS booths operated by the Theatre Development Fund. A New York tradition, TKTS has two locations in Manhattan. TKTS offers 25% and 50% discounts on same-day tickets to both Broadway and selected Off Broadway shows, music and dance events. The most famous is the booth located in the heart of Times Square at 47th Street and Broadway . Stand in the long lines here to save money for evening performances Monday through Saturday from 3 P.M. to 8 P.M. . Matinee tickets are sold on Wednesday and Saturday from 10 A.M. to 2 P.M. Sunday tickets are sold from noon to closing. If your heart's not set on any particular show, save yourself some time and get there around 6:30 P.M. or 7 P.M. when the line is usually very short and the wait is minimal. Most nights you're certain to find a few shows of merit even at the last moment.

Downtowners are served by the Lower Manhattan TKTS Center at 2 World Trade Center on the mezzanine level. This location is open Monday through Friday from 11 A.M. to 5:30 P.M. and on Saturdays from 11 A.M. to 3:30 P.M. You can buy matinee tickets the day before the performance at this location only.

Reduced price tickets are available from TKTS only for shows for that day's performances. The Theatre Development Fund has negotiated with theatre owners and producers to electronically consign unsold tickets to the two TKTS booths. There is no advance sale and *credit cards are not accepted.* Payment is by cash only. You naturally can't expect to find a hit show with great seats up there on the board the day you happen to be there. Prevent heartbreak by preparing a second, third and fourth choice. The TKTS booth is a wonderful resource if you're prepared to be flexible. There are always some good shows at extraordinary prices.

TDF

The Theatre Development Fund (TDF) is itself an excellent source of heavily discounted tickets if you qualify for membership. Ninety thousand members regularly receive offers in the mail for discounted tickets to theatre, dance and musical events. Membership is limited to students, teachers, retirees, union members, armed forces members, clergy and performing arts professionals.

Founded in 1968 to encourage the production of new plays and musicals, TDF enables attendance by those who would not ordinarily be able to afford tickets. It also encourages new productions of plays and musicals by committing to purchase from 500 to 10,000 tickets.

To receive an application for membership, send a self-addressed stamped envelope to TDF Applications, 1501 Broadway, N.Y. N.Y. 10036. There is a $14 annual fee.

TDF VOUCHERS

Here is another area in which TDF shines. Recognizing that the numbers of small dance and music groups provide so much of the excitement and uniqueness that keeps New York the artistic capital of the nation, the organization instituted its *Voucher System.*

TDF offers members packs of five vouchers which are valid for six months and may be used as tickets to dozens of events participating in the program. The vouchers insure attendance at the tiniest theatres helping to keep the theatre company solvent. At the same time, patrons are enticed into remarkable theatres they might normally never visit.

TDF has set up NYC/ONSTAGE, a telephone service operated from any touch tone phone offering a weekly menu of theatre, dance, and musical events. The number is (212) 768-1818. If you're on the Internet visit **http://www.tdf.org.**

THE HIT SHOW CLUB

The Hit Show Club offers coupons by mail to members. Join the club free by sending a self-addressed stamped envelope to the club at 630 Ninth Avenue, New York, N.Y. 10036. You'll receive a regular deluge of envelopes containing packs of tickets for the latest hit show being promoted.

Hit Show Club tickets are typically priced $49 for $75 seats and $39 for $65 seats.
To find out which shows they are discounting, call their 24-hour-line at (212) 581-4211.

The Hit Show Club also offers its immensely popular *"two-fers"*. These discount coupons are placed in thousands of shops and tourist locations throughout Manhattan where they can be easily picked up free. They are also available at the New York Tourist and Convention Bureau.

The coupons offer discounts of approximately 40% off regular box-office prices. They may be redeemed at the theatre box-office at least one hour before the performance to purchase a pair of available seats. The coupons can also be mailed to the theatre with payment and a note giving several alternative dates. You may want to call (212) 307-4100 and order your tickets by phone, referring to the code number on the "two-fer". There's a slight surcharge for this service but by using SEATS you can select the exact location you want and save more money by buying seats in the row directly behind the premium rows. The view is the same. SEATS is color-coded to show you where the prices break!

AUDIENCE EXTRAS
Top Shows for $3.00 A Pop

This is a superb ticket discount source known only to *really, really* Savvy New Yorkers. This organization fiercely avoids any publicity, does no advertising and is known through word-of-mouth only. Sort of the old Prohibition Era "Joe sent Me". Clive Barnes, in Manhattan Living, writes "*Audience Extras is the best...*" Audience Extras helps producers "paper" a house during previews while a production is trying to find its audience and get established. Word of mouth from Audience Extra members has helped shows attract thousands of bona fide ticket buyers who have made the critical difference in the solvency of a show.

The organization's brochure is loaded with caveats and warnings to keep the source of member tickets top secret: "Talk about how wonderful your AE membership is among friends. Never, never to strangers at the theatre. Don't let the cat out of the bag."

To apply for membership, call Member Services at (212) 989-9550 any Tuesday through Saturday from 10:30 A.M. to 5:30 P.M. Eastern time.

Membership costs $85 annually and they require an additional $45 reserve fund to cover their $3.00 ticket charge. If you qualify, you'll receive a membership card and a PIN number. To find out what they have available, call the 24-hour phone number they will reveal to you. Enter your member number and your PIN number and listen to the list of shows available. Making a reservation is pretty straightforward. Call the AE office. Then at the SPECIFIED time, show up at the box office and pick up your tickets. Don't forget to bring your membership card along.

WARNING. Under no conditions, ask the box office for your tickets in anything other than a soft whisper. The rules & regs read: "Have your membership card out and available for the box office person to see before approaching the box office. **Never, Never, Never say the words 'Audience Extras'** at the theatre or at the box office."

AE asks that you record your critique of each show by sending back a form that may help producers evaluate their work in its early stages of production and gives AE a sense of what sort of productions are popular with its members.

Incidentally, AE offers a small rebate to students and professionals in the entertainment industry after the first year.

HIGH 5

This little known organization brings more than 500 programs in the theatre, arts, music and museums to New York City high school students. Students from around the world are invited to participate. The offerings are so varied that they include plays in Spanish and Mandarin Chinese. The selections include Great Performances at Lincoln Center and Carnegie Hall, Jazz at Lincoln Center and music at the Japan Society as well as Broadway shows .

High School students can see the best in art, music, theatre, dance, opera and film in New York for only $5 a ticket Friday through Sunday. Students can bring a friend, family member, or teacher for $5 for two tickets on Monday through Thursday.

To participate, obtain a catalog from High 5 Tickets to the Arts, 1790 Broadway, 16th Floor, New York, N.Y. 10019. You can call them at (212) HI5-TKTS. (445-8587)

To buy tickets, select the shows you want from the catalog. Buy as early as possible, at least one day before the show. Bring money and proof of age to one of the Ticketmaster locations listed in the catalog. They are located conveniently throughout the five boroughs. Proof of age can be a high school ID, a transportation pass or anything that proves you are between 13 and 18. Be sure to ask for High 5 tickets. Arrive at the theatre or event at least one-half hour before the performance. Bring the High 5 ticket and proof of age to the box office.

Museum tickets can be purchased the same day as your museum visit and cost $5 for two tickets any day of the week. The tickets are good for one month and can be used any day.

You can reach High 5 by e-mail:
at *info@high5tix.com* or on the web at ***www.high5tix.com.***

PASSPORT TO BROADWAY

The Alliance of Resident Theatres/New York offers, on a seasonal basis, a tabloid called *Hot Seats.* The booklet lists more than 180 Off Broadway and Off-Off Broadway theaters offering discounts of up to 50%. Adventurous theatregoers have an opportunity to sample dozens of tiny experimental theatres, Spanish-language houses and children's theatres as well as opera and dance.

The discounts are listed as coupons in the 24- page *Hot Seats* tabloid. It is available at information booths in Grand Central Terminal, Penn Station, Port Authority Bus Terminal, the New York Convention and Visitors Bureau, New York City area Chase Manhattan Bank Branches and the Delta Shuttle. To receive your copy, phone (800) 610-0713.

SCHOOL THEATRE TICKET PROGRAM

Here's another great theatre ticket discount program if you're affiliated with a school in any way. If you're a student, teacher, administrator, employee, or involved with any educational institution substantial discounts are available to you.

The plan, *School Theatre Ticket Program*, distributes discount coupons to every public, private, and parochial school, junior high, high school, college and university within a 125 mile range of New York City. The coupons, resembling giant tickets, are to be found in student centers and student activity offices. About a dozen shows are available at all times.

The program is run by producer Eric Krebs, a successful impressario with important plays often running at two theatres at one time. Mr. Krebs reported that *School Theatre Ticket Program* has been in continuous existence since 1958 and has serviced over 1000 Broadway and Off-Broadway shows with a distribution of over a half-million coupons.

The exchange coupons must be brought to the box office no later than one hour before the performance to be redeemed for one or two of the best available seats. *Miss Saigon* seats were available for a two month period at $45 for $75 seats and $30 for $50 seats. *Les Miserables* seats were available at $40 for $75 seats and $25 for $40 seats. Other shows were typically offered at $12 for all seats. For opera buffs, tickets to City Opera were priced at $38 for $75 seats with 4th ring row seats at $10. If ballet is your thing, *School Theatre Program* offers $57 seats for $40 with other prices running as low at $14.

There are 9000 locations offering the coupons throughout the New York metropolitan area. If you live outside of this area, FAX

(212) 575-4740 on a school's letterhead and ask for a packet of tickets to be sent to your school.

PLAYBILL ON-LINE

Playbill On-Line is considered the single largest theatre news, information and entertainment service in cyberspace. A division of Playbill, the on-line service offers ticket discounts through Playbill On-Line Theatre Club. Membership in the club entitles you to buy discount tickets to shows around the USA and Canada. The on-line listings are updated frequently and you are notified of updates by e-mail.

To join the club, its free, go to their website at:
on the worldwide web and select "Join Our Club". You will be brought to an information page. At the bottom of this page click on REGISTER FOR THE PLAYBILL ON-LINE THEATRE CLUB. When the form opens, fill it out carefully since it will reject any error and make you do the whole process over again. Once you've filled it out with your member name and secret password, click on SUBMIT. You'll receive an e-mail message welcoming you to the club.

You must use the member name and password in exactly the same case you selected whenever you want to access the "Members Only" area to order discount tickets.

THE *"OTHER"* THEATRES

Fantastic Off-Off Broadway Theatre at Minuscule Prices

Man does not live by bread alone, neither does New York theatre live on Broadway alone. Savvy New Yorkers know the financial and artistic values available in the "other" theatres...the small obscure houses which dot Manhattan from one end to the other presenting shows that could possibly make their way to a major Broadway theatre. Welcome to the world of Off-Off Broadway. From recent drama school graduates banding together to veteran radical companies such as The Living Theatre, these troupes inhabit lofts, tiny theaters and even retired synagogues and churches, where they present experimental theatre, modern dance, avant garde concerts and expertly crafted plays which, although they may offer superb entertainment, will never make it any further.

This is the world of the true theatre buff. Off-Off Broadway offers an opportunity to see a presentation either before it hits big time or one that may never be offered again.

Off-Off Broadway is a true New York experience and is generally priced so low that tourists on modest budgets can afford tickets every night of their vacation.

Many theatres offer alluring subscription packages guaranteeing seats to what may become hot tickets to individual shows. Among the many theatres which offer money-saving programs, be sure to check out Tony Randall's National Actors' Theatre, Roundabout Theatre which offers a number of different bargain schemes, the Manhattan Theatre Club, New Federal Theatre, Playwrights Horizon, Lincoln Center Theatre, BAM, the New Group and many many others.

The granddaddy of best deals in theaterdom, the Joseph Papp Public Theatre/ New York Shakespeare Festival offers superb Shakespeare in Central Park during the summers. Tickets, 2 per customer, are **FREE**.

For its summer productions of Shakespeare in Central Park. Tickets are picked up for that evening's performance starting at 1 P.M. at the Delacorte Theatre in Central Park, tickets can also be picked up between 1 P.M. and 3 P.M. at the Public Theatre, 425 Lafayette Street.

For those in the Boroughs, tickets are available at Brooklyn Borough Hall, Brooklyn Botanic Garden and BAM Majestic Theatre. In Staten Island, tickets can be obtained at Snug Harbor Cultural Center.

In Queens tickets can be gotten from the Flushing Council on Culture & The Arts at Town Hall, Jamaica Arts Center and the Flushing YMCA. Tickets are available in the Bronx at the New York Botanical Garden, South Bronx Community Action Theatre and the Pregones Theatre. Additional Manhattan locations include El Museo del Barrio, The Harlem Victoria V Theatre and Aaron Davis Hall.

For the Public's many other distinguished events at their home on Lafayette St, check out their QuikTix program. Available tickets are available at half price 30 minutes before curtain.

For complete information contact The Public Theatre, 425 Lafayette Street, N.Y. N.Y. 10003 , Administrative offices, (212) 539-8500, FAX (212) 539-8505, Box Office (212) 260-2400

There are a number of wonderful theatres within easy striking distance of Manhattan and well worth exploring. A short and incredibly beautiful train ride up the Hudson River, about 45 minutes from Grand Central Terminal, lies the quiet village of Tarrytown, the setting of Washington Irving's *Sleepy Hollow.* At nearby Elmsford, for the past 24 years, the Westchester Broadway Theatre has been offering award winning shows complete with excellent dinners at prices far below the cost of a show alone in Manhattan. The theatre bills itself as the longest running, 52 weeks-a-year equity theatre in the history of the state of New York. Like Broadway, Westchester has eight performances each week between Wednesday and Sunday with the run of the show varying.

On Monday and Tuesday nights, special performances of music, big bands, pop singers, operetta and comedy nights often fill the house. Ticket prices for dinner and a show range between $51 and $63 plus tax. Group discounts, children's discounts and senior discounts are available for selected performance.

Westchester also offers three-show subscriptions at important savings. A regular $51 dinner-show drops to $43.35 with a three show subscription at $135.15 plus tax. Similar reductions apply to other subscriptions.

The theatre is easily reached by Metro North from Grand Central Terminal to Tarrytown. The taxi ride costs $8. Driving is also quick from New York. For the scenic route, drive up the West Side Drive to Route 9 and cruise through the river cities into Tarrytown and then to Elmsford. It's accessible from the Taconic Parkway and from the Tappan Zee Bridge. The Cross Westchester will bring you from Long Island and Connecticut.

For complete details phone (914) 592-2222 or FAX (914) 592-6917. Groups call (800) 729-7469.

CONCERTS IN THE PARK

This is another opportunity to enjoy musical concerts at the right price, **FREE**. Every season, The New York Philharmonic presents popular, familiar classical music at various parks around the boroughs of New York. Sponsored by Time Warner in conjunction with the N.Y. City Parks Commission, the Philharmonic programs start around 8 P.M. and finish with fireworks.

The programs are excellent and offer an evening's entertainment at virtually no cost.

In Manhattan the evening is generally held in Central Park at the North Meadow; Brooklyn, at Prospect Park; Bronx, Van Cortlandt Park; In nearby Westchester County, the Westchester Community College; in Queens, Cunningham Park and In Long Island, Heckscher State Park.

Recent programs have included
Dvorak: *Scherzo Capriccioso*, Copeland: *Appalachian Spring*, Bernstein: *Symphonic Dances from West Side Story*; Gershwin; *An American in Paris.*

WHERE SAVVY NEW YORKERS FIND OUT WHAT'S GOING ON

Several publications list what is playing in the major and off-beat houses with current pricing.

New York Magazine offers an excellent weekly listing of Broadway and Off-Broadway shows in its *Theater* section in the rear of the magazine. The section separates Broadway *previews and openings*, Broadway *now playing* , Off-Broadway *previews and openings* and Off-Broadway *now playing.* Pricing is listed along with a compact review.

The Sunday *Arts & Leisure* section of the ***New York Times*** offers perhaps the most comprehensive picture of the current entertainment scene in the New York area. Buried in the show's advertising you can sometimes hit upon discounts especially for long running shows, previews and faltering shows, many of which represent excellent theatre at good value.

Ads for recent Broadway plays cut prices to $40 for Orchestra seats, $30 and for Front Mezzanine. Off Broadway shows have typically been offered upon occasion for as little as $30.

The ***Times*** *Theater Directory* is really a classified ad section paid for by producers. Many small groups can't afford the steep tariff making this ***Times*** listing less than exhaustive. But it's worth keeping your eye open for the occasional ticket bargain even here. A recent listing for CATS noted a special with all tickets half-price for selected dates. Some recent Broadway shows have offered $10 student tickets. Others will cut prices to $40, $30 & $20 if you bring the listing with you.

In Theater magazine, read by professionals and theatre aficionados, covers theatre in depth with well written articles and exposes. The publication offers an extensive listing of all area theatre broken down into Broadway, Broadway coming soon, Off-Broadway, Off-Off-Broadway and On Tour listings. It includes a brief review and offers price ranges. ***In Theater*** is available on news stands and by subscription for $78. Phone (212) 719-9777.

The ***New Yorker*** keeps its theatre information in the front of the magazine. *Goings on About Town* treats its listings differently from its competitors by listing Opening and Previews for all theatre in one group. It lists Opened Recently and then Long Runs. Each listing offers a thumb-nail review but no pricing. The theatre section is followed by highly detailed listings of everything that could possibly be considered Entertainment; Dance, Night Life, Art, Photography, Orchestras, Recitals and Books.

For intensive coverage of every entertainment venue in the metropolitan area, ***Time Out New York*** lists every theatrical offering in every basement and loft calling itself a theatre. Amidst reviews and theatre advertising, ***Time Out*** offers hundreds of listings for every budget with a brief synopsis of each show.

For professionals and true aficionados, the most comprehensive publication in the entire nation may be showman Richmond Shepard's ***Performing Arts Insider.*** It lists every show in every nook and cranny of New York but also tells you what will be coming to New York as far as one year ahead. The ***Insider*** began its life some decades ago under the able stewardship of Joan Marlowe and Betty Blake who published under the title, The Theatre Information Bulletin. Richmond Shepard has continued that tradition with complete information on theatre in Los Angeles, theatre across America, Road Tours, Tryouts, Rumors, and Productions in England and Canada. Shepard includes interesting readings, backer's audtions and workshops for projects in development

The publication offers all of its information in "detail" including a brief plot summary, the producer's name, the show's publicist and their phone numbers. It also supplies theatre phone numbers which are normally impossible to find.

If you plan to visit London, the listing "Productions in England" not only lists every show in town but gives you the box office phone number allowing you to order tickets on the phone before you leave on your trip.

All of these sterling features come at sterling price. $250 a year for bi-monthly subscriptions; $150 for the basic issue once a month. Subscriptions are available by calling: (212) 262-6588. (FAX 212-262-0099) E-mail: richmond@spacelab.net.

ACKNOWLEDGMENTS

Computer artists, unshakable researchers, persistent copy-editors and a very bright financial director worked for more than 30 months to pioneer the complex computer programs, coax information from sometime reticent theatre owners and producers, gather all the other information for each page and then rush through an 18-hour-day to put the book together and keep its cutting-edge sharp and current. But for the tenacity of its staff SEATS would have been virtually impossible to produce.

The financial package required to put together a team was the task I could entrust only to my wife, **Ellin Millman** who managed the task during quiet breaks at her business, Millman's T-Shirt Factory in Poughkeepsie, N.Y.

Tireless **Sharon Lutzi** is the research editor who cajoled, threatened and pleaded with stage managers, marketing directors, producers and theatre owners to supply her with basic information. Sharon was persistent and patient. Without Sharon, this book would never have been possible.

Computer artist **Nancy Hannigan** is another whiz on the computer, working in Corel 7, and patiently patching together individual theatre seats by the thousands. Nancy greeted every request with "No Problem" and proceeded to work out seating plans that are works of art. A perfectionist, Nancy created her own programs to insure that all pages were consistent in look. She is a real pro and unfailingly creative.

Computer artist **Roch Craford** is an electronic whiz. A brilliant problem solver, he quickly became an expert in this unique project as problems manifested themselves on a daily basis. An intellectual and a talented artist, Roch is quiet and calm which was a blessing during the tense moments when Roch nursed the team through crisis after crisis as they raced to meet deadlines.

Copy Editor **Arlene LaPadura** proof-read every word, every direction, every phone number; checked every seat in every seating plan to make sure the numbers are correct and there are no seats missing. Not any extra seats either!

Linda Beasley, assisted Sharon with pricing the seats. She worked with Telecharge and Ticketmaster sales reps to give her several numbers of theatre pricing plans with each phone call.

Thanks to the many Telecharge and Ticketmaster sales reps for their cooperation.

Many thanks to computer artist **David Jones**, a talented and creative computer whiz who pioneered the complicated programs within Corel 7 that were then expanded and refined by Roch and Nancy who learned from Dave's tragic experiences with the fledgling programs when his computer froze destroying two years, work in a flash.

A warm thank you to **Robert Butler**, Manhattan computer artist, who perfected new scanning procedures that allowed us to include and improve complex stadium seating plans.

Thanks go to young and bright **Jeremy Schwartz**, my computer consultant, for teaching me all the tricks necessary to get my computer running efficiently and then teaching me word processing programs so that the introductions to this book could be written. Jeremy became my consultant when he was 10-years-old; he's now starting college.

Unlimited thanks to my agent, the lady with the rhyming name, **Lindley Kirksey**, who presented my book proposal to a dozen publishers and received three strong indications of interest within two weeks. Lin did an intensive study of all of the catalogs of the interested publishers and recommended **Glenn Young's *Applause Books.***

A salute to **Jessica Hannigan**, our messenger, who saved me hours of driving.

This smooth working team made possible the impossible and produced a work never before attempted in any theatre directory.

YOUR GUIDE TO THE BEST SEATS AT THE BEST PRICES:

SEATS

150 SEATING PLANS
to New York Metro Area Theatres, Concert Halls, & Sport Stadiums

WITH RESTAURANT COUPONS
valued up to $200

AMBASSADOR THEATRE

219 West 49th Street, New York, NY 10019

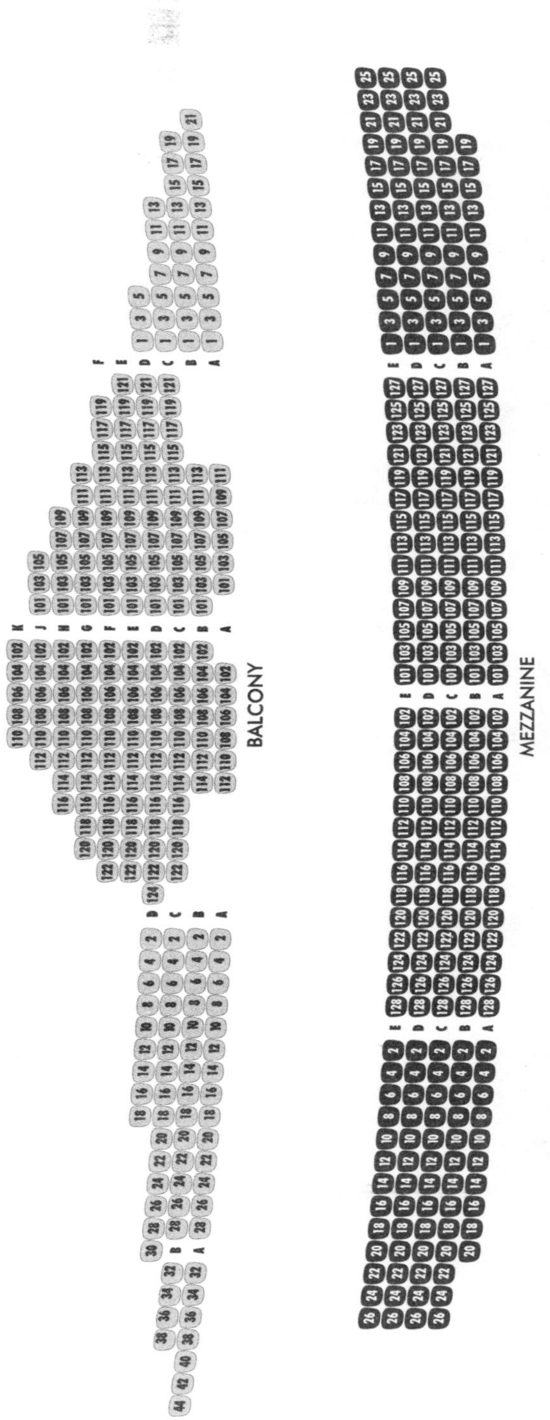

BALCONY

MEZZANINE

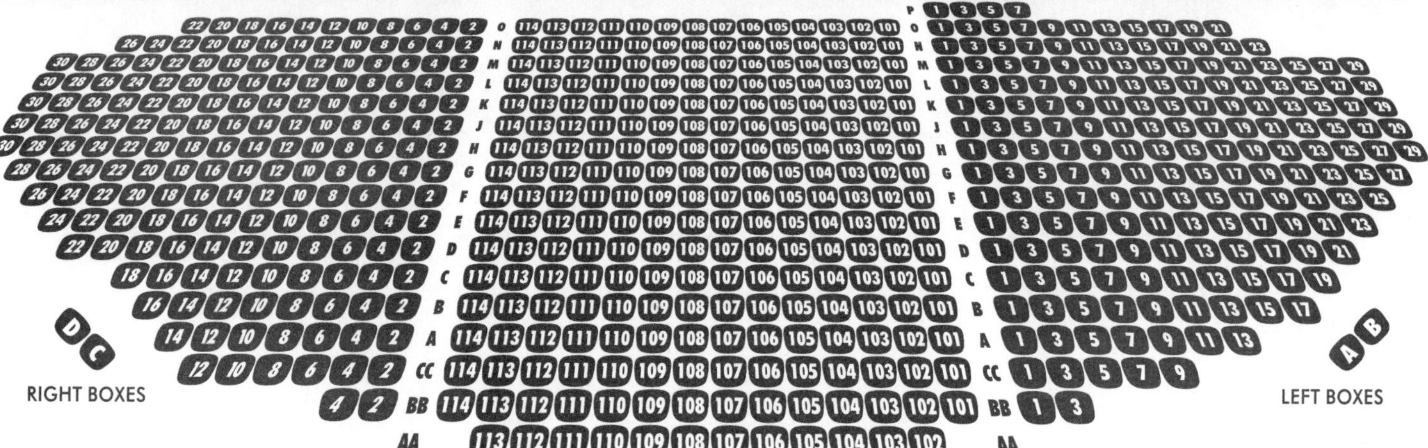

$70.00
$50.00

Mezzanine row A overhangs
Orchestra row H

Hearing devices available

STAGE

TELECHARGE (212) 239-6200

TAXI DIRECTIONS:
49th St.Westbound
(bet. Broadway & 8th Ave.)

PARKING
Edison Park Fast, 757 7th Ave.
(bet. 49th & 50th Sts.)
GMC, 225W 49th St.
(bet. Broadway & 8th Ave.)
BUS
M6,M7,M10,M27,M50,M104
SUBWAYS
1,9 to 50th St. & Broadway
C,E to 50th St. & 8th Ave.
N,R to 49th St.
B,D,F,Q to 47th-50th Sts.
& 6th Ave. Rockefeller Center

Nearby restaurants rated by
SEATS

B. SMITH'S, 771 8th Ave. at 47th St. 247-2222
SHAAN, 57 W. 48th St. 977-8400
LA PRIMAVERA, 234 W. 48th St. 586-2797
MESKEREM II, 682 11th Ave. at 49th St. 541-7858
CIRO, 813 8th Ave. at 49th St. 307-5484

BELASCO THEATRE

111 West 44th Street, New York, NY 10036

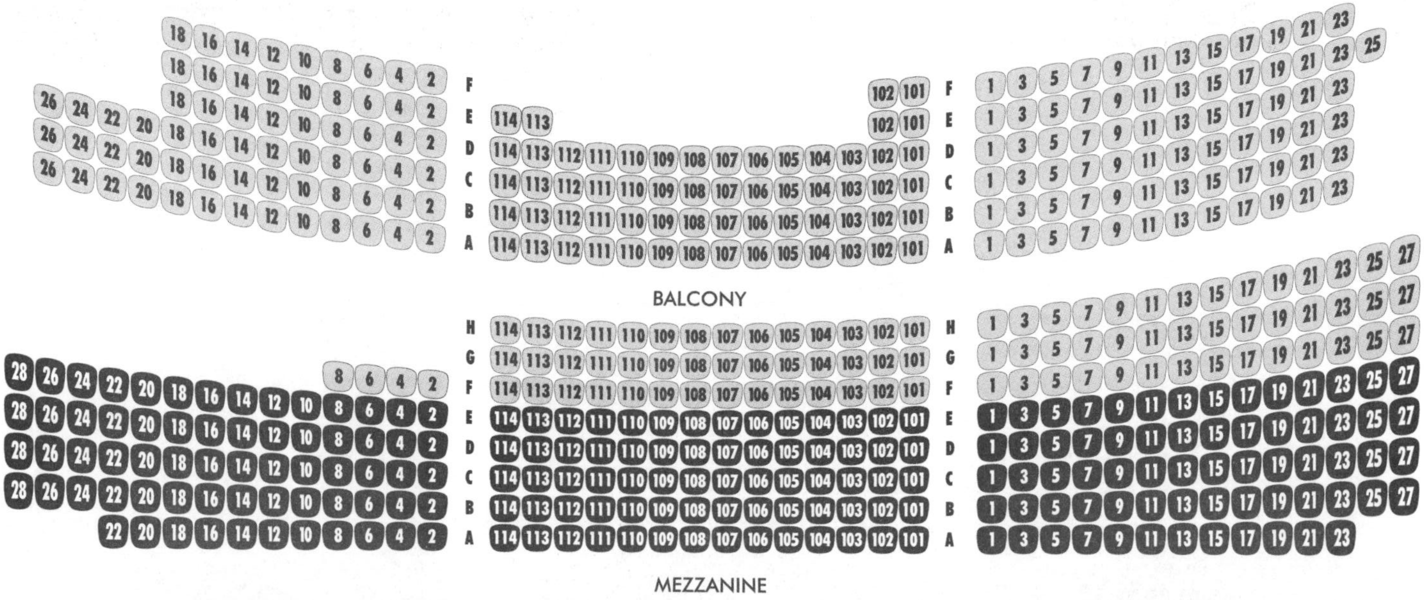

BALCONY

MEZZANINE

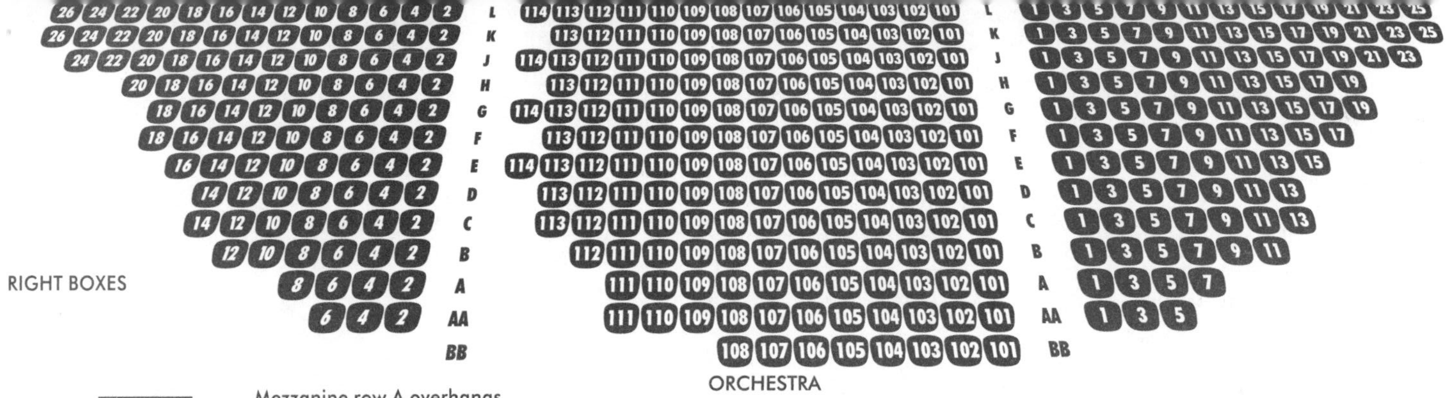

Row	Right Boxes side	Orchestra center	Row	Left side
L	26 24 22 20 18 16 14 12 10 8 6 4 2	114 113 112 111 110 109 108 107 106 105 104 103 102 101	L	1 3 5 7 9 11 13 15 17 19 21 23 25
K	26 24 22 20 18 16 14 12 10 8 6 4 2	113 112 111 110 109 108 107 106 105 104 103 102 101	K	1 3 5 7 9 11 13 15 17 19 21 23 25
J	24 22 20 18 16 14 12 10 8 6 4 2	114 113 112 111 110 109 108 107 106 105 104 103 102 101	J	1 3 5 7 9 11 13 15 17 19 21 23
H	20 18 16 14 12 10 8 6 4 2	113 112 111 110 109 108 107 106 105 104 103 102 101	H	1 3 5 7 9 11 13 15 17 19
G	18 16 14 12 10 8 6 4 2	114 113 112 111 110 109 108 107 106 105 104 103 102 101	G	1 3 5 7 9 11 13 15 17 19
F	18 16 14 12 10 8 6 4 2	113 112 111 110 109 108 107 106 105 104 103 102 101	F	1 3 5 7 9 11 13 15 17
E	16 14 12 10 8 6 4 2	114 113 112 111 110 109 108 107 106 105 104 103 102 101	E	1 3 5 7 9 11 13 15
D	14 12 10 8 6 4 2	113 112 111 110 109 108 107 106 105 104 103 102 101	D	1 3 5 7 9 11 13
C	14 12 10 8 6 4 2	113 112 111 110 109 108 107 106 105 104 103 102 101	C	1 3 5 7 9 11 13
B	12 10 8 6 4 2	112 111 110 109 108 107 106 105 104 103 102 101	B	1 3 5 7 9 11
A	8 6 4 2	111 110 109 108 107 106 105 104 103 102 101	A	1 3 5 7
AA	6 4 2	111 110 109 108 107 106 105 104 103 102 101	AA	1 3 5
BB		108 107 106 105 104 103 102 101	BB	

RIGHT BOXES

ORCHESTRA

$60.00
$45.00

Mezzanine row A overhangs orchestra row J
Balcony row A overhangs mezzanine row C

Hearing devices available

STAGE

TELECHARGE (212) 239-6200
GROUP SALES (800) 334-8457

TAXI DIRECTIONS:
44th St.Eastbound
(bet. Broadway and 6th Ave.)

PARKING
Edison Park Fast, 1120 6th Ave.
(bet. 43rd & 44th Sts.)
Kinney System,
100 West 44th St.
(bet. 6th & 7th Aves.)
BUS
M5, M6, M7, M10, M42, M104
SUBWAYS
A, C, E to 42nd St. & 8th Ave. Port Authority
N,R,1,2,3,7,9 to 42nd St. & 7th Ave. Times Square
B, D, F, Q to 42nd St. & 6th Ave.

Nearby restaurants rated by
SEATS

ORIGINAL FERRARA PASTRIES, 201 W. 42nd St. 398-6064
STARDUST DINE-O-MAT,1491 Broadway at 43rd St.768-3170
JOEY'S PAESANO, 205 W. 43rd St.997-8700
O'FLAHERTY'S ALE HOUSE, 334 W. 46th St. 246-8928

BOOTH THEATRE

222 West 45th Street, New York, NY 10036

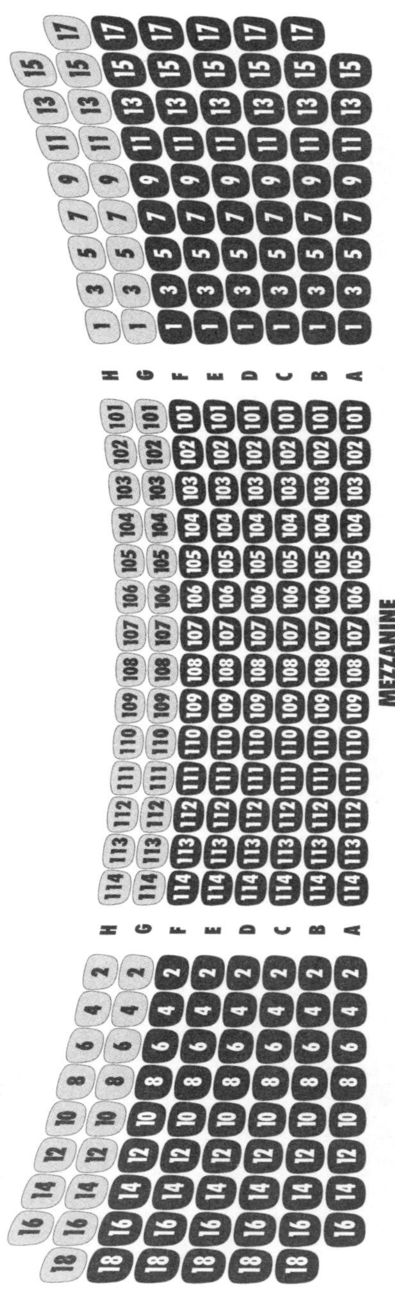

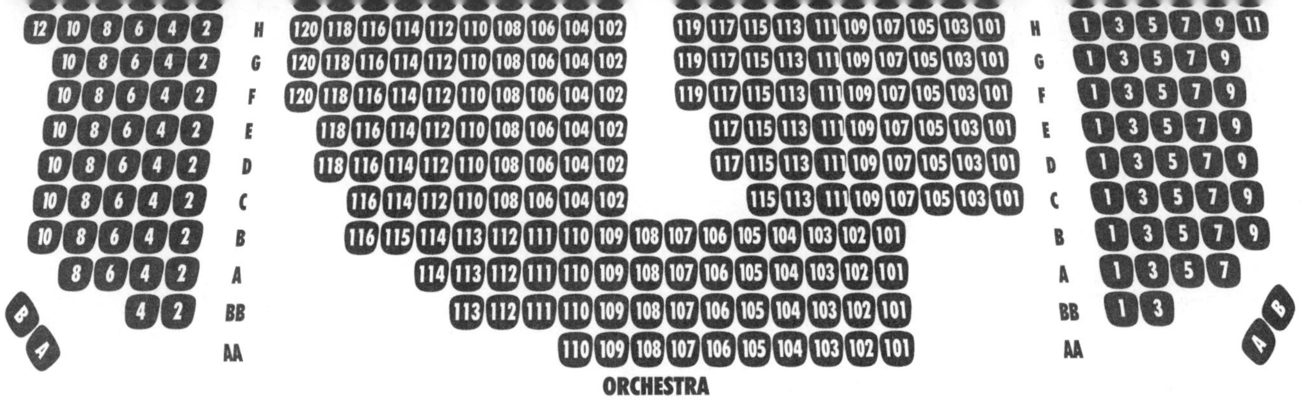

STAGE

$55.00
$45.00

Mezzanine row A overhangs
Orchestra row H

THEATRE (212) 239-6200

TAXI DIRECTIONS:
45th St.Westbound
(between Broadway and 8th Ave.)

PARKING
Edison Parking, 1120 Ave. of the Americas
(bet. 43rd & 44th Sts.)
Kinney, 100 W. 44th St.
(bet. 6th & 7th Aves.)
BUS
M6, M7, M10, M42, M104
SUBWAYS
A, C, E, to 42nd & 8th Ave. Port Authority
1,2,3,7,9,N,R,S to 42nd & 7th Ave. Times Square
B, D,F,Q to 42nd & 6th Ave.

Nearby restaurants rated by
SEATS

TURKISH CUISINE, 631 9th Ave. at 45th, 397-9650
BROADWAY JOE STEAKHOUSE, 315 W. 46th St., 246-6513
MARLOWE, 328 W. 46th St., 765-3815
O'FLAHERTY'S ALE HOUSE, 334 W. 46th St., 246-8928
DANNY'S GRAND SEA PALACE RESTAURANT,
346-348 W. 46th bet. 8th & 9th, 265-8130

BROADHURST THEATRE

235 West 44th Street, New York, NY 10036

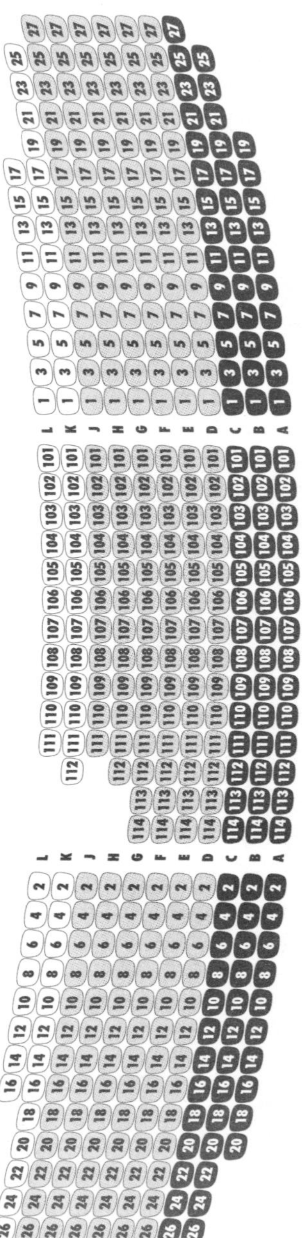

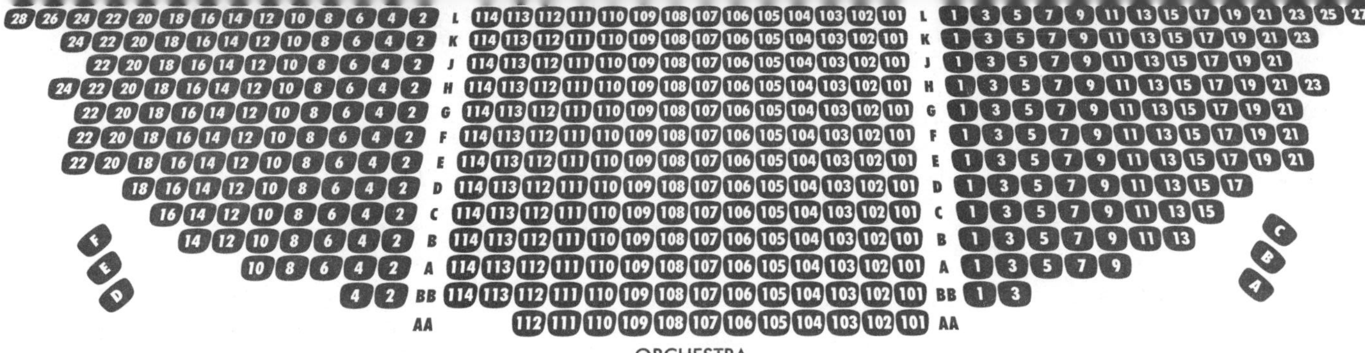

$60.00
$50.00
$40.00

Mezzanine row A overhangs
Orchestra row K

Hearing devices available

STAGE

TELECHARGE (212) 239-6200
GROUP SALES (800) 334-8457

TAXI DIRECTIONS:
44th St. Eastbound
(bet. Broadway & 8th Ave.)

PARKING
Edison Park Fast, 1120 6th Ave.
(bet. 43rd & 44th St.)
Kinney System,
100 West 44th St.
(bet. 6th & 7th Aves.)
BUS
M6,M7,M10,M42,M104
SUBWAYS
A,C,E to 42nd St. & 8th Ave. Port Authority
N,R,S,1,2,3,7,9 to 42nd St. & 7th Ave. Times Square
B,D,F,Q to 42nd St. & 6th Ave.

Nearby restaurants rated by
SEATS
ORIGINAL FERRARA PASTRIES, 201 W. 42nd St. 398-6064
STARDUST DINE-O-MAT, 1491 Broadway 768-3170
TURKISH CUISINE, 631 9th Ave. at 45th St. 397-9650
CAFE UN DEUX TROIS, 123 W. 44th St. 354-4148
VIRGIL'S, 152 W. 44th St. 921-9494

BROADWAY THEATRE

1681 Broadway, New York, NY 10019

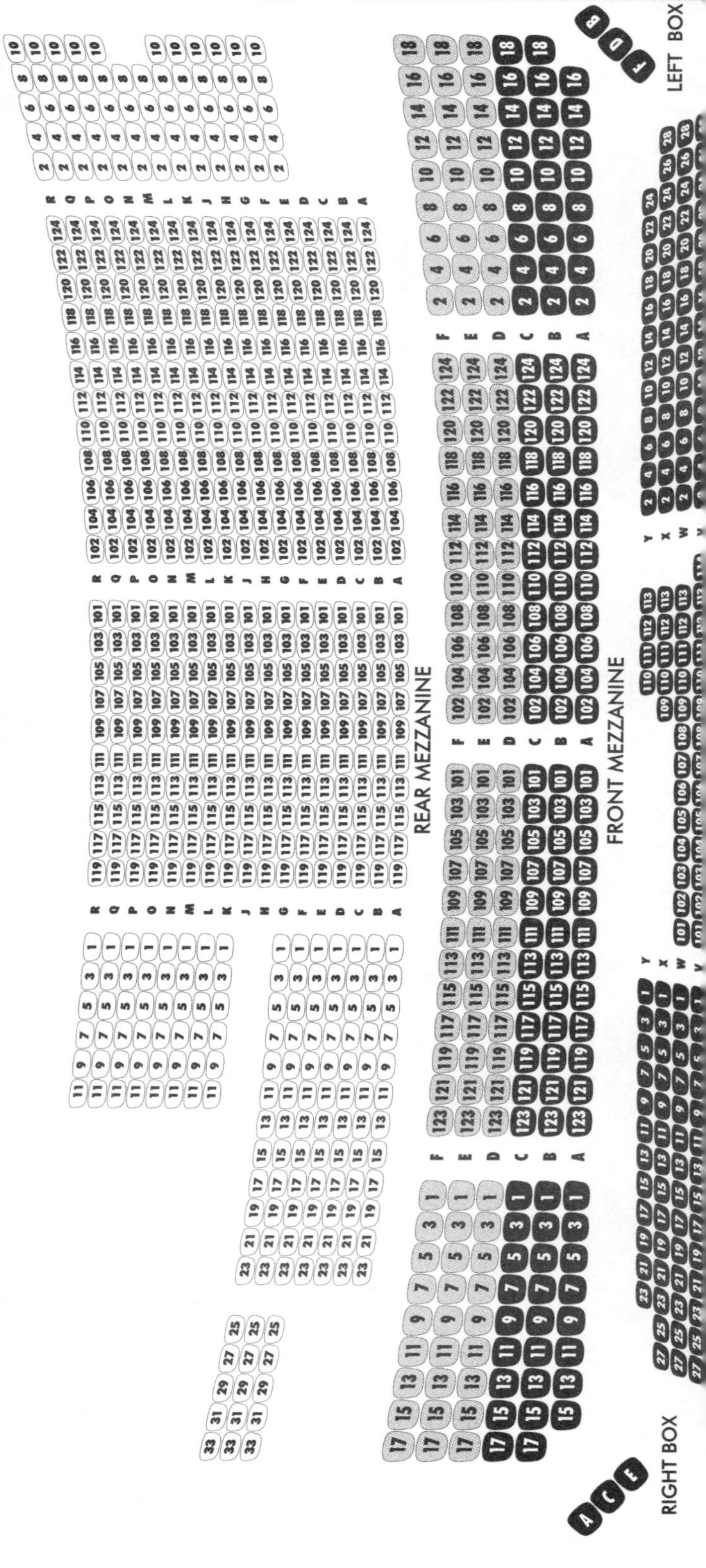

REAR MEZZANINE

FRONT MEZZANINE

LEFT BOX

RIGHT BOX

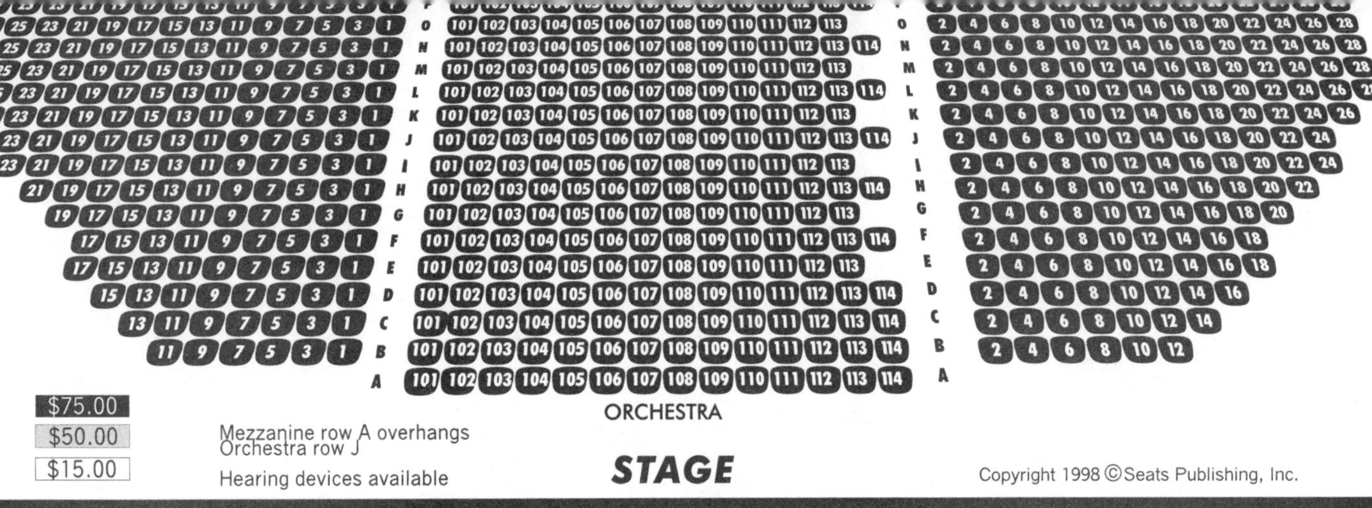

THEATRE (212) 239-6200

TAXI DIRECTIONS:
Broadway Southbound
(bet. 52nd and 53rd Sts.)

PARKING
Kinney System, 159 W. 53rd St.
(bet. 6th & 7th Aves.)
BUS
M6, M7, M10, M27, M50, M104
SUBWAYS
1,9 to 50th St.& Broadway
C,E to 50th St. & 8th Ave.
N,R to 49th St. & 7th Ave.
B,D,F,Q to 50th St. & 6th Ave. Rockefeller Center

Nearby restaurants rated by
SEATS

GALLAGHER'S STEAK HOUSE, 228 W. 52nd St. 245-5336
ORIGINAL FERRARA PASTRIES, 1700 Broadway 581-3335
GRILL 53, 111 W. 53rd St. at the N.Y. Hilton 265-1600
CARNEGIE DELI & RESTAURANT, 854 7th Ave. at 55th St. 757-2245

BROOKS ATKINSON THEATRE

256 West 47th Street, New York, NY 10036

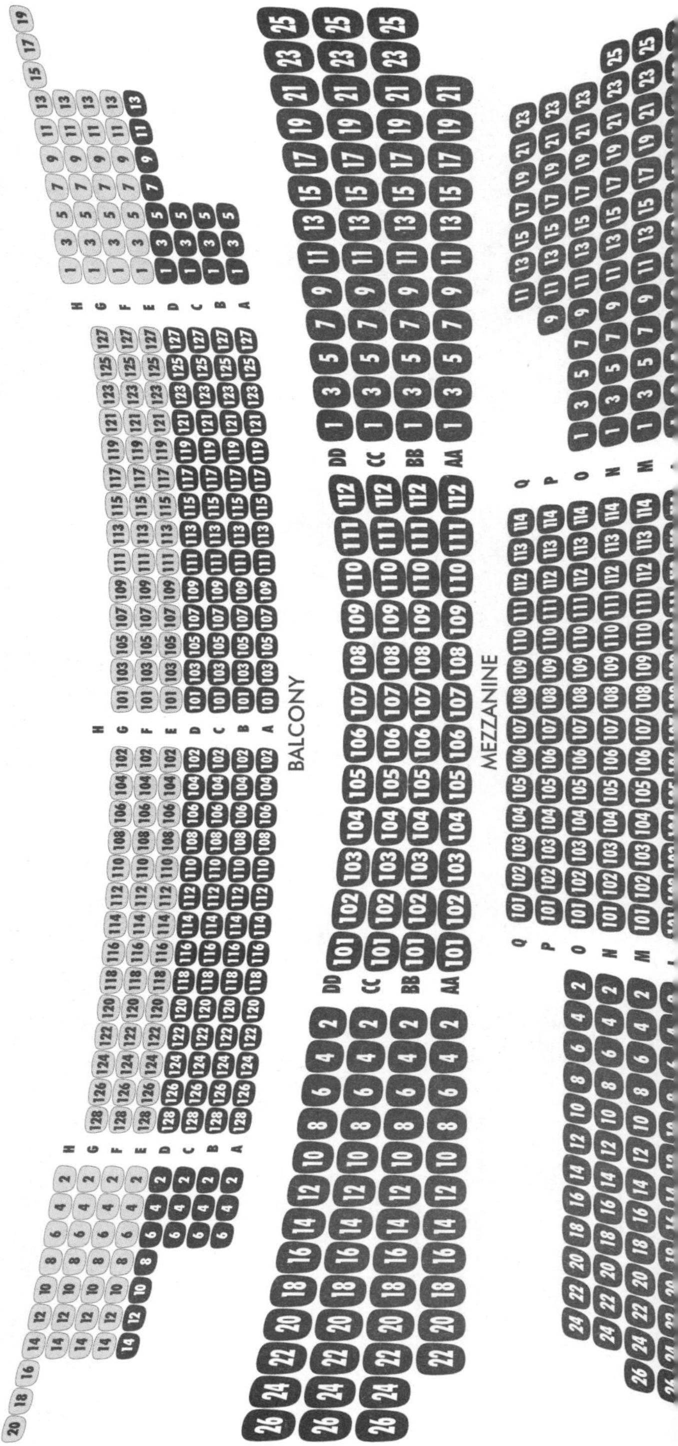

BALCONY

MEZZANINE

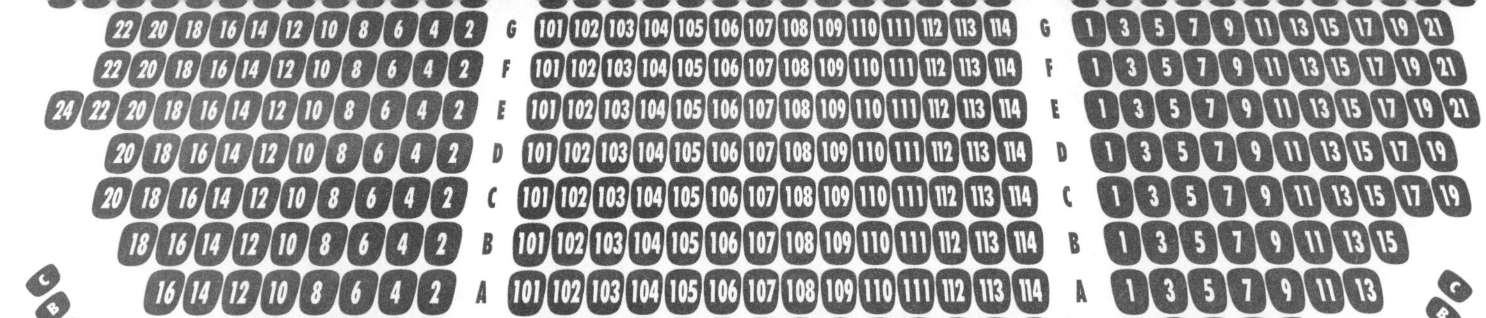

RIGHT BOXES

ORCHESTRA

LEFT BOXES

$70.00
$60.00

Mezzanine row AA overhangs
Orchestra row K

Hearing devices available

STAGE

TICKET MASTER (212) 307-4100
GROUP SALES (800) 344-8457

TAXI DIRECTIONS:
47th St. Westbound
(bet. Broadway and 8th Ave.)

PARKING
Edison Park Fast, 713-719 10th Ave.
(bet. 48th & 49th Sts.)
GMC, 257 W. 47th St.
(bet. Broadway & 8th Ave.)
Kinney System, 253 W.47th St.
(bet. Broadway & 8th Ave.)

BUS
M6, M7, M10, M27, M50, M104

SUBWAYS
1,9 to 50th St. & Broadway
C,E to 50th St. & 8th Ave.
N,R to 49th St.
B,D,F,Q to 47th - 50th Sts.& 6th Ave.
Rockefeller Center

Nearby restaurants rated by
SEATS

MESKEREM, 468 W. 47th St. 664-0520
MARLOWE, 328 W. 46th St. 765-3815
O' FLAHERTY'S ALE HOUSE, 334 W. 46th St. 246-8928
DANNY'S GRAND SEA PALACE RESTAURANT, 346-348 W. 46th St. 265-8130
LA PRIMAVERA, 234 W. 48th St. 586-2797
SHAAN, 57 W. 48th St. 977-8400
B. SMITH'S, 771 8th Ave. at 47th St. 247-2222

CIRCLE IN THE SQUARE THEATRE

1633 Broadway, New York, NY 10019

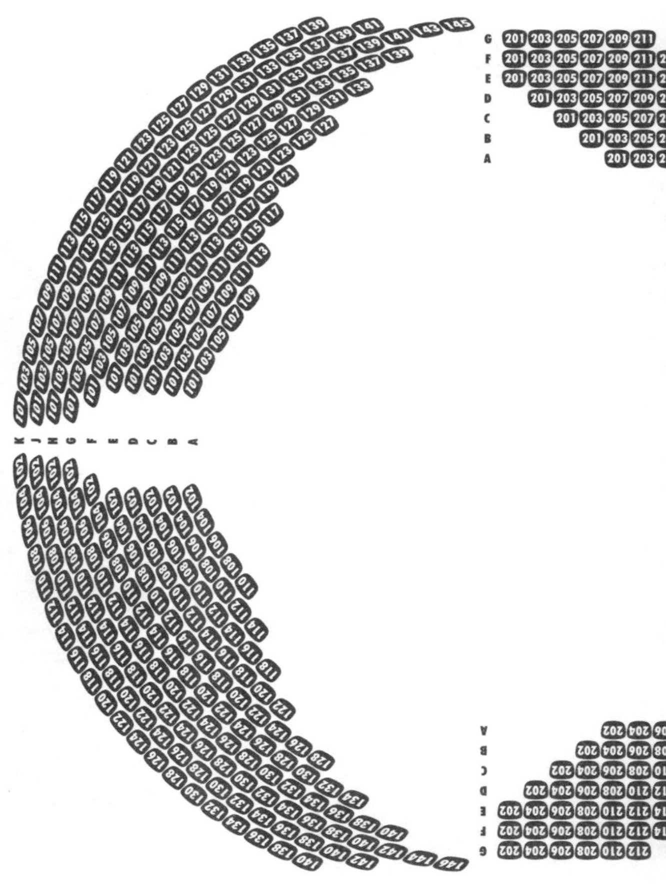

TELECHARGE (212) 239-6200

TAXI DIRECTIONS:
Broadway, Southbound
(at 50th St. Eastbound)

PARKING
Circle Parking
200-206 W. 52nd St.,
(bet. Broadway & 7th Ave.)

BUS
M6, M7, M10, M27, M50, M104

SUBWAYS
1,9 to 50th St. & Broadway
C,E to 50th St. & 8th Ave.
N,R to 49th St.
B,D,F,Q to 47th-50th St. & 6th Ave. Rockefeller Center

Nearby restaurants rated by
SEATS

SHAAN, THE RESTAURANT OF INDIA,
57 W. 48th St. 977-8400
WALLY'S & JOSEPH'S RESTAURANT,
249 W. 49th St. 582-0460
PALIO, 151 W. 51st St. 245-4850
GALLAGHER'S STEAK HOUSE,
228 W. 52nd St. 245-5336

CORT THEATRE

138 West 48th Street, New York, NY 10036

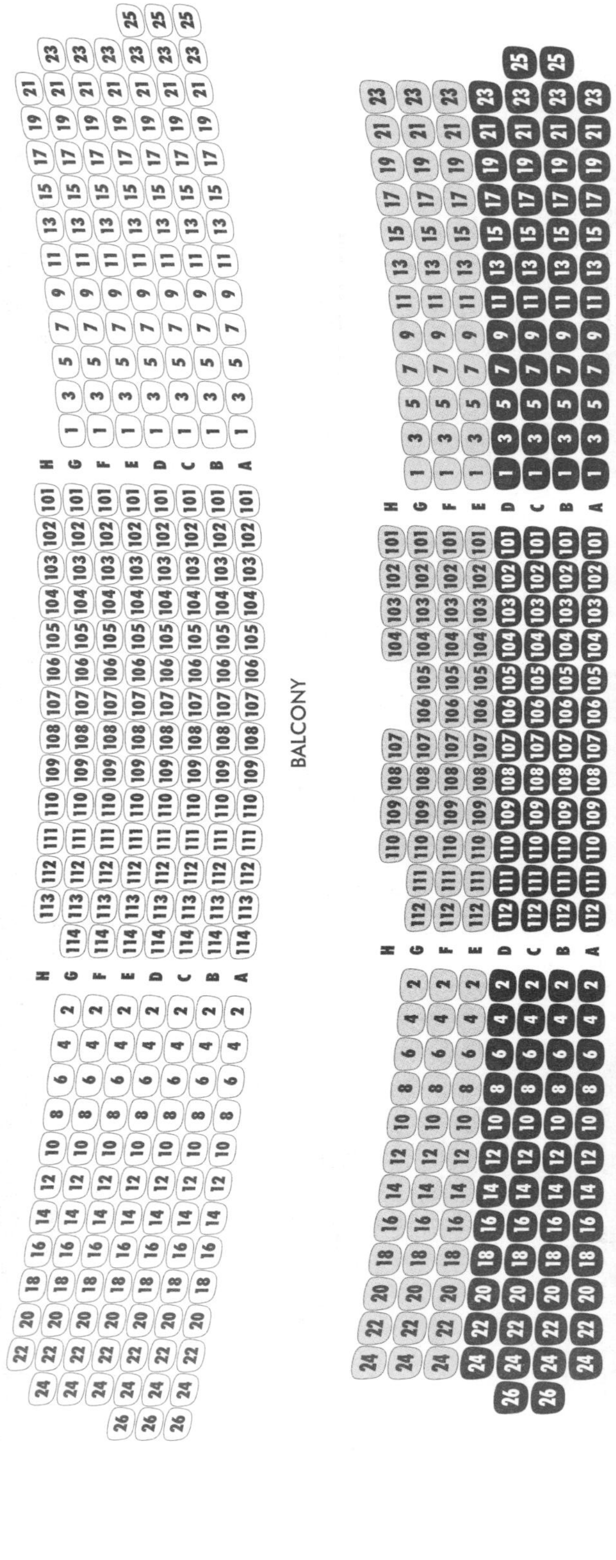

BALCONY

MEZZANINE

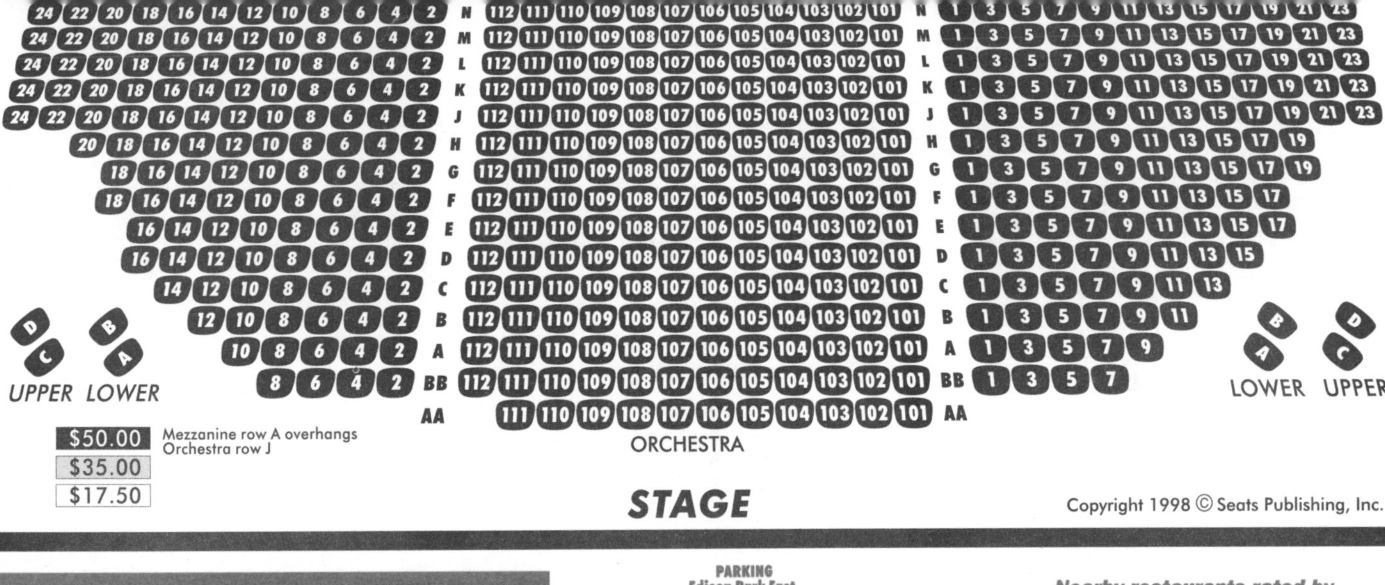

TELECHARGE (212) 239-6200

TAXI DIRECTIONS:
48th St. Eastbound
(bet. 6th & 7th Ave.)

PARKING
Edison Park Fast,
757 7th Ave.
(bet. 49th & 50th Sts.)
GMC, 148 W. 48th St.
(bet. 6th & 7th Aves.)
Kinney, 155 W. 48th St.
(bet. 6th & 7th Aves.)

BUS
M6, M7, M10, M27, M50, M104

SUBWAYS
1,9 to 50th St. & Broadway
C,E to 50th St. & 8th Ave.
N,R to 49th St.
B,D,F,Q to 47th-50th St. & 6th Ave. Rockefeller Center

Nearby restaurants rated by
SEATS

O'FLAHERTY'S ALE HOUSE, 334 W. 46th St. 246-8928
DANNY'S GRAND SEA PALACE RESTAURANT, 346-348 W. 46th St. 265-8130
B. SMITH'S, 771 8th Ave. at 47th St. 247-2222
SHAAN, 57 W. 48th St. 977-8400
LA PRIMAVERA, 234 W. 48th St. 586-2797
WALLY & JOSEPH'S RESTAURANT, 249 W. 49th St. 582-0460

ETHEL BARRYMORE THEATRE

243 West 47th Street, New York, NY 10036

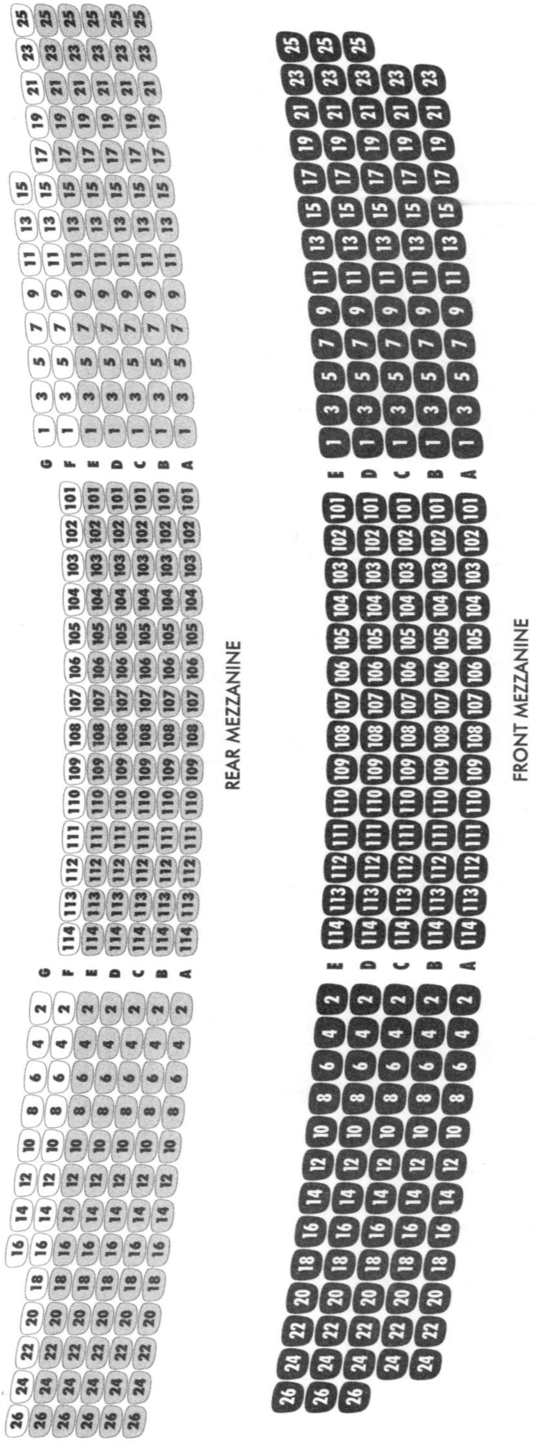

REAR MEZZANINE

FRONT MEZZANINE

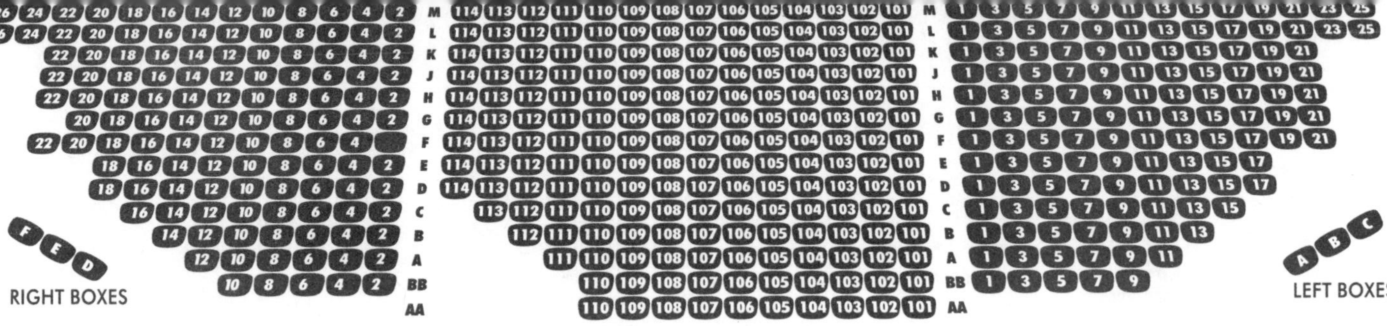

ORCHESTRA

STAGE

$75.00
$60.00
$55.00

Mezzanine row A overhangs Orchestra row K

Hearing devices available

TELECHARGE (212) 239-6200

TAXI DIRECTIONS:
47th St. Eastbound
(bet. Broadway and 8th Ave.)

PARKING
Edison Park Fast, 713-719 10th Ave.
(bet. 48th & 49th Sts.)
GMC, 257 W. 47th St.
(bet. Broadway & 8th Ave.)
Kinney System, 253 W. 47th St.
(bet. Broadway & 8th Ave)
BUS
M6, M7, M10, M27, M50, M104
SUBWAYS
1,9 to 50th St. & Broadway
C,E to 50th St. & 8th Ave.
N,R 49th St.
B,D F,Q to 47th-50th St. & 6th Ave. Rockefeller Center

Nearby restaurants rated by
SEATS
DANNY'S GRAND SEA PALACE ,
346-348 W. 46th St. 265-8130
MARLOWE, 328 W. 46th St. 765-3815
O'FLAHERTY'S ALE HOUSE, 334 W. 46th St. 246-8928
MESKEREM, 468 W.47th St. 664-0520
SHAAN, 57 W. 48th St. 977-8400

EUGENE O'NEILL THEATRE

230 West 49th Street, New York, NY 10019

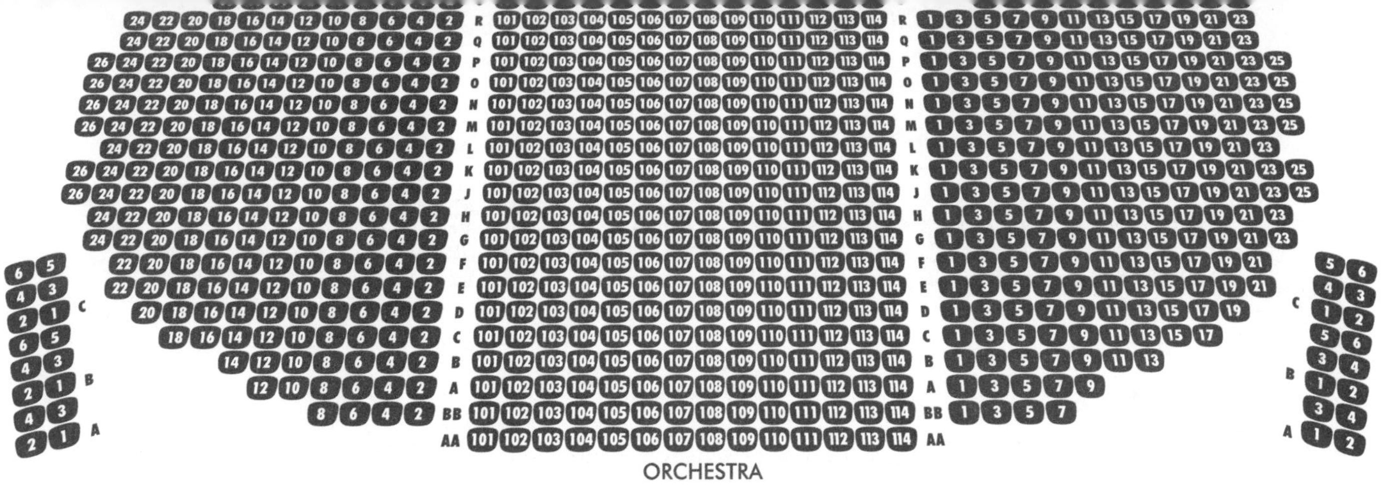

ORCHESTRA

STAGE

$67.50
$57.50

Mezzanine row A overhangs
Orchestra row K

Hearing devices available

TELECHARGE (212) 239-6200

PARKING
Edison Parking, 757 7th Ave.
(bet. 49th & 50th Sts.)
GMC, 225 W. 49th St.
(bet. Broadway & 8th Ave.)
BUS
M6, M7, M10, M27, M50, M104
SUBWAYS
C,E to 50th St. & 8th Ave.   N,R to 49th St.
1,9 to 50th St. & Broadway
B,D,F,Q to 47th-50th St. & 6th Ave. Rockefeller Center

TAXI DIRECTIONS:
49th St. Westbound
(bet. Broadway & 8th Ave.)

Nearby restaurants rated by
SEATS
B. SMITH'S, 771 8th Ave. 247-2222
SHAAN, 57 W. 48th St. 977-8400
LA PRIMAVERA, 234 W. 48th St. 586-2797
CIRO, 813 8th Ave. 307-5484
MESKEREM II, 682 11th Ave. 541-7858

FORD CENTER FOR THE PERFORMING ARTS

213 West 42nd Street, New York, NY 10036

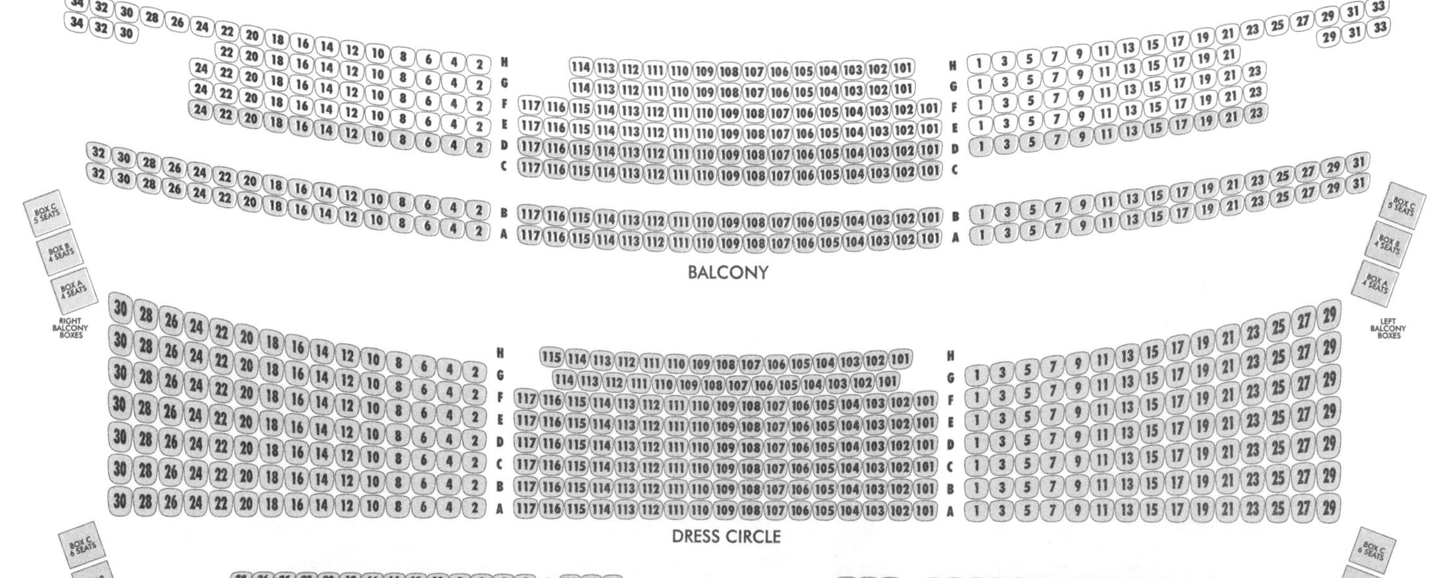

STAGE

TICKETMASTER (212) 307-4100
GROUP SALES (212) 582-1200

TAXI DIRECTIONS:
42nd St. two way
(bet. 7th & 8th Aves.)

PARKING
Square Parking, 306-332 W. 44th St.
Edison Park Fast, 401-471 W. 42nd St.
Kinney System, 250 W. 41st St.
Kinney System, 361 W. 42nd St.

BUS
M6, M7, M10, M42, M104

SUBWAYS
A, C, E to 42nd St. & 8th Ave. Port Authority
N,R,S,1,2,3,7,9 to 42nd St. & 7th Ave. Times Square
B, D, F, Q to 42nd St. & 6th Ave.

Nearby restaurants rated by
SEATS
BRYANT PARK GRILL, 20 W. 40th St. 840-6500
ORIGINAL FERRARA PASTRIES, 201 W. 42nd St. 398-6064
STARDUST DINE-O-MAT, 1491 Broadway 768-3170
JOEY'S PAESANO, 205 W. 43rd St. 997-8700

GERSHWIN THEATRE

222 West 51st Street, New York, NY 10019

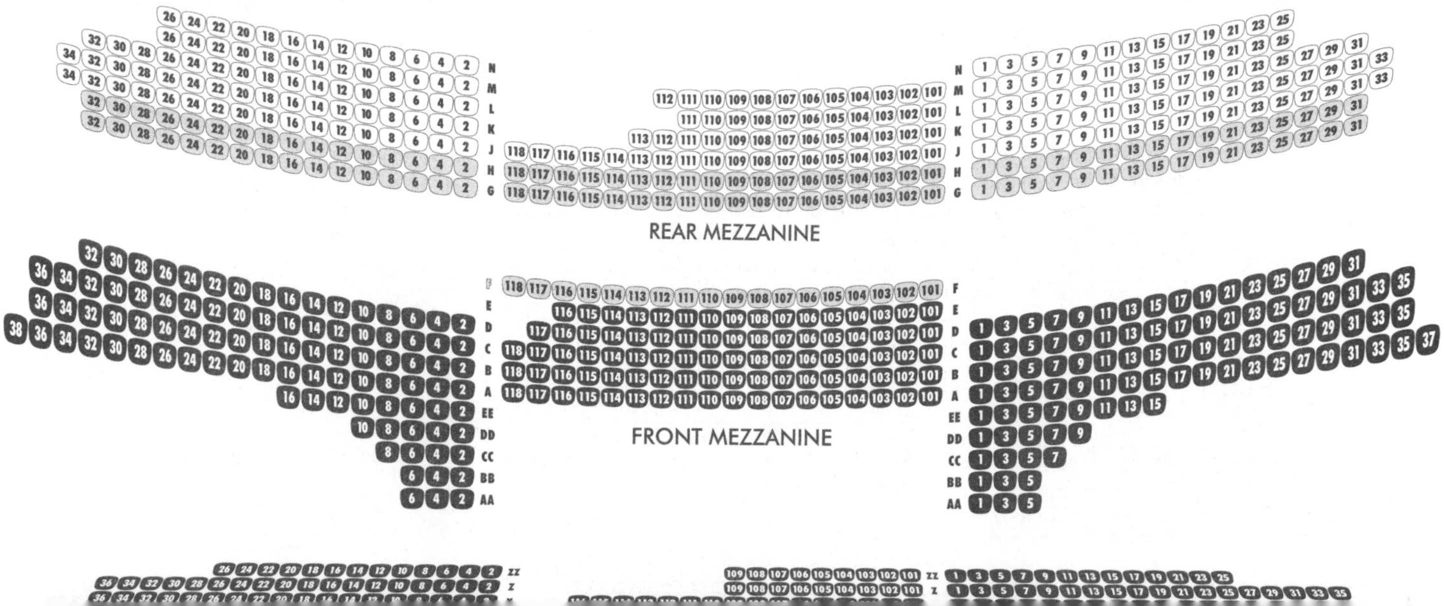

REAR MEZZANINE

FRONT MEZZANINE

ORCHESTRA

$75.00
$55.00
$20.00

Front mezzanine row A overhangs orchestra row N

STAGE

TICKETMASTER (212) 307-4100

TAXI DIRECTIONS:
51st St. Westbound
(bet. Broadway & 8th Ave.)

PARKING
Edison Park Fast, 757 7th Ave.
(bet. 49th & 50th Sts.)
GMC, 218 W. 50th St.
(bet. Broadway & 8th Ave.)
Kinney System, 1633 Broadway at 51st St.

BUS
M6, M7, M10, M27, M50, M104

SUBWAYS
1,9 to 50th St. & Broadway
C,E to 50th St. & 8th Ave.
N,R to 49th St.
B,D,F,Q to 47th-50th St. & 6th Ave.

Nearby restaurants rated by
SEATS

LA PRIMAVERA, 234 W. 48th St. 586-2797
MESKEREM II, 682 11th Ave. 541-7858
CIRO, 813 8th Ave. 307-5484
VICTOR'S CAFE 52, 236 W. 52nd St. 586-7714

HELEN HAYES THEATRE

240 West 44th Street, New York, NY 10036

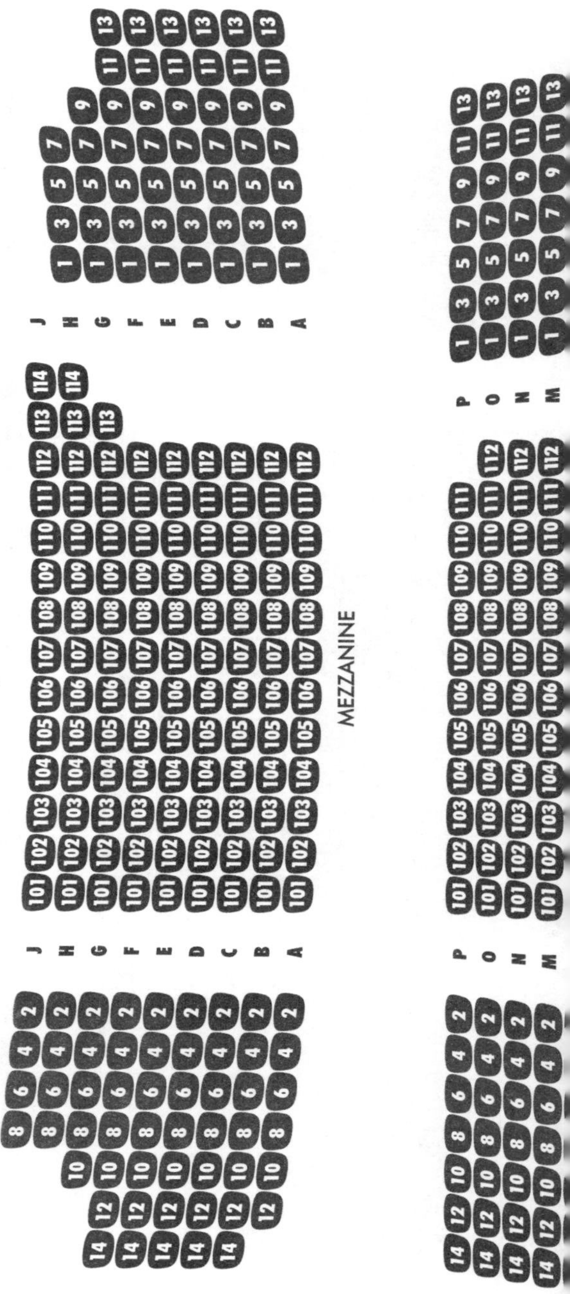

MEZZANINE

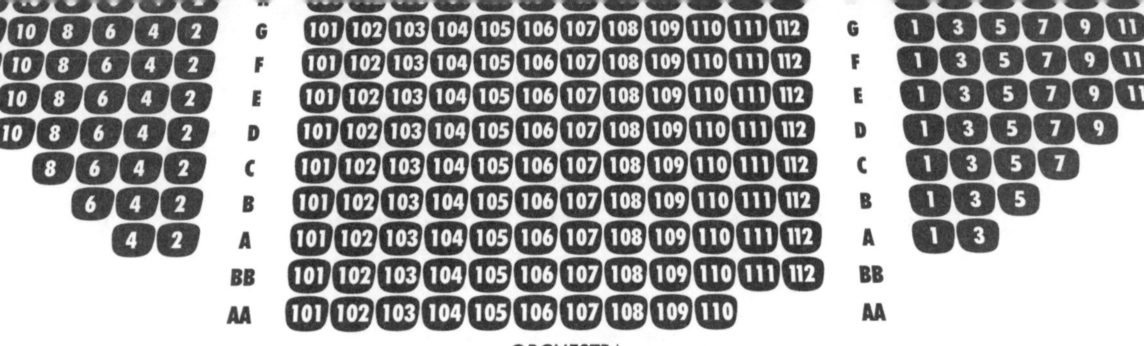

STAGE

All Seats $55.00

Mezzanine row A overhangs
Orchestra row K

Hearing devices available

TICKETMASTER (212) 307-4100
GROUP SALES (212) 889-4300

TAXI DIRECTIONS:
44th St. Eastbound
(bet. 7th & 8th Aves.)

PARKING
Edison Park Fast, 1120 6th Ave,
(bet. 43rd & 44th Sts.)
Kinney System, 100 W. 44th St.
(bet. 6th & 7th Aves.)

BUS
M6, M7, M10, M42, M104

SUBWAYS
A, C, E to 42nd St. & 8th Ave. Port Authority
N,R,S,1,2,3,7,9,to 42nd St. & 7th Ave. Times Square
B, D, F, Q to 42nd St. & 6th Ave.

Nearby restaurants rated by
SEATS

ORIGINAL FERRARA PASTRIES, 201 W. 42nd St. 398-6064
STARDUST DINE-O-MAT, 1491 Broadway 768-3170
TURKISH CUISINE, 631 9th Ave. at 45th St. 397-9650
CAFE UN DEUX TROIS,123 W. 44th St. 354-4148
VIRGIL'S, 152 W. 44th St. 921-9494

IMPERIAL THEATRE

249 West 45th Street, New York, NY 10036

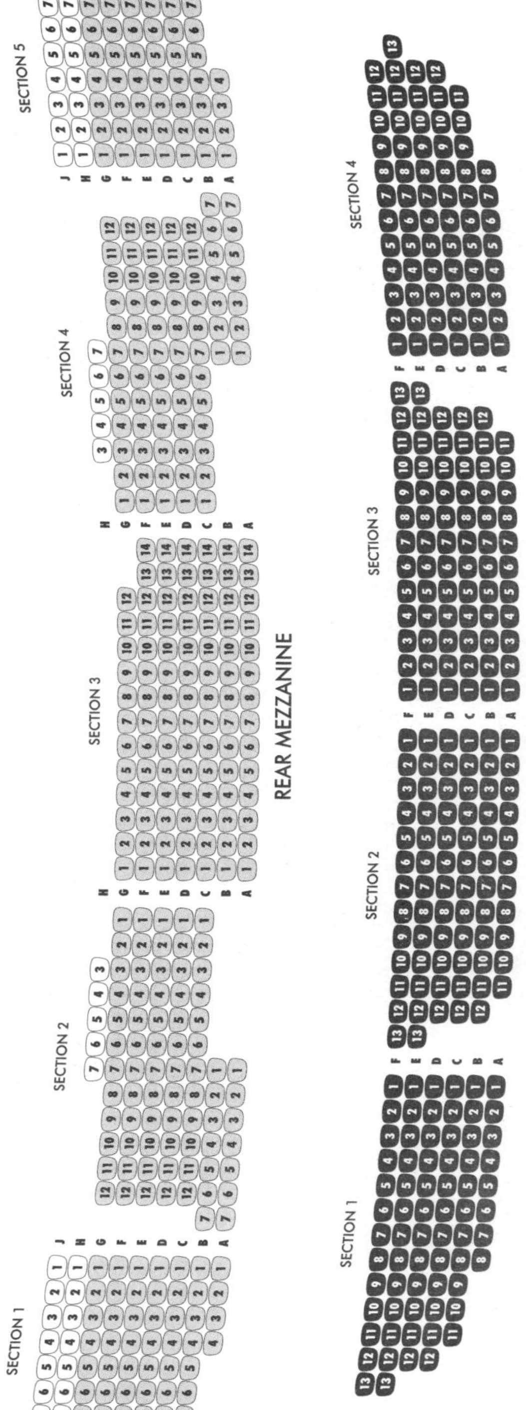

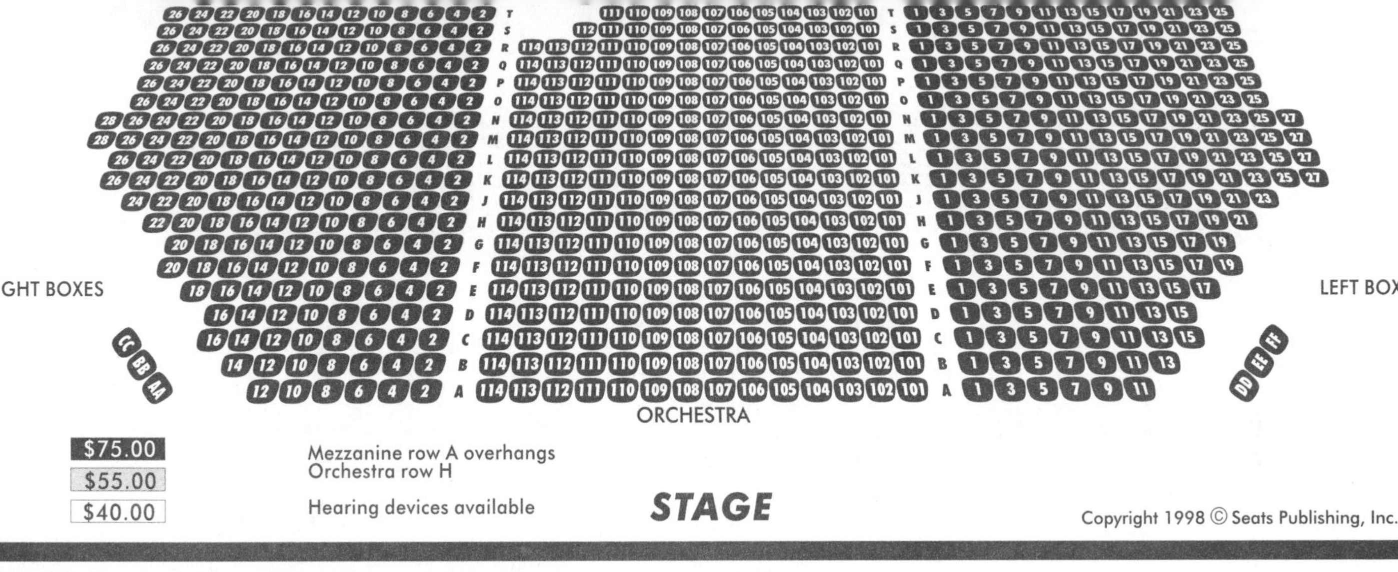

TELECHARGE (212) 239-6200

TAXI DIRECTIONS:
45th St. Westbound
(bet. Broadway & 8th Ave.)

PARKING
Edison Park Fast, 1120 6th Ave.
(bet. 43rd & 44th Sts.)
Kinney System,
100 W. 44th St.
(bet. 6th & 7th Aves.)

BUS
M6, M7, M10, M42, M104

SUBWAYS
A, C, E to 42nd St. & 8th Ave. Port Authority
N,R,S,1,2,3,7,9 to 42nd St. & 7th Ave. Times Square
B, D, F, Q to 42nd St. & 6th Ave.

Nearby restaurants rated by
SEATS

TURKISH CUISINE, 631 9th Ave. at 45th St. 397-9650
BROADWAY JOE STEAK HOUSE, 315 W. 46th St. 246-6513
MARLOWE, 328 W 46th St. 765-3815
O'FLAHERTY'S ALE HOUSE, 334 W. 46th St. 246-8928
DANNY'S GRAND SEA PALACE RESTAURANT,
346-348 W. 46th St, 265-8130

JOHN GOLDEN THEATRE

252 West 45th Street, New York, NY 10036

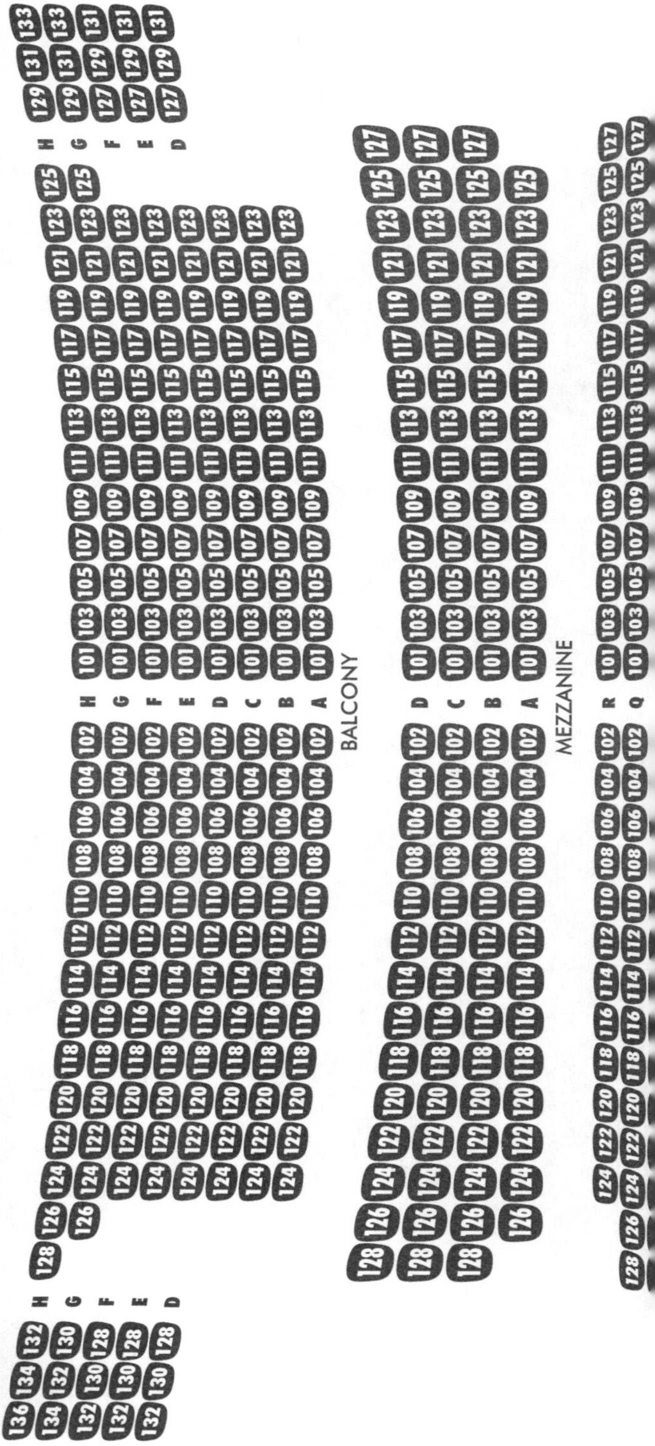

BALCONY

MEZZANINE

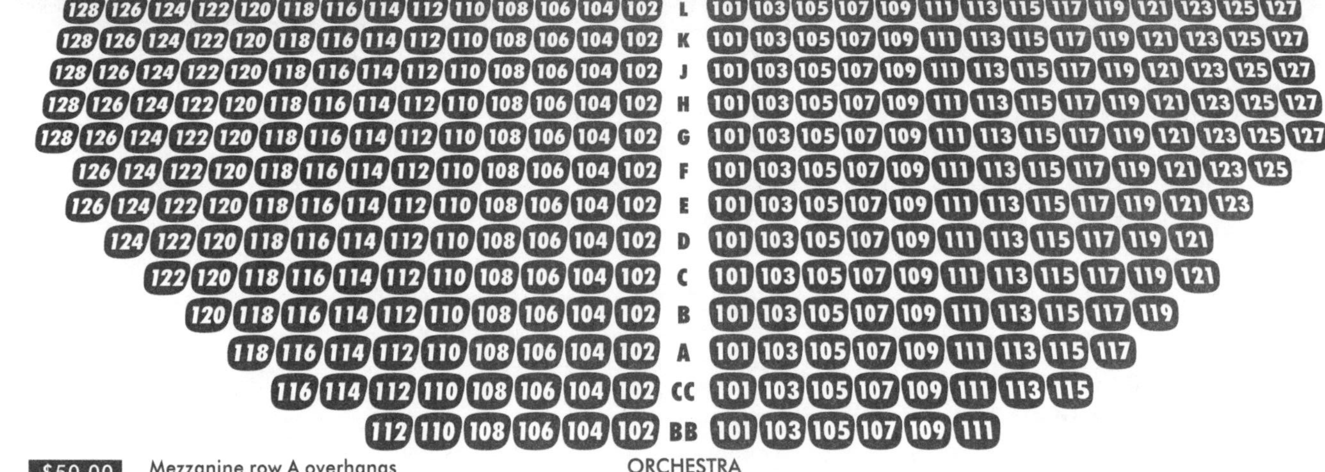

TELECHARGE (212) 239-6200

TAXI DIRECTIONS:
45th St. Westbound
(bet. Broadway & 8th Ave.)

PARKING
Edison Park Fast, 1120 6th Ave.
(bet. 43rd & 44th Sts.)
Kinney System,
100 West 44th St.
(bet. 6th & 7th Aves.)

BUS
M6, M7, M10, M42, M104

SUBWAYS
A, C, E to 42nd St. & 8th Ave. Port Authority
N,R,S,1,2,3,7,9 to 42nd St. & 7th Ave. Times Square
B, D, F, Q to 42nd St. & 6th Ave.

Nearby restaurants rated by
SEATS

TURKISH CUISINE, 631 9th Ave. at 45th St. 397-9650
BROADWAY JOE STEAK HOUSE, 315 W. 46th St. 246-6513
MARLOWE, 328 W. 46th St. 765-3815
O'FLAHERTY'S ALE HOUSE, 334 W. 46th St. 246-8928
DANNY'S GRAND SEA PALACE RESTAURANT,
346-348 W. 46th St, 265-8130

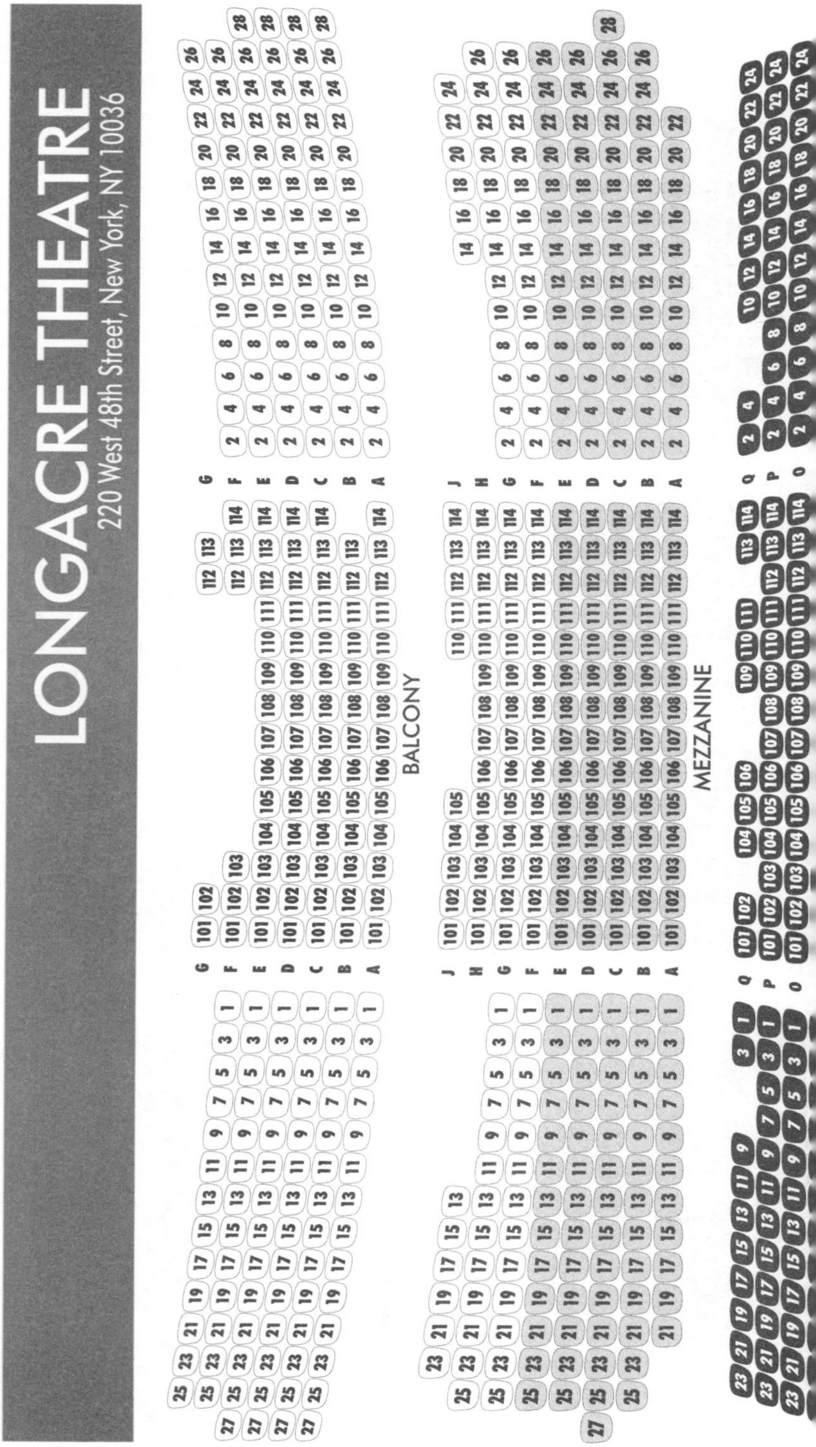

LONGACRE THEATRE

220 West 48th Street, New York, NY 10036

BALCONY

MEZZANINE

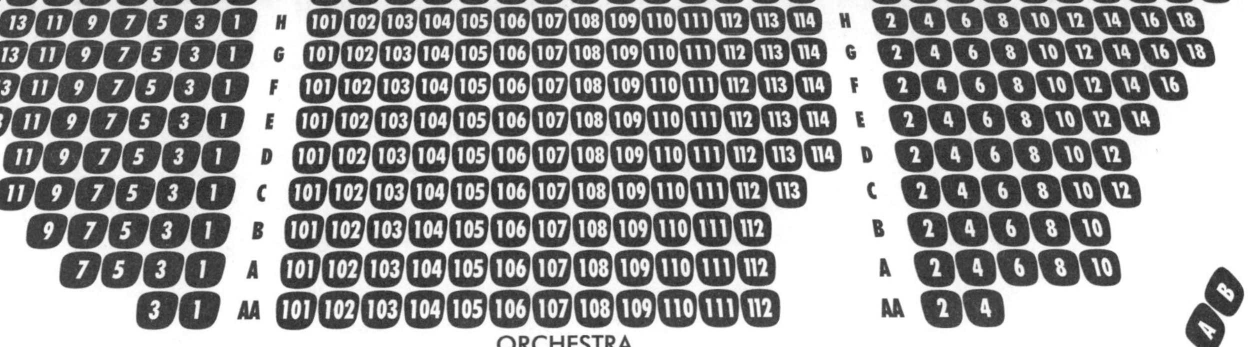

$70.00
$45.00
$38.50

Mezzanine row A overhangs Orchestra row K
Balcony row A overhangs Mezzanine row B

STAGE

THEATRE (212) 239-6200

TAXI DIRECTIONS:
48th St. Eastbound
(bet. Broadway & 8th Ave.)

PARKING
Edison Parking, 757 7th Ave.
(bet. 49th & 50th Sts.)
GMC 148 W. 48th
(bet. 6th & 7th Aves.)
Kinney, 155 W. 48th St.
(bet. 6th & 7th Aves.)

BUS
M6, M7, M10, M27, M50, M104

SUBWAY
1,9 TO 50th St. & Broadway
C,E to 50th St. & 8th Ave.
N,R to 49th St.
B,D,F,Q to 47th St. & 6th Ave.
Rockefeller Center

Nearby restaurants rated by
SEATS

B. SMITH'S, 771 8th Ave. at 47th St. 247-2222
SHAAN, 57 W. 48th St. 977-8400
LA PRIMAVERA, 234 W. 48th St. 586-2797
MESKEREM II, 682 11th Ave. at 49th St. 541-7858
CIRO, 813 8th Ave. at 49th St. 307-5484
WALLY'S & JOSEPH'S RESTAURANT, 249 W. 49th St. 582-0460

LUNT-FONTANNE THEATRE

205 West 46th Street, New York, NY 10036

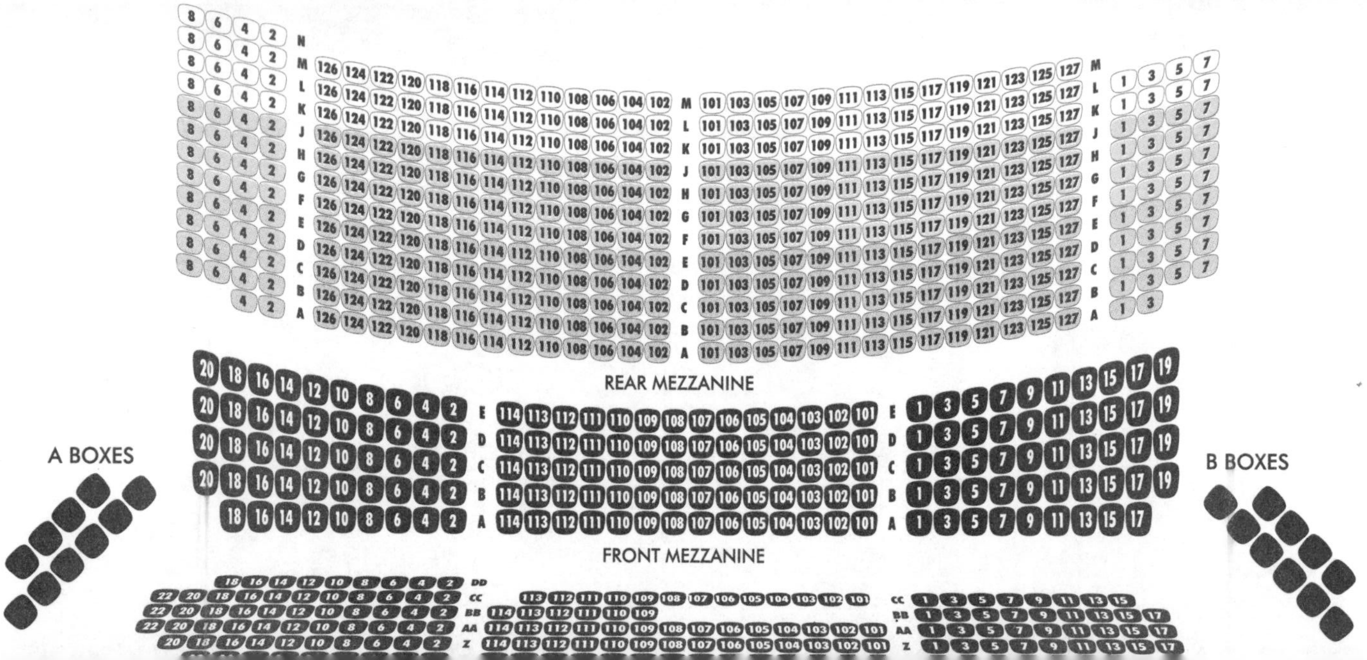

REAR MEZZANINE

A BOXES

B BOXES

FRONT MEZZANINE

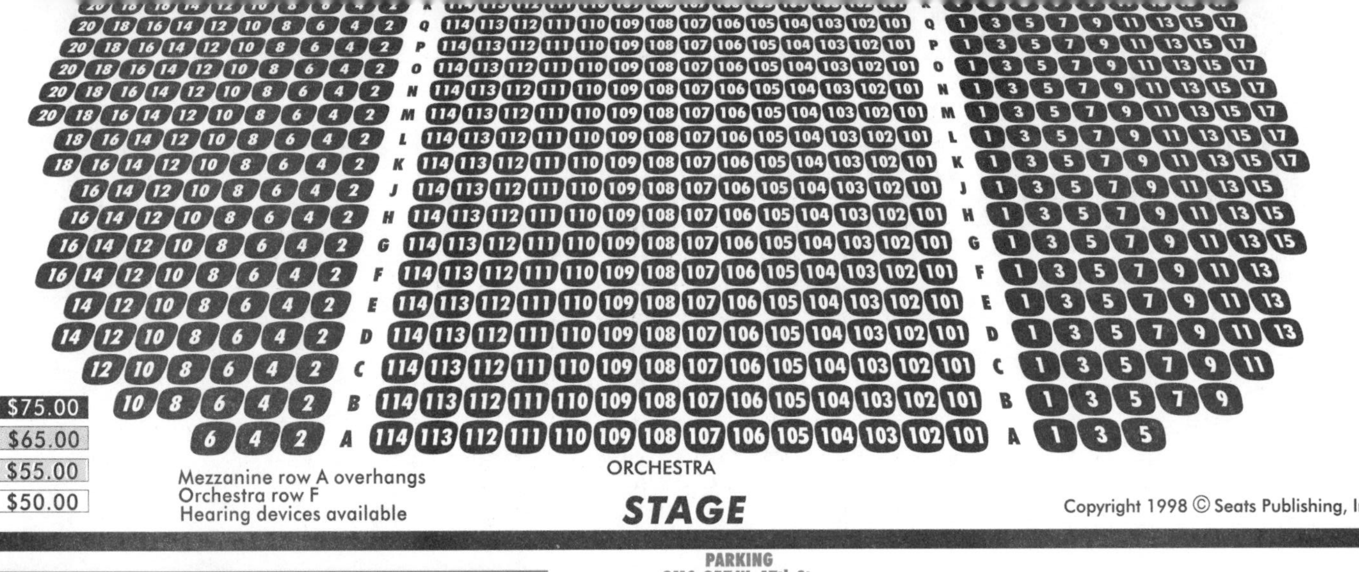

TICKETMASTER (212) 307-4100

TAXI DIRECTIONS:
46th St. Eastbound
(bet. Broadway & 8th Ave.)

PARKING
GMC, 257 W. 47th St.
(bet. Broadway & 8th Ave.)
Kinney System,
38 W. 46th St.
(bet. 5th & 6th Aves.)
253 W. 47th St.
(bet. Broadway & 8th Ave.)

BUS
M6, M7, M10, M42, M104

SUBWAYS
A,C,E to 42nd & 8th Ave. Port Authority
N,R,S,1,2,3,7,9 to 42nd St. & 7th Ave. Times Square
B,D,F,Q to 42nd & 6th Ave.

Nearby restaurants rated by
SEATS

TURKISH CUISINE, 631 9th Ave. at 45th St. 397-9650
MARLOWE, 328 W. 46th St. 765-3815
O'FLAHERTY'S ALE HOUSE, 334 W. 46th St. 246-8928
DANNY'S GRAND SEA PALACE RESTAURANT, 346-348 W. 46th St. 265-8130
MESKEREM, 468 W. 47th St. 664-0520
B. SMITH, 771 8th Ave. at 47th St. 247-2222

LYCEUM THEATRE

149 West 45th Street, New York, NY 10036

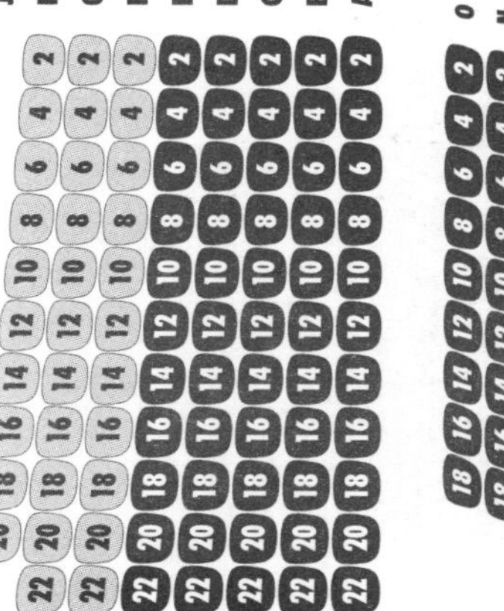

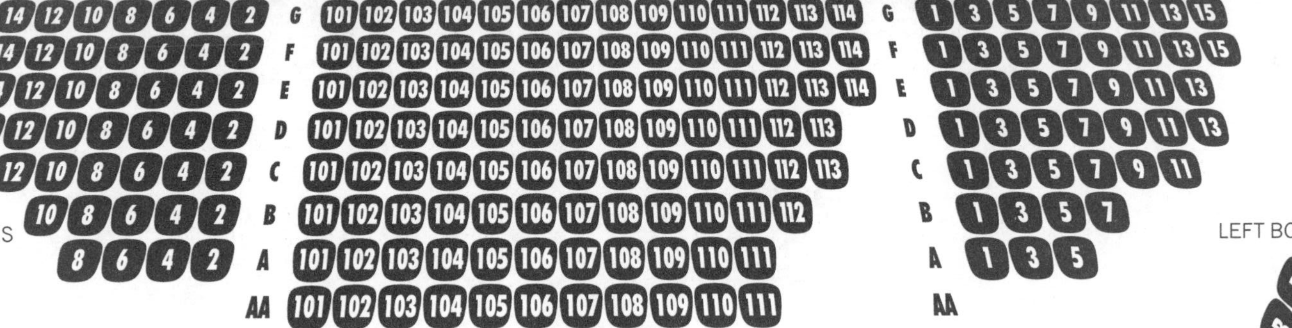

ORCHESTRA

STAGE

Mezzanine row A overhangs
Orchestra row L
Balcony row A overhangs
Mezzanine row C

THEATRE (212) 239-6200

TAXI DIRECTIONS:
45th St, Westbound
(bet. Broadway & 6th Ave.)

PARKING
Edison Park Fast, 757 7th Ave. (bet. 49th & 50th Sts.)
GMC, 148 W. 48th St. (bet. 6th & 7th Aves.)
Kinney System, 155 W. 48th St. (bet. 6th & 7th Aves.)

BUS
M5, M6, M7, M10, M42, M104

SUBWAYS
B, D, F,Q to 42nd St. & 6th Ave.
1,2,3,7,9,N,R,S to 42nd St.& 7th Ave.Times Square,
A, C, E to 42nd St. & 8th Ave. Port Authority

Nearby restaurants rated by
SEATS

O' FLAHERTY'S ALE HOUSE, 334 W. 46th St. 246-8928
DANNY'S GRAND SEA PALACE RESTAURANT, 346-348 W. 46th (bet. 8th & 9th Aves.) 265-8130
B. SMITH'S, 771 8th Ave. at 47th St. 247-2222
SHAAN, 57 W. 48th St., 977- 8400
LA PRIMAVERA, 234 W. 48th St. 586-2797
WALLY & JOSEPH'S RESTAURANT, 249 W. 49th St. 582-0460

MAJESTIC THEATRE

245 West 44th Street, New York, NY 10036

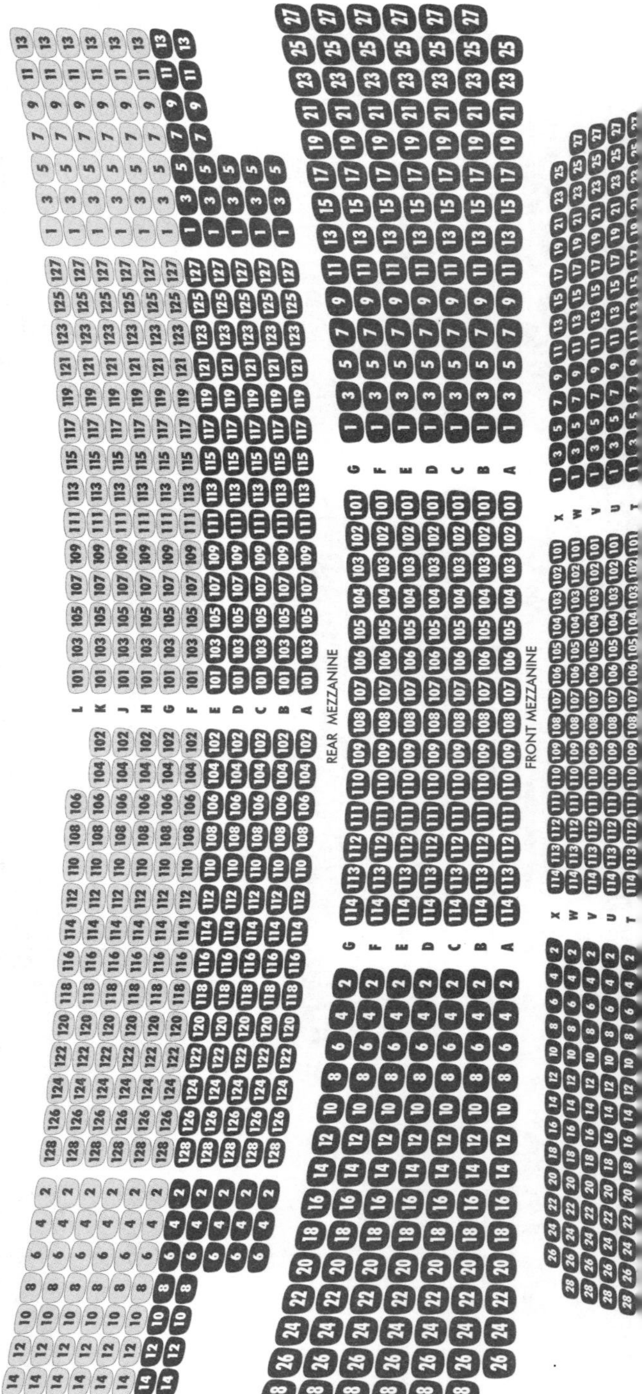

REAR MEZZANINE

FRONT MEZZANINE

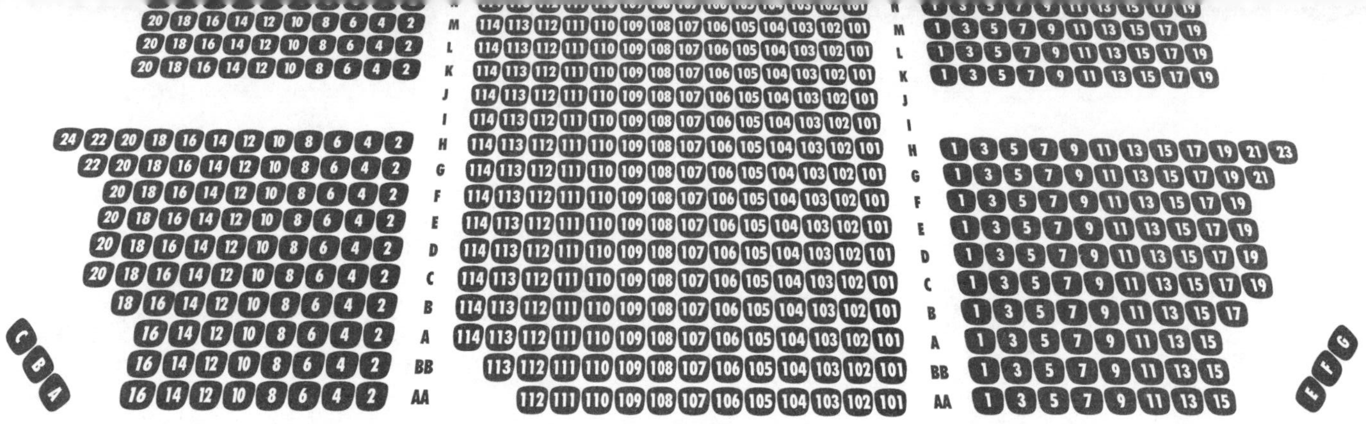

ORCHESTRA

$75.00
$50.00

Front Mezzanine Row A overhangs Orchestra Row J

Hearing devices available

STAGE

THEATRE (212) 239-6200
GROUP SALES (800) 334-8457

TAXI DIRECTIONS:
44th St. Eastbound
(bet. Broadway & 8th Ave.)

PARKING
Edison Park Fast, 1120 Ave. of the Americas (bet. 43rd & 44th Sts.)
Kinney System, 100 W. 44th St. (bet. 6th & 7th Aves.)

BUS
M6, M7, M10, M42, M104

SUBWAYS
B, D, F, Q to 42nd St. & 6th Ave.
1,2,3,7,9,N,R,S to 42nd St. & 7th Ave. Times Square
A, C, E to 42nd St. & 8th Ave. Port Authority

Nearby restaurants rated by
SEATS

ORIGINAL FERRARA PASTRIES, 201 W. 42nd St. 398-6064
STARDUST DINE O-MAT, 1491 Broadway at 43rd St. 768-3170
CAFE UN DEUX TROIX, 123 W. 44th St. 354-4148
VIRGIL'S, 152 W. 44th St. 921-9494
TURKISH CUISINE, 631 9th Ave. at 45th St. 397-9650

MARQUIS THEATRE

1535 Broadway, New York, NY 10036

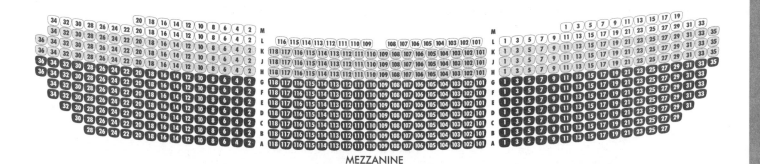

MEZZANINE

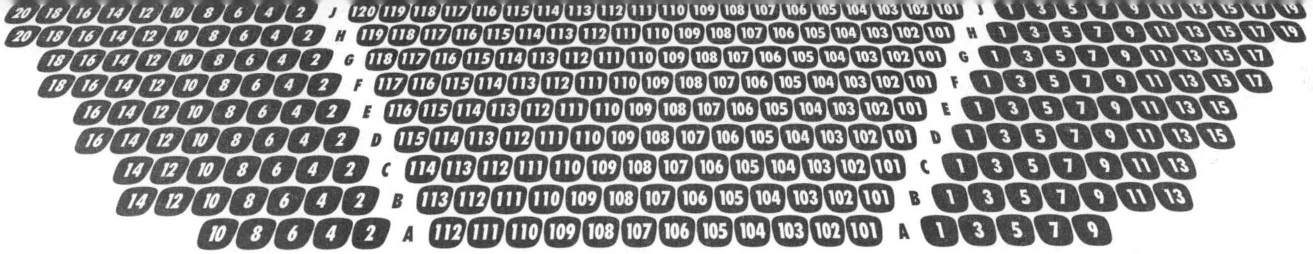

J 20 18 16 14 12 10 8 6 4 2 J 120 119 118 117 116 115 114 113 112 111 110 109 108 107 106 105 104 103 102 101 J 1 3 5 7 9 11 13 15 17 19
H 20 18 16 14 12 10 8 6 4 2 H 119 118 117 116 115 114 113 112 111 110 109 108 107 106 105 104 103 102 101 H 1 3 5 7 9 11 13 15 17 19
G 18 16 14 12 10 8 6 4 2 G 118 117 116 115 114 113 112 111 110 109 108 107 106 105 104 103 102 101 G 1 3 5 7 9 11 13 15 17
F 18 16 14 12 10 8 6 4 2 F 117 116 115 114 113 112 111 110 109 108 107 106 105 104 103 102 101 F 1 3 5 7 9 11 13 15 17
E 16 14 12 10 8 6 4 2 E 116 115 114 113 112 111 110 109 108 107 106 105 104 103 102 101 E 1 3 5 7 9 11 13 15
D 16 14 12 10 8 6 4 2 D 115 114 113 112 111 110 109 108 107 106 105 104 103 102 101 D 1 3 5 7 9 11 13 15
C 14 12 10 8 6 4 2 C 114 113 112 111 110 109 108 107 106 105 104 103 102 101 C 1 3 5 7 9 11 13
B 14 12 10 8 6 4 2 B 113 112 111 110 109 108 107 106 105 104 103 102 101 B 1 3 5 7 9 11 13
A 10 8 6 4 2 A 112 111 110 109 108 107 106 105 104 103 102 101 A 1 3 5 7 9

ORCHESTRA

STAGE

$75.00
$65.00
$55.00

Mezzanine row A overhangs
Orchestra row M

Hearing devices available

TICKETMASTER (212) 307-4100

TAXI DIRECTIONS:
Broadway Southbound
(bet. 45th and 46th Sts.)

PARKING
GMC, 257 W 47th St.
(bet. Broadway & 8th Ave.)
Kinney System, 38 W. 46th St.
(bet. 5th & 6th Aves.)
253 W. 47th St.
(bet. Broadway & 8th Ave.)
BUS
M6,M7,M10,M42,M104
SUBWAYS
A,C,E to 42nd & 8th Ave. Port Authority
N,R,S,1,2,3,7,9 to 42nd St. & 7th Ave. Times Square
B,D,F,Q to 42nd St. & 6th Ave.

Nearby restaurants rated by
SEATS
TURKISH CUISINE, 631 9th Ave. at 45th St. 397-9650
MARLOWE, 328 W. 46th St. 765-3815
O'FLAHERTY'S ALE HOUSE, 334 W. 46th St. 246-8928
DANNY'S GRAND SEA PALACE RESTAURANT,
346-348 W. 46th St. 265-8130
MESKEREM, 468 W. 47th St. 664-0520

MARTIN BECK THEATRE

302 West 45th Street, New York, NY 10036

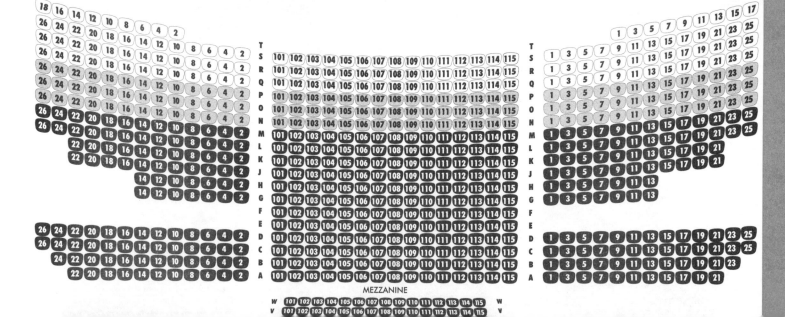

MEZZANINE

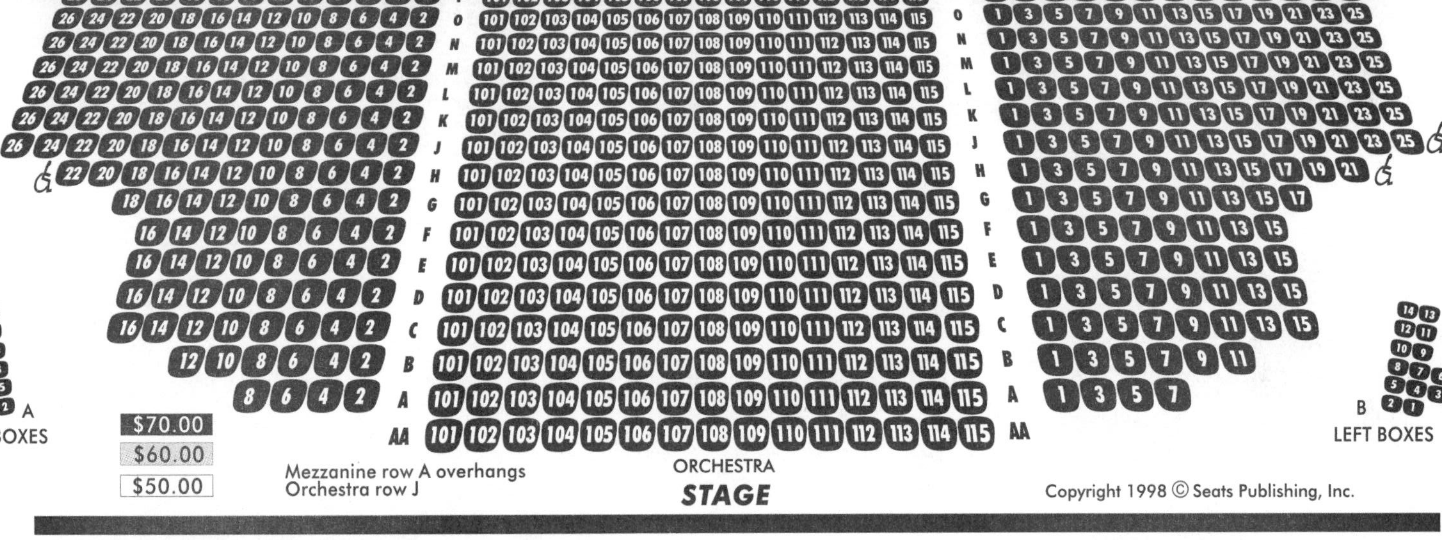

THEATRE (212) 239-6200

TAXI DIRECTIONS:
45th St. Westbound
(bet. 8th & 9th Aves.)

PARKING
Edison Park Fast, 1120 6th Ave.
(bet. 43rd & 44th Sts.)
Kinney System, 100 W. 44th St.
(bet. 6th & 7th Aves.)

BUS
M6, M7, M10, M11, M42, M104

SUBWAYS
A,C,E to 42nd St. & 8th Ave. Port Authority
1,2,3,7,9,N,R,S to 42nd St. & 7th Ave. Times Square

Nearby restaurants rated by
SEATS

TURKISH CUISINE, 631 9th Ave. at 45th St. 397-9650
BROADWAY JOE STEAK HOUSE, 315 W. 46th St. 246-6513
MARLOWE, 328 W. 46th St. 765-3815
O' FLAHERTY'S ALE HOUSE, 334 W. 46th St. 246-8928
DANNY'S GRAND SEA PALACE RESTAURANT,
346-348 W. 46th St. 265-8130

MINSKOFF THEATRE

200 West 45th Street, New York, NY 10036

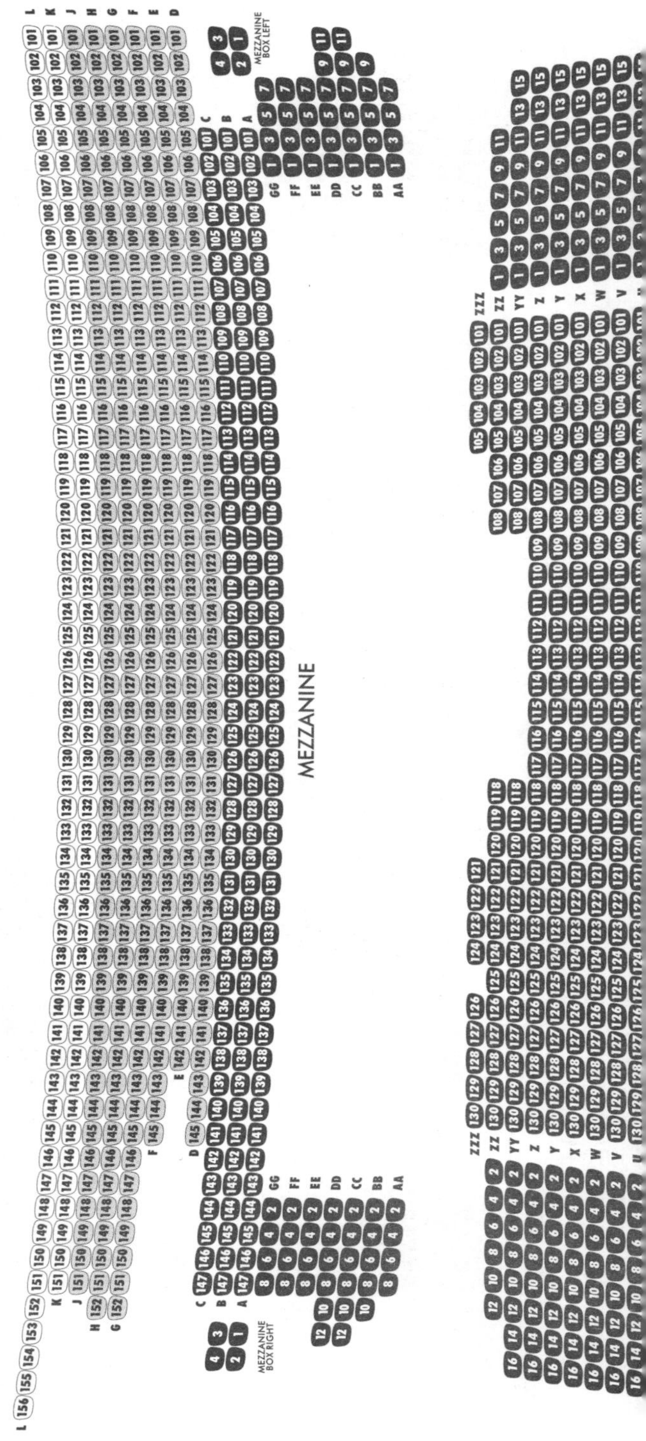

MEZZANINE

MEZZANINE BOX RIGHT

MEZZANINE BOX LEFT

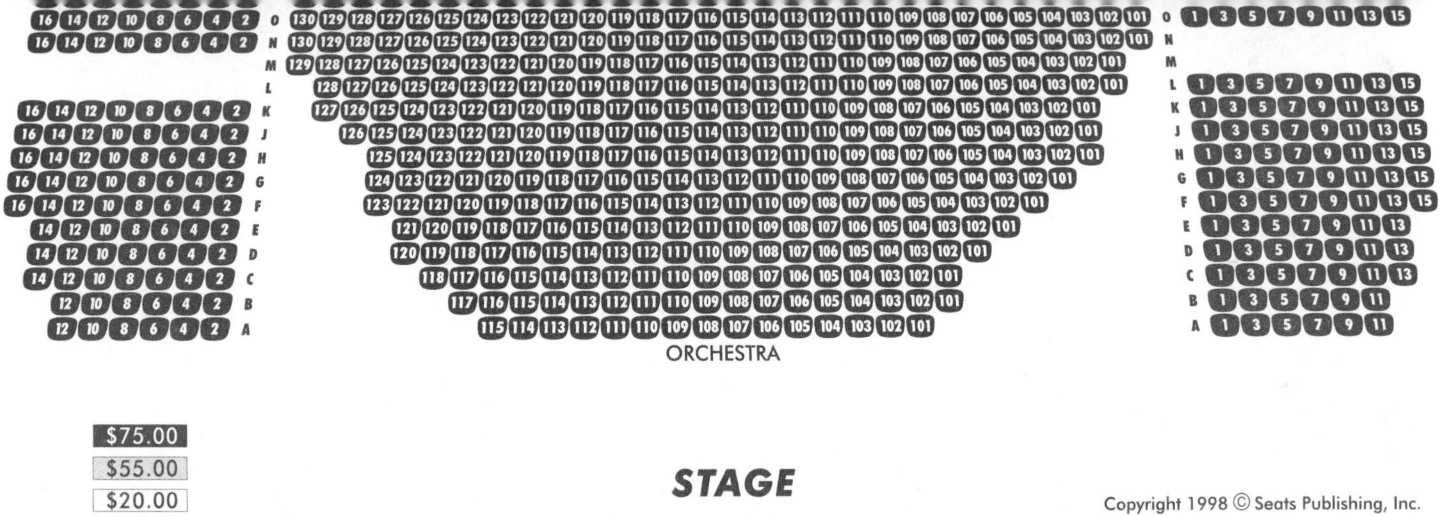

ORCHESTRA

$75.00

$55.00

$20.00

STAGE

TICKETMASTER (212) 307-4100

TAXI DIRECTIONS:
45th St. Westbound
(bet. 7th & 8th Aves.)

PARKING
Edison Park Fast, 1120 6th Ave.
(bet. 43rd & 44th St.)
Kinney System,
100 W. 44th St.
(bet. 6th & 7th Aves.)

BUS
M6, M7, M10, M42, M104

SUBWAYS
A, C, E to 42nd St. & 8th Ave. Port Authority
N,R,S,1,2,3,7,9 to 42nd St. & 7th Ave. Times Square
B, D, F, Q to 42nd St. & 6th Ave.

Nearby restaurants rated by
SEATS

TURKISH CUISINE, 631 9th Ave. at 45th St. 397-9650
BROADWAY JOE STEAK HOUSE, 315 W. 46th St. 246-6513
MARLOWE, 328 W. 46th St. 765-3815
O'FLAHERTY'S ALE HOUSE, 334 W. 46th St.246-8928
DANNY'S GRAND SEA PALACE RESTAURANT,
346-348 W. 46th St., 265-8130

MUSIC BOX THEATRE

239 West 45th Street, New York, NY 10036

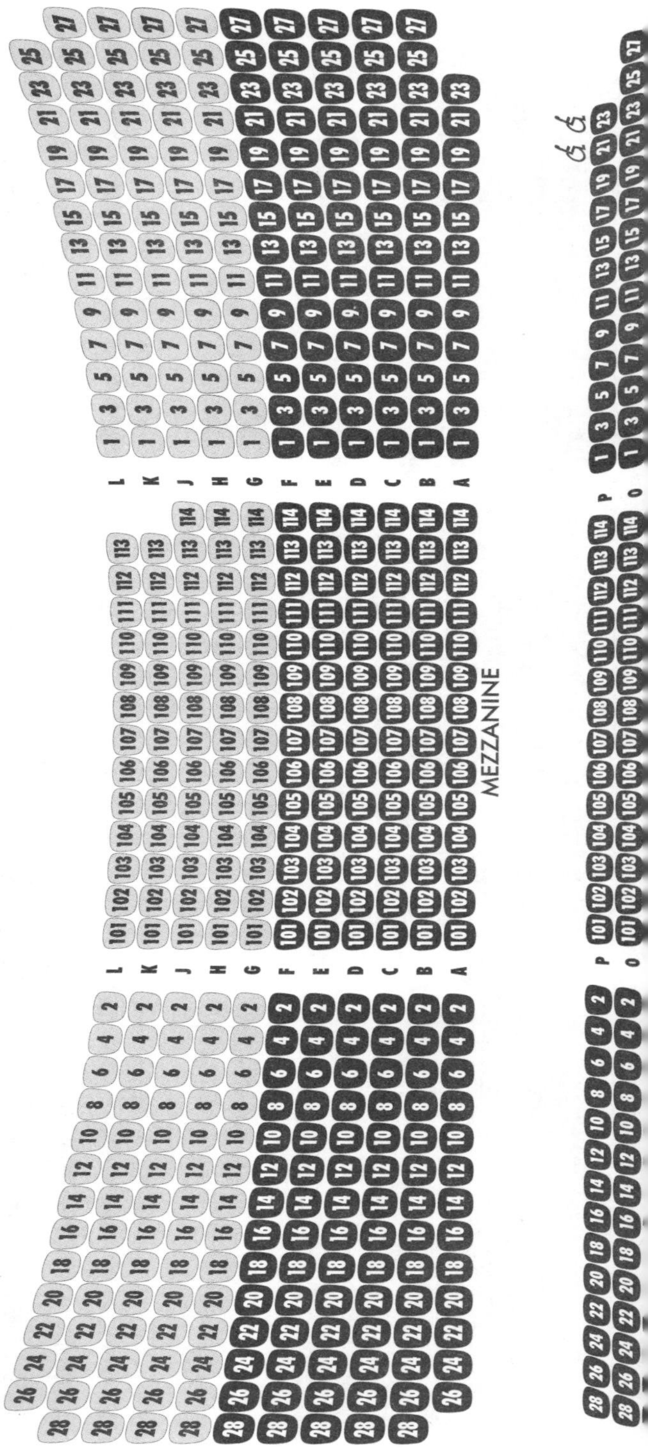

MEZZANINE

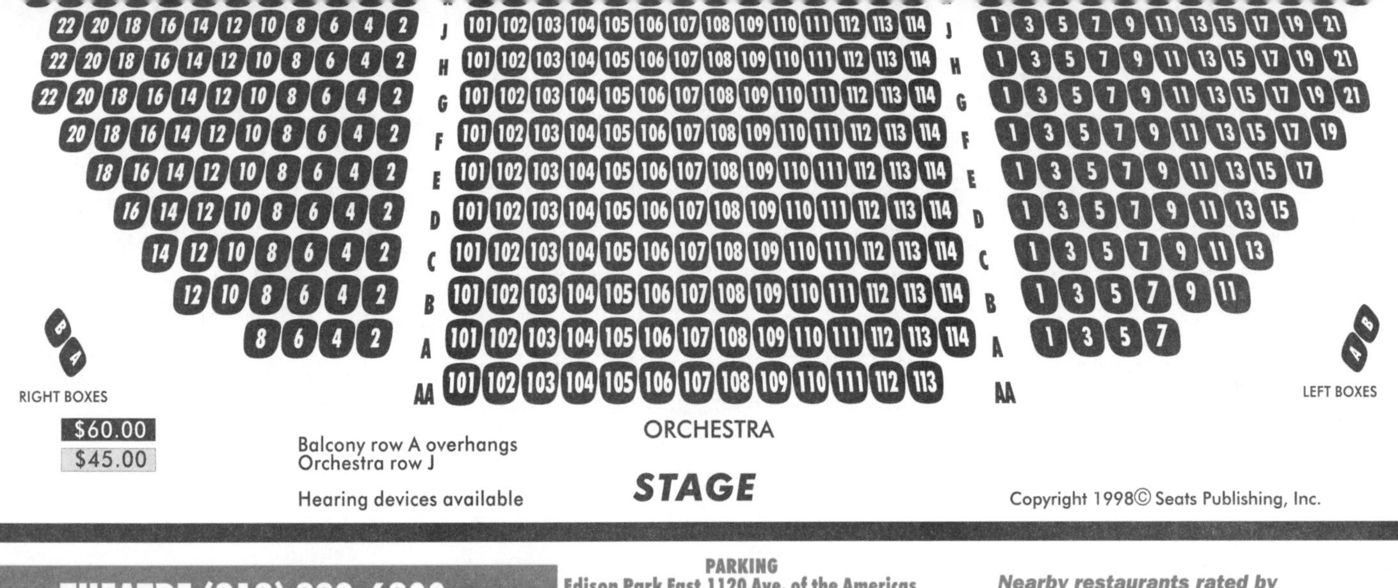

THEATRE (212) 239-6200

TAXI DIRECTIONS:
45th St. Westbound
(bet. Broadway & 8th Ave.)

PARKING
Edison Park Fast, 1120 Ave. of the Americas
(bet. 43rd & 44th Sts.)
Kinney System, 100 W. 44th St.
(bet. 6th & 7th Aves.)

BUS
M6, M7, M10, M42, M104

SUBWAYS
B, D, F, Q to 42nd St. & 6th Ave.
1,2,3,7,9,N,R,S to 42nd St. & 7th Ave. Times Square
A, C, E to 42nd St. & 8th Ave. Port Authority

Nearby restaurants rated by
SEATS

TURKISH CUISINE, 631 9th Ave. at 45th St. 397-9650
BROADWAY JOE STEAK HOUSE, 315 W. 46th St. 246-6513
MARLOWE, 328 W. 46th St. 765-3815
O' FLAHERTY'S ALE HOUSE, 334 W. 46th St. 246-8928
DANNY'S GRAND SEA PALACE RESTAURANT,
346-348 W. 46th St. 265-8130

NEDERLANDER THEATRE

208 West 41st Street, New York, NY 10036

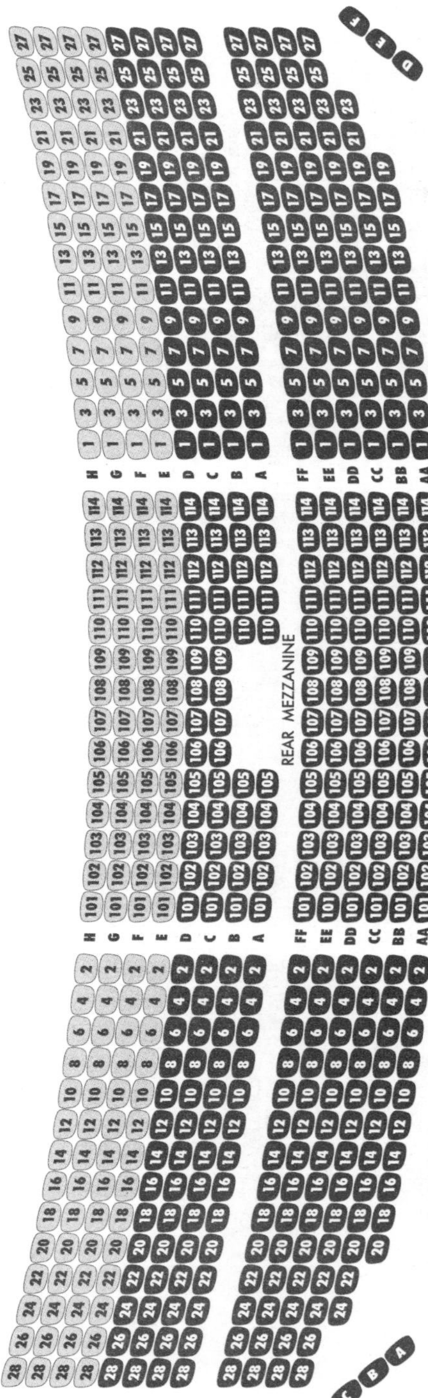

$75.00 Mezzanine row AA overhangs
$35.00 Orchestra row G

Hearing devices available

TICKETMASTER (212) 307-4100
GROUP SALES (800) 334-8457

TAXI DIRECTIONS:
41st St. Westbound
(bet. 7th & 8th Aves.)

PARKING
Edison Park Fast, 401-471 W. 42nd St.
(bet. 9th & 10th Aves.)
Kinney System,
250 W. 41st St.
(bet. 7th & 8th Aves.)
361 W. 42nd St.
(bet. 8th & 9th Aves.)

BUS
M6, M7, M10, M42, M104

SUBWAYS
A,C,E to 42nd St. & 8th Ave. Port Authority
N,R,S,1,2,3,7,9 to 42nd St. & 7th Ave. Times Square
B,D,F,Q to 42nd St. & 6th Ave.

Nearby restaurants rated by
SEATS

BRYANT PARK GRILL, 20 W. 40th St. 840-6500
ORIGINAL FERRARA PASTRIES, 201 W. 42nd St. 398-6064
STARDUST DINE-O-MAT, 1491 Broadway 768-3170
JOEY'S PAESANO, 205 W. 43rd St. 997-8700

NEIL SIMON THEATRE

250 West 52nd Street, New York, NY 10019

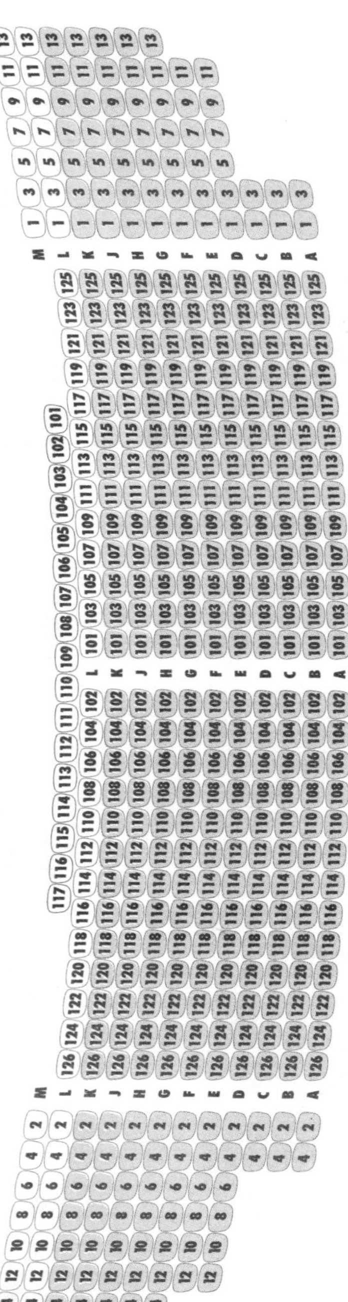

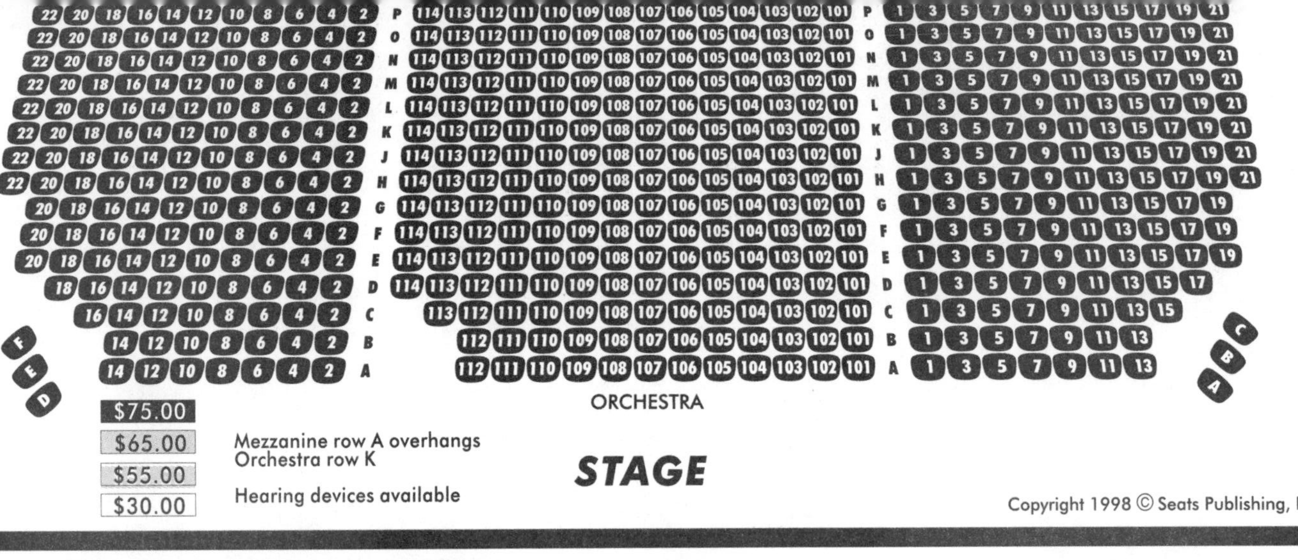

TICKETMASTER (212) 307-4100

TAXI DIRECTIONS:
52nd St. Eastbound
(bet. Broadway & 8th Ave.)

PARKING
Kinney System,
159 W. 53rd St. (bet. 6th & 7th Aves.)
301 W. 53rd St. (bet. 8th & 9th Aves.)
BUS
M6, M7, M10, M27, M50, M104
SUBWAYS
1,9 to 50th St. & Broadway
C,E to 50th St. & 8th Ave.
N,R to 49th St.
B,D,F,Q to 47th-50th St. & 6th Ave. Rockefeller Center

Nearby restaurants rated by
SEATS
LES PYRENEES, 251 W. 51st St. 246-0044
GALLAGHER'S STEAK HOUSE, 228 W. 52nd St. 245-5336
ORIGINAL FERRARA PASTRIES,
1700 Broadway 581-3335
GRILL 53,
111 W. 53rd St. at the New York Hilton 265-1600

NEW AMSTERDAM THEATRE

214 West 42nd Street, New York, NY 10036

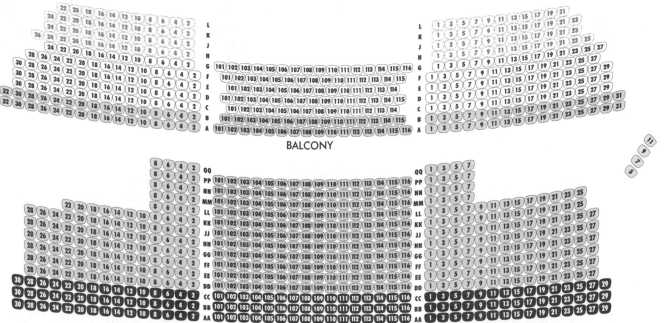

BALCONY

MEZZANINE

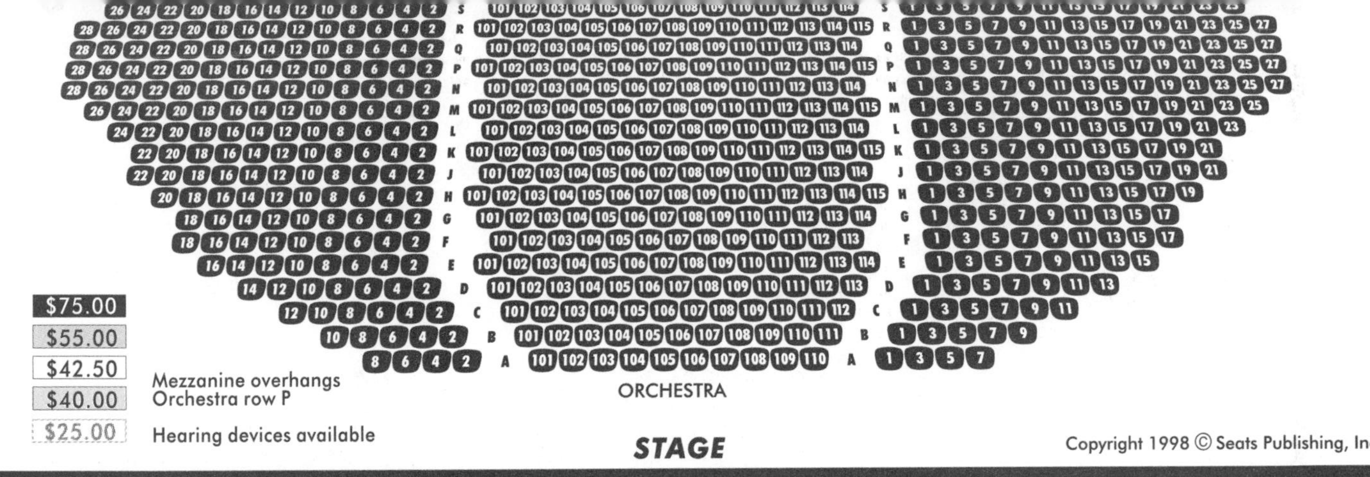

TICKETMASTER (212) 307-4100

PARKING
Square Parking, 306-332 W. 44th St.
Edison Park Fast, 401-471 W. 42nd St.
Kinney System, 250 W. 41st St.
Kinney System, 361 W. 42nd St.

BUS
M6, M7,M10, M42, M104

SUBWAYS
A, C, E to 42nd St. & 8th Ave. Port Authority
N,R,S,1,2,3,7,9,to 42nd St. & 7th Ave. Times Square
B, D, F, Q to 42nd St. & 6th Ave.

Nearby restaurants rated by
SEATS

BRYANT PARK GRILL, 20 W. 40th St. 840-6500
ORIGINAL FERRARA PASTRIES, 201 W. 42nd St. 398-6064
STARDUST DINE-O-MAT, 1491 Broadway 768-3170

TAXI DIRECTIONS:
42nd St. two way
(bet. 7th & 8th Aves.)

NEW VICTORY THEATRE

209 West 42nd Street, New York, NY 10036

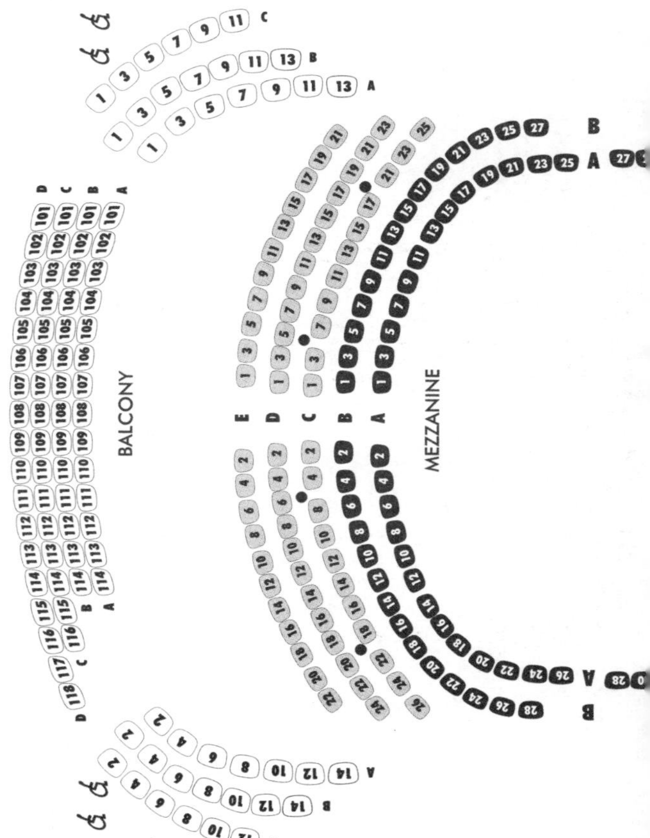

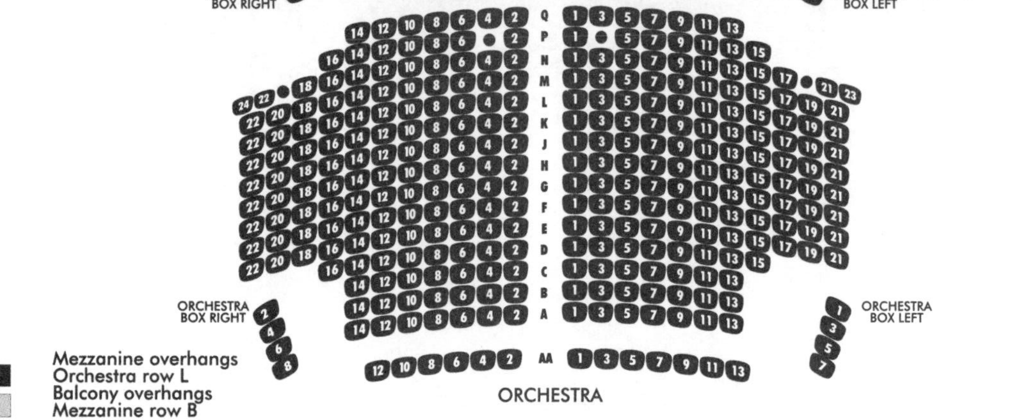

$25.00 Mezzanine overhangs

$20.00 Orchestra row L

$10.00 Balcony overhangs Mezzanine row B

STAGE

THEATRE (212) 239-6200
GROUP SALES (212) 564-4222
Membership Hotline (212) 382-4020

TAXI DIRECTIONS:
42nd St. two way
(bet. Broadway and 8th Ave.)

PARKING
Sauare Parking, 306-332 W. 44th St.
Edison Park Fast, 401-471 W. 42nd St.
Kinney System, 250 W. 41st St.
Kinney System, 361 W. 42nd St.

BUS
M6, M7, M10, M42, M104

SUBWAY
A,C,E, to 42nd St. & 8th Ave. Port Authority
N,R,S, 1,2,3,7,9, to 42nd St. & 7th Ave. Times Square
B,D,F,Q to 42nd St. & 6th Ave.

Nearby restaurants rated by
SEATS

BRYANT PARK GRILL, 20 W. 40th St. 840-6500
ORIGINAL FERRARA PASTRIES, 201 W. 42nd St. 398-6064
STARDUST DINE-O-MAT, 1491 Broadway at 43rd St. 768-3170

PALACE THEATRE

1564 Broadway at 47th Street, New York, NY 10036

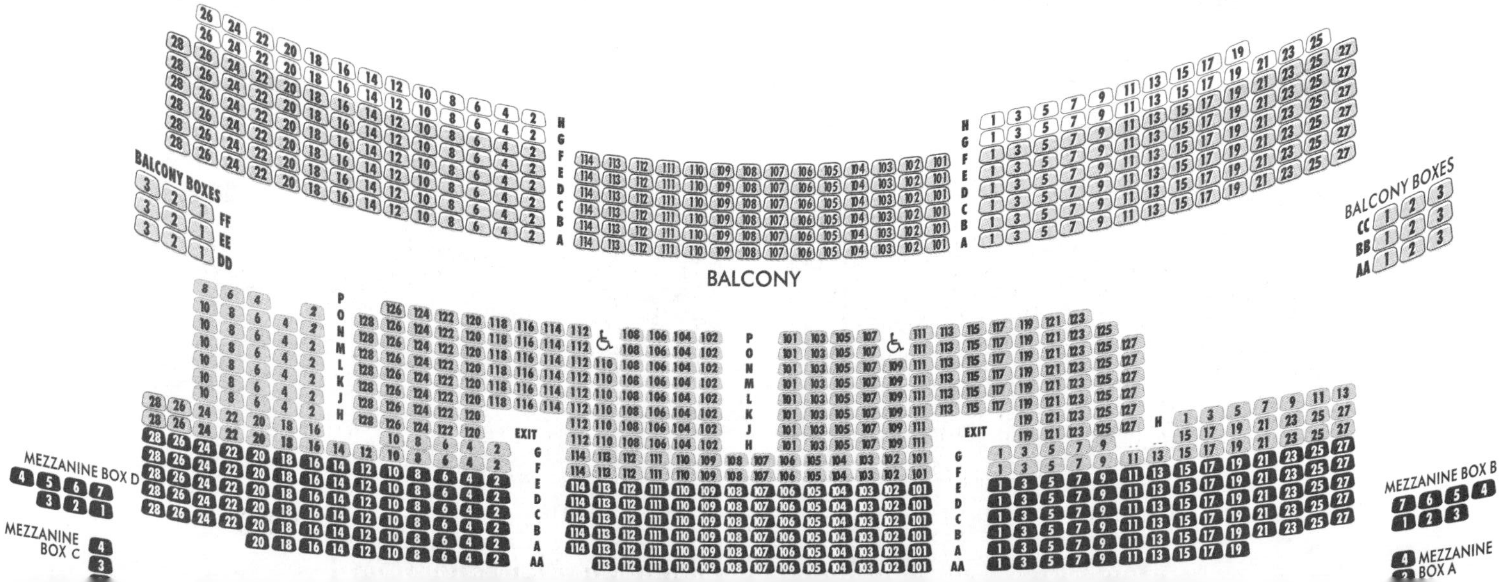

BALCONY BOXES

BALCONY

MEZZANINE BOX D

MEZZANINE BOX C

MEZZANINE BOX B

MEZZANINE BOX A

EXIT

EXIT

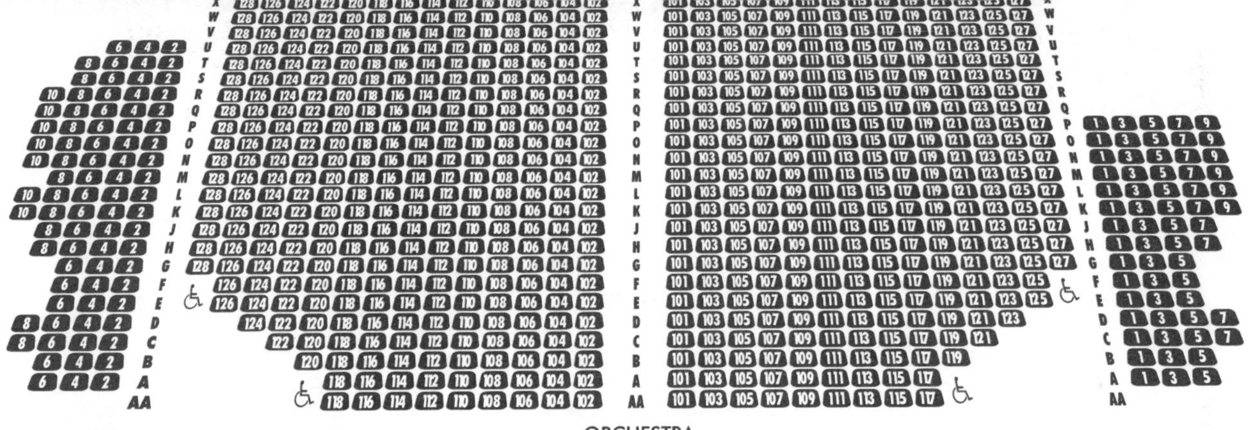

ORCHESTRA

STAGE

$70.00
$55.00
$38.50
$22.50

Mezzanine row A overhangs
Orchestra row K
Balcony row A overhangs
Mezzanine row G

TICKETMASTER (212) 307-4100

Taxi Directions:
Broadway is Southbound
(bet. 46th & 47th Sts.)

PARKING
GMC, 257 W. 47th St.
(bet. Broadway & 8th Ave.)
Kinney System, 253 W. 47th St.
(bet. Broadway & 8th Ave.)

BUS
M5, M6, M7 M10, M27, M50 M104

SUBWAYS
A,C,E to 42nd St. & 8th Ave. Port Authority
N, R, 1,2,3,7,9,S to 42nd St. & 7th Ave. Times Square
B,D,F,Q, to 42nd St. & 6th Ave.

Nearby restaurants rated by
SEATS

BROADWAY JOE STEAK HOUSE, 315 W. 46th St. 246-6513
O'FLAHERTY'S ALE HOUSE, 334 W. 46th St. 246-8928
DANNY'S GRAND SEA PALACE RESTAURANT, 346 W. 46th St. 265-8130
MESKEREM, 468 W. 47th St. 664-0520
SHAAN, 57 W. 48th St. 977-8400
B. SMITH'S, 771 8th at 47th St. 247-2222
LA PRIMAVERA, 234 W. 48th St. 586-2797
CIRO, 813 8th Ave. at 49th St. 307-5484

PLYMOUTH THEATRE

236 West 45th Street, New York, NY 10036

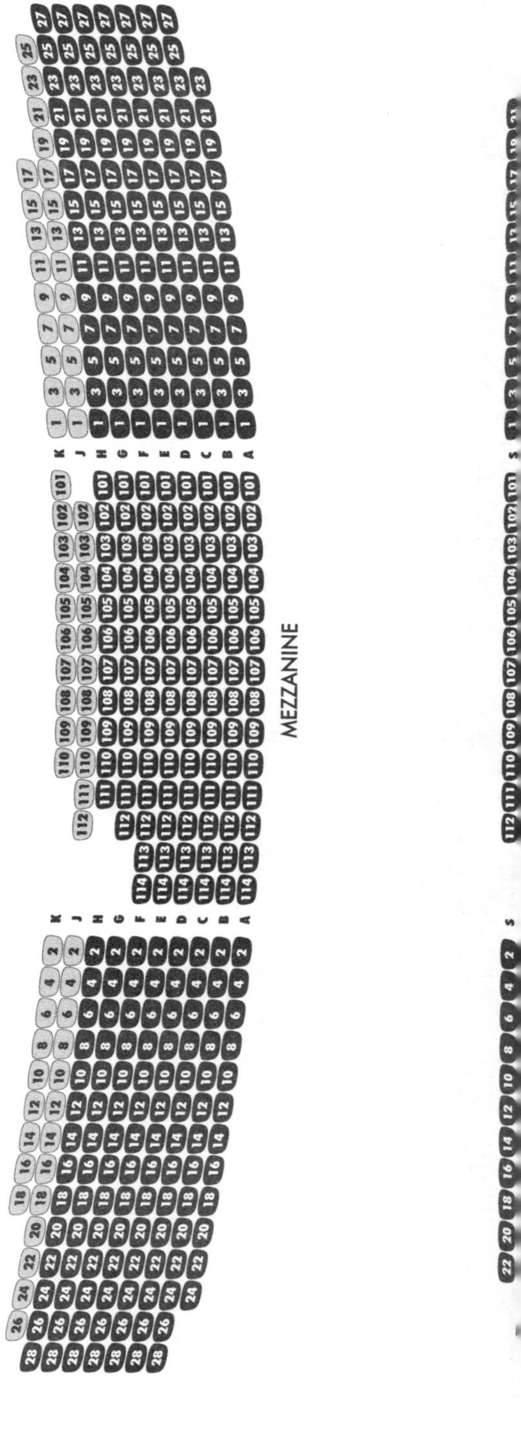

MEZZANINE

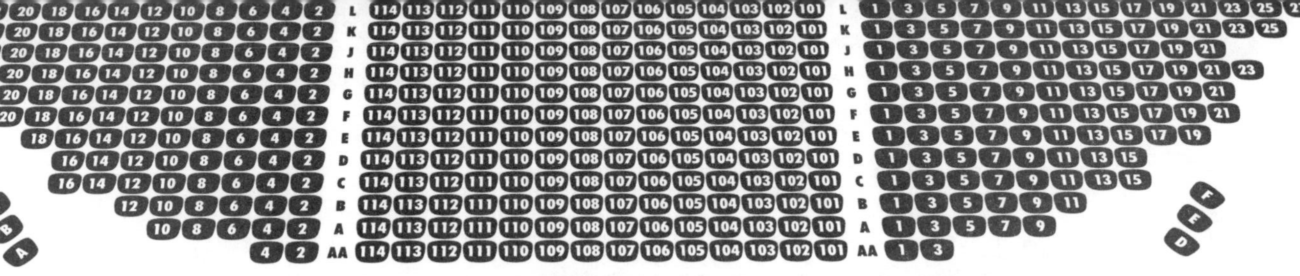

STAGE

$75.00

$55.00

Front mezzanine row A overhangs orchestra row J

Hearing devices available

TELECHARGE (212) 239-6200

TAXI DIRECTIONS:
45th St. Westbound
(bet. Broadway & 8th Ave.)

PARKING
Edison Park Fast, 1120 6th Ave.
(bet. 43rd & 44th St.)
Kinney System,
100 W. 44th St.
(bet. 6th & 7th Ave.)
BUS
M6, M7, M10,M42, M104
SUBWAYS
A, C, E to 42nd St. & 8th Ave. Port Authority
N,R,S,1,2,3,7,9 to 42nd St. & 7th Ave. Times Square
B, D, F, Q to 42nd St. & 6th Ave.

Nearby restaurants rated by
SEATS
TURKISH CUISINE, 631 9th Ave. at 45th St. 397-9650
BROADWAY JOE STEAK HOUSE, 315 W. 46th St. 246-6513
MARLOWE, 328 W. 46th St. 765-3815
O'FLAHERTY'S ALE HOUSE, 334 W. 46th St. 246-8928
DANNY'S GRAND SEA PALACE RESTAURANT,
346-348 W. 46th St. 265-8130

RICHARD RODGERS THEATRE

226 West 46th Street, New York, NY 10036

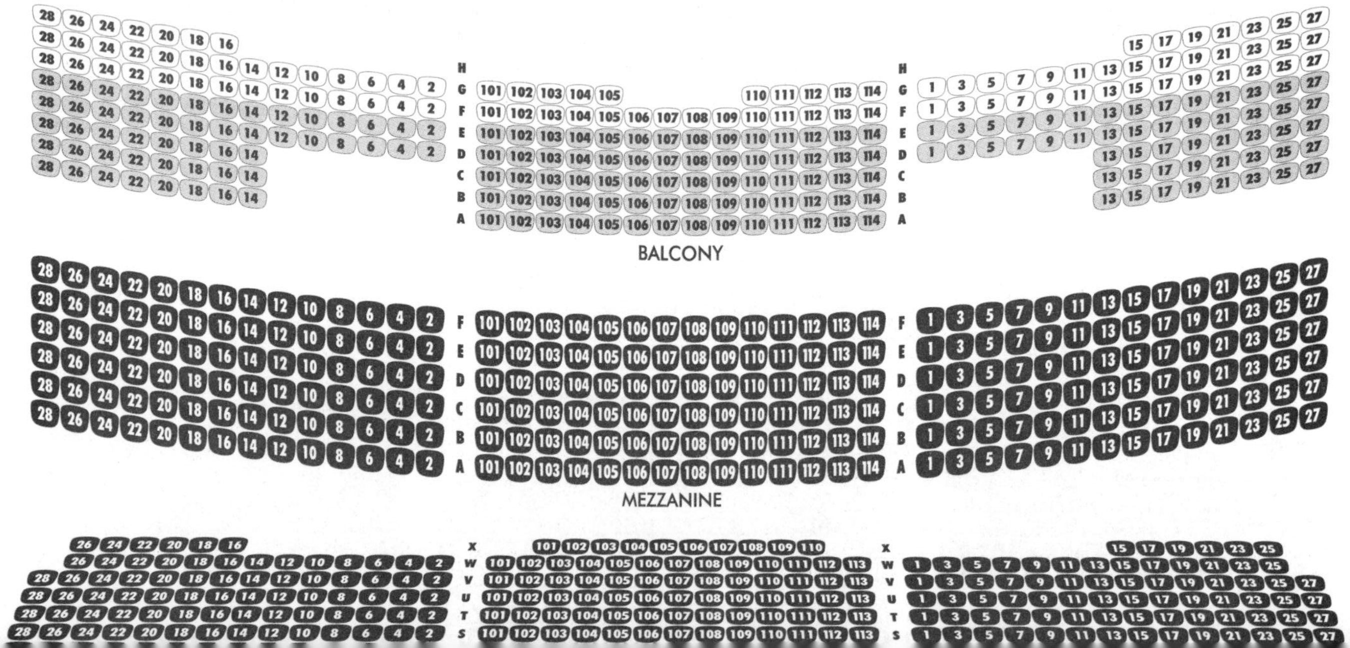

BALCONY

MEZZANINE

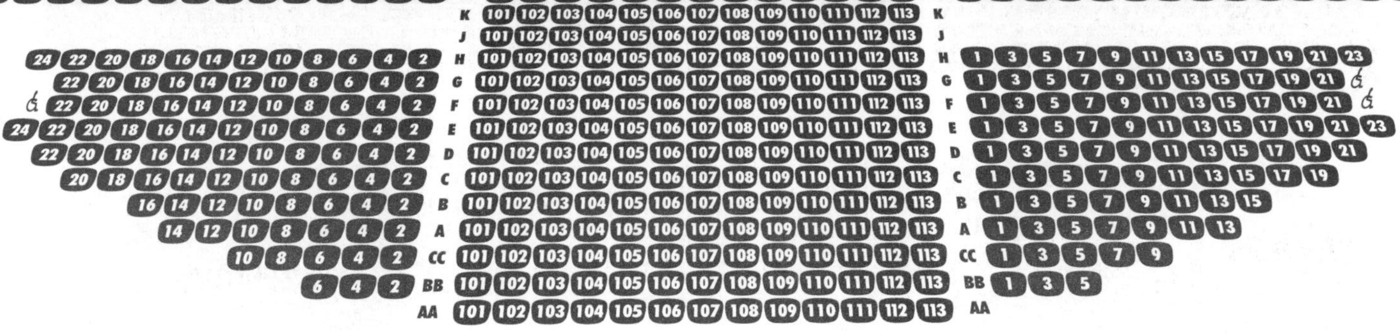

ORCHESTRA

Mezzanine row A overhangs
Orchestra row L

Hearing devices available

$75.00
$60.00
$45.00

STAGE

TICKETMASTER (212) 307-4100

TAXI DIRECTIONS:
46th St. Eastbound
(bet. Broadway & 8th Ave.)

PARKING
GMC, 257 W. 47th St.
(bet. Broadway & 8th Ave.)
Kinney System, 38 W. 46th St.
(bet. 5th & 6th Aves.)
BUS
M6, M7, M10, M42, M104
SUBWAYS
A,C,E to 42nd & 8th Ave. Port Authority
N,R,S,1,2,3,7,9, to 42nd St. & 7th Ave. Times Square
B,D,F,Q to 42nd St. & 6th Ave.

Nearby restaurants rated by
SEATS
TURKISH CUISINE, 631 9th Ave. at 45th St. 397-9650
MARLOWE, 328 W. 46th St. 765-3815
O'FLAHERTY'S ALE HOUSE, 334 W. 46th St. 246-8928
DANNY'S GRAND SEA PALACE RESTAURANT,
346-348 W. 46th St. 265-8130
MASKEREM, 468 W. 47th St. 664-0520

ROUNDABOUT THEATRE COMPANY

1530 Broadway, New York, NY 10036

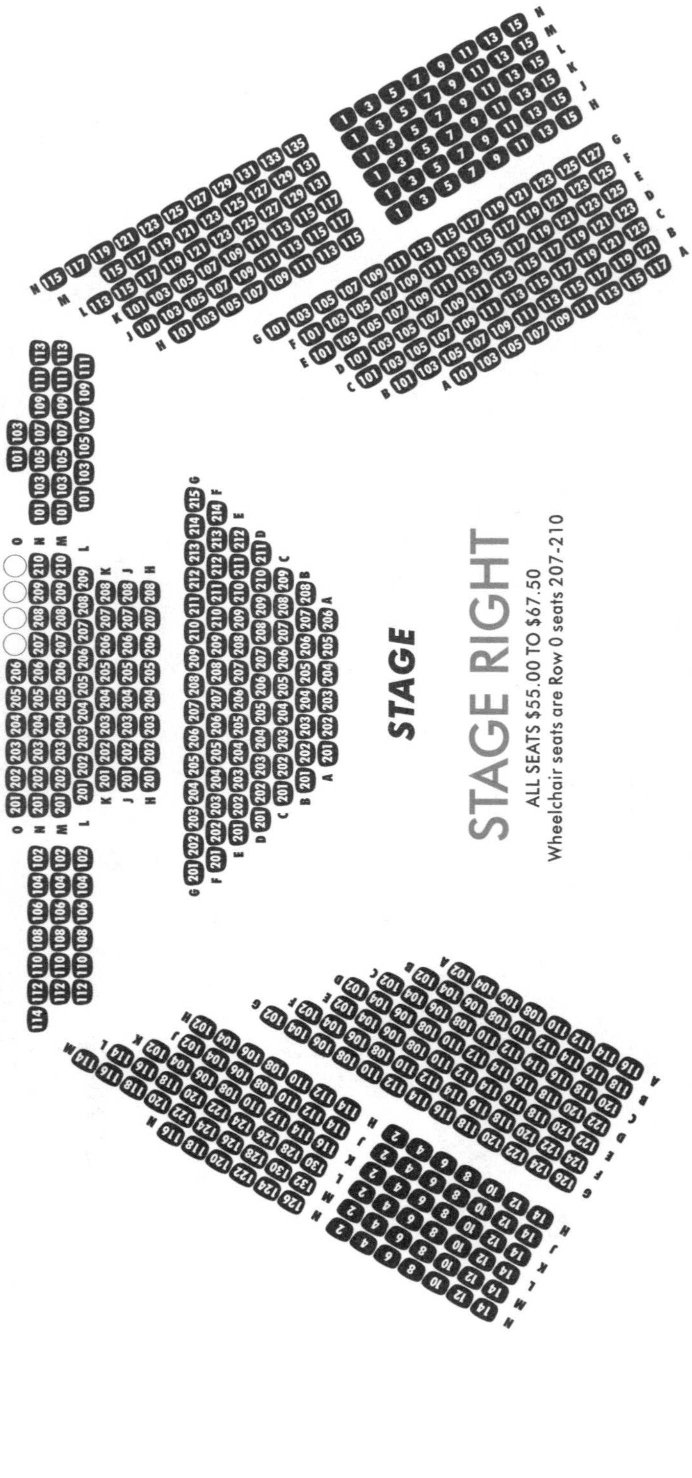

STAGE

STAGE RIGHT

ALL SEATS $55.00 TO $67.50

Wheelchair seats are Row 0 seats 207-210

LAURA PELS

ALL SEATS $45.00
Wheelchair in boxes

Row	Box	Left	Center	Right	Box
RR		14 12 10 8 6 4 2	101 102 103 104 105 106 107 108 109 110 111 112 113 114 115 116	1 3 5 7 9 11 13	
QQ		16 14 12 10 8 6 4 2	101 102 103 104 105 106 107 108 109 110 111 112	1 3 5 7 9 11 13	
PP		16 14 12 10 8 6 4 2	101 102 103 104 105 106 107 108 109 110 111 112	1 3 5 7 9 11 13	
OO		16 14 12 10 8 6 4 2	101 102 103 104 105 106 107 108 109 110 111 112	1 3 5 7 9 11 13	
NN		12 10 8 6 4 2	101 102 103 104 105 106 107 108 109 110 111 112	1 3 5 7 9 11	
MM		12 10 8 6 4 2	101 102 103 104 105 106 107 108 109 110 111 112	1 3 5 7 9 11	
LL		10 8 6 4 2	101 102 103 104 105 106 107 108 109 110 111 112	1 3 5 7 9	
KK		14 12 10 8 6 4 2	101 102 103 104 105 106 107 108 109 110 111 112	1 3 5 7 9 11 13	
JJ		14 12 10 8 6 4 2	101 102 103 104 105 106 107 108 109 110 111 112	1 3 5 7 9 11 13	
HH		14 12 10 8 6 4 2	101 102 103 104 105 106 107 108 109 110 111 112	1 3 5 7 9 11 13	
GG		12 10 8 6 4 2	101 102 103 104 105 106 107 108 109 110 111 112	1 3 5 7 9 11	
FF		12 10 8 6 4 2	101 102 103 104 105 106 107 108 109 110 111 112	1 3 5 7 9 11	
EE	EE8	6 4 2	101 102 103 104 105 106 107 108 109 110 111 112	1 3 5	EE7
DD	DD6	4 2	101 102 103 104 105 106 107 108 109 110 111 112	1 3	DD5
CC	CC6	4 2	101 102 103 104 105 106 107 108 109 110 111 112	1 3	CC5
BB	BB6	4 2	101 102 103 104 105 106 107 108 109 110 111 112	1 3	BB5
AA		4 2	101 102 103 104 105 106 107 108 109 110 111 112	1 3	

STAGE

TICKETS (212) 869-8400

TAXI DIRECTIONS:
Broadway Southbound
(bet. 44th & 45th Sts.)

PARKING
Edison Park Fast,
1120 6th Ave.
(bet. 43rd & 44th Sts.)
Kinney System, 100 W. 44th St.
(bet. 6th & 7th Aves.)
Hippodrome, 50 W. 44th St.

BUS
M5, M6, M7, M10, M42, M104

SUBWAYS
1,2,3,7,9,R,N,S to 42nd & 7th Ave. Times Square
A,C,E to 42nd St. & 8th Ave. Port Authority
B,D,F,Q, to 42nd St. & 6th Ave.

Nearby restaurants rated by
SEATS

BROADWAY JOE'S STEAK HOUSE, 315 W. 46th St. 246-6513
TURKISH CUISINE, 631 9th Ave. at 45th St. 397-9650
O'FLAHERTY'S ALE HOUSE, 334 W. 46th St. 246-8928
VIRGIL'S, 152 W. 44th St. 921-9494
DANNY'S GRAND SEA PALACE RESTAURANT,
346 W. 46th St. 265-8130

ROYALE THEATRE

242 West 45th Street, New York, NY 10036

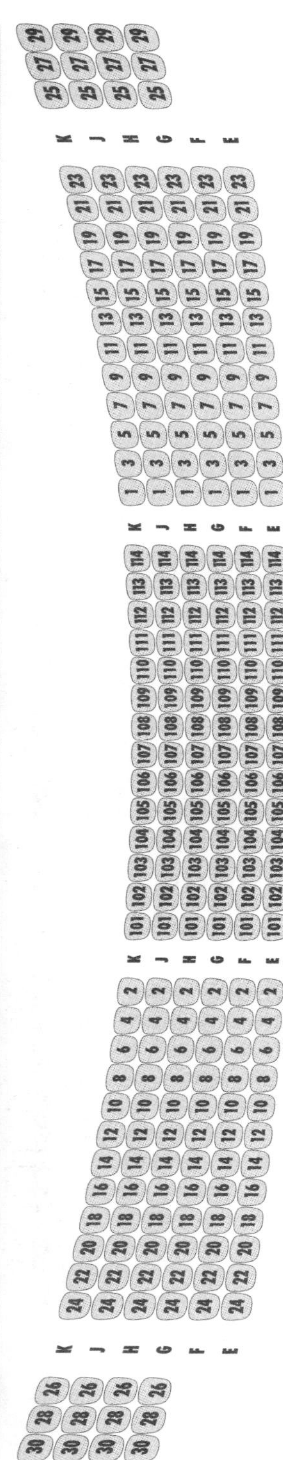

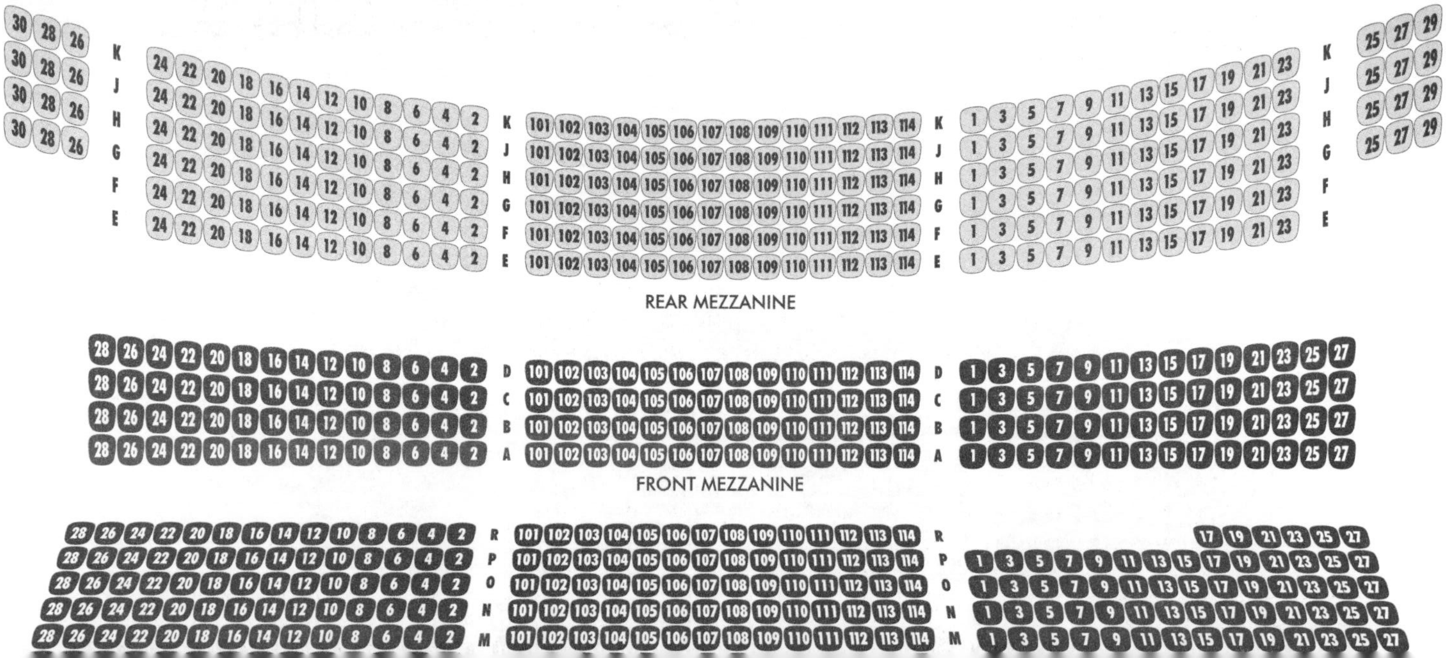

REAR MEZZANINE

FRONT MEZZANINE

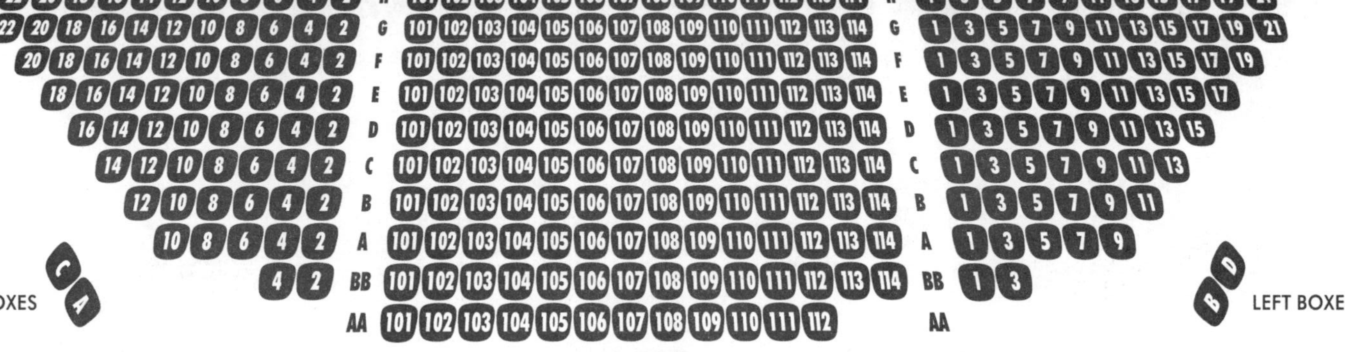

$75.00
$55.00

Mezzanine row A overhangs Orchestra row I

Hearing devices available

STAGE

THEATRE (212) 239-6200
GROUP SALES (800) 223-7565

TAXI DIRECTIONS:
45th St. Westbound
(bet. Broadway & 8th Ave.)

PARKING
Edison Park Fast, 1120 Ave. of the Americas
(bet. 43rd & 44th Sts.)
Kinney System, 100 W. 44th St.
(bet. 6th & 7th Ave.)

BUS
M6, M7, M10, M42, M104

SUBWAYS
B, D, F, Q to 42nd St. & 6th Ave.
1,2,3,7,9,N,R,S to 42nd St. & 7th Ave.
Times Square
A, C, E to 42nd & 8th Ave. Port Authority

Nearby restaurants rated by
SEATS

TURKISH CUISINE, 631 9th Ave. at 45th St. 397-9650
BROADWAY JOE STEAK HOUSE, 315 W. 46th St. 246-6513
MARLOWE, 328 W. 46th St. 765-3815
O' FLAHERTY'S ALE HOUSE, 334 W. 46th St. 246-8928
DANNY'S GRAND SEA PALACE RESTAURANT,
346-348 W. 46th St. 265-8130

ST. JAMES THEATRE

246 West 44th Street, New York, NY 10036

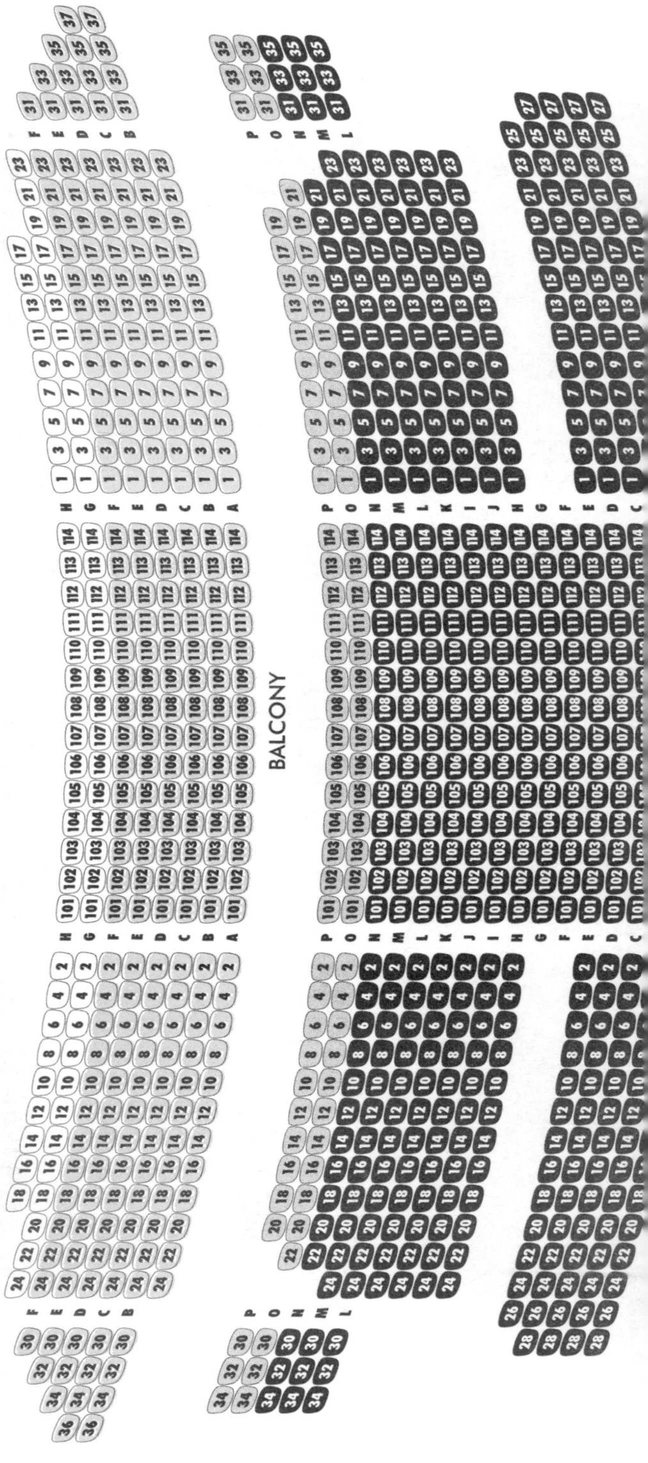

BALCONY

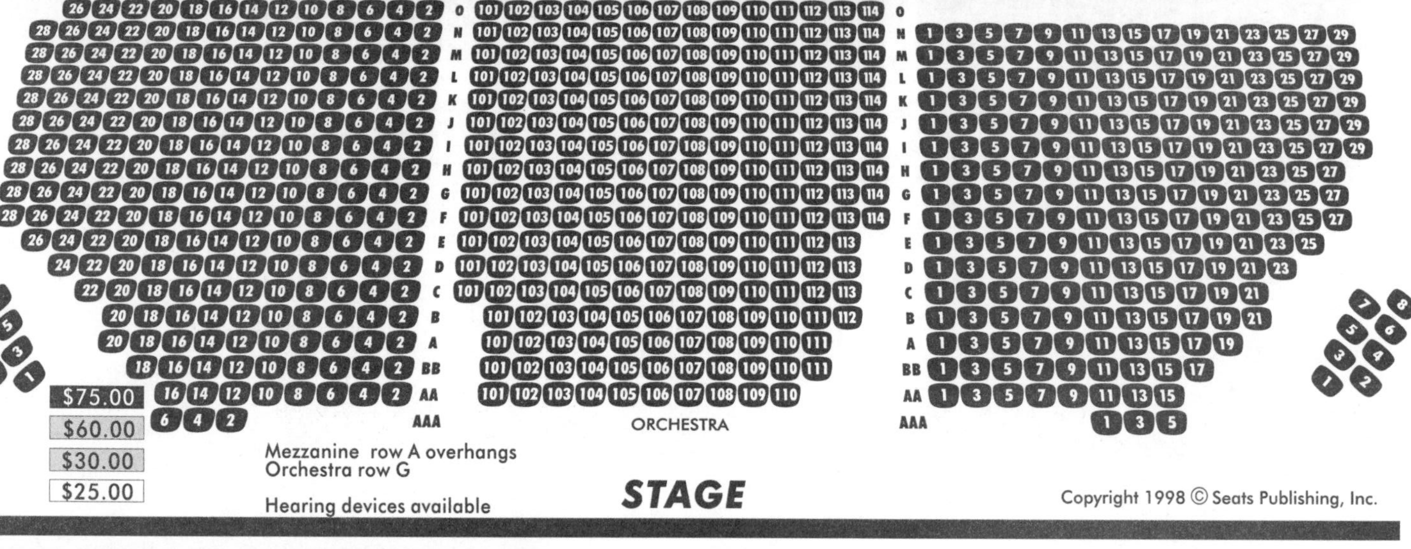

TELECHARGE (212) 239-6200

TAXI DIRECTIONS:
44th St. Easttbound
(bet. 7th & 8th Aves.)

PARKING
Edison Park Fast, 1120 6th Aves.
(bet. 43rd & 44th Sts.)
Kinney System,
100 W. 44th St.
(bet. 6th & 7th Aves.)
BUS
M6, M7, M10, M42, M104
SUBWAYS
A,C,E to 42nd St. & 8th Ave. Port Authority
N,R,S,1,2,3,7,9 to 42nd St. & 7th Ave. Times Square
B,D,F,Q to 42nd St. & 6th Ave.

Nearby restaurants rated by
SEATS
ORIGINAL FERRARA PASTRIES, 201 W. 42nd St. 398-6064
STARDUST DINE-O-MAT, 1491 Broadway 768-3170
TURKISH CUISINE, 631 9th Ave. at 45th St. 397-9650
CAFE UN DEUX TROIS, 123 W. 44th St. 354-4148
VIRGIL'S, 152 W. 44th St. 921-9494

SHUBERT THEATRE

225 West 44th Street, New York, NY 10036

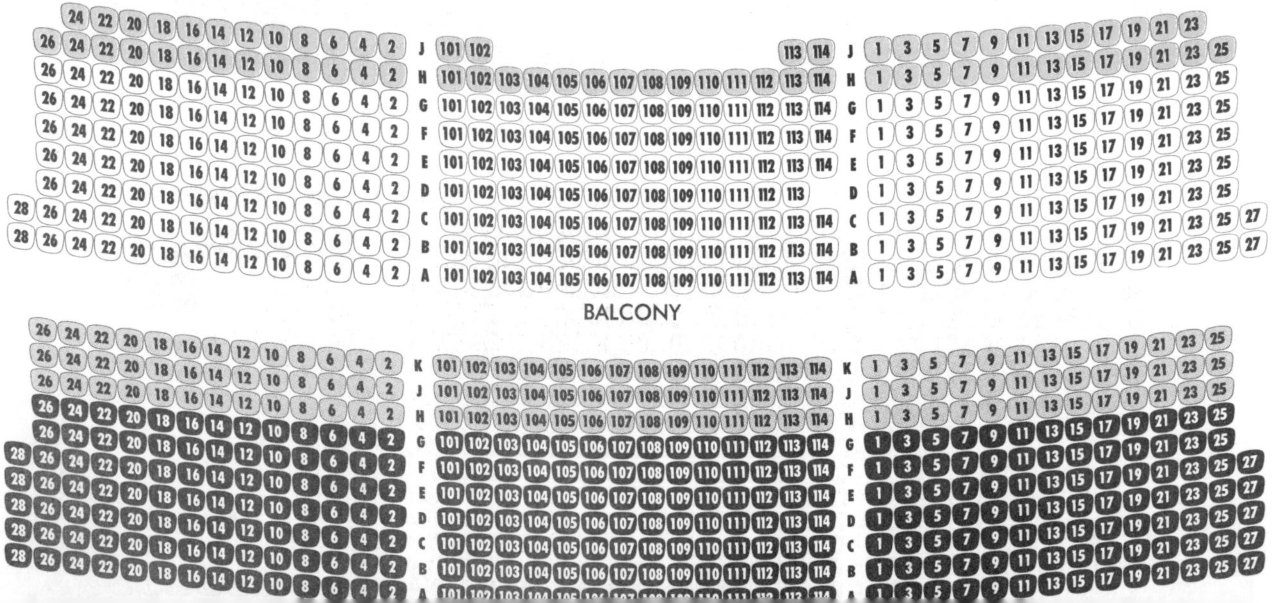

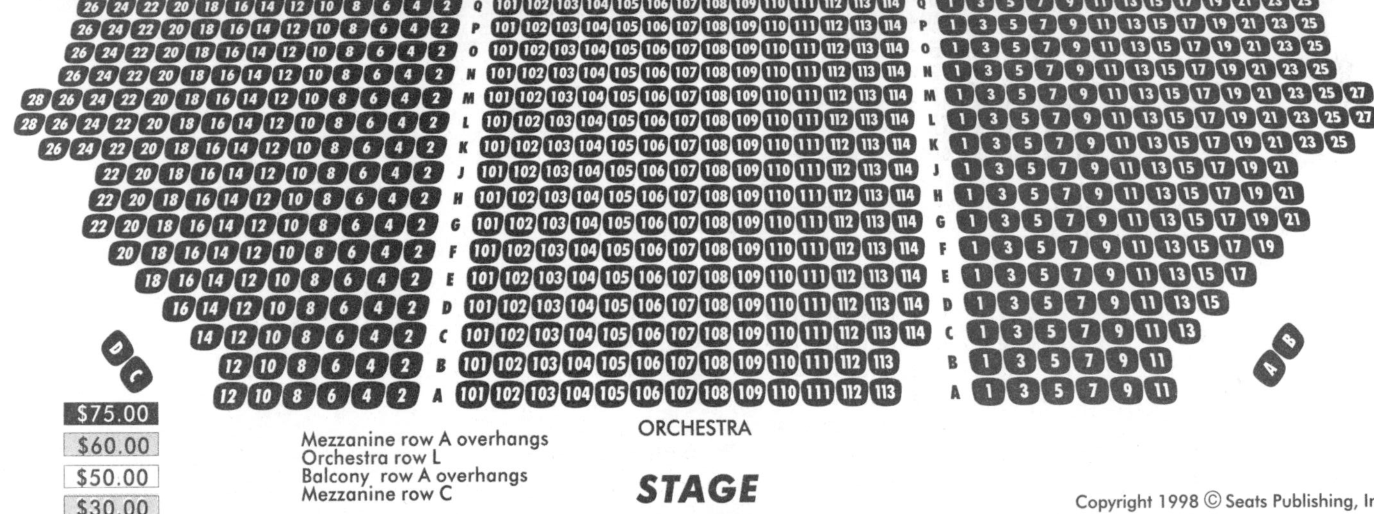

TELECHARGE (212)239-6200

TAXI DIRECTIONS:
44th St. Eastbound
(bet. 7th & 8th Aves.)

PARKING
Edison Park Fast, 1120 6th Ave.
(bet. 43rd & 44th Sts.)
Kinney System,
100 W. 44th St.
(bet. 6th & 7th Aves.)
BUS
M6, M7, M10, M42, M104
SUBWAYS
A, C, E to 42nd St. & 8th Ave. Port Authority
N,R,S,1,2,3,7,9 to 42nd St. & 7th Ave. Times Square
B, D, F, Q to 42nd St. & 6th Ave.

Nearby restaurants rated by
SEATS
ORIGINAL FERRARA PASTRIES, 201 W. 42nd St. 398-6064
STARDUST DINE-O-MAT, 1491 Broadway 768-3170
TURKISH CUISINE, 631 9th Ave. at 45th St. 397-9650
CAFE UN DEUX TROIS, 123 W. 44th St. 354-4148
VIRGIL'S, 152 W. 44th St. 921-9494

VIRGINIA THEATRE

245 West 52nd Street, New York, NY 10019

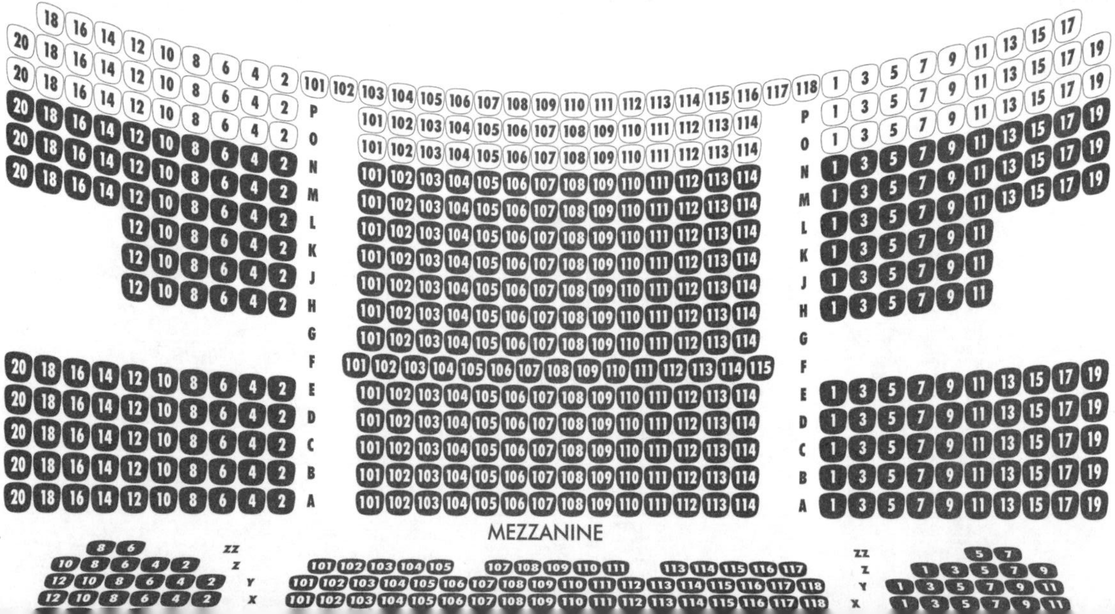

MEZZANINE

$75.00
$35.00

Mezzanine row A overhangs Orchestra row A

ORCHESTRA

STAGE

TELECHARGE (212) 239-6200

TAXI DIRECTIONS:
52nd St.Eastbound
(bet. Broadway & 8th Ave.)

PARKING
Kinney System, 159 W. 53rd St.
(bet. 6th & 7th Aves.)
Kinney System, 301 W. 53rd St
(bet. 8th & 9th Aves.)

BUS
M6, M7, M10, M27, M50, M104

SUBWAYS
1,9 to 50th St. & Broadway
C,E to 50th St. & 8th Ave.
N,R to 49th St.
B,D,F,Q to 47th-50th St. & 6th Ave. Rockefeller Center

Nearby restaurants rated by
SEATS

LES PYRENEES, 251 W. 51st St. 246-0064
GALLAGHER'S STEAK HOUSE, 228 W. 52nd St. 245-5336
ORIGINAL FERRARA PASTRIES,
1700 Broadway 581-3335
GRILL 53, 111 W. 53rd St.
at the New York Hilton. 265-1600

WALTER KERR THEATRE

219 West 48th Street, New York, NY 10036

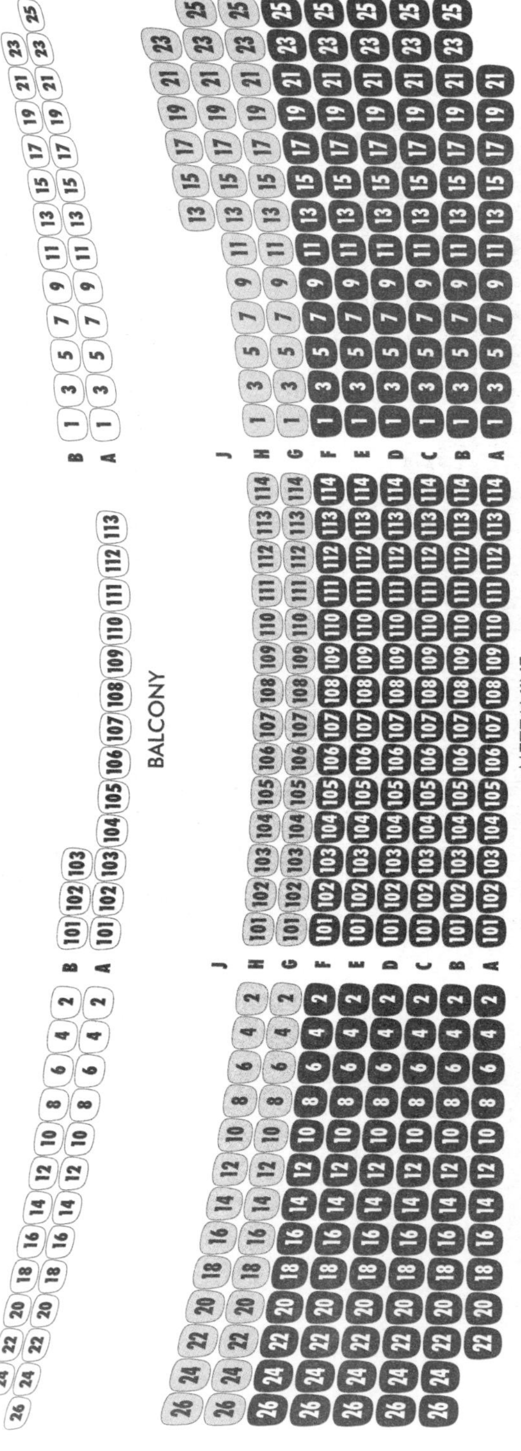

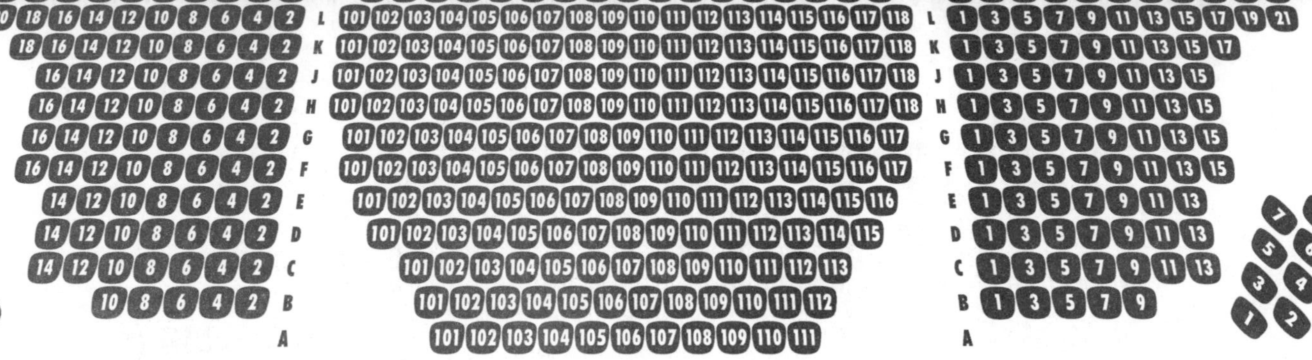

$75.00
$55.00
$20.00

Mezzanine row A overhangs
Orchestra row J

STAGE

TELECHARGE (212) 239-6200
GROUP SALES (800) 677-1164

TAXI DIRECTIONS:
48th St. Eastbound
(bet. Broadway & 8th Ave.)

PARKING
Edison Parking, 757 7th Ave.
(bet. 49th & 50th Sts.)
GMC, 148 W. 48th St.
(bet. 6th & 7th Aves.)
Kinney, 155 W. 48th St.
(bet. 6th & 7th Aves.)

BUS
M6, M7, M10, M27, M50, M104

SUBWAYS
1,9 to 50th St. & Broadway
C,E to 50th St. & 8th Ave.
N,R to 49th St.
B,D,F,Q to 47th-50th St. & 6th Ave. Rockefeller Center

Nearby restaurants rated by
SEATS

B. SMITH'S, 771 8th Ave. 247-2222
SHAAN, 57 W. 48th St. 977-8400
LA PRIMAVERA, 234 W. 48th St. 586-2797
MESKEREM II, 682 11th Ave. 541-7858
CIRO, 813 8th Ave. 307-5484
WALLY'S & JOSEPH'S RESTAURANT, 249 W. 49th St. 582-0460

WINTER GARDEN THEATRE

1634 Broadway, New York, NY 10019

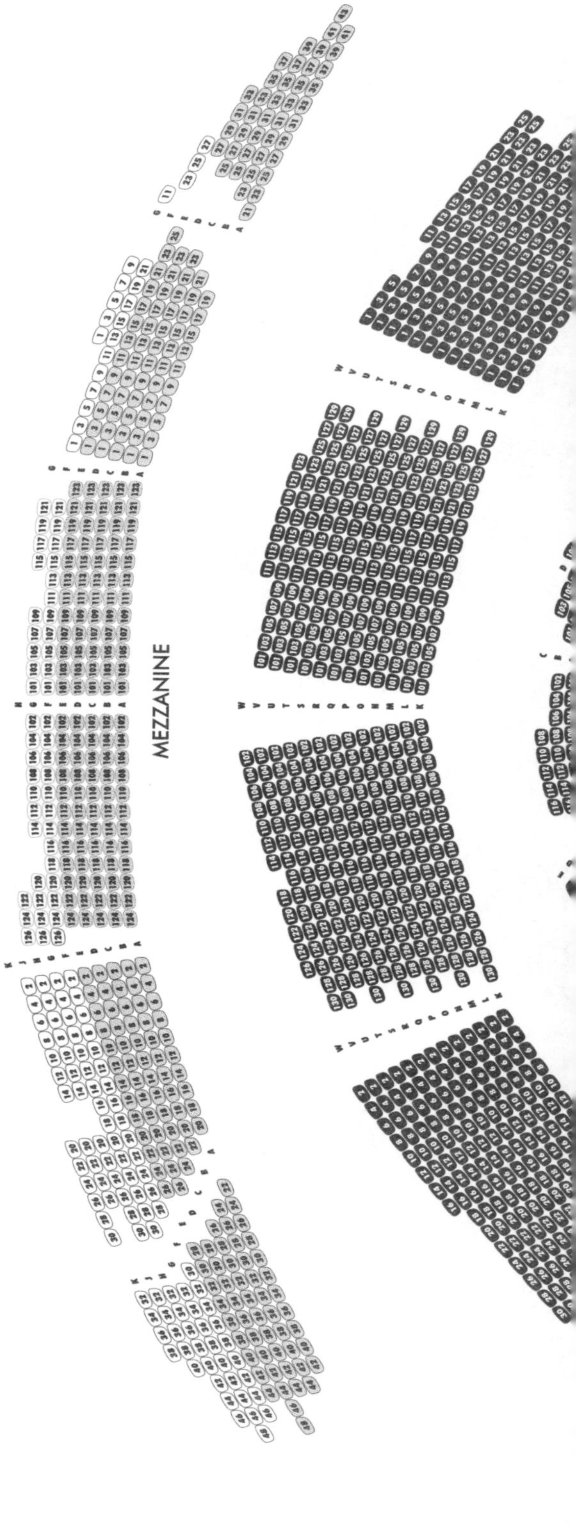

MEZZANINE

STAGE

$70.00
$57.50
$42.50

Hearing devices available

TELECHARGE (212) 239-6200
GROUP SALES (212) 239-6262

TAXI DIRECTIONS:
Broadway Southbound
(bet. 50th & 51st Sts.)

PARKING
Edison Park Fast, 713-719 10th Ave.
(bet. 48th & 49th Sts.)
GMC, 218 W 50th St.
(bet. Broadway & 8th Ave.)
BUS
M6, M7, M10, M27, M50, M104
SUBWAYS
1,9 to 50th St. & Broadway
C,E to 50th St. & 8th Ave.
N,R to 49th St.
B,D,F,Q to 47th-50th St. & 6th Ave. Rockefeller Center

Nearby restaurants rated by
SEATS
SHAAN, THE RESTAURANT OF INDIA,
57 W. 48th St. 977-8400
WALLY'S & JOSEPH'S RESTAURANT,
249 W. 49th St. 582-0460
PALIO, 151 W. 51st St. 245-4850
GALLAGHER'S STEAK HOUSE,
228 W. 52nd St. 245-5336

ACTORS' PLAYHOUSE

100 Seventh Avenue South, New York, NY 10014

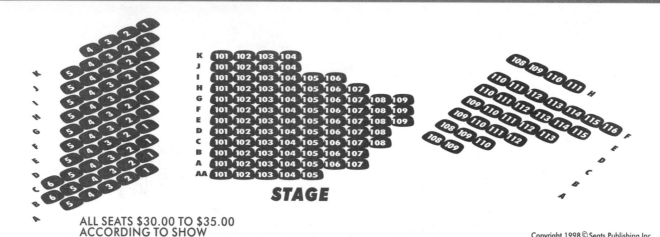

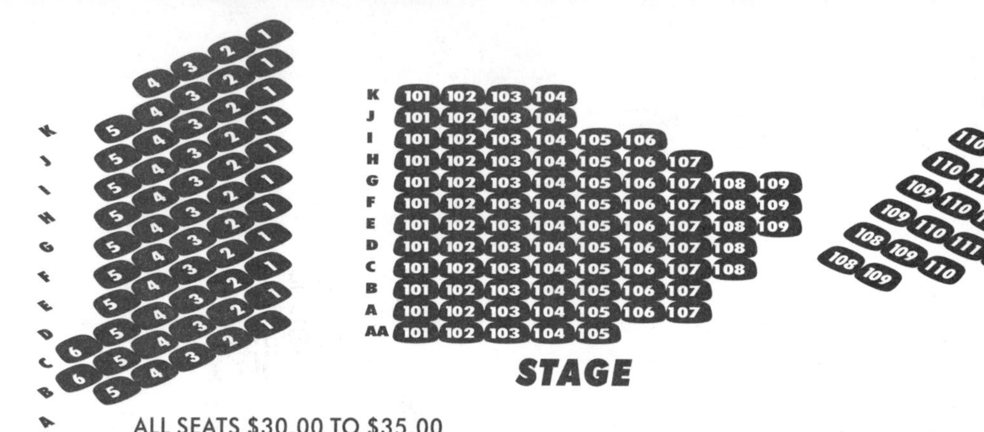

ALL SEATS $30.00 TO $35.00
ACCORDING TO SHOW

TELECHARGE (212) 239-6200

Taxi Directions:
From West Side 7th Ave. Southbound (bet. Bleeker & Christopher Sts.)
From East Side West at Houston St.

PARKING
Kinney System, 18 Morton St. (bet. Bleeker St. & 7th Ave. South)
BUS
M8, M10
SUBWAYS
1,9 to Christopher St. & 7th Ave. Sheridan Square

Nearby restaurants rated by
SEATS

CAFE TORINO 139 W. 10th St. (bet. Greenwich St. & 7th Ave.) 675-5554
SUZIE'S RESTAURANT, 163 Bleeker St. 777-1395
CALIENTE CAB CO. 61 7th Ave, South 243-8517

AMERICAN JEWISH THEATRE

307 West 26th Street, New York, NY 10001

E 201 202 203 204 205 206 207 208 209 210 211 212 E
D 201 202 203 204 205 206 207 E E 210 211 212 213 214 215 216 D
C 201 202 203 204 205 206 207 E E 210 211 212 213 214 215 216 C
B 201 202 203 204 205 206 207 208 209 210 211 212 B
A 201 202 203 204 205 206 207 208 209 210 211 212 A

A 101 102 103 104 105 106 A
B 101 102 103 104 105 106 B
C 101 102 103 104 105 106 107 C
D 101 102 103 104 105 106 107 D
E 101 102 103 104 105 106 107 E
F 101 102 103 104 105 106 107 F
G 101 102 103 104 105 106 G

A 301 302 303 304 305 306 A
B 301 302 303 304 305 306 B
C 301 302 303 304 305 306 307 C
D 301 302 303 304 305 306 307 D
E 301 302 303 304 305 E
F 301 302 303 304 305 306 307 F

STAGE

ALL SEATS $30.00

THEATRE (212) 633-9797

Taxi Directions:
26th St. Eastbound
at 8th Ave. Northbound

PARKING
Central System, 252 W. 26th St.
BUS
M10, M11, M23
SUBWAYS
1,9,to 28th St. & 7th Ave.
C,E to 23rd St. & 8th Ave.

Nearby restaurants rated by
SEATS

ZUCCA RESTAURANT, 227 10th Ave.
bet. 23rd & 24th Sts. 741-1970
LUMA RESTAURANT, 200 9th Ave.
bet. 22nd & 23rd Sts. 633-8033
CHELSEA COMMONS RESTAURANT, 463 W. 24th St,
at 10th Ave. 924-6737

THE AMERICAN PLACE THEATRE

111 West 46th Street, New York, NY 10036

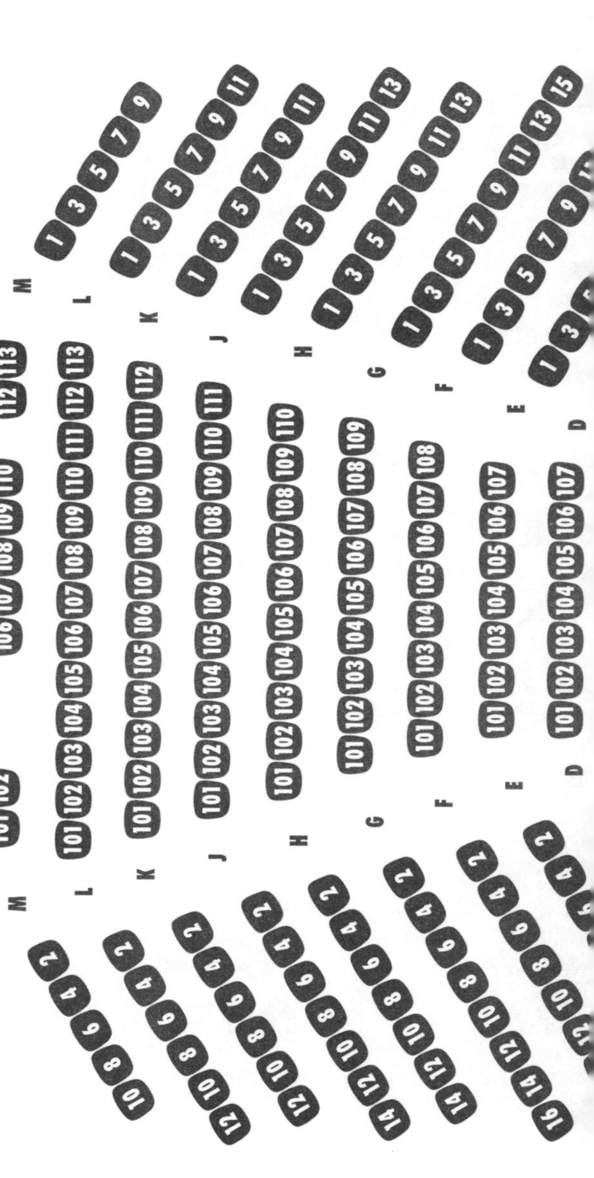

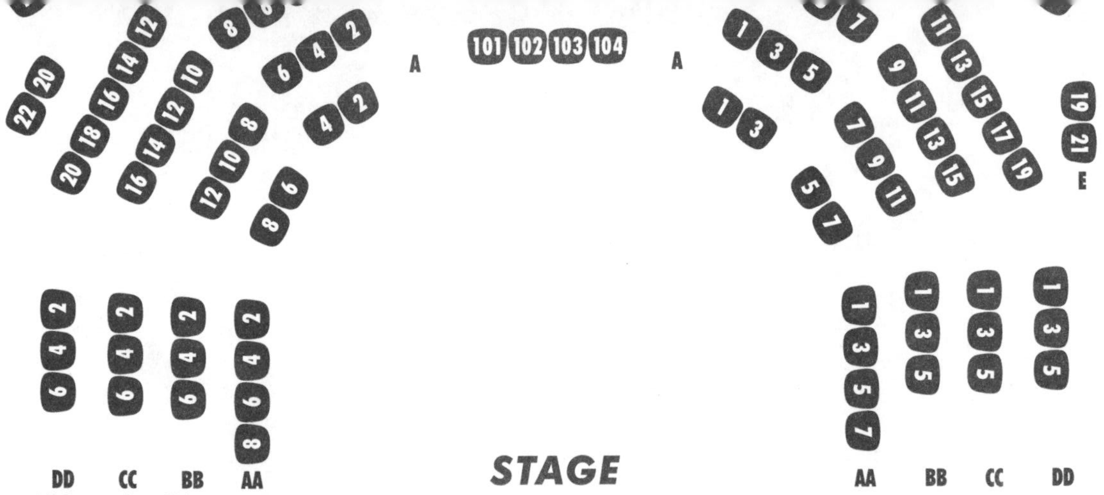

STAGE

All Seats One Price
Hearing devices available
♿ Wheelchair seating available

TICKETS (212) 239-6200
GROUP SALES (212) 889-4300

TAXI DIRECTIONS:
46th St. Eastbound
(bet. 6th and 7th Aves.)

PARKING
Edison Park Fast, 757 7th Ave.
(bet. 49th & 50th Sts.)
GMC, 148 W. 48th St.
(bet. 6th & 7th Aves.)
Kinney System, 155 W. 48th St.
(bet. 6th & 7th Aves.)

BUS
M5, M6, M7, M10, M42, M104

SUBWAYS
B, D, F, Q to 42nd St. & 6th Ave.
1,2,3,7,9,N,R,S to 42nd St. & 7th Ave. Times Square
A, C, E to 42nd St. & 8th Ave. Port Authority

Nearby restaurants rated by
SEATS

O' FLAHERTY'S ALE HOUSE, 334 W. 46th St. 246-8928
DANNY'S GRAND SEA PALACE RESTAURANT, 346-348 W. 46th St. 265-8130
B. SMITH'S, 771 8th Ave. at 47th St. 247-2222
SHAAN, 57 W. 48th St. 977-8400
LA PRIMAVERA, 234 W. 48th St. 586-2797
WALLY'S & JOSEPH'S RESTAURANT, 249 W. 49th St. 582-0460

ASTOR PLACE THEATRE

434 Lafayette Street, NY 10003

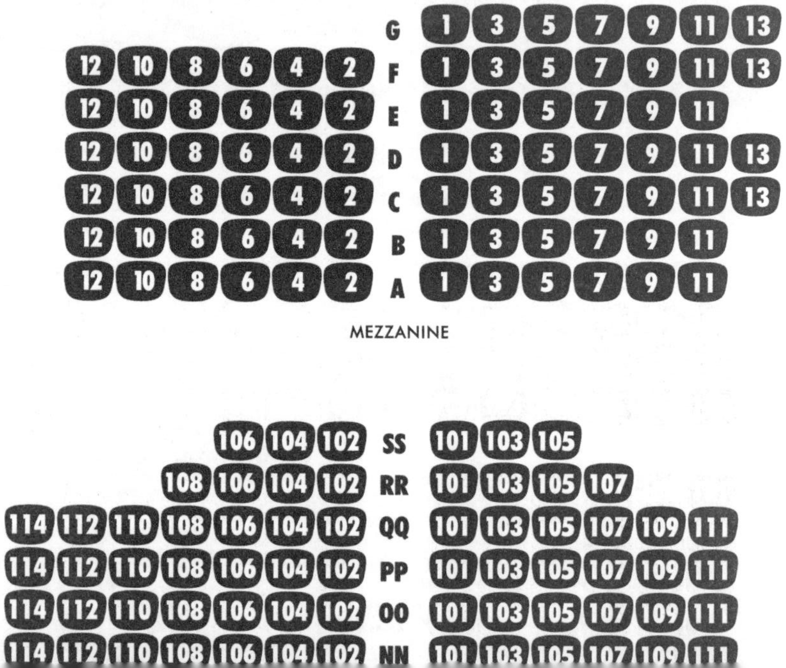

MEZZANINE

G		1 3 5 7 9 11 13
F	12 10 8 6 4 2	1 3 5 7 9 11 13
E	12 10 8 6 4 2	1 3 5 7 9 11
D	12 10 8 6 4 2	1 3 5 7 9 11 13
C	12 10 8 6 4 2	1 3 5 7 9 11 13
B	12 10 8 6 4 2	1 3 5 7 9 11
A	12 10 8 6 4 2	1 3 5 7 9 11

SS	106 104 102	101 103 105
RR	108 106 104 102	101 103 105 107
QQ	114 112 110 108 106 104 102	101 103 105 107 109 111
PP	114 112 110 108 106 104 102	101 103 105 107 109 111
OO	114 112 110 108 106 104 102	101 103 105 107 109 111
NN	114 112 110 108 106 104 102	101 103 105 107 109 111

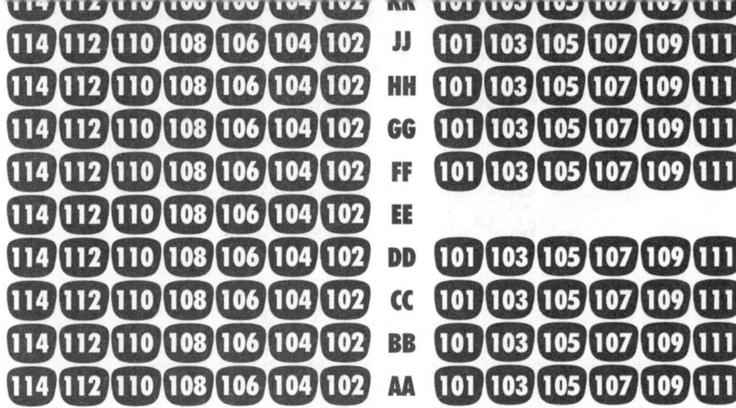

All Seats $49.00

STAGE

TICKETMASTER (212) 307-4100

TAXI DIRECTIONS:
Lafayette St. Northbound
(bet. Astor Place & W. 4th St.)

PARKING
Stop & Park, 410-420 Lafayette St.
BUS
M10, M11, M23
SUBWAYS
6 to Astor Place
N,R to 8th St. & Broadway

Nearby restaurants rated by
SEATS
INDOCHINE, 430 Lafayette St. 505-5111
HELENA'S, 432 Lafayette St. 677-5151

ATLANTIC THEATRE

336 West 20th Street, New York, NY 10011

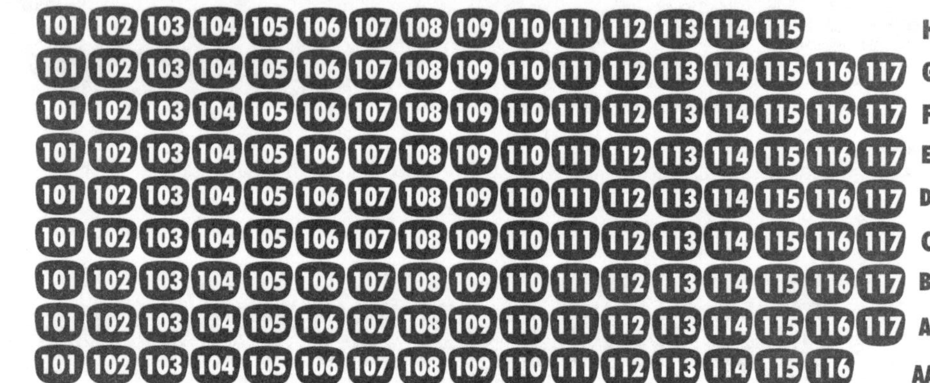

All Seats One Price

STAGE

THEATRE (212) 845-8015
TELECHARGE (212) 239-6200

Taxi Directions:
20th St. Eastbound
(bet. 8th & 9th Aves.)

PARKING
19th Street Garage
250 W. 19th St.
(bet. 7th & 8th Aves.)
Discount for ticket holders
Kinney System, 435 W. 23rd St.,
(bet. 9th & 10th Aves.)

BUS
M10, M11, M23

SUBWAYS

Nearby restaurants rated by
SEATS

ZUCCA, 227 10th Ave. 741-1970
LUMA, 200 9th Ave. 633-8033

CLASSIC STAGE THEATRE

136 East 13th Street, New York, NY 10003

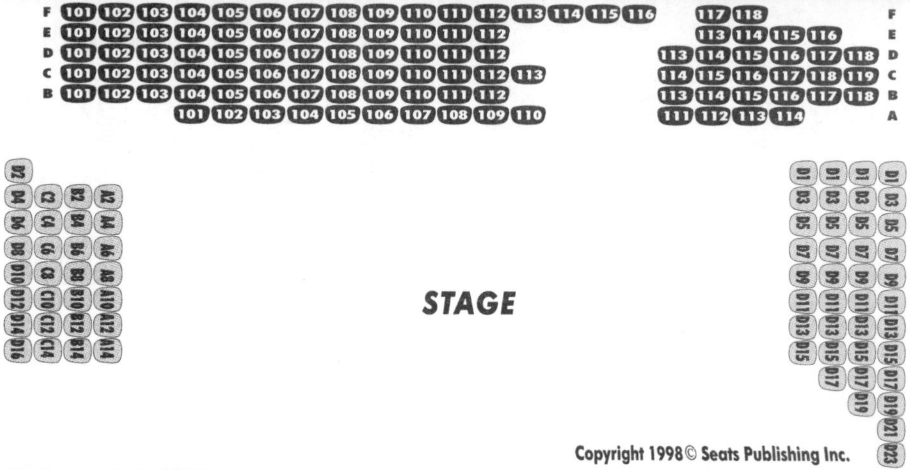

F 101 102 103 104 105 106 107 108 109 110 111 112 113 114 115 116 117 118 F
E 101 102 103 104 105 106 107 108 109 110 111 112 113 114 115 116 E
D 101 102 103 104 105 106 107 108 109 110 111 112 113 114 115 116 117 118 D
C 101 102 103 104 105 106 107 108 109 110 111 112 113 114 115 116 117 118 119 C
B 101 102 103 104 105 106 107 108 109 110 111 112 113 114 115 116 117 118 B
101 102 103 104 105 106 107 108 109 110 111 112 113 114 A

D2 D4 D6 D8 D10 D12 D14 D16
C2 C4 C6 C8 C10 C12 C14
B2 B4 B6 B8 B10 B12 B14
A2 A4 A6 A8 A10 A12 A14

STAGE

D1 D3 D5 D7 D9 D11 D13 D15
D1 D3 D5 D7 D9 D11 D13 D15 D17
D1 D3 D5 D7 D9 D11 D13 D15 D17 D19
D1 D3 D5 D7 D9 D11 D13 D15 D17 D19 D21 D23

$33.00
$30.00

THEATRE (212) 677-4210

Taxi Directions:
13th St. Westbound
(bet. 3rd & 4th Aves.)

PARKING
GMC, 21 E. 12th St.
Enter on
12th St. or University Place
Kinney System, 310 E. 11th St.
BUS
M1, M3, M9, M14, M18, M101
M102
SUBWAY
L, N, R, 4, 5, 6 to 14th St. Union Square

Nearby restaurants rated by
SEATS
THE COTTAGE, 33 Irving Place 505-8600
IN PADELLA 145 2nd Ave. 598-9800
SHARAKU, 14 Stuyvesant St. 598-0403
GUS'S PLACE, 148 Waverly Place 645-8511
A TASTE OF SIAM, 180 2nd Ave. 420-8280
VESELKA, 144 2nd Ave. 228-9682
ZEN PALATE, 24 East Union Square 995-9668

CHERRY LANE THEATRE

38 Commerce Street, New York, NY 10014

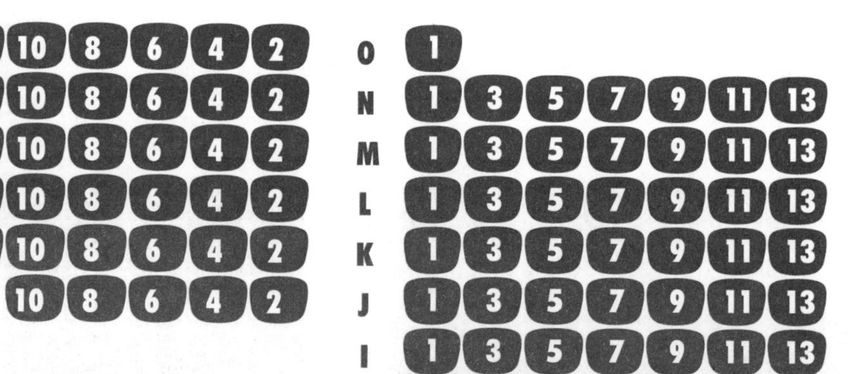

Prices vary from $25.00
to $40 according to show

STAGE

TELECHARGE (212) 239-6200

Taxi Directions:
Commerce St. Westbound
(bet. 7th Ave. and Hudson St.)

PARKING
GMC, 160 W. 10th St. at
the corner of 7th Ave. South
BUS
M8, M10
SUBWAYS
1, 9 to Christopher St.

Nearby restaurants rated by
SEATS
GRANGE HALL, 50 Commerce St.
924-5246
THOMAS SCOTT'S ON BEDFORD, 72 Bedford St.
627-4011
CHUMLEY'S, 86 Bedford St.
675-4449

DOUGLAS FAIRBANKS THEATRE

432 West 42nd Street, New York, NY 10036

N					12	11	10	9	8	7	6	5	4	3	2	1	N
M			14	13	12	11	10	9	8	7	6	5	4	3	2	1	M
L	16	15	14	13	12	11	10	9	8	7	6	5	4	3	2	1	L
K	16	15	14	13	12	11	10	9	8	7	6	5	4	3	2	1	K
J	16	15	14	13	12	11	10	9	8	7	6	5	4	3	2	1	J
H	16	15	14	13	12	11	10	9	8	7	6	5	4	3	2	1	H
G	16	15	14	13	12	11	10	9	8	7	6	5	4	3	2	1	G
F	15	14	13	12	11	10	9	8	7	6	5	4	3	2	1		F

STAGE

All Seats One Price

TELECHARGE (212) 239-6200

TAXI DIRECTIONS:
42nd St., two way
(bet. 9th & 10th Aves.)

PARKING
Edison Parking,
401-471 W 42nd St.
(bet. 9th & 10th Aves.)
Kinney,
352 W 43rd St.
(bet 8th & 9th Aves.)
BUS
M10, M11, M16, M42
SUBWAYS
A,C,E to 42nd St. & 8th Ave. Port Authority
1,2,3,7,9,N,R to 42nd St. & 7th Ave. Times Square

Nearby restaurants rated by
SEATS
CHEZ JOSEPHINE, 414 W 42nd St. 594-1925
WEST BANK CAFE, 407 W 42nd St. 695-6909
RACHEL's AMERICAN BISTRO,
608 9th Ave. at 43rd St. 957-9050

DUFFY THEATER

1553 Broadway, New York, NY 10019

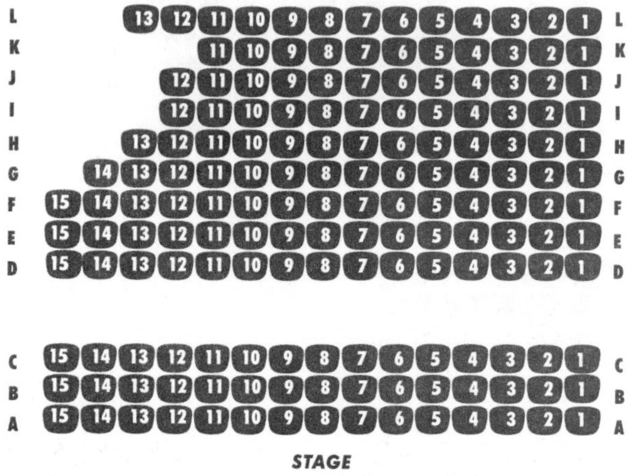

Row																Row
L			13	12	11	10	9	8	7	6	5	4	3	2	1	L
K					11	10	9	8	7	6	5	4	3	2	1	K
J				12	11	10	9	8	7	6	5	4	3	2	1	J
I				12	11	10	9	8	7	6	5	4	3	2	1	I
H			13	12	11	10	9	8	7	6	5	4	3	2	1	H
G		14	13	12	11	10	9	8	7	6	5	4	3	2	1	G
F	15	14	13	12	11	10	9	8	7	6	5	4	3	2	1	F
E	15	14	13	12	11	10	9	8	7	6	5	4	3	2	1	E
D	15	14	13	12	11	10	9	8	7	6	5	4	3	2	1	D
C	15	14	13	12	11	10	9	8	7	6	5	4	3	2	1	C
B	15	14	13	12	11	10	9	8	7	6	5	4	3	2	1	B
A	15	14	13	12	11	10	9	8	7	6	5	4	3	2	1	A

STAGE

All Seats One Price

THEATER (212) 695-3401
TICKETMASTER (212) 307-4100

TAXI DIRECTIONS:
Broadway Southbound at 46th St. Eastbound

PARKING
GMC, 257 W. 47th St. (bet. Broadway & 8th Ave.)
Kinney System, 38 W. 46th St. (bet. 5th & 6th Aves.)
Kinney System, 253 W. 47th St. (bet. Broadway & 8th Aves.)

BUS
M6, M7, M10, M27, M50, M104

SUBWAYS
B, D, F, Q to 42nd & 6th Ave.

Nearby restaurants rated by **SEATS**

SOUTHSIDE CAFE, 252 W. 47th St. 719-5694
TURKISH CUISINE, 631 9th Ave. 397-9650
MARLOWE, 328 W. 46th St. 765-3815
O' FLAHERTY'S ALE HOUSE, 334 W. 46th St. 246-8928
DANNY'S GRAND SEA PALACE, 346-348 W. 46th St. 265-8130

THE IRISH REPERTORY THEATRE

132 West 22nd Street, New York, NY 10011

THEATRE(212) 727-2737

Taxi Directions:
22nd St. Eastbound
(bet. 6th and 7th Aves.)

PARKING
Flannery Parking System, 129 W. 21st St.
Kinney System, 235 W. 22nd St.(bet. 7th & 8th Aves.)
514 West Corporation, 514 W. 23rd St.
BUS
M5, M6, M7, M10, M23
SUBWAYS
1,9 TO 23rd St. & 7th Ave.
F to 23rd St. & 6th Ave.
C,E, TO 23rd St. & 8th Ave.

Nearby restaurants rated by
SEATS

LOLA'S, 30 W. 22nd St. 675-6700
ZUCCA RESTAURANT, 227 10th Ave. at 23rd St. 741-1970
CHELSEA COMMONS RESTAURANT, 463 W. 24th St. at 10th Ave. 924-6737
LUMA RESTAURANT, 200 9th Ave. (bet. 22nd and 23rd Sts.) 633-8033

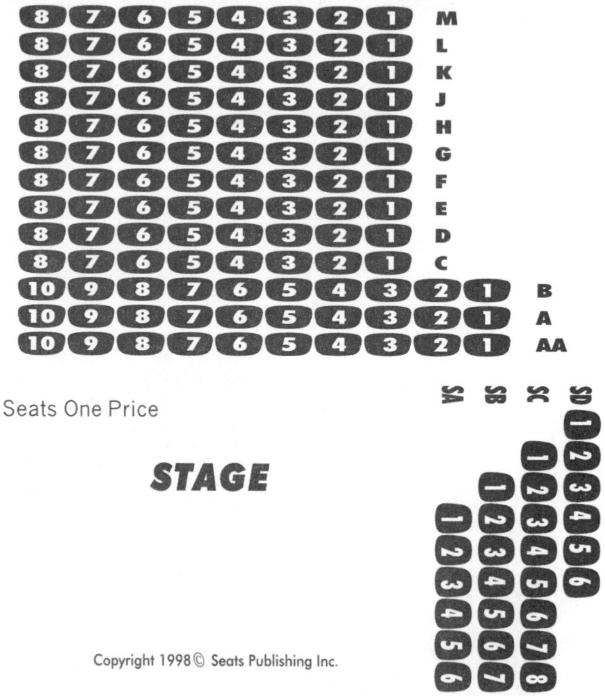

Row	Seats
M	8 7 6 5 4 3 2 1
L	8 7 6 5 4 3 2 1
K	8 7 6 5 4 3 2 1
J	8 7 6 5 4 3 2 1
H	8 7 6 5 4 3 2 1
G	8 7 6 5 4 3 2 1
F	8 7 6 5 4 3 2 1
E	8 7 6 5 4 3 2 1
D	8 7 6 5 4 3 2 1
C	8 7 6 5 4 3 2 1
B	10 9 8 7 6 5 4 3 2 1
A	10 9 8 7 6 5 4 3 2 1
AA	10 9 8 7 6 5 4 3 2 1
SA	1 2 3 4 5 6
SB	1 2 3 4 5 6 7
SC	1 2 3 4 5 6 7 8
SD	1 2 3 4 5 6

All Seats One Price

STAGE

GRAMERCY ARTS THEATRE
& REPERTORIO ESPANOL

138 East 27th Street, New York, NY 10016

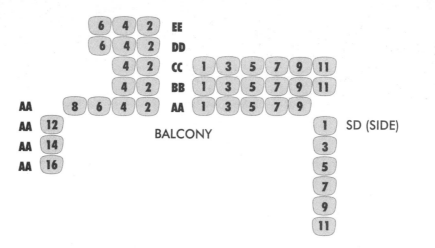

6 4 2 EE

6 4 2 DD

4 2 CC 1 3 5 7 9 11

4 2 BB 1 3 5 7 9 11

AA 8 6 4 2 AA 1 3 5 7 9

AA 12

AA 14

AA 16

BALCONY

SD (SIDE) 1 3 5 7 9 11

8 6 4 N

8 6 4 2 M 1 3

10 8 6 4 2 L 1 3

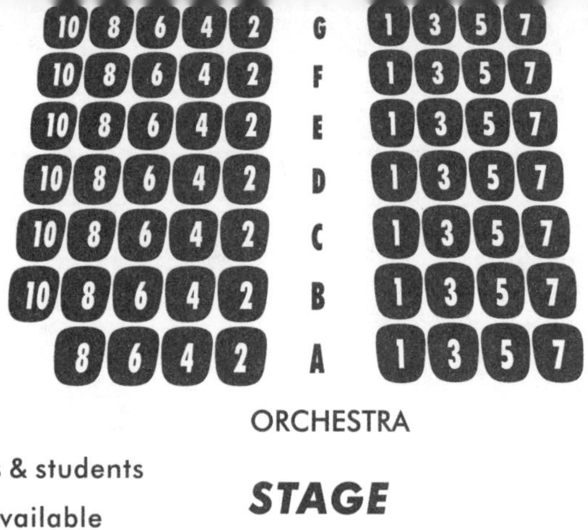

					Row				
10	8	6	4	2	G	1	3	5	7
10	8	6	4	2	F	1	3	5	7
10	8	6	4	2	E	1	3	5	7
10	8	6	4	2	D	1	3	5	7
10	8	6	4	2	C	1	3	5	7
10	8	6	4	2	B	1	3	5	7
	8	6	4	2	A	1	3	5	7

ORCHESTRA

STAGE

$25.00
$20.00

Discounts for Seniors & students
Spoken in Spanish.
Translation devices available

THEATRE (212) 889-2850

TAXI DIRECTIONS:
27th St. runs Westbound between Lexington Ave. & 3rd Ave.

PARKING
Peter Operative Corp. 26th St. (bet. 2nd & 3rd Aves.)
BUS
M23, M101, M102
SUBWAYS
6 to 28th St. & Park Avenue South
N,R to 28th St. & Broadway

Nearby restaurants rated by
SEATS
PATRIA, 250 Park Avenue South 777-6211
I TRULLI, 122 E.27th St. 481-7372
LA COLOMBE D'OR, 134 E. 26th St. 689-0666

JOHN HOUSEMAN THEATRE

450 West 42nd Street, New York, NY 10036

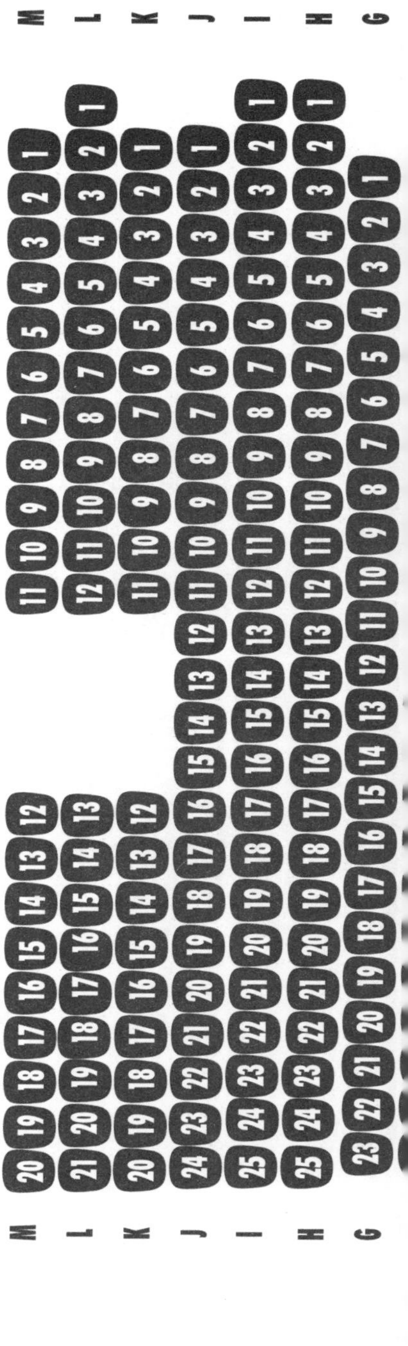

M 20 19 18 17 16 15 14 13 12 11 10 9 8 7 6 5 4 3 2 1 M

L 21 20 19 18 17 16 15 14 13 12 11 10 9 8 7 6 5 4 3 2 1 L

K 20 19 18 17 16 15 14 13 12 11 10 9 8 7 6 5 4 3 2 1 K

J 24 23 22 21 20 19 18 17 16 15 14 13 12 11 10 9 8 7 6 5 4 3 2 1 J

I 25 24 23 22 21 20 19 18 17 16 15 14 13 12 11 10 9 8 7 6 5 4 3 2 1 I

H 25 24 23 22 21 20 19 18 17 16 15 14 13 12 11 10 9 8 7 6 5 4 3 2 1 H

G 23 22 21 20 19 18 17 16 15 14 13 12 11 10 9 8 7 6 5 4 3 2 1 G

STAGE

All Seats One Price

TELECHARGE (212) 239-6200
OUTSIDE NY 1-800-543-4835

TAXI DIRECTIONS:
42nd St. two way
(bet. 9th & 10th Aves.)

PARKING
Edison Parking, 401-471 W. 42nd St.
(bet. 9th & 10th Aves.)
Kinney System, 352 W. 43rd St.
(bet. 8th & 9th Aves.)

Bus
M10, M11, M16, M42

SUBWAYS
1,2,3,7,9,N,R to 42nd St. & 7th Ave.
Times Square
A, C, E to 42nd St. & 8th Ave. Port Authority

Nearby restaurants rated by
SEATS
CHEZ JOSEPHINE, 414 W. 42nd St.
594-1925
WEST BANK CAFE, 407 W. 42nd St.
695-6909
RACHEL'S AMERICAN BISTRO, 608 9th Ave.
at 43rd St. 957-9050

JOSEPH PAPP PUBLIC THEATRE

425 Lafayette Street, New York, NY 10003

ANSPACHER THEATER

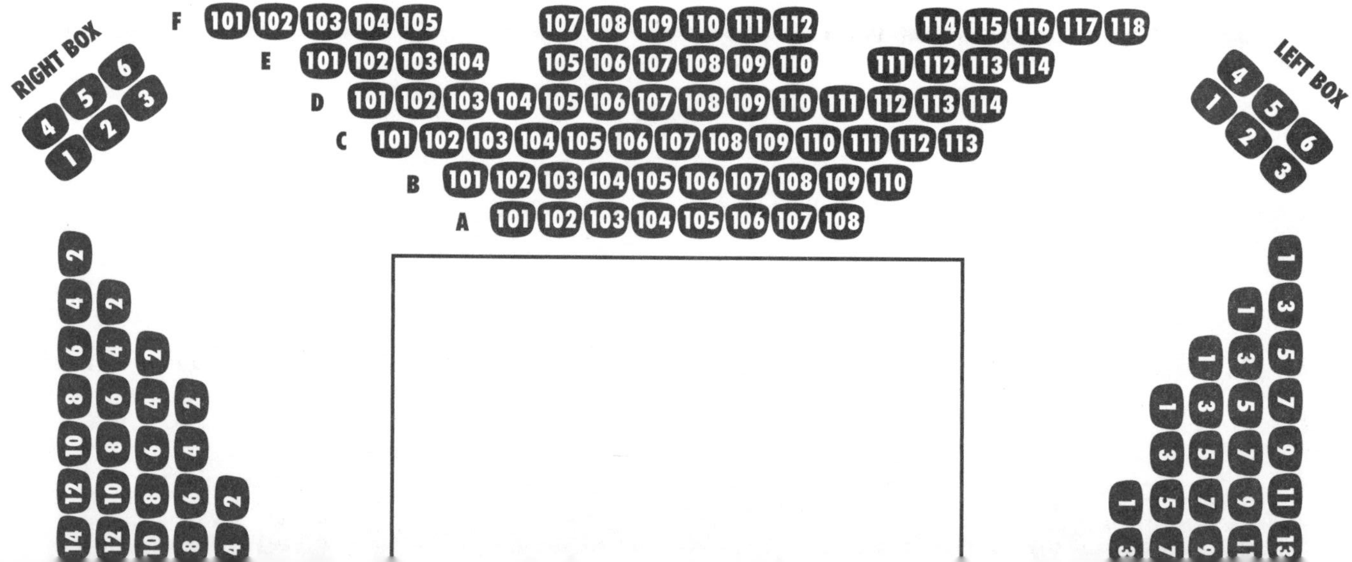

RIGHT BOX

LEFT BOX

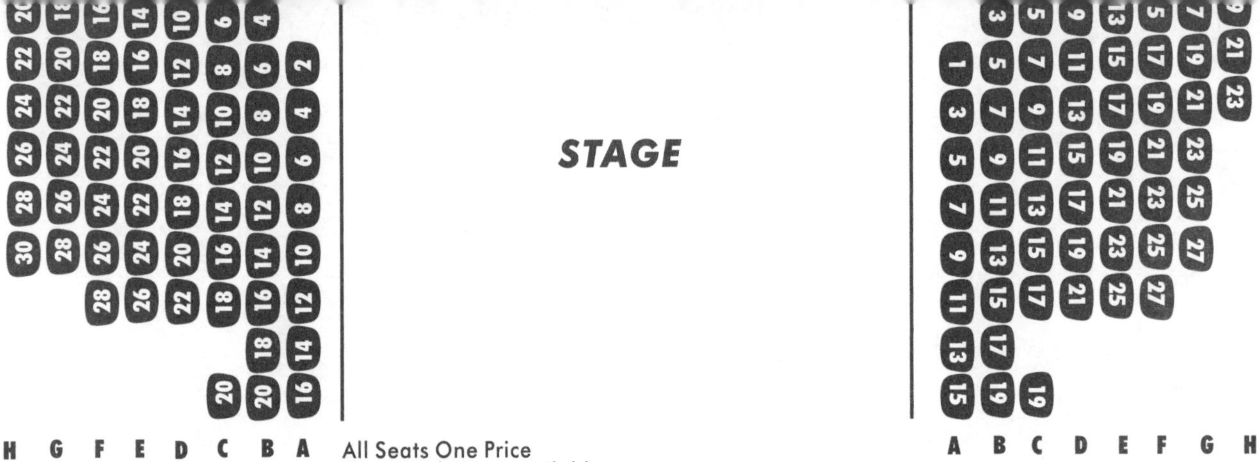

STAGE

H G F E D C B A

All Seats One Price
Hearing devices available

A B C D E F G H

TELECHARGE (212) 239-6200

PARKING
Stop and Park
410-420 Lafayette St.
BUS
M10, M11, M101, M102
SUBWAYS
6 to Astor Place
N, R to 8th St.

Nearby restaurants rated by
SEATS
INDOCHINE RESTARURANT, 430 Lafayette St. 505-5111
HELENA'S, 432 Lafayette St. 677-5151

TAXI DIRECTIONS:
Lafayette Northbound
(bet. Astor & 4th Sts.)

JOSEPH PAPP PUBLIC THEATRE

425 Lafayette Street, New York, NY 10003

NEWMAN THEATER

Row																			
S	1	2	3	4	5	6	7	8	9	10	11	12	13	14	15	16	17	18	
R	1	2	3	4	5	6	7	8	9	10	11	12	13	14	15	16	17	18	19
Q	1	2	3	4	5	6	7	8	9	10	11	12	13	14	15	16	17	18	19
P	1	2	3	4	5	6	7	8	9	10	11	12	13	14	15	16	17	18	19
O	1	2	3	4	5	6	7	8	9	10	11	12	13	14	15	16	17	18	19
N	1	2	3	4	5	6	7	8	9	10	11	12	13	14	15	16	17	18	19
M	1	2	3	4	5	6	7	8	9	10	11	12	13	14	15	16	17	18	19
L	1	2	3	4	5	6	7	8	9	10	11	12	13	14	15	16	17	18	19
K	1	2	3	4	5	6	7	8	9	10	11	12	13	14	15	16	17	18	19
J	1	2	3	4	5	6	7	8	9	10	11	12	13	14	15	16	17	18	19
H	1	2	3	4	5	6	7	8	9	10	11	12	13	14	15	16	17	18	

STAGE

All Seats One Price
Hearing devices available

TELECHARGE (212) 239-6200

PARKING
Stop and Park
410-420 Lafayette St.
BUS
M10 ,M11, M101, M102
SUBWAYS
6 to Astor Place
N, R to 8th St.

Nearby restaurants rated by
SEATS
INDOCHINE RESTARURANT,430 Lafayette St. 505-5111
HELENA'S, 432 Lafayette St. 677-5151

TAXI DIRECTIONS:
Lafayette Northbound
(bet. Astor & 4th Sts.)

JOYCE THEATRE

175 8th Avenue, New York, NY 10011

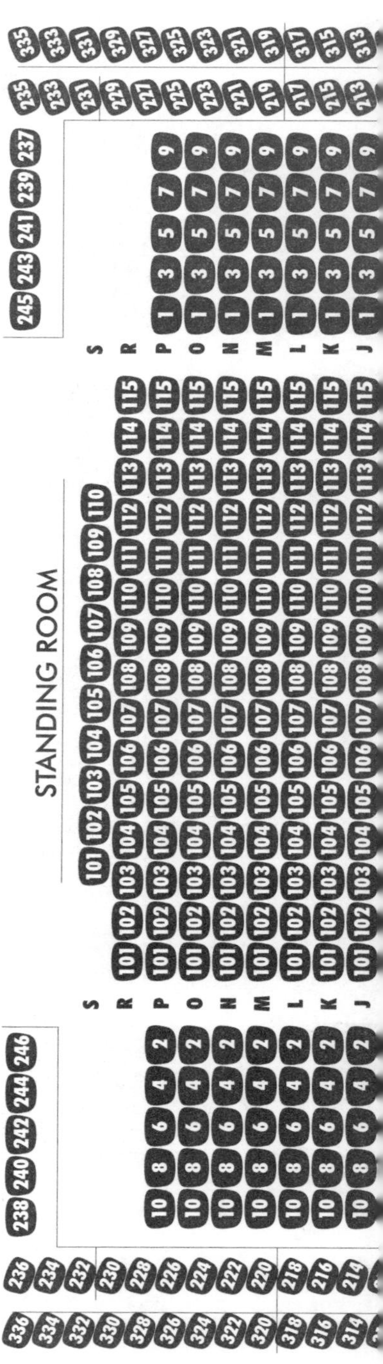

STANDING ROOM

	302	202																											201	301
D			10	8	6	4	2	101	102	103	104	105	106	107	108	109	110	111	112	113	114	115	1	3	5	7	9			
C								101	102	103	104	105	106	107	108	109	110	111	112	113	114	115								
B			10	8	6	4	2	101	102	103	104	105	106	107	108	109	110	111	112	113	114	115	1	3	5	7	9			
A			10	8	6	4	2	101	102	103	104	105	106	107	108	109	110	111	112	113	114	115	1	3	5	7	9			

LOGE

ORCHESTRA

LOGE

STAGE

All Seats One Price

Prices will vary from
$26.00 to $34.00
according to show

THEATRE (212) 242-0800
Call & ask for membership information, members receive a discount

TAXI DIRECTIONS:
8th Ave. Northbound
(at 19th St. Westbound)

PARKING
Meyers Parking, 111 8th Ave.
(bet. 15th & 16th Sts.)
discounts for members
Garage Corp., 250 W. 19th St.
(bet. 7th & 8th Aves.)
BUS
M10, M11, M23
SUBWAYS
A, C, E to 14th St. & 8th Ave.
1,9 to 18th St. and 7th Ave.

Nearby restaurants rated by
SEATS

CAFE INFERNO, 165 8th Ave. 989-2330
MAN RAY, 169 8th Ave. 627-4220
TIZIANO, 165 8th Ave. 989-2330

THE LAMB'S THEATRE

130 West 44th Street, New York, NY 10036-4078

FF 213 212 211 210 209 208 107 106 105 104 103 102 101 FF
EE 210 209 208 207 206 105 104 103 102 101 EE
DD 212 211 210 209 208 207 106 105 104 103 102 101 DD
CC 114 113 112 111 110 109 108 107 106 105 104 103 102 101 CC
BB 117 116 115 114 113 112 111 110 109 108 107 106 105 104 103 102 101 BB
AA 115 114 113 112 111 110 109 108 107 106 105 104 103 102 101 AA

BB 2 4 6 8
AA 2 4 6 8 10 12 14 16

MEZZANINE

AA 1 3 5 7 9 11 13 15
BB 1 3 5 7

H 118 117 116 115 114 113 112 111 110 109 108 107 106 105 104 103 102 101 H

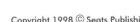

A 108 107 106 105 104 103 102 101 A

ORCHESTRA

STAGE

$30.00
$25.00

Mezzanine row AA overhangs
Orchestra row E

TELECHARGE (212) 239-6200

TAXI DIRECTIONS:
44th St. Eastbound
(bet. Broadway & 6th Ave.)

PARKING
Edison Fast Park, 1120 6th Ave.
bet. 43rd & 44th St.
Kinney System,
100 West 44th St. bet. 6th & 7th Ave.
Hippodrome, 50 West 44th St.

BUS
M5, M6, M7, M10, M27 M42, M104

SUBWAYS
1,2,3,7.9,N,R,S to 42nd St. & 7th Ave. Times Square
B, D, F, Q to 42nd St. & 6th Ave.
A, C, E to 42nd St. & 8th Ave. Port Authority

Nearby restaurants rated by
SEATS

ORIGINAL FERRARA PASTRIES,
201 W. 42nd St. 398-6064
STARDUST DINE-O-MAT,
1491 Broadway at 43rd St. 768-3170
O'FLAHERTY'S ALE HOUSE, 334 W. 46th St. 246-8928
JOEY'S PAESANO, 205 W. 43rd St. 997-8700

LUCILLE LORTEL THEATRE

121 Christopher Street, New York, NY 10014

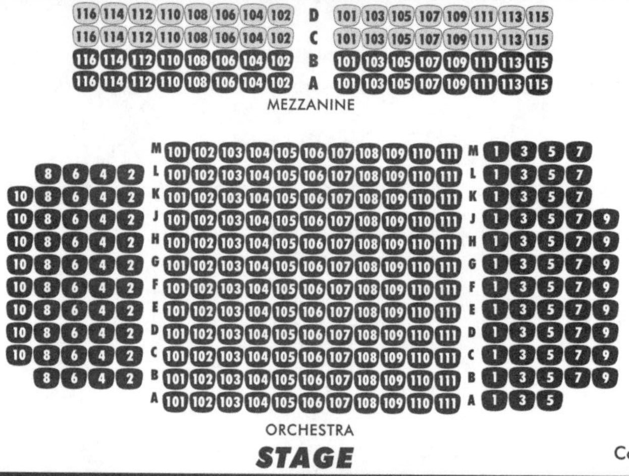

MEZZANINE

Left	Row	Right
116 114 112 110 108 106 104 102	D	101 103 105 107 109 111 113 115
116 114 112 110 108 106 104 102	C	101 103 105 107 109 111 113 115
116 114 112 110 108 106 104 102	B	101 103 105 107 109 111 113 115
116 114 112 110 108 106 104 102	A	101 103 105 107 109 111 113 115

ORCHESTRA

Left	Row	Center	Row	Right
	M	101 102 103 104 105 106 107 108 109 110 111	M	1 3 5 7
8 6 4 2	L	101 102 103 104 105 106 107 108 109 110 111	L	1 3 5 7
10 8 6 4 2	K	101 102 103 104 105 106 107 108 109 110 111	K	1 3 5 7
10 8 6 4 2	J	101 102 103 104 105 106 107 108 109 110 111	J	1 3 5 7 9
10 8 6 4 2	H	101 102 103 104 105 106 107 108 109 110 111	H	1 3 5 7 9
10 8 6 4 2	G	101 102 103 104 105 106 107 108 109 110 111	G	1 3 5 7 9
10 8 6 4 2	F	101 102 103 104 105 106 107 108 109 110 111	F	1 3 5 7 9
10 8 6 4 2	E	101 102 103 104 105 106 107 108 109 110 111	E	1 3 5 7 9
10 8 6 4 2	D	101 102 103 104 105 106 107 108 109 110 111	D	1 3 5 7 9
10 8 6 4 2	C	101 102 103 104 105 106 107 108 109 110 111	C	1 3 5 7 9
8 6 4 2	B	101 102 103 104 105 106 107 108 109 110 111	B	1 3 5 7 9
	A	101 102 103 104 105 106 107 108 109 110 111	A	1 3 5

STAGE

$45.00
$40.00

Mezzanine row A overhangs orchestra row F

TELECHARGE (212) 239-6200

TAXI DIRECTIONS:
Christopher St. Westbound
(bet. Bleecker & Hudson)

PARKING
Apple West, 741-9079
GMC 160 W. 10th St.
BUS
M8, M10
SUBWAYS
1,9 to Christopher St.

Nearby restaurants rated by
SEATS
POT BELLY STOVE CAFE, 94 Christopher St. 242-9652
GROVE RESTAURANT, 314 Bleecker St. 675-9463

MANHATTAN THEATRE CLUB

131 West 55th Street, New York, NY 10019

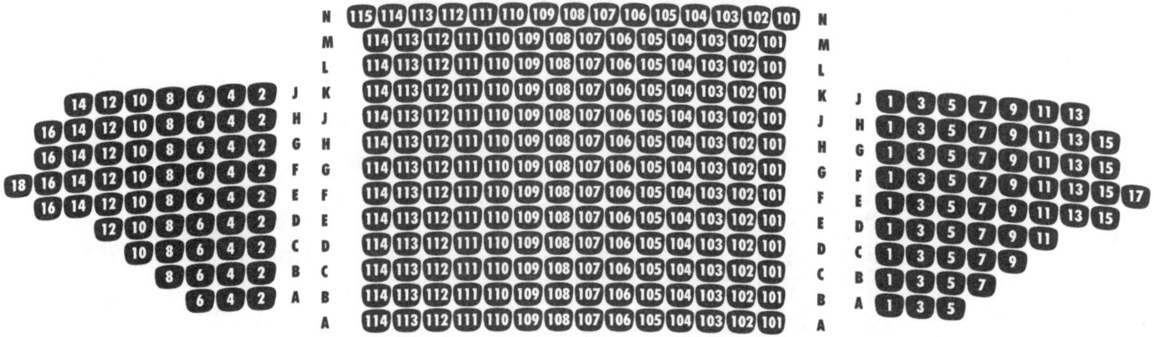

Row	Seats
J	14 12 10 8 6 4 2
H	16 14 12 10 8 6 4 2
G	16 14 12 10 8 6 4 2
F	18 16 14 12 10 8 6 4 2
E	16 14 12 10 8 6 4 2
D	12 10 8 6 4 2
C	10 8 6 4 2
B	8 6 4 2
A	6 4 2

Row	Seats
N	115 114 113 112 111 110 109 108 107 106 105 104 103 102 101
M	114 113 112 111 110 109 108 107 106 105 104 103 102 101
L	114 113 112 111 110 109 108 107 106 105 104 103 102 101
K	114 113 112 111 110 109 108 107 106 105 104 103 102 101
J	114 113 112 111 110 109 108 107 106 105 104 103 102 101
H	114 113 112 111 110 109 108 107 106 105 104 103 102 101
G	114 113 112 111 110 109 108 107 106 105 104 103 102 101
F	114 113 112 111 110 109 108 107 106 105 104 103 102 101
E	114 113 112 111 110 109 108 107 106 105 104 103 102 101
D	114 113 112 111 110 109 108 107 106 105 104 103 102 101
C	114 113 112 111 110 109 108 107 106 105 104 103 102 101
B	114 113 112 111 110 109 108 107 106 105 104 103 102 101
A	114 113 112 111 110 109 108 107 106 105 104 103 102 101

Row	Seats
J	1 3 5 7 9 11 13
H	1 3 5 7 9 11 13 15
G	1 3 5 7 9 11 13 15
F	1 3 5 7 9 11 13 15 17
E	1 3 5 7 9 11 13 15
D	1 3 5 7 9 11
C	1 3 5 7 9
B	1 3 5 7
A	1 3 5

STAGE

All Seats One Price

CITY TIX (212) 581-1212

Taxi Directions:
55th St. Westbound
(bet. 6th & 7th Aves.)

PARKING
1345 Garage, 101 W. 54th St.
Kinney Garage, 888 7th Ave.
Entrance on 56th St.
GMC, 156 W. 56th St.

BUS
M5, M6, M7, M30, M31, M57

SUBWAYS
N,R, 57th St. & Broadway
Q 57th St. & 6th Ave.
B,D,E,N,R to 57th St. & 7th Ave.
1, 9 to 59th Sts. & Broadway Columbus Circle

Nearby restaurants rated by
SEATS

ORIGINAL FERRARA PASTRIES, 1700 Broadway (bet. 53rd & 54th Sts.) 581-3335
HARLEY DAVIDSON CAFE, 1370 Ave. of the Americas at 56th St. 245-6000
PATSY'S ITALIAN RESTAURANT, 236 W. 56th St. 247-3491
RUMPELMAYER'S RESTAURANT, 50 Central Park South at the St. Moritz, 755-5800

MINETTA LANE THEATRE

18 Minetta Lane, New York, NY 10012

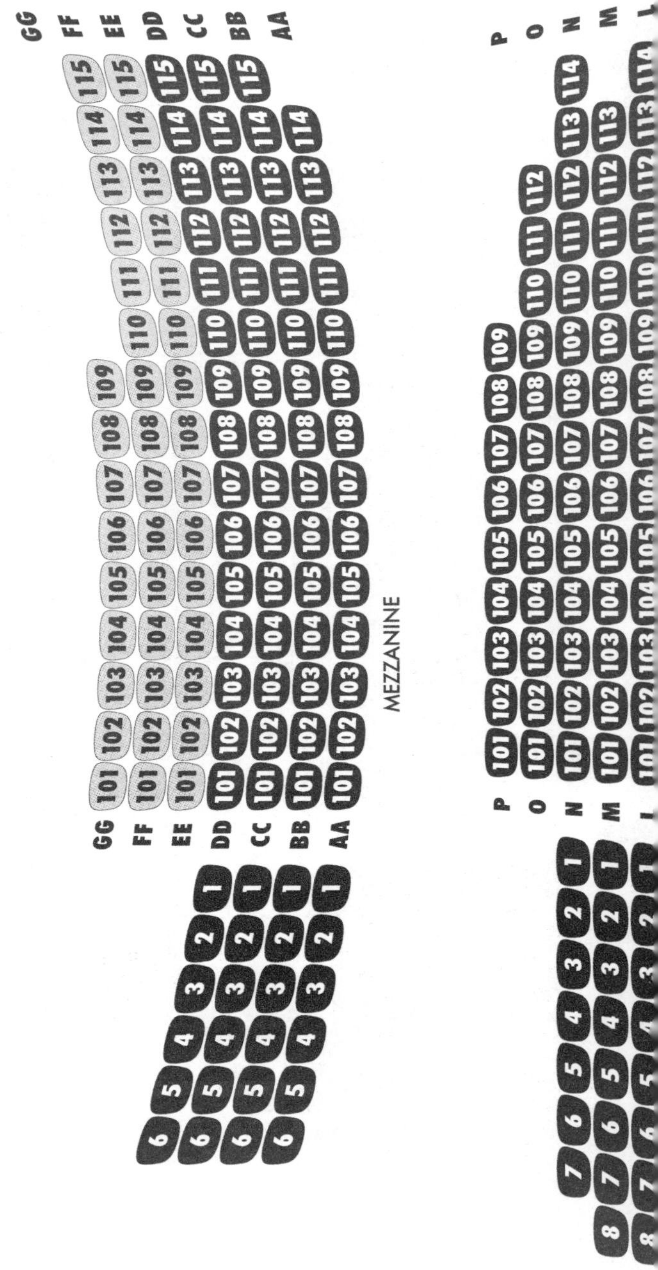

MEZZANINE

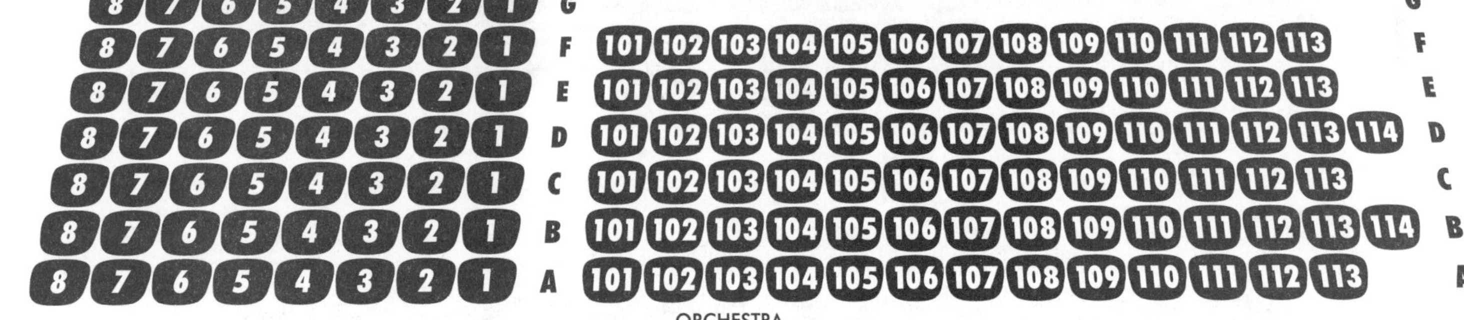

$47.50
$29.50

Mezzanine row A overhangs
Orchestra row J

STAGE

TICKETMASTER (212) 307-4100
BOX OFFICE (212) 420-8000

TAXI DIRECTIONS:
Minetta Lane Eastbound
(bet. 6th Ave. & Macdougal St.)

PARKING
GMC, 122 W. 3rd St.
BUS
M5, M6
SUBWAYS
A, C,E,B,F,Q to W. 4th St. & 6th Ave. Washington Square

♿ Wheelchair accessible
Infrared devices available

Nearby restaurants rated by
SEATS
LA BOHEME RESTAURANT, 24 Minetta Lane 473-6447
GRAND TICINO, 228 Thompson 777-5922
MINETTA TAVERN, 113 Macdougal 475-3850

ORPHEUM THEATRE

126 Second Avenue, New York, NY 10003

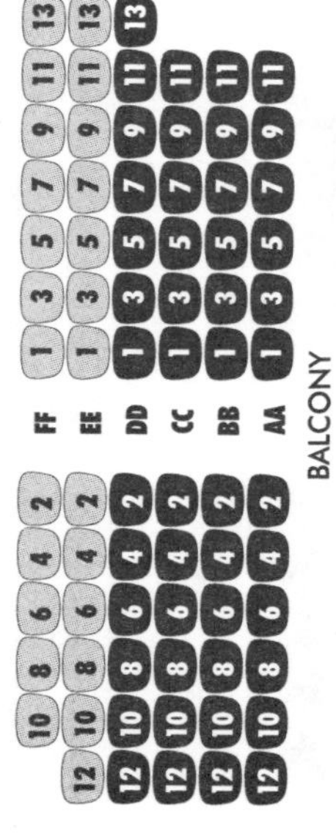

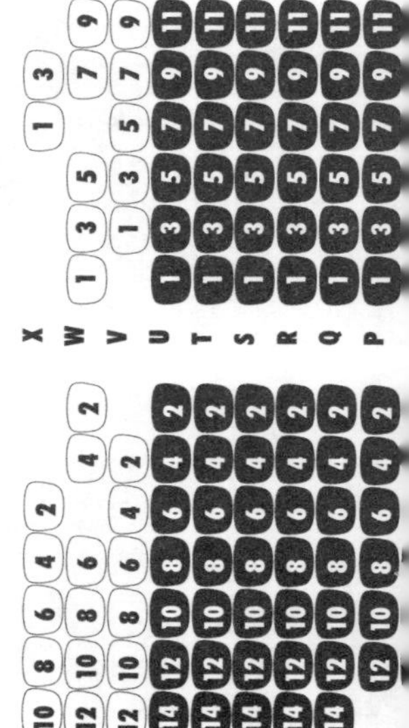

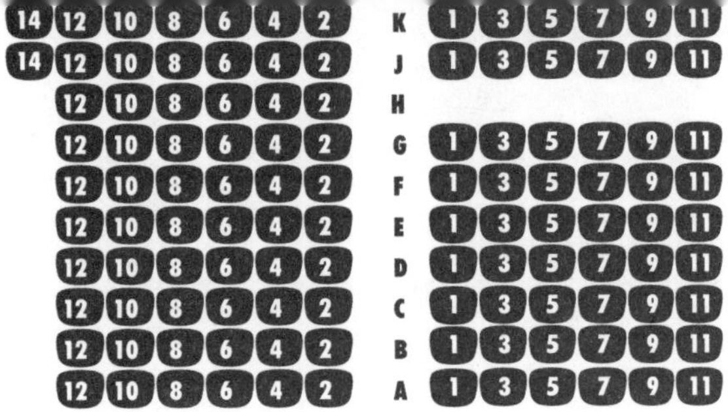

							Row						
14	12	10	8	6	4	2	K	1	3	5	7	9	11
14	12	10	8	6	4	2	J	1	3	5	7	9	11
	12	10	8	6	4	2	H						
	12	10	8	6	4	2	G	1	3	5	7	9	11
	12	10	8	6	4	2	F	1	3	5	7	9	11
	12	10	8	6	4	2	E	1	3	5	7	9	11
	12	10	8	6	4	2	D	1	3	5	7	9	11
	12	10	8	6	4	2	C	1	3	5	7	9	11
	12	10	8	6	4	2	B	1	3	5	7	9	11
	12	10	8	6	4	2	A	1	3	5	7	9	11

ORCHESTRA

$47.50
$29.50
$24.50

STAGE

TICKETMASTER (212) 307-4100
BOX OFFICE (212) 477-2477

TAXI DIRECTIONS:
Second Ave. Southbound at 8th St. Eastbound

PARKING
Kinney System, 220 E.9th St. (bet. 2nd & 3rd Aves.)
BUS
M8,M15, M103
SUBWAYS
R,N to 8th St. & Broadway
6 to Astor Place

Nearby restaurants rated by **SEATS**
VIRAGE, 118 2nd Ave. 253-0425
CIRCA, 102 2nd Ave. 777-4120

THE PEARL THEATRE CO. INC.

80 St. Marks Place, New York, NY 10003

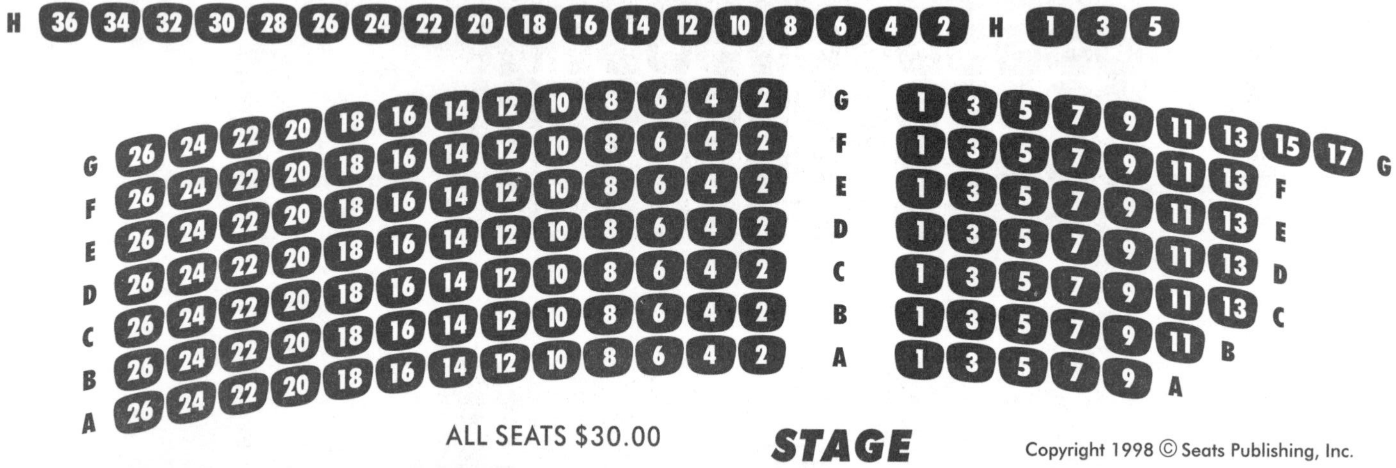

H 36 34 32 30 28 26 24 22 20 18 16 14 12 10 8 6 4 2 H 1 3 5

G 26 24 22 20 18 16 14 12 10 8 6 4 2 G 1 3 5 7 9 11 13 15 17 G
F 26 24 22 20 18 16 14 12 10 8 6 4 2 F 1 3 5 7 9 11 13 F
E 26 24 22 20 18 16 14 12 10 8 6 4 2 E 1 3 5 7 9 11 13 E
D 26 24 22 20 18 16 14 12 10 8 6 4 2 D 1 3 5 7 9 11 13 D
C 26 24 22 20 18 16 14 12 10 8 6 4 2 C 1 3 5 7 9 11 13 C
B 26 24 22 20 18 16 14 12 10 8 6 4 2 B 1 3 5 7 9 11 B
A 26 24 22 20 18 16 14 12 10 8 6 4 2 A 1 3 5 7 9 A

ALL SEATS $30.00

STAGE

THEATER (212) 598-9802

Taxi Directions:
St. Mark's Place
(bet. 1st & 2nd Aves.)

PARKING
On 9th Street
(bet. 2nd & 3rd Aves.)
BUS
M1,M15 to 8th & 9th St. & 2nd Ave.
SUBWAYS
N,R to 8th St. & Broadway
4,5,6 to 8th St. & Lafayette
L to 4th St

Nearby restaurants rated by
SEATS

YAFFA CAFE, 101 St. Mark's Place, 674-9302
MIRACLE GRILL, 112 1st Ave. 254-2353
CUCINA DE PESCE, 87 E.4th St. 260-6800
ELVIE'S TURO-TURO, 214 1st Ave. 473-7785

PLAYWRIGHTS HORIZONS THEATRE

416 West 42nd Street, New York, NY 10003

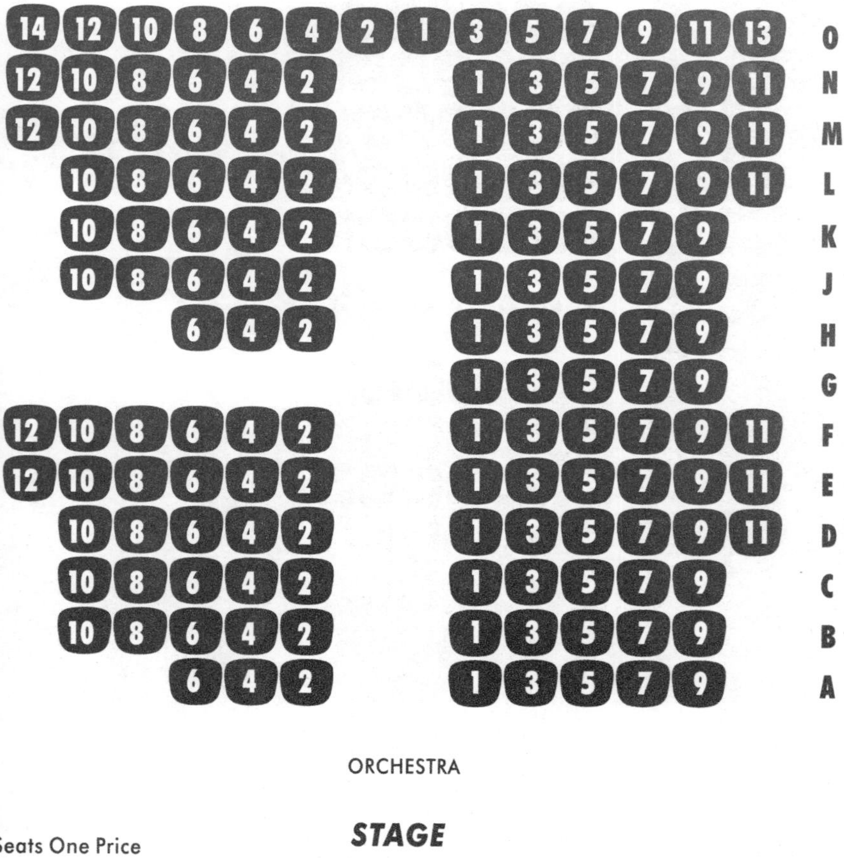

Row	Left side	Right side
O	14 12 10 8 6 4 2	1 3 5 7 9 11 13
N	12 10 8 6 4 2	1 3 5 7 9 11
M	12 10 8 6 4 2	1 3 5 7 9 11
L	10 8 6 4 2	1 3 5 7 9 11
K	10 8 6 4 2	1 3 5 7 9
J	10 8 6 4 2	1 3 5 7 9
H	6 4 2	1 3 5 7 9
G		1 3 5 7 9
F	12 10 8 6 4 2	1 3 5 7 9 11
E	12 10 8 6 4 2	1 3 5 7 9 11
D	10 8 6 4 2	1 3 5 7 9 11
C	10 8 6 4 2	1 3 5 7 9
B	10 8 6 4 2	1 3 5 7 9
A	6 4 2	1 3 5 7 9

ORCHESTRA

STAGE

Seats One Price

KETS (212) 279-4200

IRECTIONS:
St. Two Way
9th & 10th Aves.)

PARKING
Edison Parking,
401-471 W. 42nd St.
(bet. 9th & 10th Aves.)
BUS
M10, M11, M16, M42
SUBWAYS
1, 2, 3, 7, 9, N, R
to 42nd St. & 7th Ave.
A,C,E to 42nd St. & 8th Ave.
Port Authority

Nearby restaurants rated by
SEATS

CHEZ JOSEPHINE, 414 W. 42nd St. 594-1925
WEST BANK CAFE, 407 W. 42nd St. 695-6909
RACHEL'S AMERICAN BISTRO, 608 9th Ave.
at 43rd St. 957-9050

PLAYHOUSE 91

316 East 91st Street, New York, NY 10128

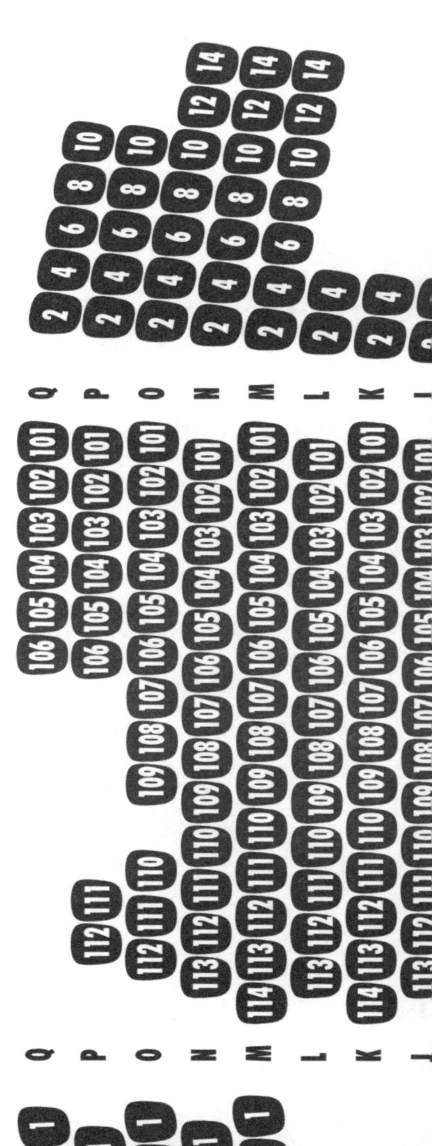

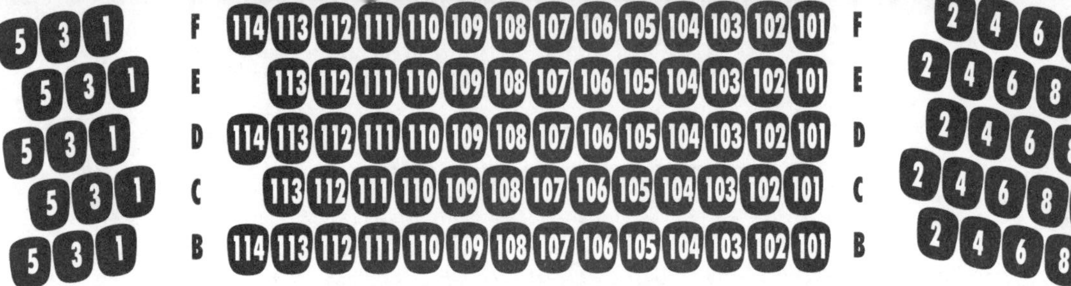

All Seats $35.00

TICKETS (212) 831-2001

TAXI DIRECTIONS:
91st St. Westbound
(bet. 1st & 2nd Aves.)

PARKING
David's Garage, 422 E.91st St.
GMC, 340 E. 93rd St.
BUS
M15, M31, M86
SUBWAY
4,5,6, to 86th St. and Lexington Ave.

Nearby restaurants rated by
SEATS

TALLULAHS, 1744 2nd Ave. 289-7510

PROMENADE THEATRE

2162 Broadway, New York, NY 10024

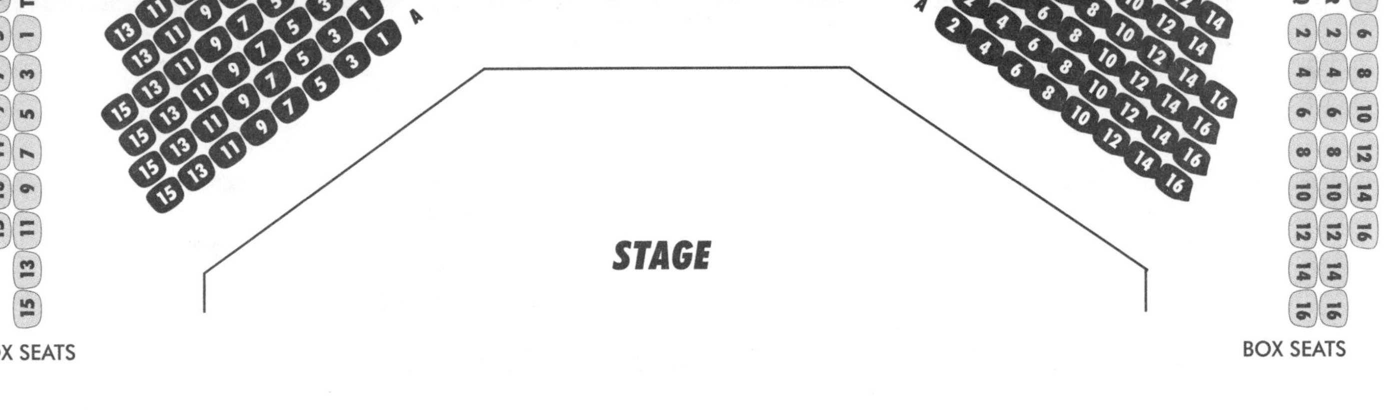

$47.50 / $42.50 — Prices may vary according to show

THEATRE (212) 580-1313
TELECHARGE (212) 239-6200

TAXI DIRECTIONS
45th St. westbound
(bet. Broadway & 8th Ave.)

PARKING
Kinney System, 201 W. 75th St.

BUS
M7, M11, M79, M104

SUBWAYS
1,9,to 79th St. & Broadway

Nearby restaurants rated by **SEATS**
222, 222 W. 79th St. 799-0400
ERNIE'S, 2150 Broadway 496-1588

SECOND STAGE THEATRE

2162 Broadway, New York, NY 10024

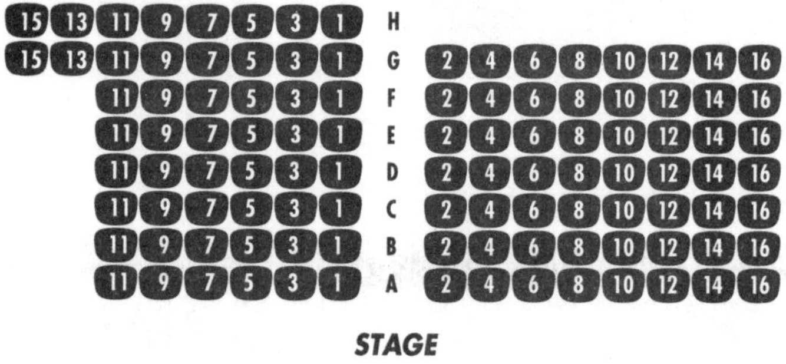

								Row								
15	13	11	9	7	5	3	1	H								
15	13	11	9	7	5	3	1	G	2	4	6	8	10	12	14	16
		11	9	7	5	3	1	F	2	4	6	8	10	12	14	16
		11	9	7	5	3	1	E	2	4	6	8	10	12	14	16
		11	9	7	5	3	1	D	2	4	6	8	10	12	14	16
		11	9	7	5	3	1	C	2	4	6	8	10	12	14	16
		11	9	7	5	3	1	B	2	4	6	8	10	12	14	16
		11	9	7	5	3	1	A	2	4	6	8	10	12	14	16

STAGE

All Seats One Price

TICKETS (212) 787-3392

TAXI DIRECTIONS:
Broadway two way

PARKING
Kinney System, 201 W.75th St.
BUS
M7, M11, M79, M104
SUBWAYS
1,9 to 79th St. and Broadway

Nearby restaurants rated by
SEATS
222, 222 W. 79th St. 799-0400

ST. LUKES CHURCH THEATRE

308 W. 46th Street, New York, NY 10036

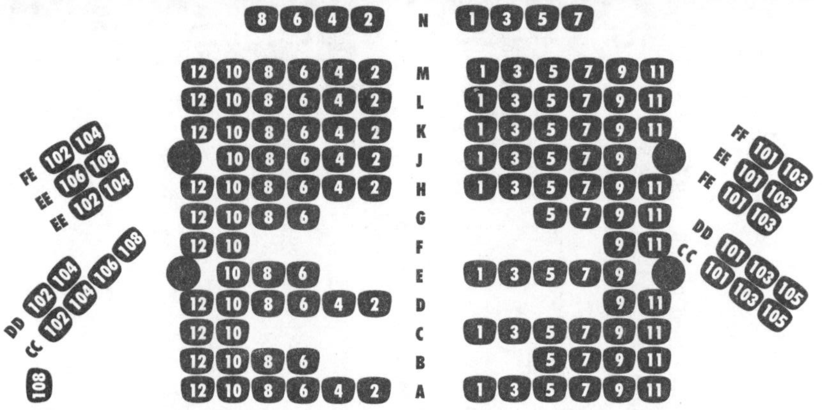

Left	Row	Right
8 6 4 2	N	1 3 5 7
12 10 8 6 4 2	M	1 3 5 7 9 11
12 10 8 6 4 2	L	1 3 5 7 9 11
12 10 8 6 4 2	K	1 3 5 7 9 11
10 8 6 4 2	J	1 3 5 7 9
12 10 8 6 4 2	H	1 3 5 7 9 11
12 10 8 6	G	5 7 9 11
12 10	F	9 11
10 8 6	E	1 3 5 7 9
12 10 8 6 4 2	D	9 11
12 10	C	1 3 5 7 9 11
12 10 8 6	B	5 7 9 11
12 10 8 6 4 2	A	1 3 5 7 9 11

FE 102 104
EE 106 108
EE 102 104
DD 102 104
CC 102 104 106 108
108

FF 101 103
EE 101 103
FE 101 103
DD 101 103 105
CC 101 103 105

All Seats One Price

STAGE

TELECHARGE (212) 239-6200

TAXI DIRECTIONS:
46th St. Eastbound
(bet. 8th & 9th Aves.)

PARKING
Edison Parking, 713 - 719 10th Ave.
(bet. 48th & 49th Sts.)
Kinney, 253 W. 47th St.
GMC, 257 W. 47th St.
(both are bet. Broadway & 8th Ave.)

BUS
M6, M7, M10, M11, M42, M104

SUBWAYS
1,2,3,7,9,N,R,S to 42nd St. & 7th Ave. Times Square
A, C, E to 42nd St. & 8th Ave. Port Authority

Nearby restaurants rated by
SEATS

MESKEREM, 468 W. 47th St. 664-0520
B. SMITH'S, 771 8th Ave at 47th St. 247-2222
MARLOWE, 328 W. 46th St. 765-3815
O' FLAHERTY'S ALE HOUSE, 334 W. 46th St. 246-8928
DANNY'S GRAND SEA PALACE , 346-348 W. 46th St. 265-8130
LA PRIMAVERA, 234 W. 48th St. 586-2797

SOHO PLAYHOUSE

15 Vandam Street, New York NY 10013

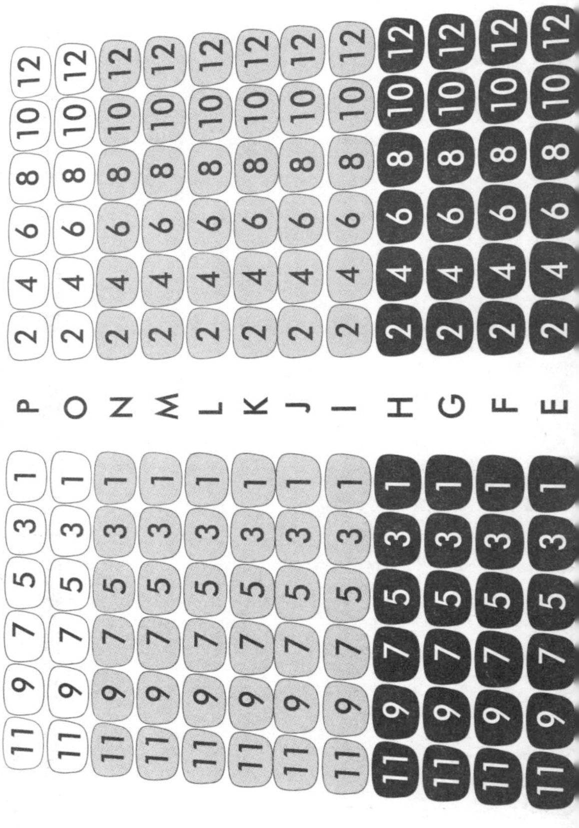

						Row						
11	9	7	5	3	1	P	2	4	6	8	10	12
11	9	7	5	3	1	O	2	4	6	8	10	12
11	9	7	5	3	1	N	2	4	6	8	10	12
11	9	7	5	3	1	M	2	4	6	8	10	12
11	9	7	5	3	1	L	2	4	6	8	10	12
11	9	7	5	3	1	K	2	4	6	8	10	12
11	9	7	5	3	1	J	2	4	6	8	10	12
11	9	7	5	3	1	I	2	4	6	8	10	12
11	9	7	5	3	1	H	2	4	6	8	10	12
11	9	7	5	3	1	G	2	4	6	8	10	12
11	9	7	5	3	1	F	2	4	6	8	10	12
11	9	7	5	3	1	E	2	4	6	8	10	12

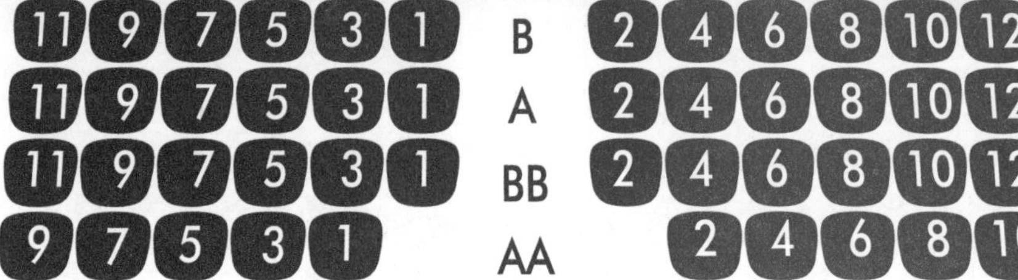

STAGE

$47.50
$42.50
$37.50

THEATRE (212) 691-1555
GROUP SALES (212) 974-2060

TAXI DIRECTIONS:
Vandam St. Westbound
(bet. 6th & 7th Aves.)

BUS
M21 to 6th Ave. & Houston
M10 to Varick & Vandam St.
M5 to Houston & 6th Ave. Walk South to Vandam

SUBWAYS
E,C, to Spring St.
1,2,3,9 to Houston St. transfer to E to Spring St.
B, D,F, Q to W. 46th St. transfer to E to Spring St.

Nearby restaurants rated by
SEATS

TRIPLETS ROUMANIAN STEAKHOUSE,
11-17 Grand St. 925-9303
TENNESSEE MOUNTAIN,
143 Spring St. 431-3993

SULLIVAN STREET PLAYHOUSE

181 Sullivan Street, New York, NY 10012

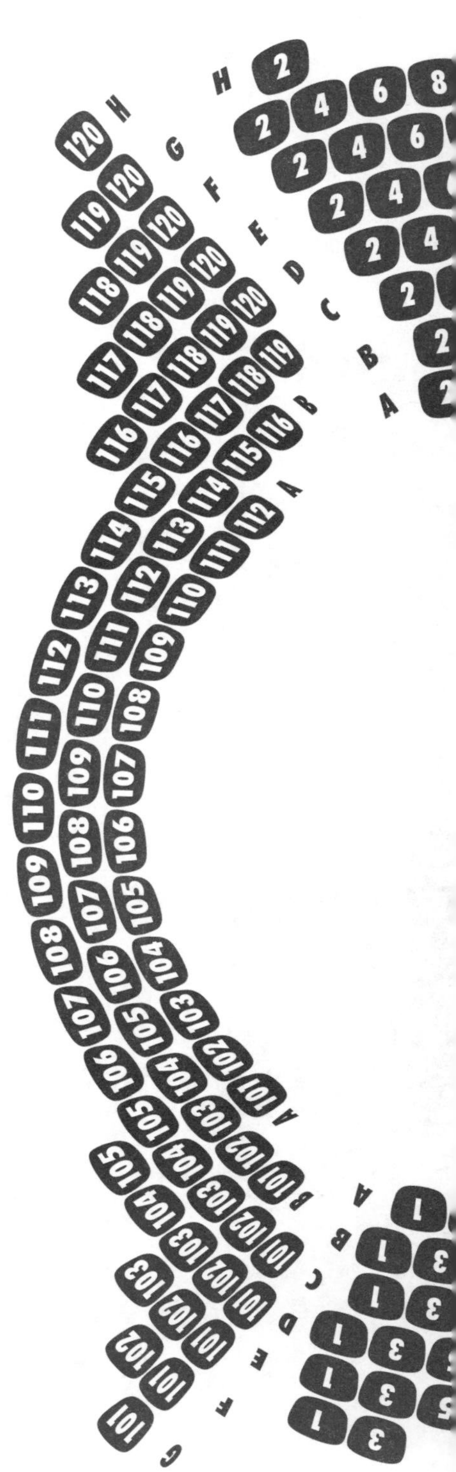

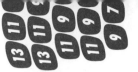

$37.50 All Seats One Price

TICKETS (212) 674-3838

BUS
M1,M5, M6, M21
SUBWAYS
A,B,C,D,E,F
to West 4th St. at Washington Square

Nearby restaurants rated by
SEATS
VILLA MOSCONI, 69 MacDougal St. 673-0390
CHEZ JACQUELINE, 72 MacDougal St. 505-0727
DERBY, 109 MacDougal St. 475-0520

TAXI DIRECTIONS:
Sullivan St. Northbound
(bet. Houston & Bleeker Sts.)

UNION SQUARE THEATRE

100 East 17th Street, New York, NY 10003

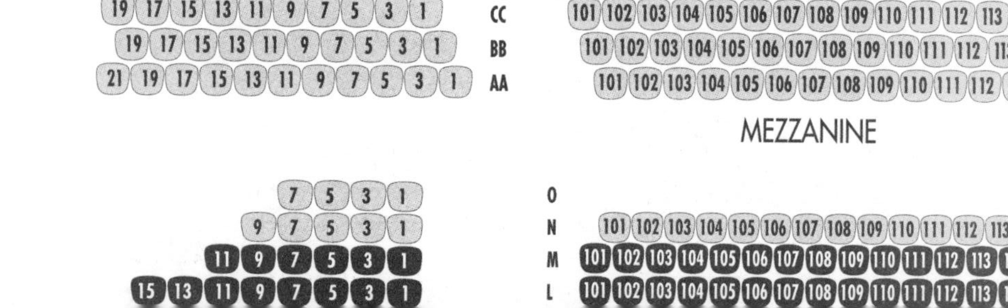

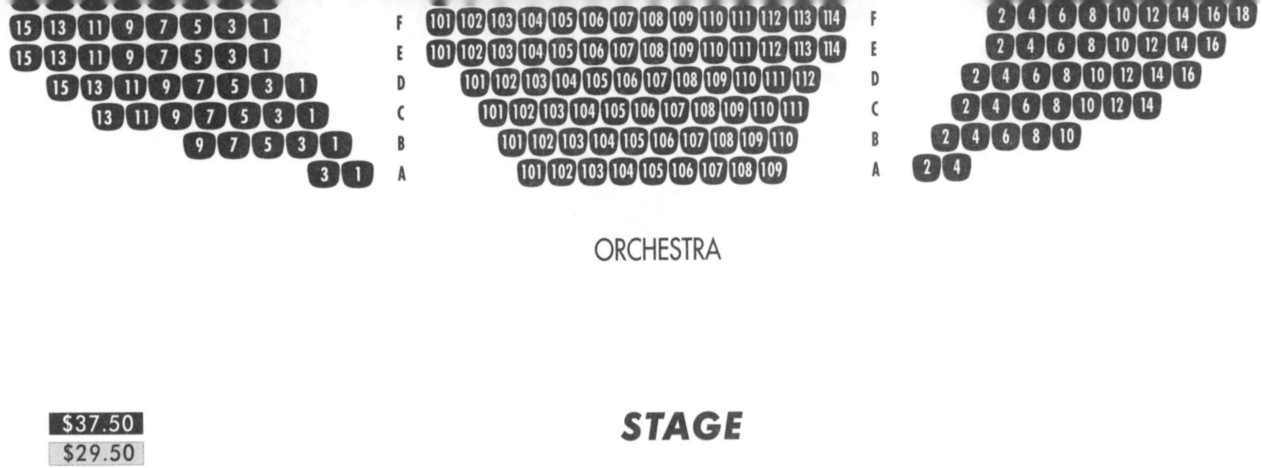

Row	Left	Center	Right	Row
F	15 13 11 9 7 5 3 1	101 102 103 104 105 106 107 108 109 110 111 112 113 114	2 4 6 8 10 12 14 16 18	F
E	15 13 11 9 7 5 3 1	101 102 103 104 105 106 107 108 109 110 111 112 113 114	2 4 6 8 10 12 14 16	E
D	15 13 11 9 7 5 3 1	101 102 103 104 105 106 107 108 109 110 111 112	2 4 6 8 10 12 14 16	D
C	13 11 9 7 5 3 1	101 102 103 104 105 106 107 108 109 110 111	2 4 6 8 10 12 14	C
B	9 7 5 3 1	101 102 103 104 105 106 107 108 109 110	2 4 6 8 10	B
A	3 1	101 102 103 104 105 106 107 108 109	2 4	A

ORCHESTRA

$37.50
$29.50

STAGE

TICKETMASTER (212) 307-4100
BOX OFFICE (212) 505-0700

TAXI DIRECTIONS:
17th St. Westbound
(bet. Park Ave. South & Irving Place)

PARKING
GMC, 144 E. 17th St.
(bet. Lexington & 3rd Aves.)
Kinney System, 202 E. 10th St.
(bet. 2nd & 3rd Aves.)
BUS
M1, M2, M3, M5, M14,
M101, M102, M103
SUBWAYS
4,5,6,L,M,R to 14th St. Union Square
F Path to 14th St. & 6th Ave.

Nearby restaurants rated by
SEATS
ZEN PALATE, 34 Union Square 614-9291
PARK AVALON, 225 Park Ave. South 533-2500
SAL ANTHONY'S, 55 Irving Place 692-9030

VARIETY ARTS THEATRE

110 Third Avenue, New York, NY 10003

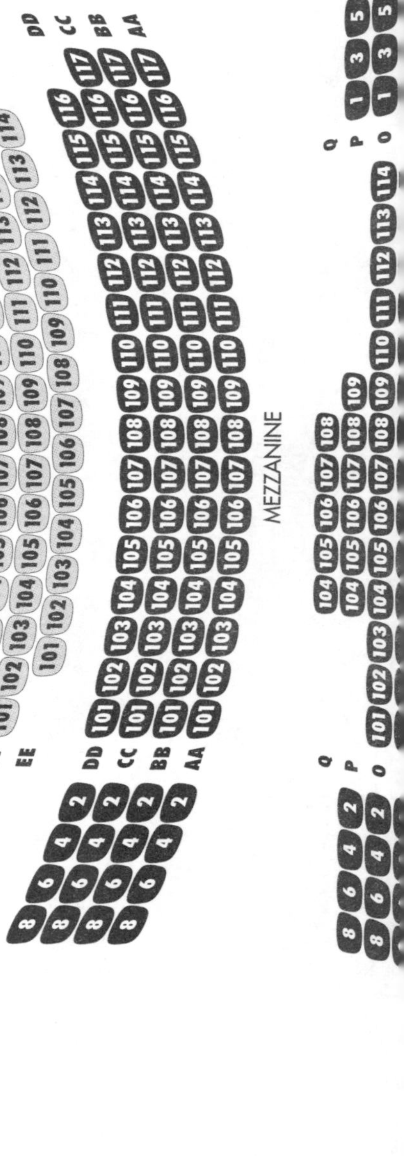

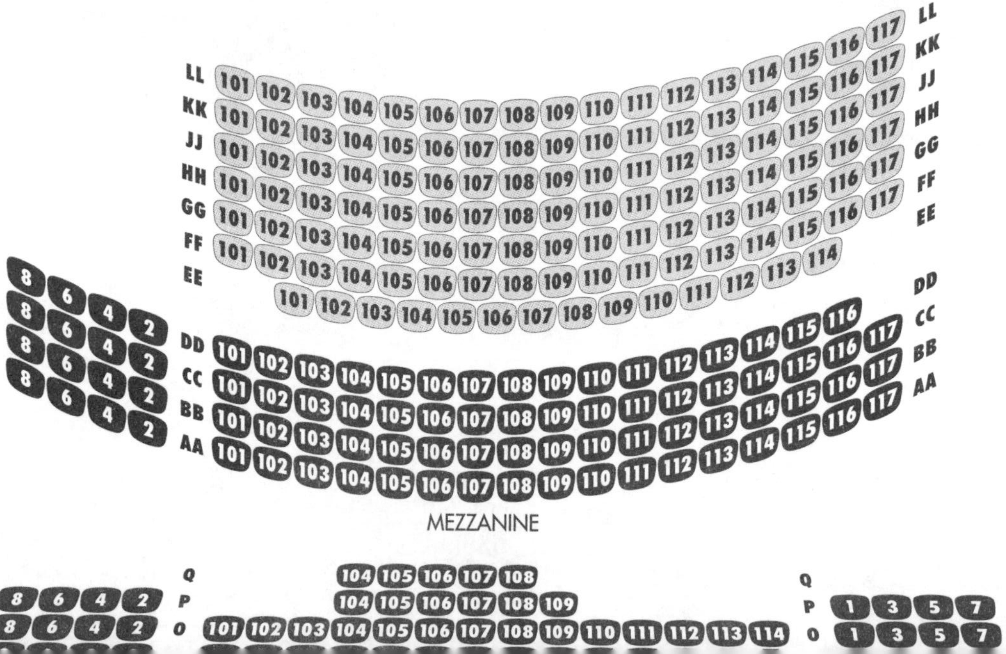

MEZZANINE

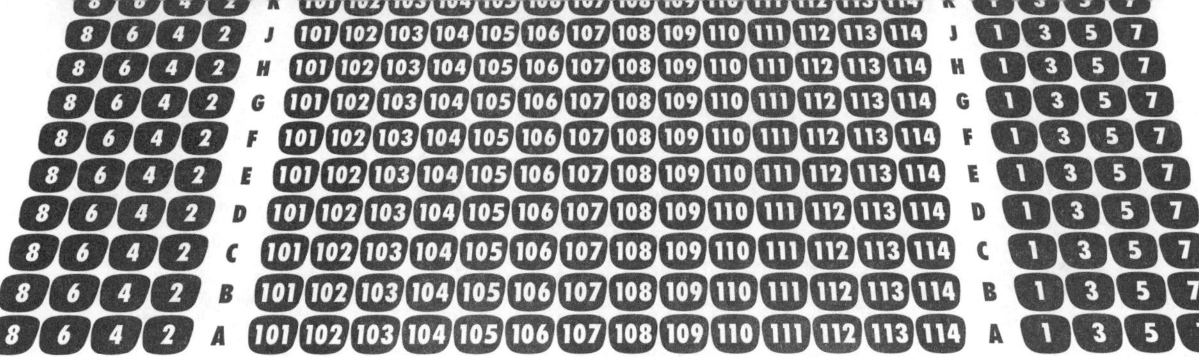

$45.00
$40.00

Mezzanine row AA overhangs Orchestra row F

TELECHARGE (212) 239-6200

TAXI DIRECTIONS:
3rd Ave. two way
(bet. 13th & 14th Sts.)

PARKING
GMC, 144 E. 17th St.
(bet. Irving Place & 3rd Ave.)
Kinney System,
311 E. 11th St.
(bet. 1st & 2nd Aves.)
BUS
M14, M101, M202
SUBWAYS
L to 3rd Ave.
4,5,6,N,R to 14th St.

Nearby restaurants rated by
SEATS

WESTSIDE THEATRE

407 West 43rd Street, New York, NY 10036

DOWNSTAIRS THEATRE

A 101 102 103 104 105 106 107 108 A

STAGE

Prices vary per performance.
Neither theatre is wheelchair accessible
Free Sennheiser infrared listening system available

TELECHARGE (212) 239-6200

TAXI DIRECTIONS:
43rd St. Westbound
(bet. 9th & 10th Aves.)

PARKING
Allure Parking, 500 W. 43rd St.
Discount available
(bet. 10th & 11th Aves.)
Edison Park Fast, 401-471 W. 42nd St.
(bet. 9th & 10th Aves.)
Kinney System, 352 W. 43rd St.
(bet. 8th & 9th Aves.)
BUS
M10, M11, M16, M42
SUBWAYS
A,C,E, to 42nd St. & 8th Ave. Port Authority
1,2,3,7,9,S,N,R to 42nd St. & 7th Ave. Times Square

Nearby restaurants rated by
SEATS
WEST BANK CAFE, 407 W. 42nd St. 695-6909
CHEZ JOSEPHINE, 414 W. 42nd St. 594-1925
LE MADELEINE, 403 W. 43rd St. 246-2993
ZUNI, 598 9th Ave. at 43rd St. 765-7626
RACHEL'S AMERICAN BISTRO,
608 9th Ave. at 43rd St. 957-9050
TURKISH CUISINE, 631 9th Ave. at 45th St.
397-9650

WESTSIDE THEATRE

407 West 43rd Street, New York, NY 10036

UPSTAIRS THEATRE

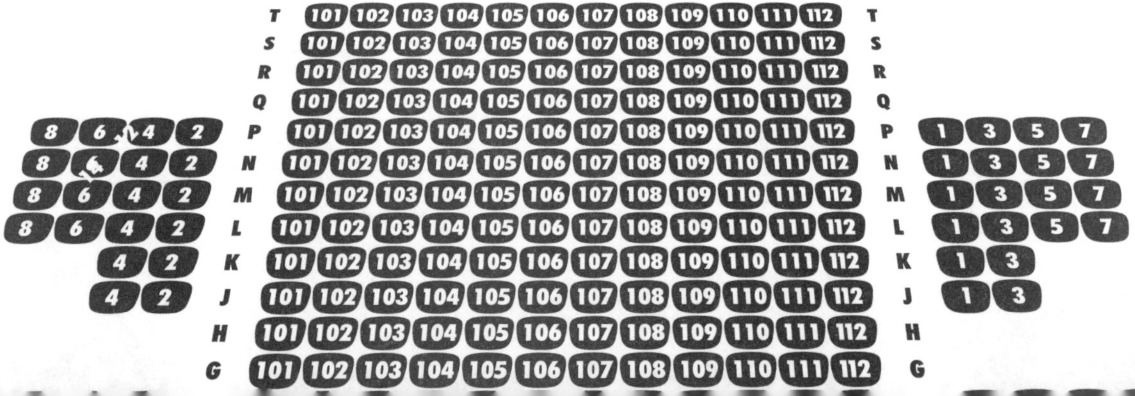

				Row													Row				
				T	101	102	103	104	105	106	107	108	109	110	111	112	T				
				S	101	102	103	104	105	106	107	108	109	110	111	112	S				
				R	101	102	103	104	105	106	107	108	109	110	111	112	R				
				Q	101	102	103	104	105	106	107	108	109	110	111	112	Q				
8	6	4	2	P	101	102	103	104	105	106	107	108	109	110	111	112	P	1	3	5	7
8	6	4	2	N	101	102	103	104	105	106	107	108	109	110	111	112	N	1	3	5	7
8	6	4	2	M	101	102	103	104	105	106	107	108	109	110	111	112	M	1	3	5	7
8	6	4	2	L	101	102	103	104	105	106	107	108	109	110	111	112	L	1	3	5	7
		4	2	K	101	102	103	104	105	106	107	108	109	110	111	112	K	1	3		
		4	2	J	101	102	103	104	105	106	107	108	109	110	111	112	J	1	3		
				H	101	102	103	104	105	106	107	108	109	110	111	112	H				
				G	101	102	103	104	105	106	107	108	109	110	111	112	G				

Row				Row													Row			
	6	4	2	B	101	102	103	104	105	106	107	108	109	110	111	112	B	1	3	5
	6	4	2	A	101	102	103	104	105	106	107	108	109	110	111		A	1	3	5

STAGE

Prices vary per performance.
Neither theatre is wheelchair accessible
Free Sennheiser infrared listening system available

TELECHARGE (212) 239-6200

TAXI DIRECTIONS:
43rd St. Westbound
(bet. 9th & 10th Aves.)

PARKING
Allure Parking, 500 W. 43rd St.
Discount available
(bet. 10th & 11th Aves.)
Edison Park Fast, 401-471 W. 42nd St.
(bet. 9th & 10th Aves.)
Kinney System, 352 W. 43rd St.
(bet. 8th & 9th Aves.)

BUS
M10, M11, M16, M42

SUBWAYS
A,C,E, to 42nd St. & 8th Ave. Port Authority
1,2,3,7,9,S,N,R to 42nd St. & 7th Ave. Times Square

Nearby restaurants rated by
SEATS
WEST BANK CAFE, 407 W. 42nd St. 695-6909
CHEZ JOSEPHINE, 414 W. 42nd St. 594-1925
LE MADELEINE, 403 W. 43rd St. 246-2993
ZUNI, 598 9th Ave. at 43rd St. 765-7626
RACHEL'S AMERICAN BISTRO, 608 9th Ave. at 43rd St. 957-9050
TURKISH CUISINE, 631 9th Ave. at 45th St. 397-9650

AMATO OPERA THEATRE

319 Bowery, New York, NY 10003

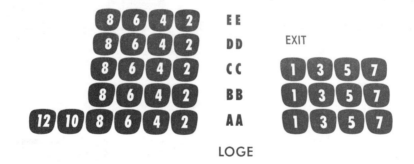

						Row				
		8	6	4	2	EE				
		8	6	4	2	DD	EXIT			
		8	6	4	2	CC	1	3	5	7
		8	6	4	2	BB	1	3	5	7
12	10	8	6	4	2	AA	1	3	5	7

LOGE

						Row				
						J	1	3	5	7
				EXIT		H	1	3	5	7
10	8	6	4	2	G	G	1	3	5	7

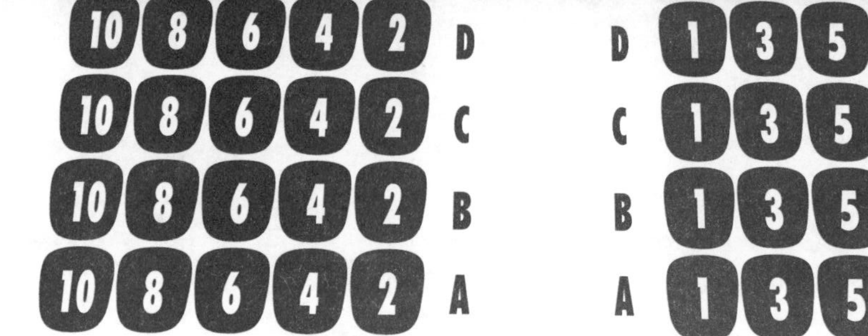

All Seats One Price

TICKETS (212) 228-8200

TAXI DIRECTIONS:
Bowery two-way at 2nd St.
Theatre on eastside of Bowery

PARKING
321 Bowery Corporation,
321Bowery at 2nd St.
BUS
M102
SUBWAYS
F,B,D, to Broadway - Lafayette St.
6 to Bleecker St.

Nearby restaurants rated by
SEATS

FRITTO DE - MARE, 84 E. 4th St. 979-2034
LANZA RESTAURANT, 168 1st Ave. 674-7014

PRIMARY STAGES THEATRE

354 West 45th Street, New York, NY 10036

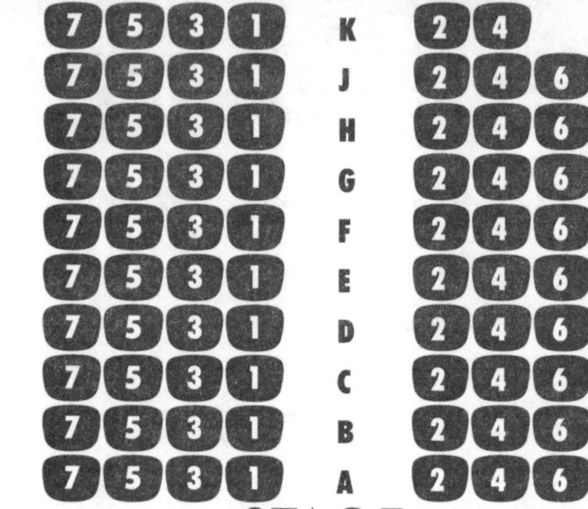

ALL SEATS $35.00

THEATRE (212) 333-4052

Taxi Directions:
45th St. Westbound
(bet. 8th & 9th Aves.)

PARKING
Edison Park Fast, 1120
Avenue of the Americas
(bet. 43rd & 44th Sts.)
Kinney System, 100 W. 44th St.
(bet. 6th & 7th Aves.)
BUS
M6, M7, M10, M42, M104
SUBWAY
A,C,E to 42nd St. & 8th Ave. Port Authority
N,R,S,1,2,3,7,9 to 42nd St. & 7th Ave. Times Square

Nearby restaurants rated by
SEATS

TURKISH CUISINE, 631 9th Ave. at 45th St., 397-9650
BROADWAY JOE STEAK HOUSE, 315 W. 46th St., 246-6513
MARLOWE, 328 W. 46th St. 765-3815
O' FLAHERTY'S ALE HOUSE, 334 W. 46th St. 246-8928
DANNY'S GRAND SEA PALACE RESTAURANT,
346-348 W. 46th St. bet. 8th & 9th Aves. 265-8130

ST. CLEMENTS CHURCH THEATRE

423 West 46th Street, New York, N.Y. 10036

Row	Seats
J	1 2 3 4 5 6 7 8 9 10 11 12
H	1 2 3 4 5 6 7 8 9 10 11 12 13 14 15
G	1 2 3 4 5 6 7 8 9 10 11 12 13 14 15 16
F	1 2 3 4 5 6 7 8 9 10 11 12 13 14 15
E	1 2 3 4 5 6 7 8 9 10 11 12 13 14 15 16
D	1 2 3 4 5 6 7 8 9 10 11 12 13 14 15
C	1 2 3 4 5 6 7 8 9 10 11 12 13 14 15 16
B	1 2 3 4 5 6 7 8 9 10 11 12 13 14 15
A	1 2 3 4 5 6 7 8 9 10 11 12 13 14 15 16
AA	1 2 3 4 5 6 7 8 9 10 11 12 13 14 15

All Seats One Price

STAGE

TICKETS (212) 246-7277

TAXI DIRECTIONS:
46th St. Eastbound
(bet. 9th & 10th Aves.)

PARKING
GMC, 257 W. 47th St.
(bet. Broadway & 8th Ave.)
Kinney System, 253 W. 47th St.
(bet. Broadway & 8th Ave.)

BUS
M10, M11, M42 , M104

SUBWAY
A,C,E to 42nd & 8th Ave.
1,2,3,9,7,S,N to 42nd St. & 7th Ave.

Nearby restaurants rated by
SEATS

DANNY'S GRAND SEA PALACE, 346-348 W. 46th St. 265-8130
MARLOWE, 328 W. 46th St. 765-3815
O' FLAHERTY'S, 334 W. 46th St. 246-8928
MESKEREM 468 W. 47th St. 664-0520
B.SMITH'S, 771 8th Ave. at 47th St. 247-2222
LA PRIMAVERA, 234 W. 48th St. 586-2797

THE SYLVIA & DANNY KAYE PLAYHOUSE

Hunter College, New York, NY 10021

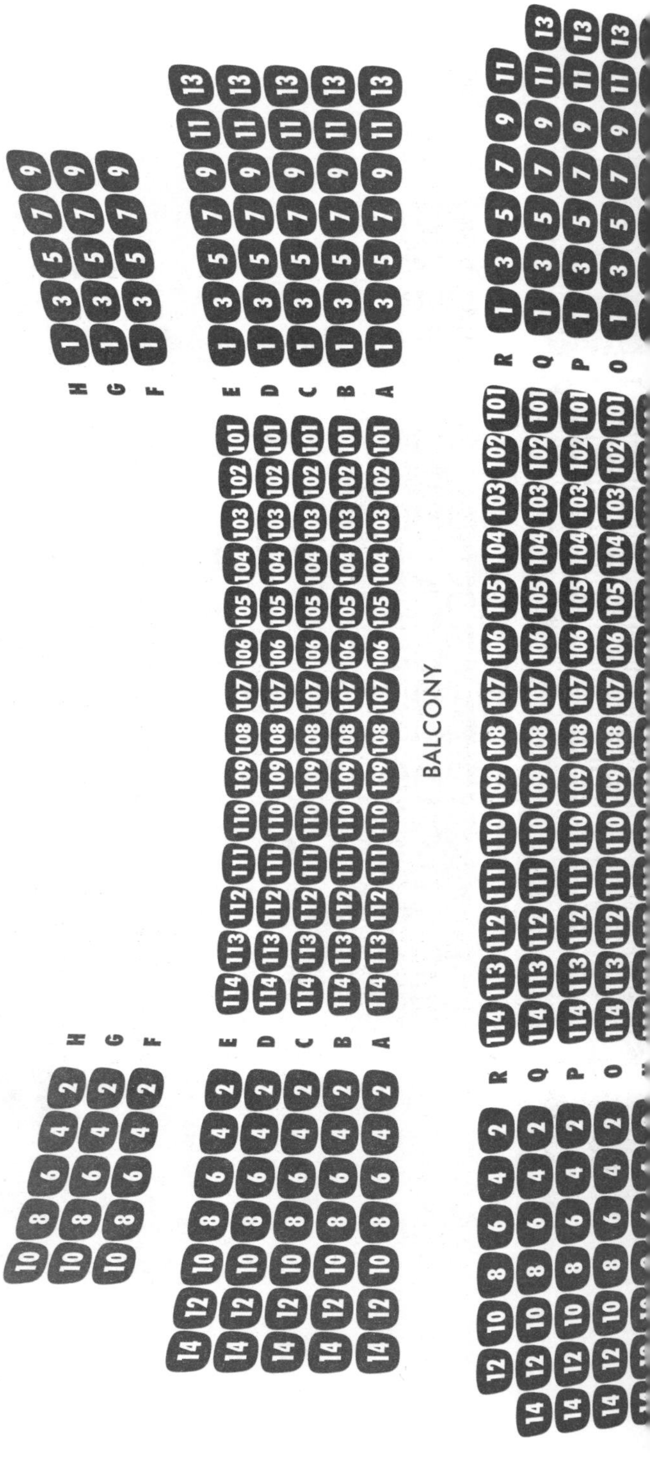

BALCONY

Seats (left)	Row	Seats (center)	Row	Seats (right)
14 12 10 8 6 4 2	J	114 113 112 111 110 109 108 107 106 105 104 103 102 101	J	1 3 5 7 9 11 13
14 12 10 8 6 4 2	H	114 113 112 111 110 109 108 107 106 105 104 103 102 101	H	1 3 5 7 9 11 13
14 12 10 8 6 4 2	G	114 113 112 111 110 109 108 107 106 105 104 103 102 101	G	1 3 5 7 9 11 13
	F	114 113 112 111 110 109 108 107 106 105 104 103 102 101	F	
	E	114 113 112 111 110 109 108 107 106 105 104 103 102 101	E	
14 12 10 8 6 4 2	D	114 113 112 111 110 109 108 107 106 105 104 103 102 101	D	1 3 5 7 9 11 13
12 10 8 6 4 2	C	114 113 112 111 110 109 108 107 106 105 104 103 102 101	C	1 3 5 7 9 11
12 10 8 6 4 2	B	114 113 112 111 110 109 108 107 106 105 104 103 102 101	B	1 3 5 7 9 11
10 8 6 4 2	A	114 113 112 111 110 109 108 107 106 105 104 103 102 101	A	1 3 5 7 9

ORCHESTRA

STAGE

Balcony begins over Orchestra row K

♿ Room for 16 wheelchairs in the theatre

Infrared devices available

All Seats $24.00
Seniors $18.00
Students $10.00

TICKETS (212) 772-4448

TAXI DIRECTIONS:
68th St. Eastbound
(bet. Park & Lexington Aves.)

PARKING
Kinney System, 301 E. 69th St.
(Bet. 1st & 2nd Aves.)
Kinney System, 301 E. 66th St.
(Bet. 1st & 2nd Aves.)
BUS
M101, M102, M103, M66
SUBWAY
6 to 68th St.
Q to 63rd St. & Lexington Ave.

Nearby restaurants rated by
SEATS

ANCHE VIVOLO, 222 E. 58th St. 308-0112
CAFE WORD OF MOUTH, 1012 Lexington Ave. 249-5351
CIRCUS, 808 Lexington Ave. 223-2566
GINO, 780 Lexington Ave. 758-4466
LE PETIT HULOT, 973 Lexington Ave. 749-9800
THE SIGN OF THE DOVE, 1110 3rd Ave. 861-8080
TOSCANA, 843 Lexington Ave. 517-2288
VIVOLO, 140 E. 74th St. 737-3533

WPA THEATER

519 West 23rd Street, New York, NY 10011

THEATER (212) 206-0523

Taxi Directions:
23rd St. East and Westbound at 10th Ave.

PARKING
Kinney System, 235 W. 22rd St.
(bet 7th and 8th Aves.)
514 West Corporation, 514 W. 23rd St.
BUS
M23
SUBWAYS
C,E to 23rd St.& 8th Ave.
1,9 to 23rd St. & 7th Ave.

Nearby restaurants rated by

SEATS

ZUCCA RESTAURANT, 227 10th Ave. 741-1970
CHELSEA COMMONS RESTAURANT, 463 W. 24th St. At 10th Ave. 924-6737
LUMA RESTAURANT, 200 9th Ave. 633-8033

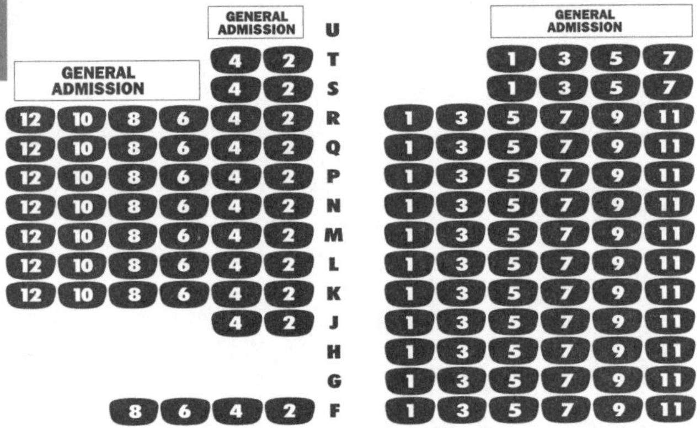

Row	Left section	Right section
U	GENERAL ADMISSION	GENERAL ADMISSION
T	4 2	1 3 5 7
S	4 2 (GENERAL ADMISSION)	1 3 5 7
R	12 10 8 6 4 2	1 3 5 7 9 11
Q	12 10 8 6 4 2	1 3 5 7 9 11
P	12 10 8 6 4 2	1 3 5 7 9 11
N	12 10 8 6 4 2	1 3 5 7 9 11
M	12 10 8 6 4 2	1 3 5 7 9 11
L	12 10 8 6 4 2	1 3 5 7 9 11
K	12 10 8 6 4 2	1 3 5 7 9 11
J	4 2	1 3 5 7 9 11
H		1 3 5 7 9 11
G		1 3 5 7 9 11
F	8 6 4 2	1 3 5 7 9 11

STAGE

All Seats One Price
Prices Range from
$25.00-$40.00

♿ Wheelchair seating available.

YORK THEATRE COMPANY

St. Peter's Church, 619 Lexington Avenue, New York, NY 10022

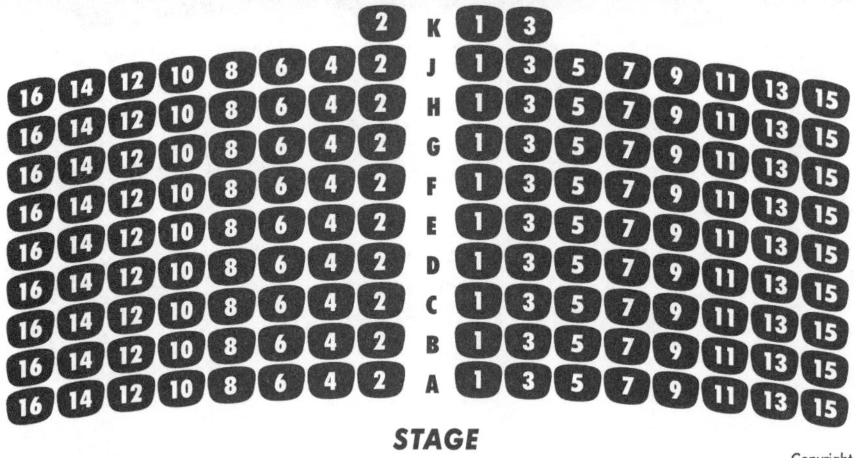

								Row								
							2	K	1	3						
	14	12	10	8	6	4	2	J	1	3	5	7	9	11	13	
16	14	12	10	8	6	4	2	H	1	3	5	7	9	11	13	15
16	14	12	10	8	6	4	2	G	1	3	5	7	9	11	13	15
16	14	12	10	8	6	4	2	F	1	3	5	7	9	11	13	15
16	14	12	10	8	6	4	2	E	1	3	5	7	9	11	13	15
16	14	12	10	8	6	4	2	D	1	3	5	7	9	11	13	15
16	14	12	10	8	6	4	2	C	1	3	5	7	9	11	13	15
16	14	12	10	8	6	4	2	B	1	3	5	7	9	11	13	15
16	14	12	10	8	6	4	2	A	1	3	5	7	9	11	13	15

STAGE

All Seats One Price

THEATRE (212) 935-5820

Taxi Directions:
Lexington Ave.Southbound
at 54th St. Eastbound

PARKING
Hawthorne Garage, 211 E. 53rd St.
Obtain parking validation sticker
GMC, 229 E. 55th St.
(bet. 2nd & 3rd Aves.)

BUS
M27, M31, M50, M57, M101, M102,M103

SUBWAYS
E, F TO 53rd St. & Lexington Ave.
6 to 51st St. & Lexington Ave.

BEACON THEATRE

2124 Broadway, New York, NY 10023

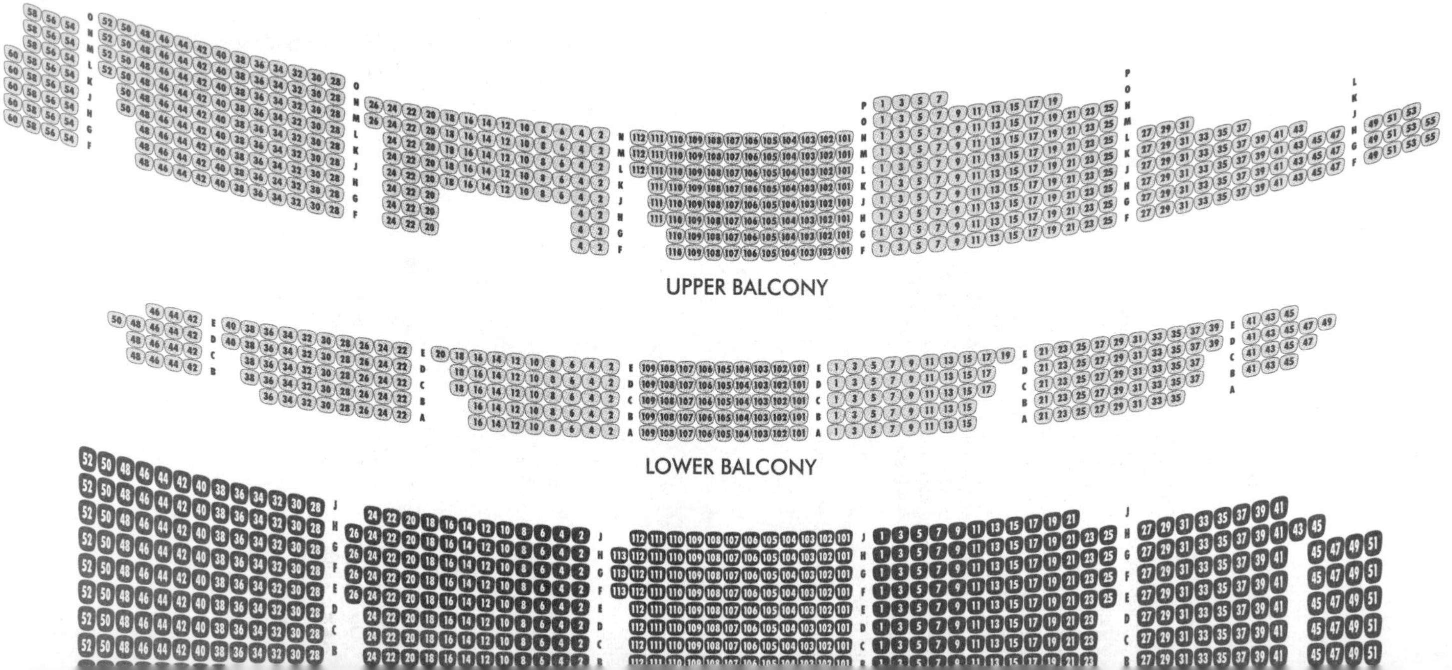

UPPER BALCONY

LOWER BALCONY

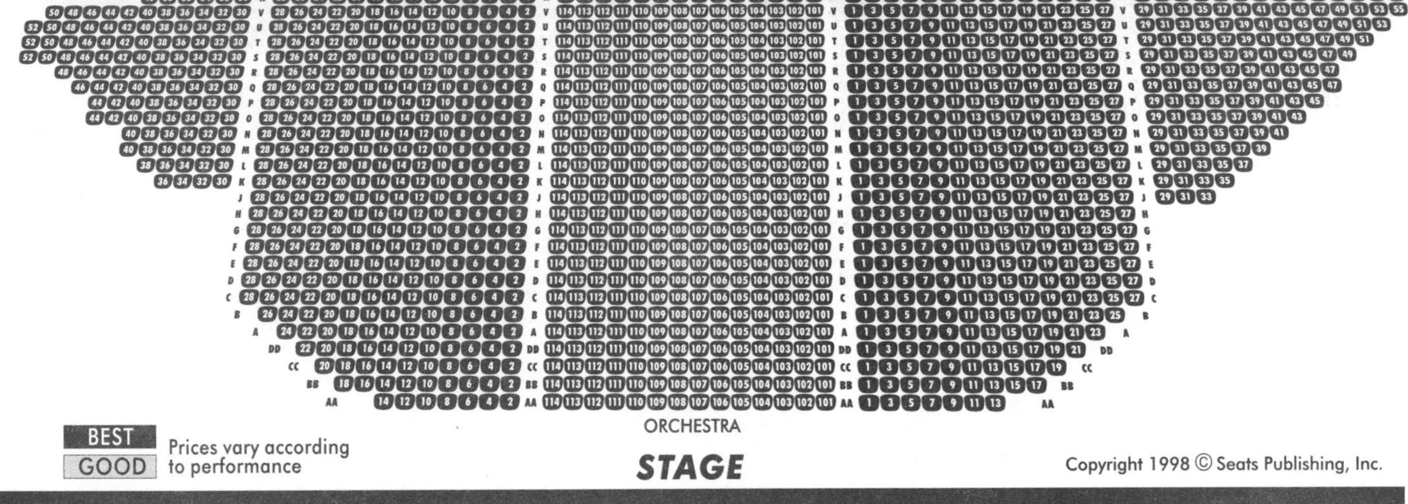

TICKETMASTER (212) 307-7171
PRE-RECORDED INFORMATION (212) 496-7070

TAXI DIRECTIONS:
Broadway, two way
(bet. 74th & 75th Sts.)

PARKING
Kinney System,
201 W. 75th St.
(bet. Broadway & Amsterdam Ave.)
BUS
M5, M7, M11, M72, M104
SUBWAYS
1,9,2,3 to 72nd St. & Broadway

Nearby restaurants rated by
SEATS
ERNIE'S, 2150 Broadway 496-1588
NIKO'S, 2161 Broadway 873-7000

BROOKLYN ACADEMY OF MUSIC

MAJESTIC THEATRE

30 Lafayette Avenue, Brooklyn, NY 11217

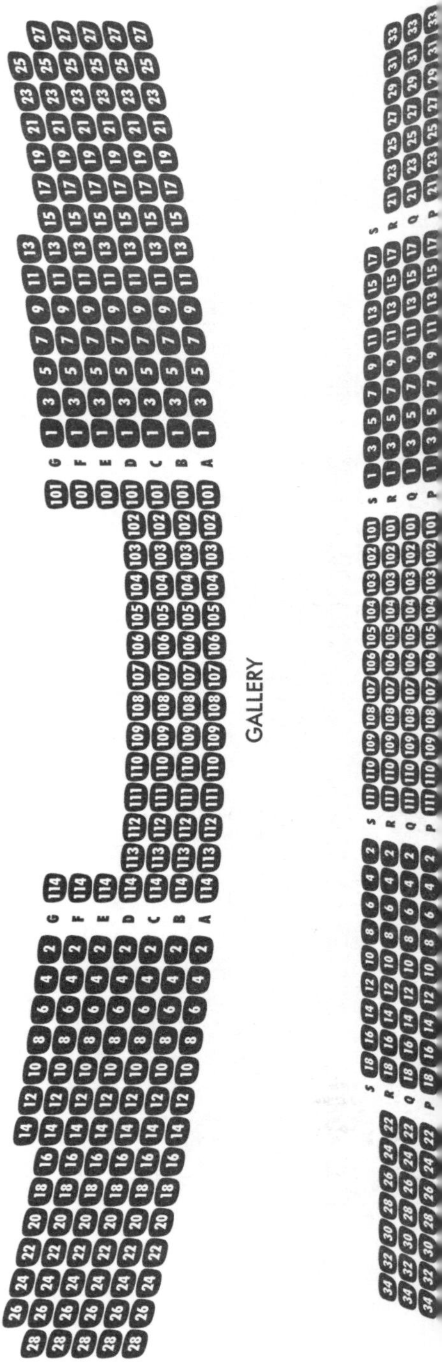

GALLERY

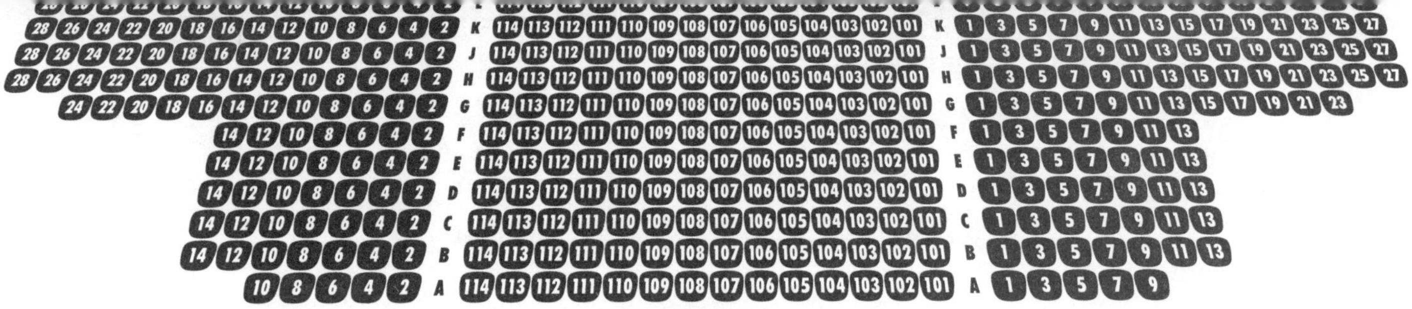

Row	Left	Center	Right
K	28 26 24 22 20 18 16 14 12 10 8 6 4 2	114 113 112 111 110 109 108 107 106 105 104 103 102 101	1 3 5 7 9 11 13 15 17 19 21 23 25 27
J	28 26 24 22 20 18 16 14 12 10 8 6 4 2	114 113 112 111 110 109 108 107 106 105 104 103 102 101	1 3 5 7 9 11 13 15 17 19 21 23 25 27
H	28 26 24 22 20 18 16 14 12 10 8 6 4 2	114 113 112 111 110 109 108 107 106 105 104 103 102 101	1 3 5 7 9 11 13 15 17 19 21 23 25 27
G	24 22 20 18 16 14 12 10 8 6 4 2	114 113 112 111 110 109 108 107 106 105 104 103 102 101	1 3 5 7 9 11 13 15 17 19 21 23
F	14 12 10 8 6 4 2	114 113 112 111 110 109 108 107 106 105 104 103 102 101	1 3 5 7 9 11 13
E	14 12 10 8 6 4 2	114 113 112 111 110 109 108 107 106 105 104 103 102 101	1 3 5 7 9 11 13
D	14 12 10 8 6 4 2	114 113 112 111 110 109 108 107 106 105 104 103 102 101	1 3 5 7 9 11 13
C	14 12 10 8 6 4 2	114 113 112 111 110 109 108 107 106 105 104 103 102 101	1 3 5 7 9 11 13
B	14 12 10 8 6 4 2	114 113 112 111 110 109 108 107 106 105 104 103 102 101	1 3 5 7 9 11 13
A	10 8 6 4 2	114 113 112 111 110 109 108 107 106 105 104 103 102 101	1 3 5 7 9

ORCHESTRA

Gallery row A overhangs
Orchestra row N

♿ Wheelchair accesible

STAGE

Prices vary according to event.

TELECHARGE (212) 307-4100
INFORMATION (718) 636-4100
MEMBERSHIPS AVAILABLE
www.bam.org

PARKING
Edison Park Fast, Ashland Place
BUS
call the BAMbus (718) 636-4100
SUBWAYS
2,3,4,5,D,Q to Atlantic Ave.
B, N,M,R to Pacific St.
G to Fulton St.
LIRR to Flatbush

Nearby restaurants rated by
SEATS
CAFE LE PERCQ, at the Academy
GAGE & TOLLNER, 372 Fulton St. (718) 875-5181
JUNIOR'S, 386 Flatbush Ave. Ext. (718) 852-5257

BROOKLYN ACADEMY OF MUSIC

OPERA HOUSE

30 Lafayette Avenue, Brooklyn, NY 11217

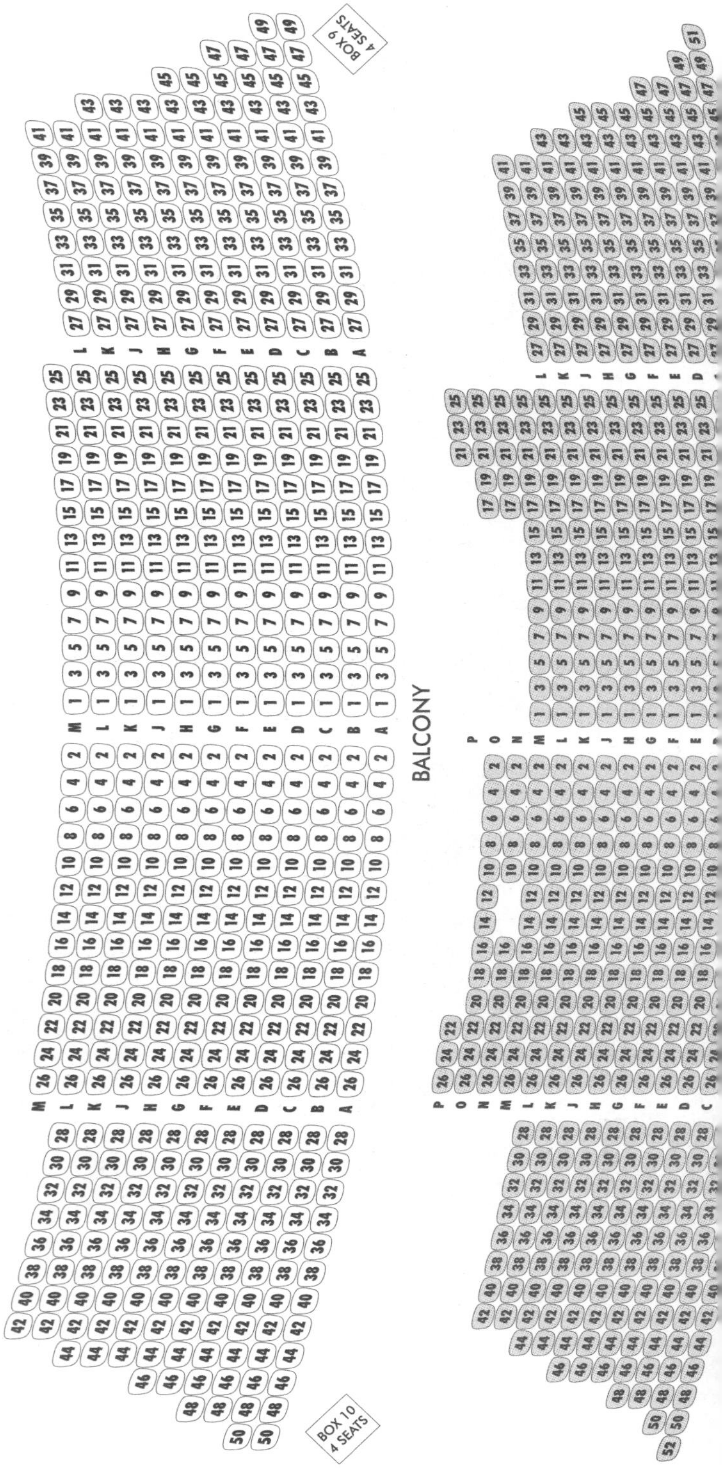

BOX 10
4 SEATS

BOX 9
4 SEATS

BALCONY

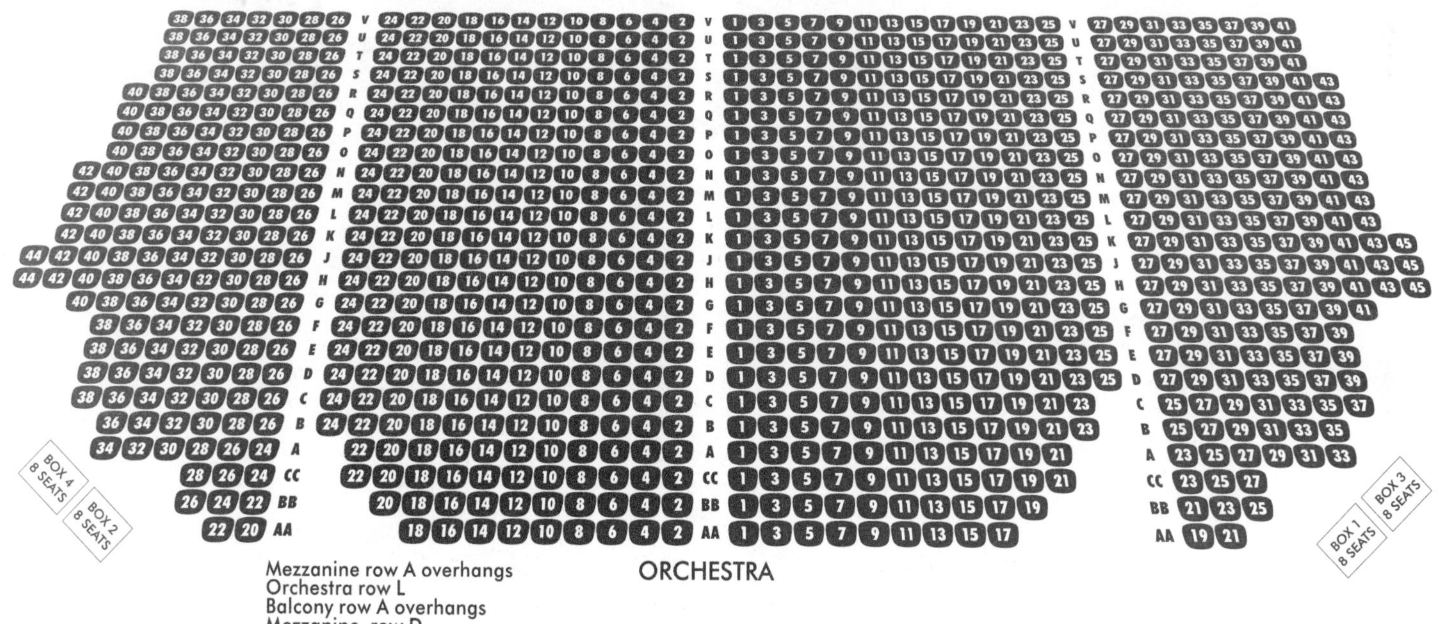

Mezzanine row A overhangs
Orchestra row L
Balcony row A overhangs
Mezzanine row D

Prices vary according to event.

CARNEGIE HALL

881 Seventh Avenue, New York, NY 10019-3210

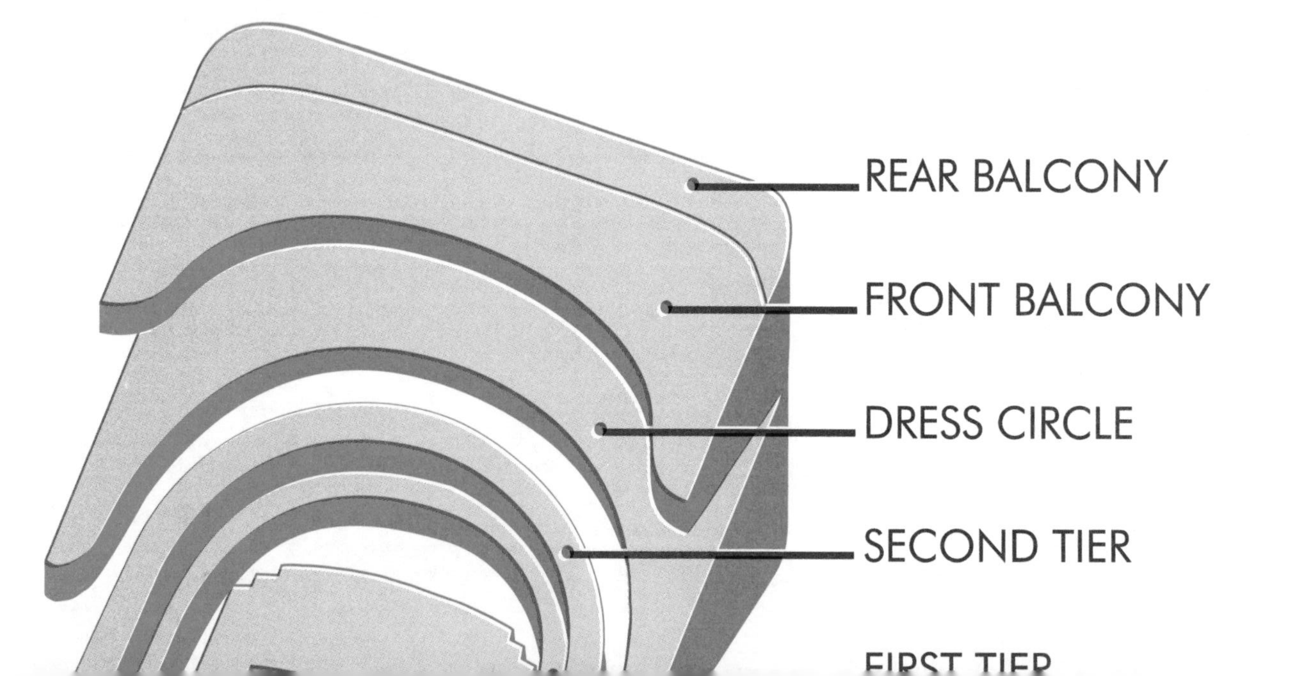

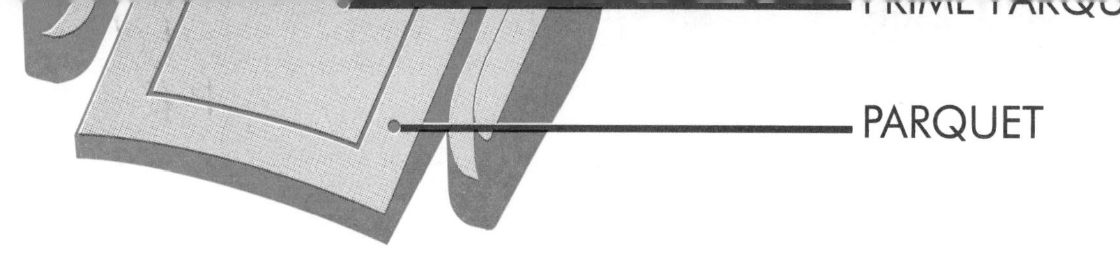

CARNEGIE HALL SEATING CHART

Prices vary according to event.

CARNEGIE CHARGE (212) 247-7800
GROUP SALES (212) 903-9705

TAXI DIRECTIONS
Seventh Avenue, Southbound
(at 57th Street, two way street)

ONLINE
www.carnegiehall.org

PARKING
GMC, 200 Central Park South

BUS
M5,M6,M7,M10,M30,M31,M57,M104

SUBWAYS
1,9,A, B,C,D to 59th St. & Broadway, Columbus Circle
Q to 57th and 6th Ave.
R,N, to 57th St. and 7th Ave.
B,D,E to 53rd St. And 7th Ave.

Nearby restaurants rated by **SEATS**

CARNEGIE HALL EAST ROOM, 881 7th Ave. 903-9689
CAFÉ DELL' ARTE, 900 7th Ave. At 57th St. 245-9800
MOTOWN CAFÉ, 104 W 57th St. 581-8030
LUCKY'S BAR & GRILL, 60 W 57th St. 582-4000
HARD ROCK CAFÉ, 221 W 57th St. 489-6565
MICKEY MANTLE'S RESTAURANT SPORTS BAR 42 Central Park South 688-7777
PETROSSIAN, 182 W. 58th St. 245-2214

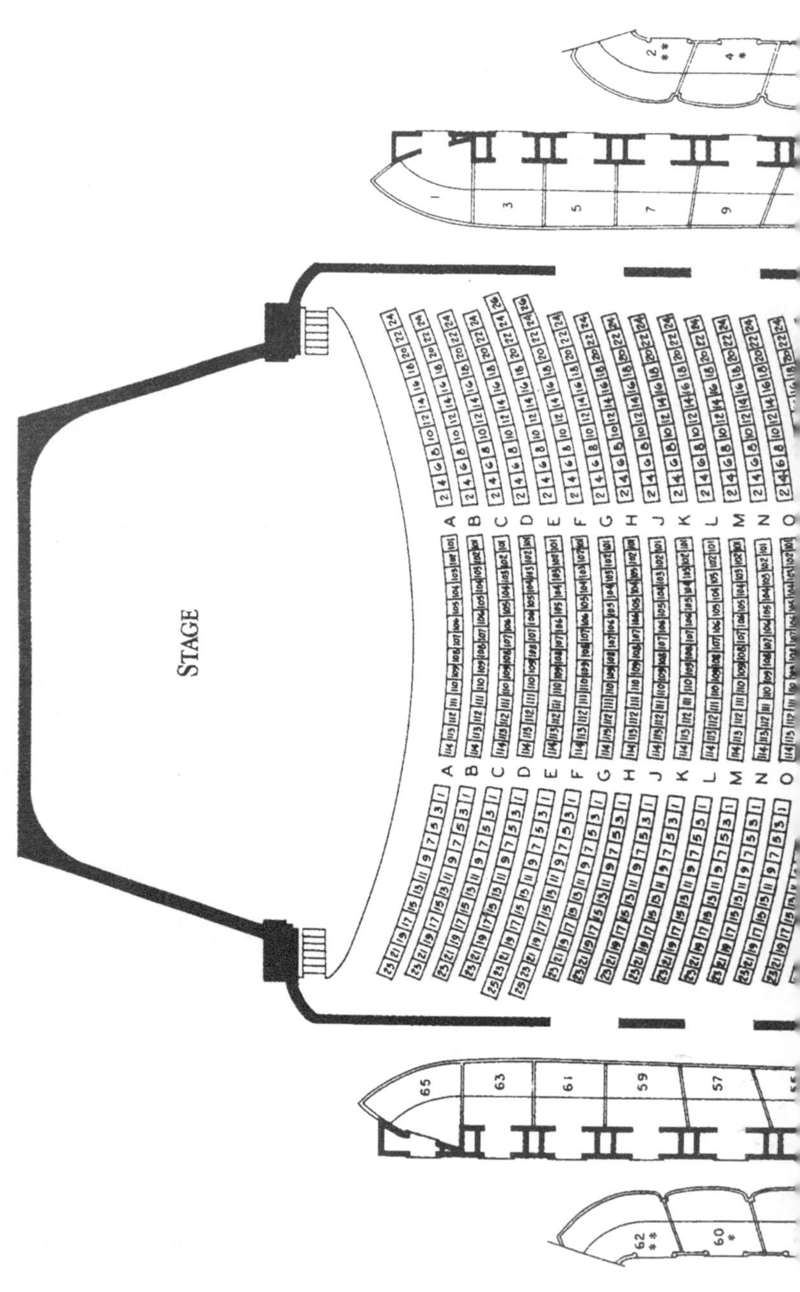
STAGE

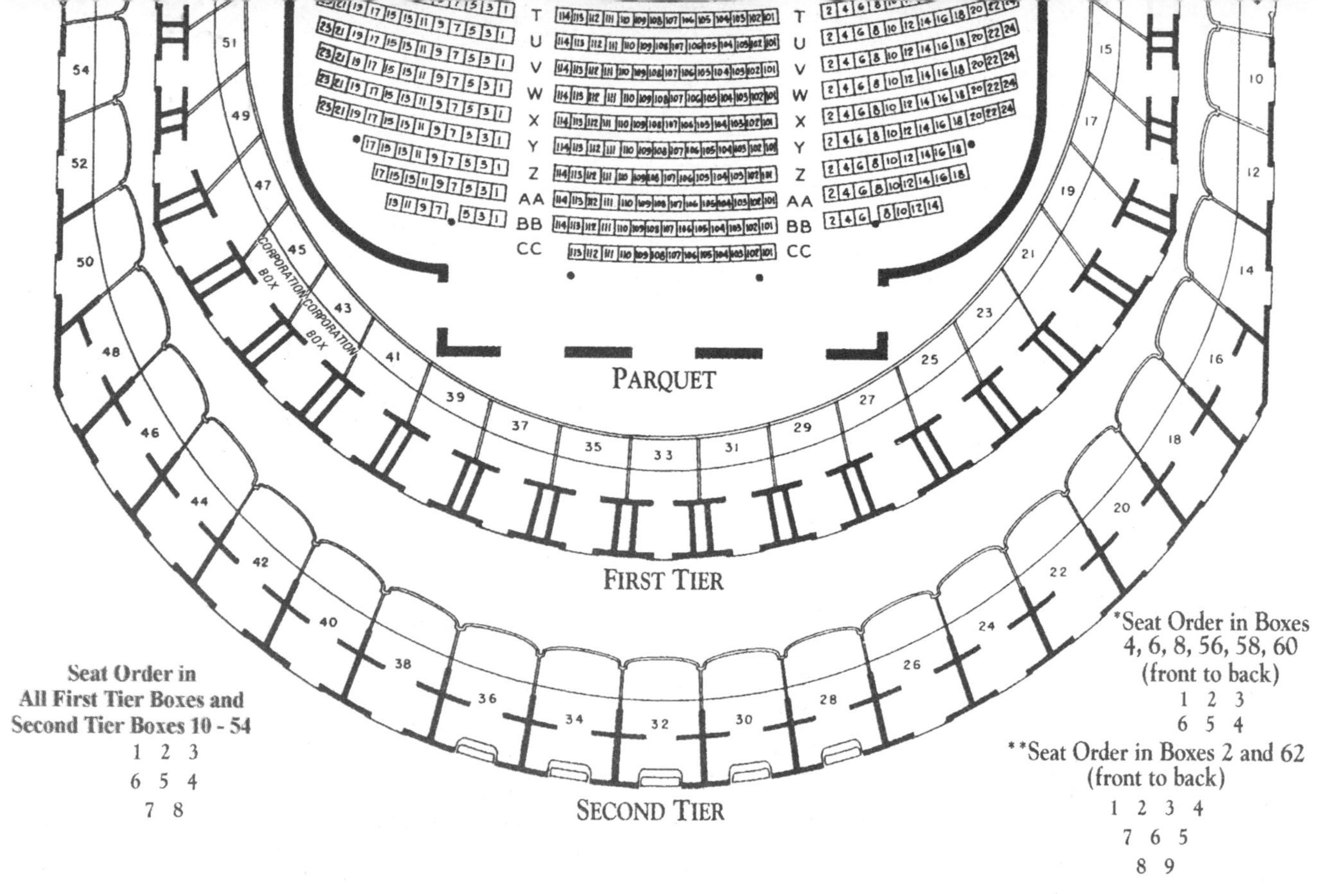
PARQUET
FIRST TIER
SECOND TIER
CORPORATION BOX
CORPORATION BOX
Seat Order in All First Tier Boxes and Second Tier Boxes 10 - 54
1 2 3
6 5 4
7 8
*Seat Order in Boxes 4, 6, 8, 56, 58, 60 (front to back)
1 2 3
6 5 4
**Seat Order in Boxes 2 and 62 (front to back)
1 2 3 4
7 6 5
8 9

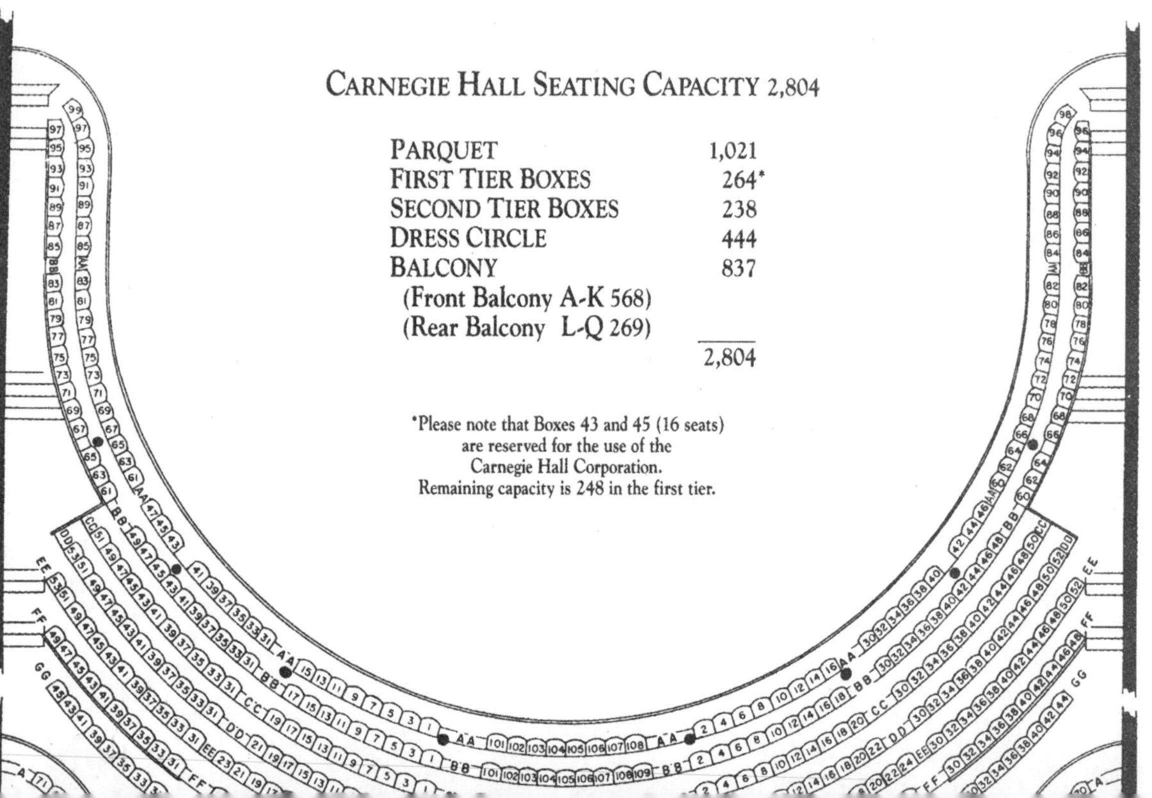

CARNEGIE HALL SEATING CAPACITY 2,804

PARQUET	1,021
FIRST TIER BOXES	264*
SECOND TIER BOXES	238
DRESS CIRCLE	444
BALCONY	837
(Front Balcony A-K 568)	
(Rear Balcony L-Q 269)	
	2,804

*Please note that Boxes 43 and 45 (16 seats) are reserved for the use of the Carnegie Hall Corporation. Remaining capacity is 248 in the first tier.

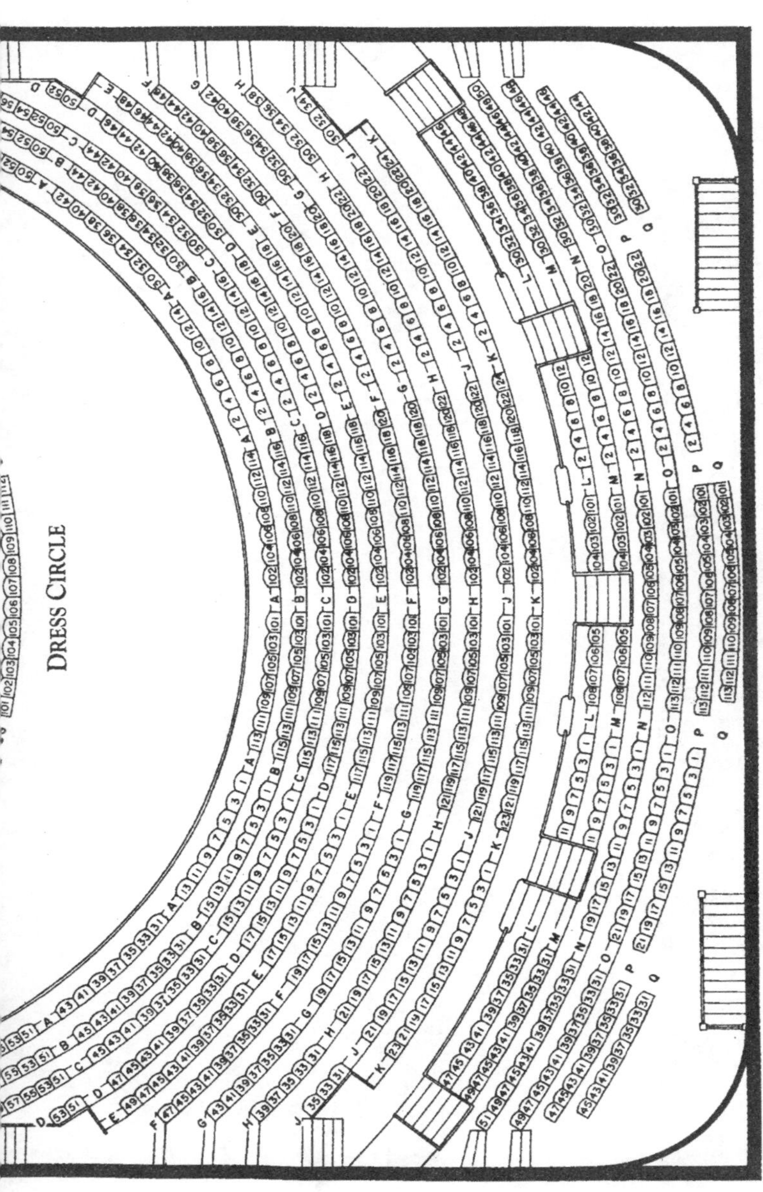
DRESS CIRCLE
BALCONY

CITY CENTER

West 55th Street, New York, NY 10019

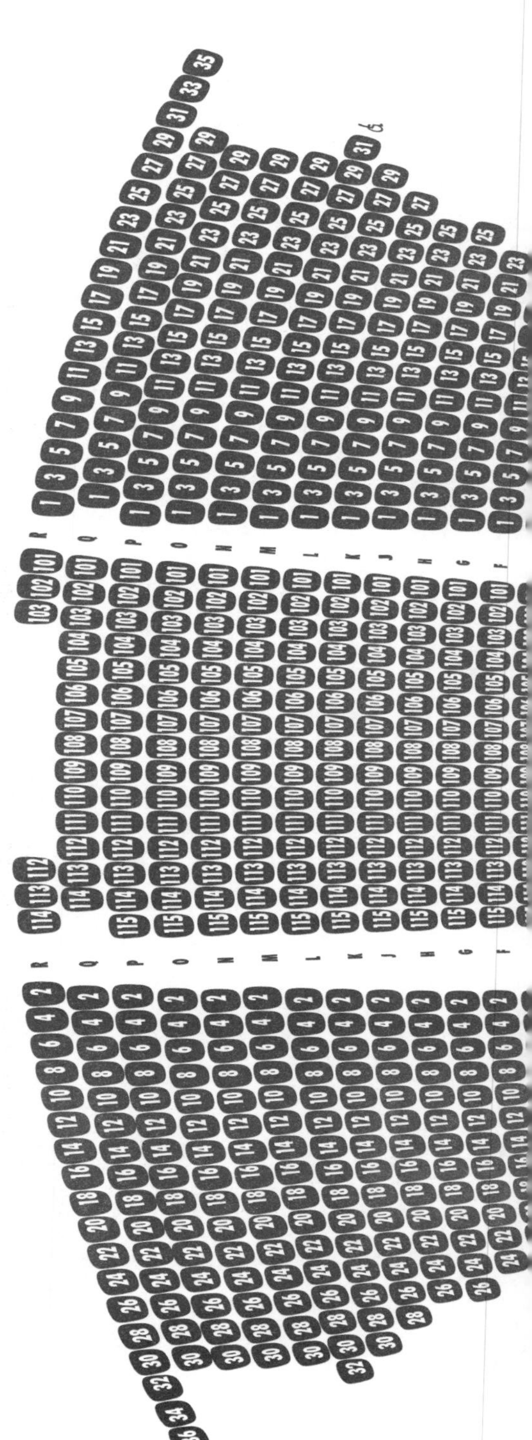

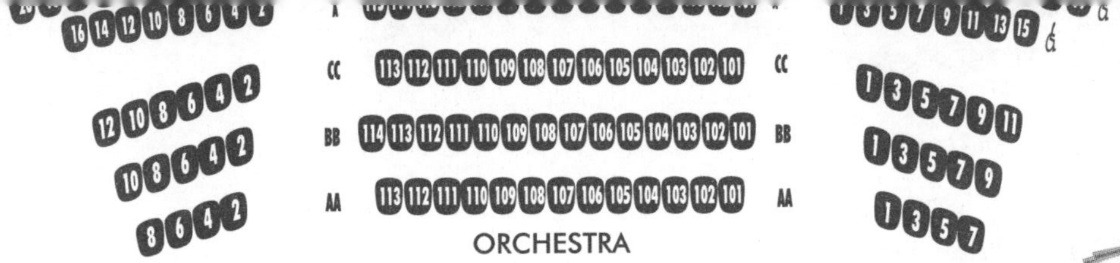

CC 12 10 8 6 4 2 | 113 112 111 110 109 108 107 106 105 104 103 102 101 | 1 3 5 7 9 11 CC

BB 10 8 6 4 2 | 114 113 112 111 110 109 108 107 106 105 104 103 102 101 | 1 3 5 7 9 BB

AA 8 6 4 2 | 113 112 111 110 109 108 107 106 105 104 103 102 101 | 1 3 5 7 AA

ORCHESTRA

Grand Tier row A overhangs
Orchestra row G

$55.00
$45.00
$40.00
$25.00
$20.00

Prices may vary according to show

STAGE

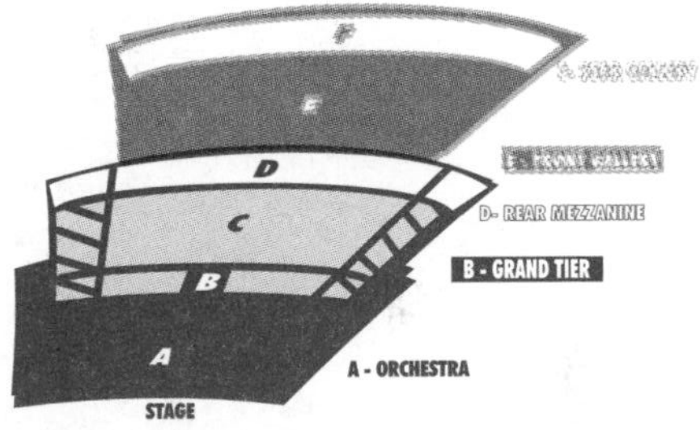

F
E
D
C
B
A
STAGE

D- REAR MEZZANINE
B - GRAND TIER
A - ORCHESTRA

CITY TIX (212) 581-1212
GROUP SALES (212) 889-4300

TAXI DIRECTIONS:
55th St. Westbound
(bet. 6th & 7th Aves.)

PARKING
1345 Garage, 101 W. 54th St.
Kinney System, 888 7th Ave. Entrance on 56th St.
GMC, 156, W. 56th St.
(bet. 6th & 7th Aves.)

BUS
M5, M6, M7, M30, M31, M57

SUBWAYS
B,D,E,N,R, to 57th St. & 7th Ave.
1,9, to 59th St. & Broadway Columbus Circle

Nearby restaurants rated by
SEATS

ORIGINAL FERRARA PASTRIES, 1700 Broadway (bet. 53rd & 54th Sts.) 581-3335
HARLEY DAVIDSON CAFE, 1370 Ave. of the Americas at 56th St. 245-6000
PATSY'S ITALIAN RESTAURANT, 236 W. 56th St. 247-3491
RUMPELMAYER'S RESTAURANT, 50 Central Park South at the St. Mortiz 755-5800

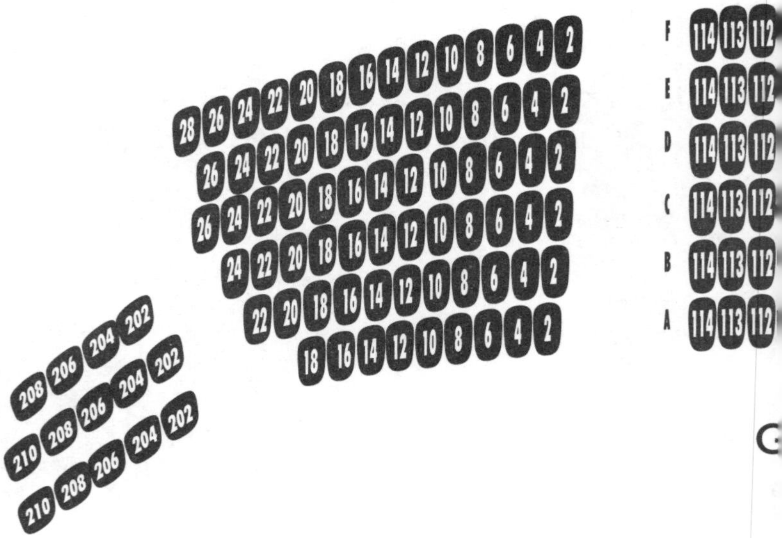

CI

F 114 113 112
E 114 113 112
D 114 113 112
C 114 113 112
B 114 113 112
A 114 113 112

28 26 24 22 20 18 16 14 12 10 8 6 4 2

G

$55.00
$45.00
$40.00
$25.00
$20.00

Prices may vary according to show

Grand Tier row A overhangs Orchestra row G

ENTER

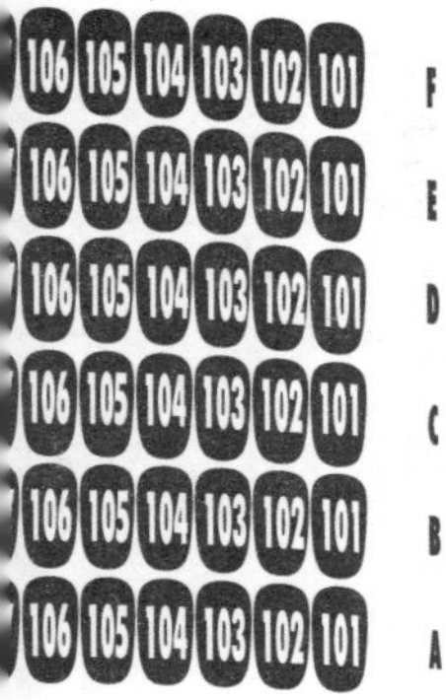

106 105 104 103 102 101 F
106 105 104 103 102 101 E
106 105 104 103 102 101 D
106 105 104 103 102 101 C
106 105 104 103 102 101 B
106 105 104 103 102 101 A

1 3 5 7 9 11 13 15 17 19 21 23 25 27
201 203 205 207 209

TIER

F
E
D
C
B
A
E - FRONT GALLERY
D- REAR MEZZANINE
B - GRAND TIER
A - ORCHESTRA
STAGE

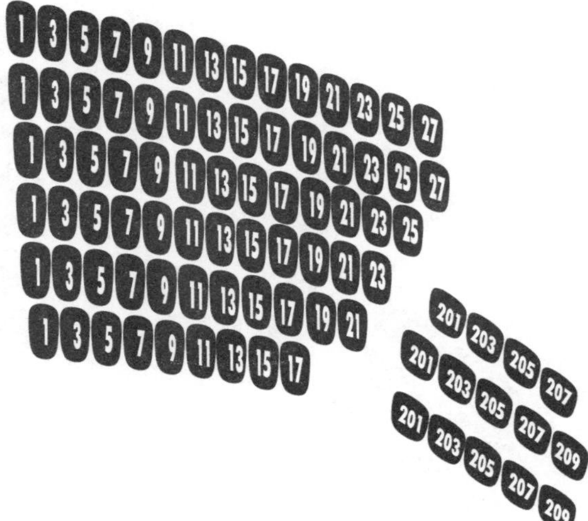

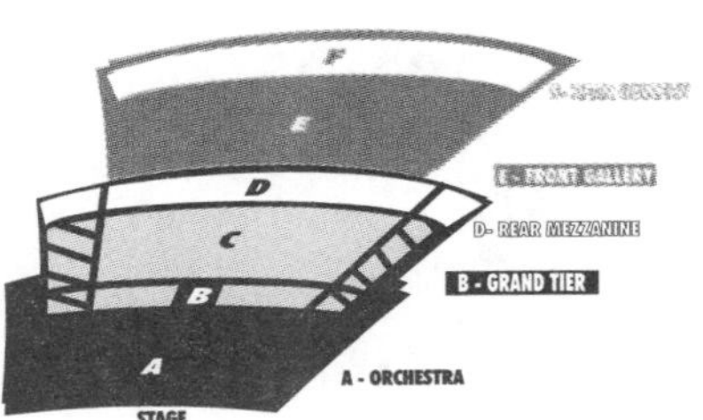

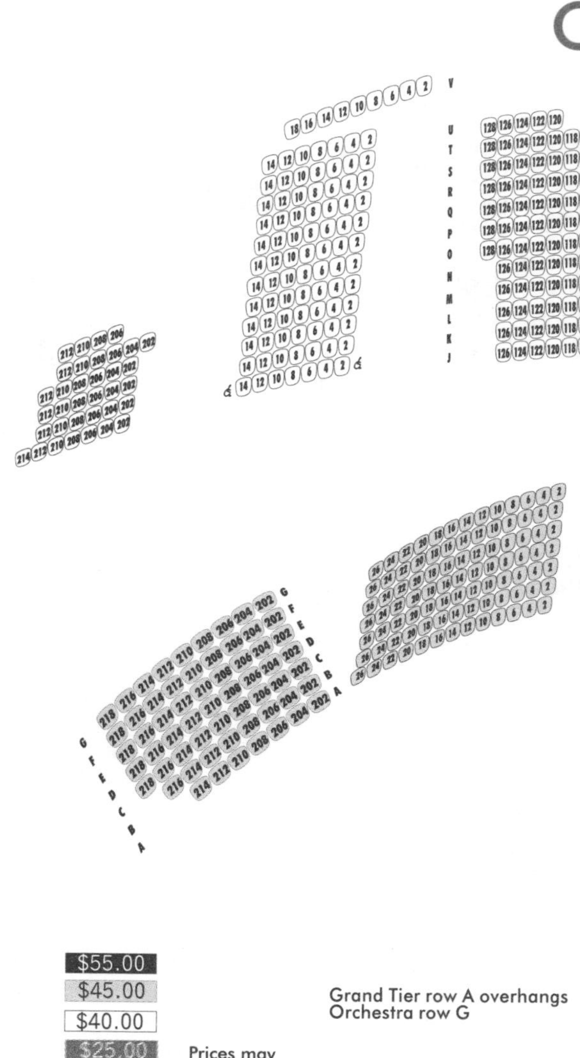

$55.00
$45.00
$40.00
$25.00
$20.00

Prices may vary according to show

Grand Tier row A overhangs Orchestra row G

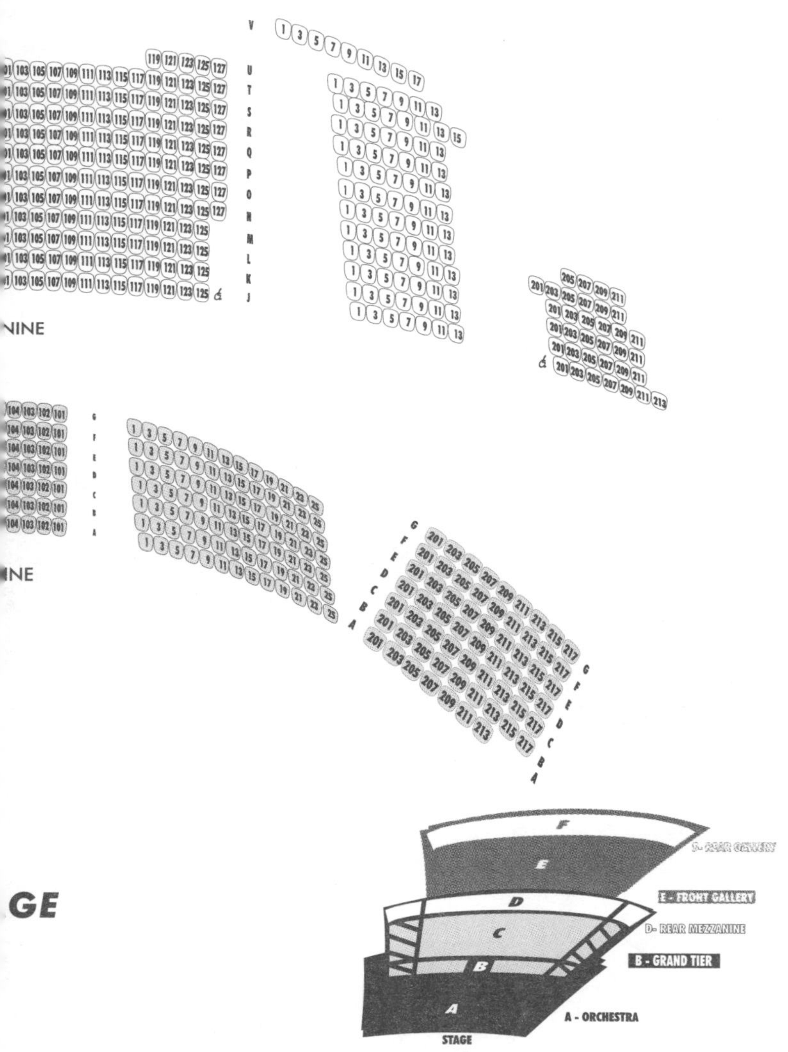

ENTER
NINE
NE
GE
F - REAR GALLERY
E - FRONT GALLERY
D- REAR MEZZANINE
B - GRAND TIER
A - ORCHESTRA
STAGE

CIT

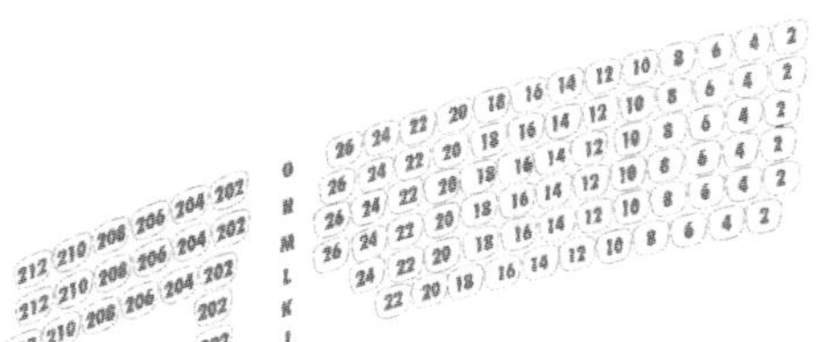

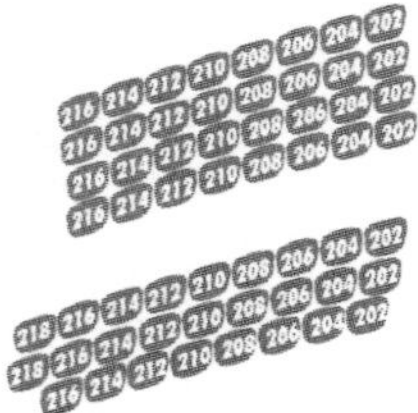

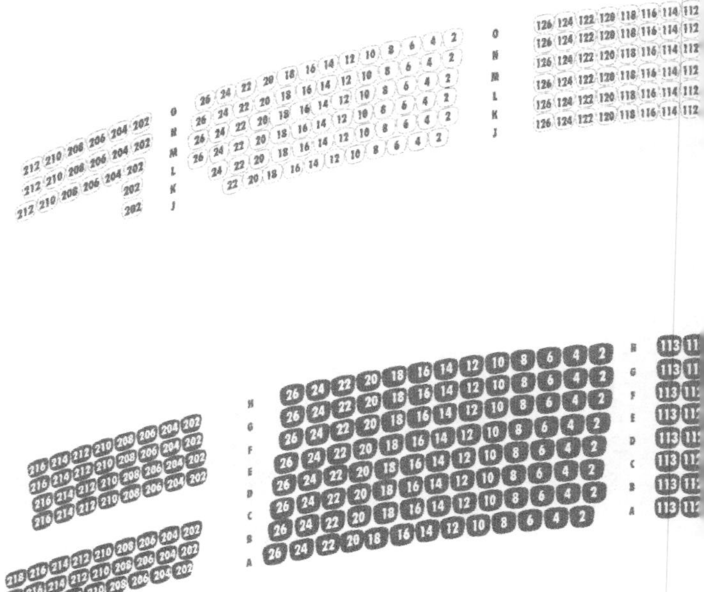

$55.00

$45.00

$40.00

$25.00

$20.00

Prices may vary according to show

Grand Tier row A overhangs Orchestra row G

ENTER

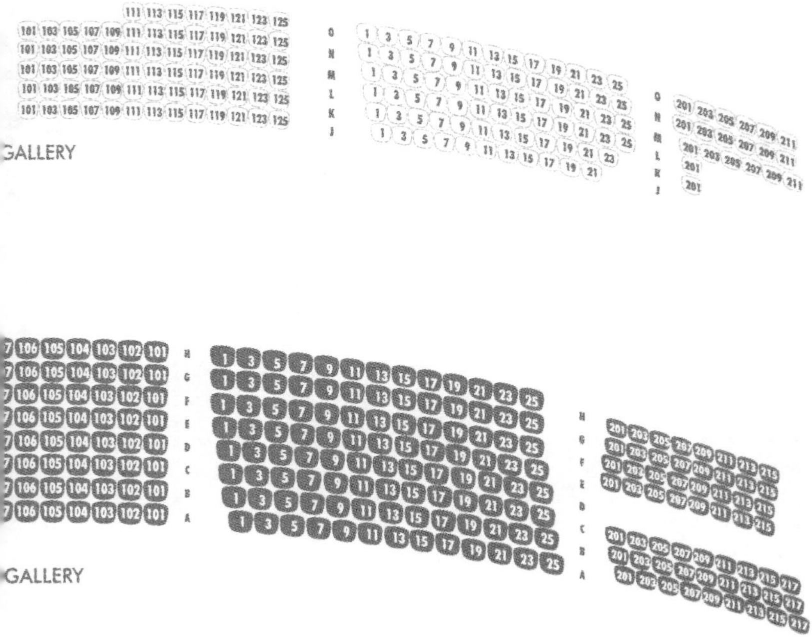

GALLERY

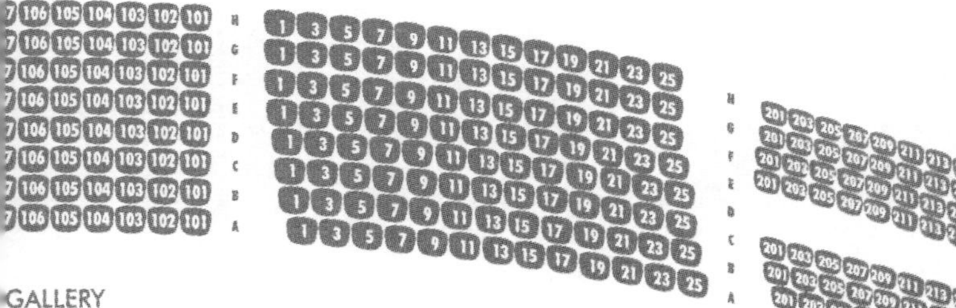

GALLERY

GE

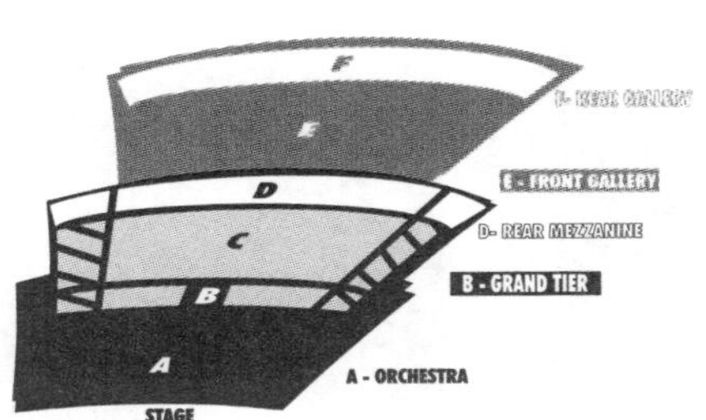

KAUFMANN CONCERT HALL

92nd Street YM-YWHA, 1395 Lexington Avenue at 92nd Street, New York, NY 10128

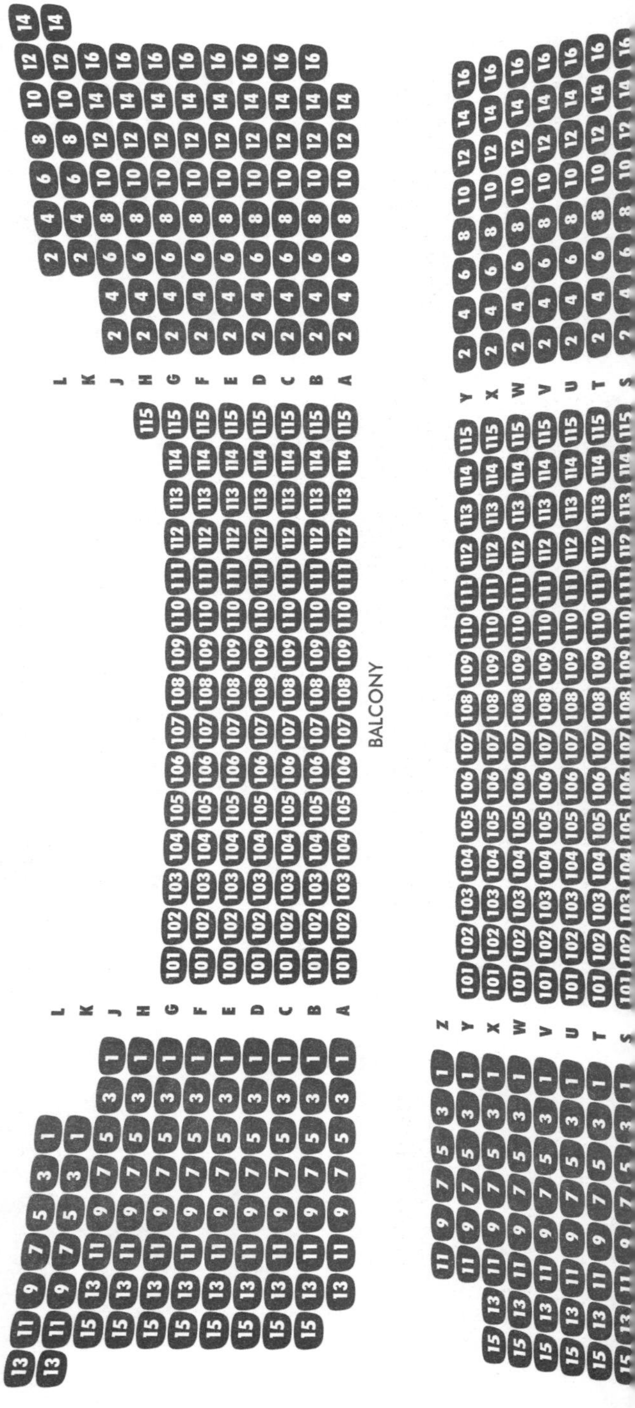

BALCONY

ORCHESTRA

Prices vary according to event
William Sound devices available
Wheelchair accessible

Balcony row A overhangs
Orchestra row S

STAGE

THEATRE (212) 996-1100
GROUP SALES (212) 415-5440

TAXI DIRECTIONS:
Lexington Ave. Southbound
(bet. 91st & 92nd St.)

PARKING
David's Garage, 422 E. 91st St.
GMC, 340 E. 93rd St.
(bet. 2nd & 3rd Aves.)
Kinney System, 200 E. 89th St.
BUS
M15, M31, M86
SUBWAYS
4,5,6 to 86th St. and Lexington Ave.

Nearby restaurants rated by
SEATS

TALLULAH'S, 1744 2nd Ave. 289-7510

LINCOLN CENTER

1941 Broadway, New York, NY 10023

ALICE TULLY HALL

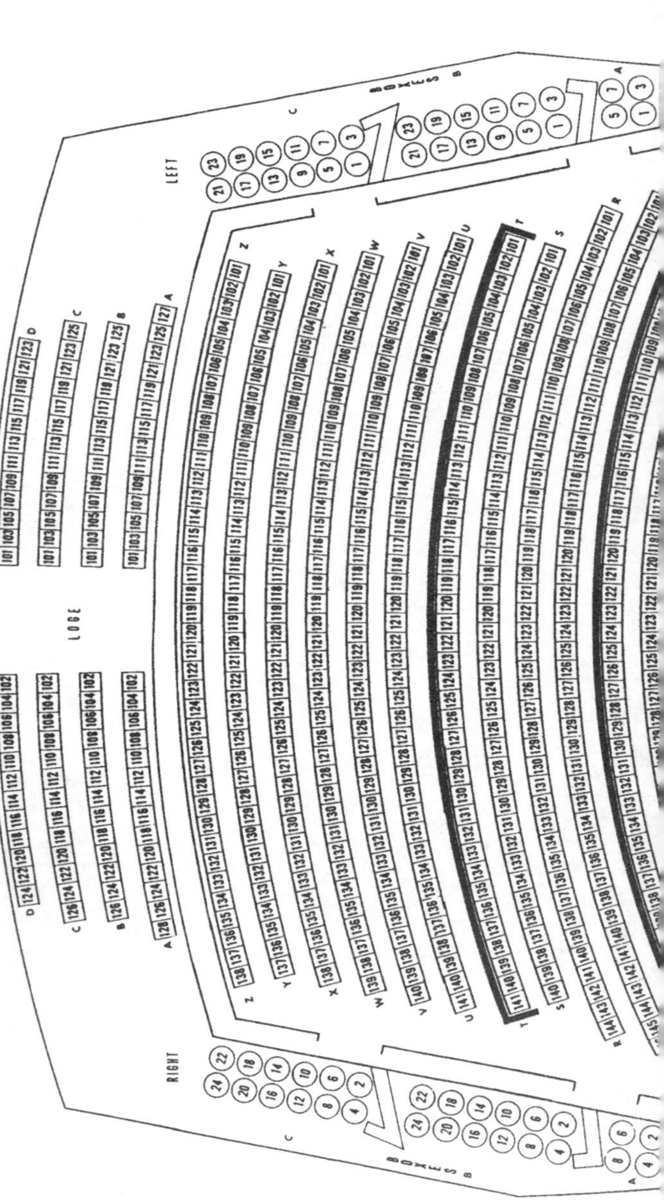

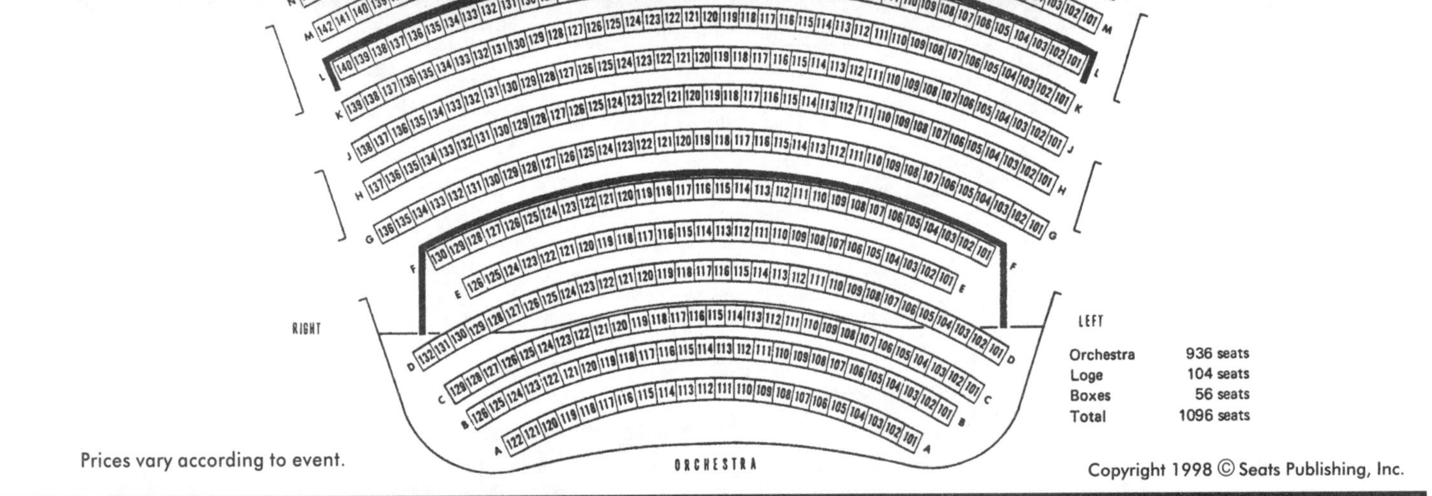

Orchestra	936 seats
Loge	104 seats
Boxes	56 seats
Total	1096 seats

Prices vary according to event.

CENTER CHARGE (212) 721-6500
CHAMBER MUSIC SOCIETY
(212) 875-5788

TAXI DIRECTIONS:
Broadway at 65th St. Eastbound

PARKING
Lincoln Center Underground Park & Lock
enter on 65th St.
(bet. Amsterdam Ave. & Broadway)
GMC, 2000 Broadway, enter on 68th St.
(bet. Broadway & Columbus Ave.)

BUS
M5, M7, M10, M11, M66, M104

SUBWAYS
1, 9 to 66th St. & Broadway

Nearby restaurants rated by
SEATS

PANEVINO RISTORANTE at Avery Fisher Hall 874-7000
CAFE VIENNA at Avery Fisher Hall 874-7000
SHUN LEE WEST, 43 W. 65th St. 595-8895
CAFFE LA FENICE, 2014 Broadway 579-1337
FEDERICO'S, 1981 Broadway 873-4210
OLLIE'S, 1991 Broadway 595-8181

LINCOLN CENTER

10 Lincoln Center Plaza, New York, NY 10023

AVERY FISHER HALL

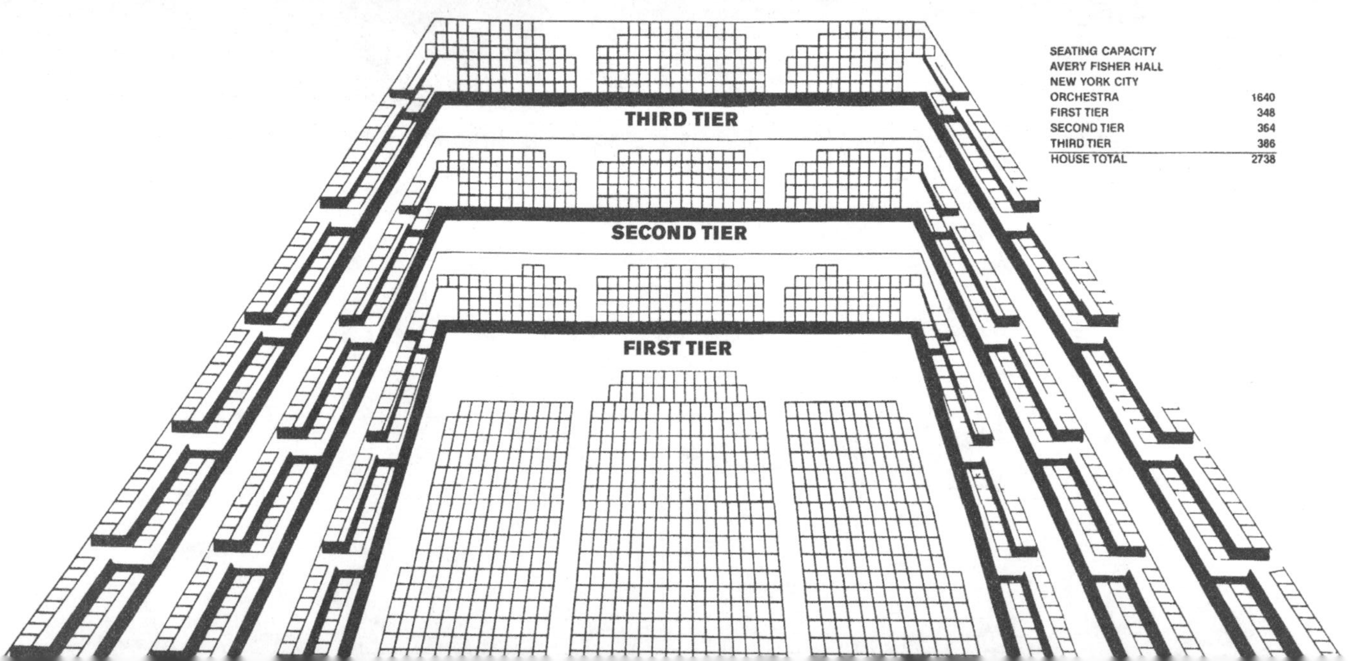

SEATING CAPACITY
AVERY FISHER HALL
NEW YORK CITY

ORCHESTRA	1640
FIRST TIER	348
SECOND TIER	364
THIRD TIER	386
HOUSE TOTAL	2738

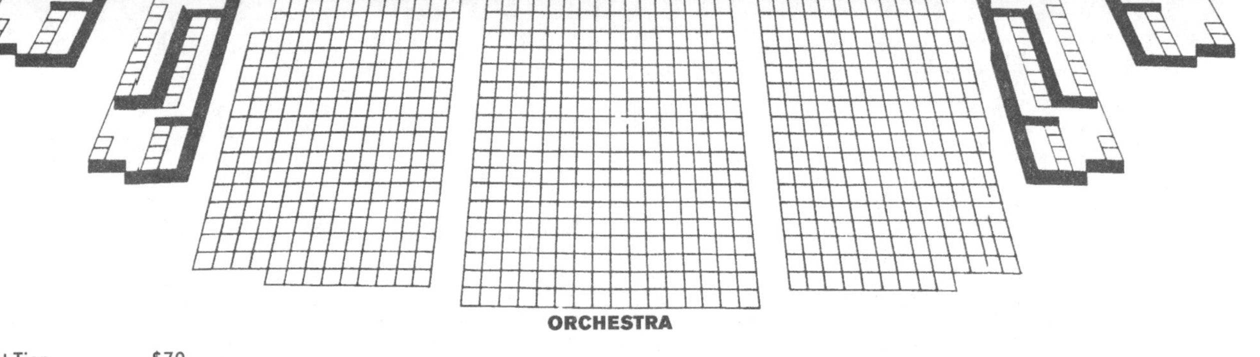

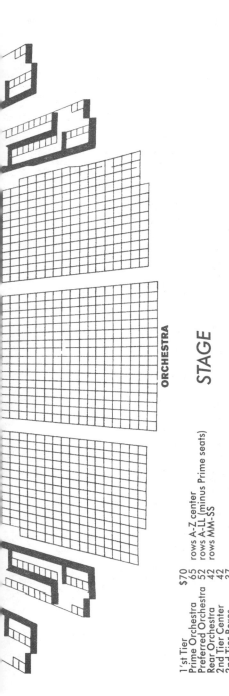

1'st Tier	$70	
Prime Orchestra	65	rows A-Z center
Preferred Orchestra	52	rows A-LL (minus Prime seats)
Rear Orchestra	42	rows MM-SS
2nd Tier Center	42	
2nd Tier Boxes	37	
3rd Tier Center	32	
3rd Tier Boxes	16	

CENTERCHARGE (212) 721-6500
NY PHILHARMONIC (212) 875-5656
GROUP SALES (212) 875-5408

ON-LINE: www.newyorkphilharmonic.org

TAXI DIRECTIONS
Broadway, at 65th St. Eastbound

PARKING
Lincoln Center Underground Park & Lock
enter on 65th St.
Between Amsterdam & Broadway
GMC, 2000 Broadway
enter on 68th St.

BUS
M5, M7, M10, M11, M66, M104

SUBWAYS
1, 9 to 66th St. and Broadway

Nearby restaurants rated by
SEATS

PANEVINO RISTORANTE at Avery Fisher Hall, 874-7000
CAFE VIENNA at Avery Fisher Hall, 873-7411
SHUN LEE WEST, 43 W. 65th St. 595-8895
JOHN'S PIZZERIA, 48 West 65th St. 721-7001
LINCOLN TAVERN, 51 W. 64th St. 721-8271
ORLOFF'S DELI & RESTAURANT, 2 Lincoln Square 799-4000

AVERY FISHER HALL

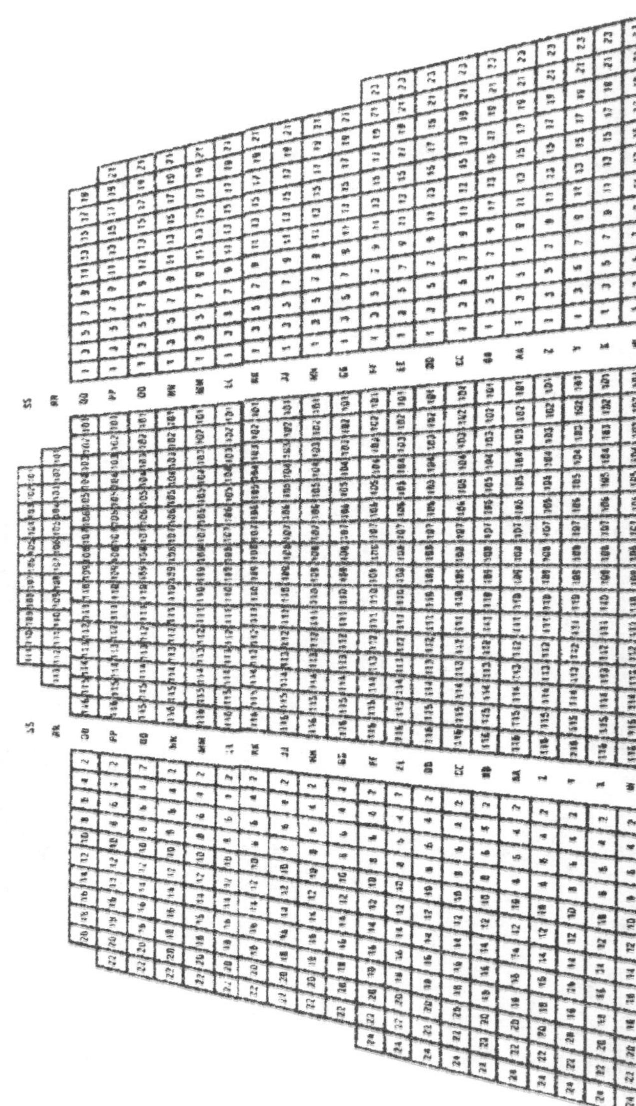

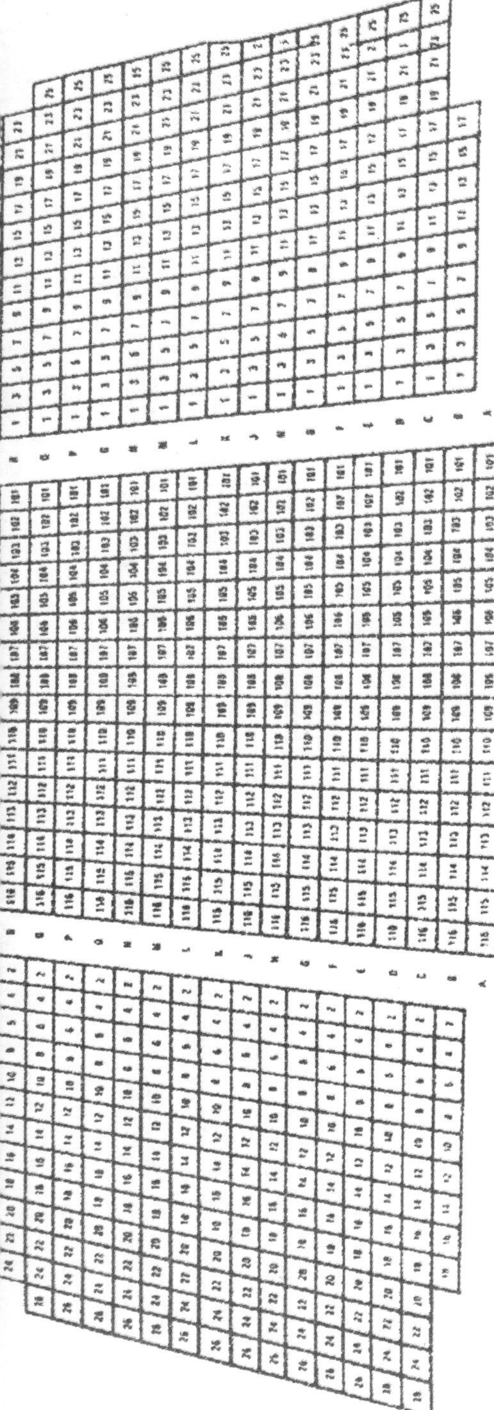

ORCHESTRA

STAGE

AVERY FISHER HALL

MIDDLE TIER

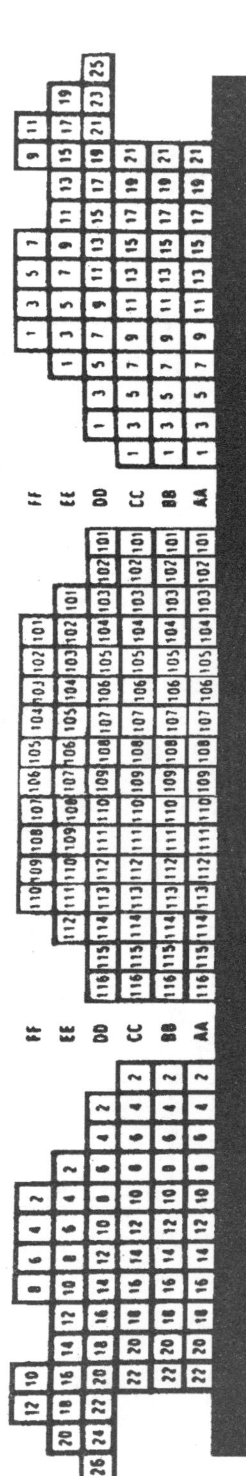

THIRD TIER

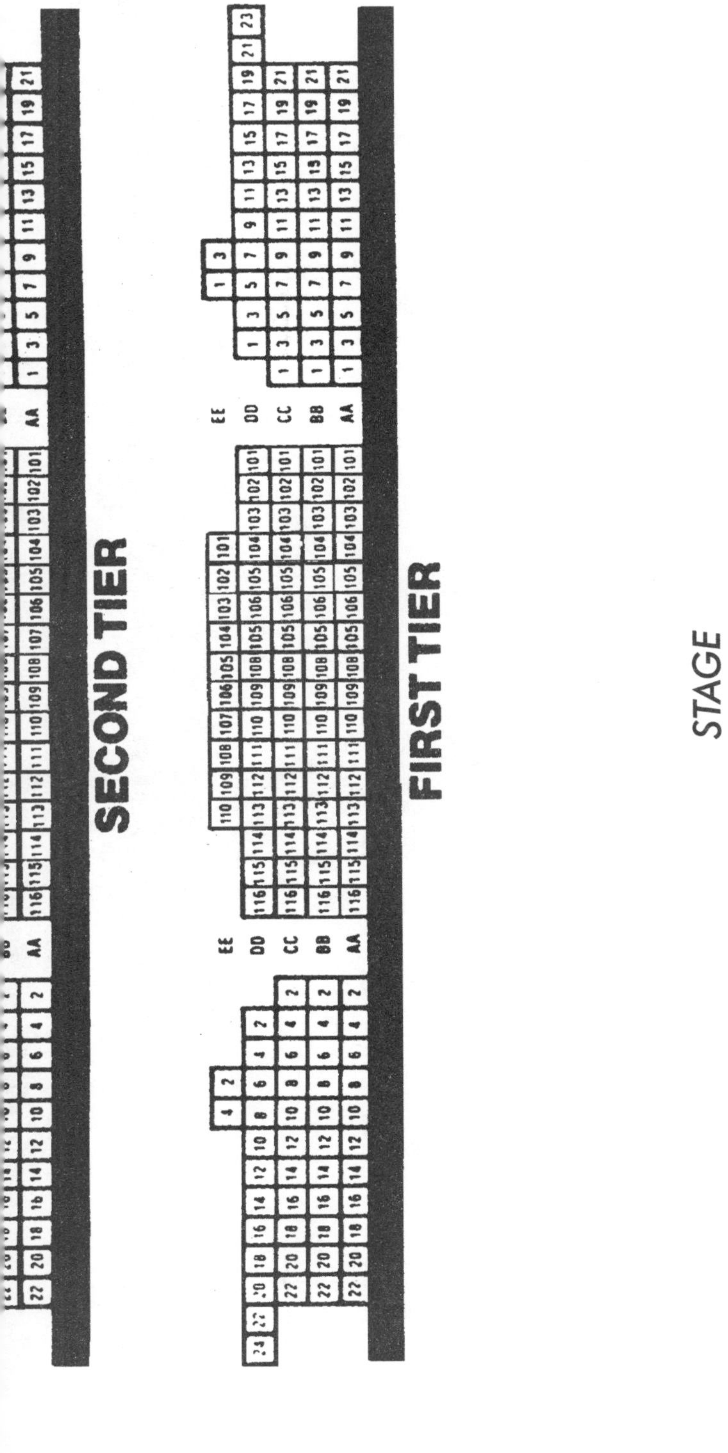

SECOND TIER

FIRST TIER

STAGE

AVERY FISHER HALL

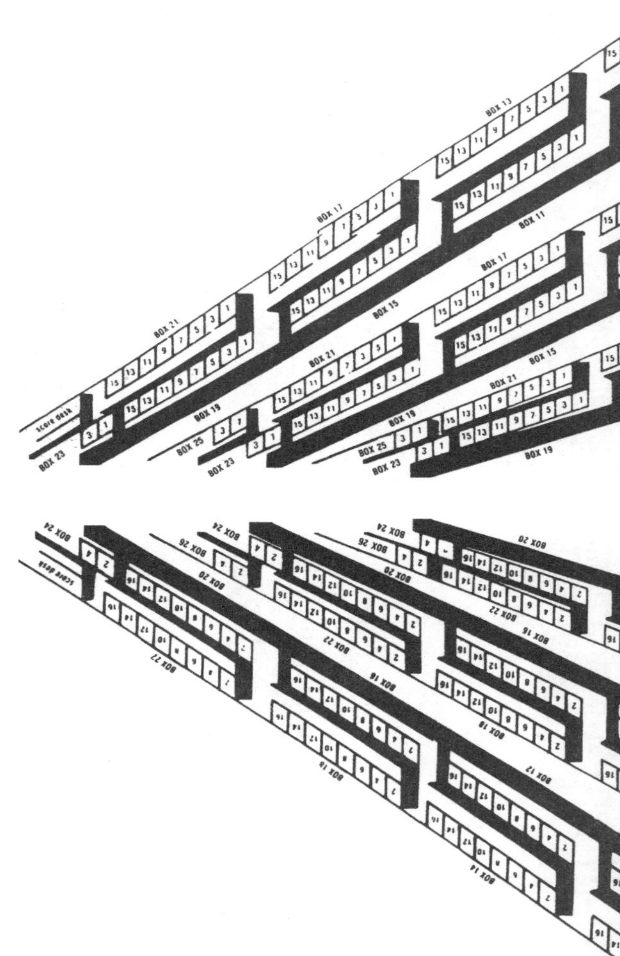

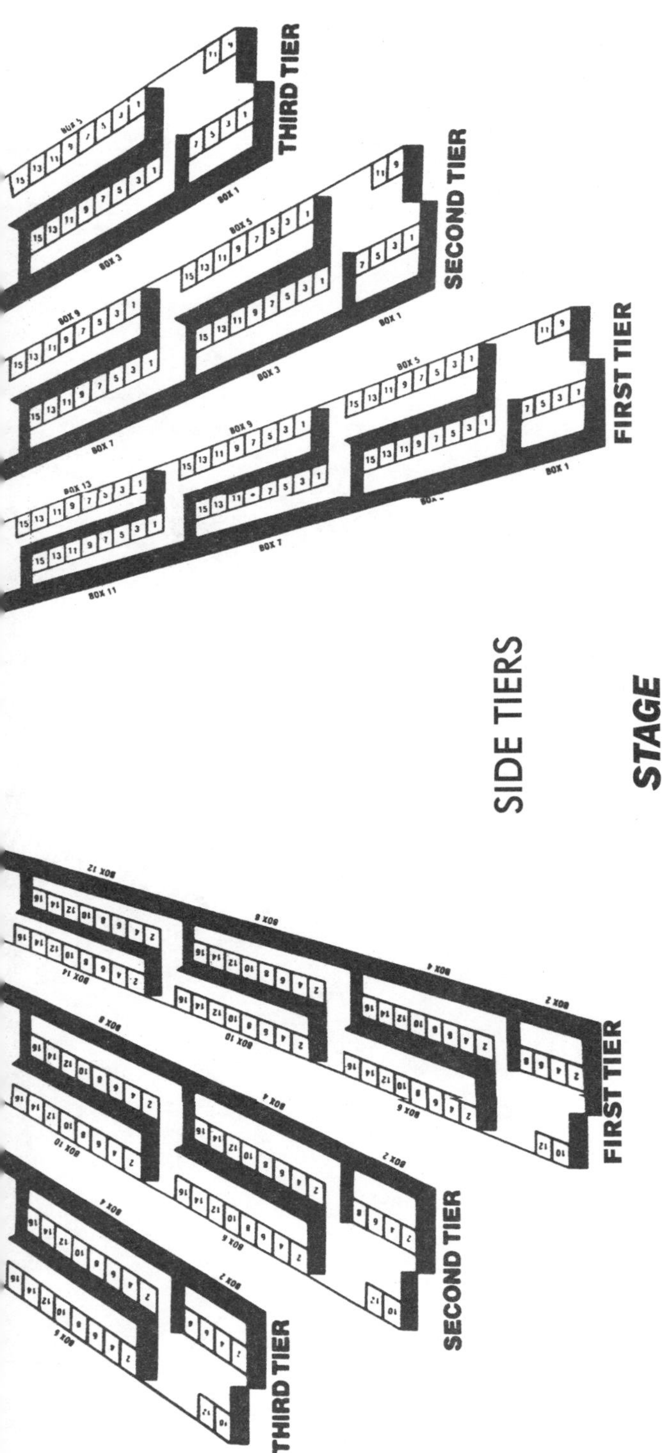
THIRD TIER
SECOND TIER
FIRST TIER
SIDE TIERS
STAGE
FIRST TIER
SECOND TIER
THIRD TIER

LINCOLN CENTER

30 Lincoln Center Plaza, New York, NY 10023

METROPOLITAN OPERA HOUSE

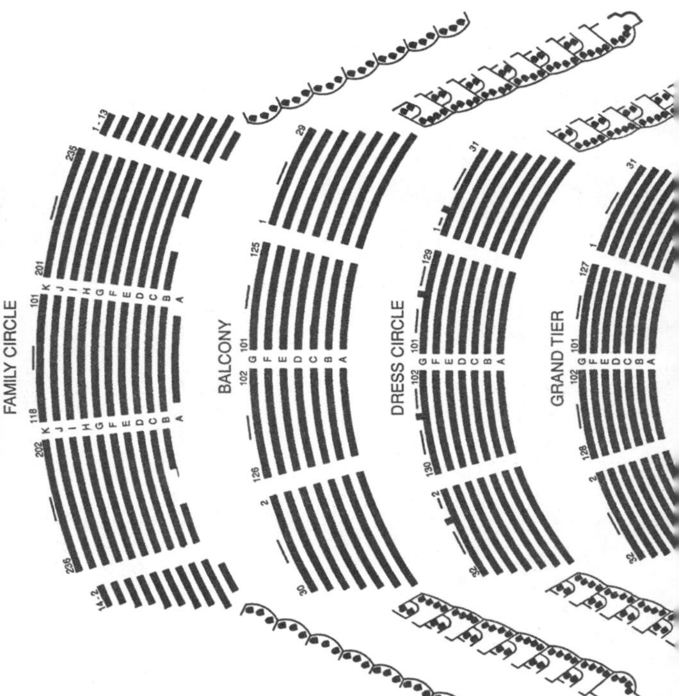

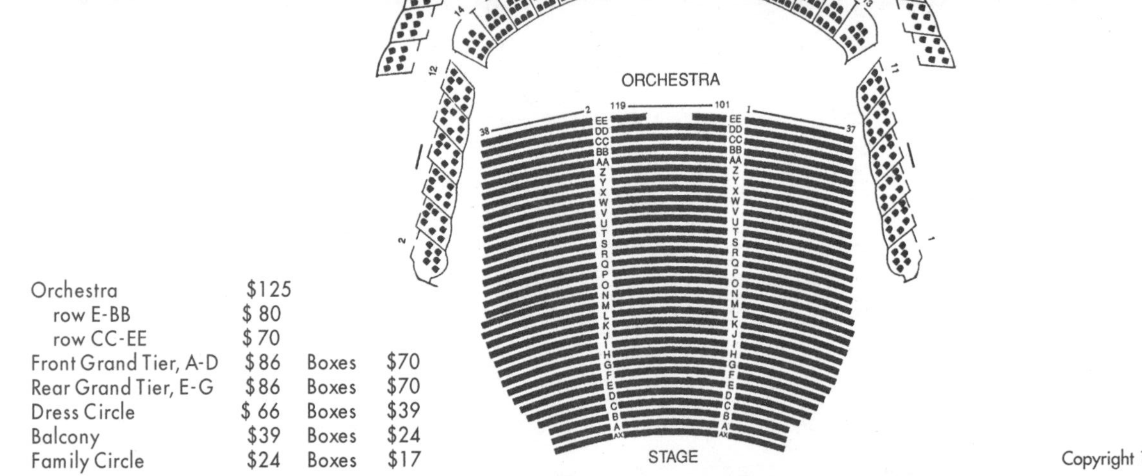

Orchestra	$125		
row E-BB	$ 80		
row CC-EE	$ 70		
Front Grand Tier, A-D	$86	Boxes	$70
Rear Grand Tier, E-G	$86	Boxes	$70
Dress Circle	$ 66	Boxes	$39
Balcony	$39	Boxes	$24
Family Circle	$24	Boxes	$17

TICKETS (212) 362-6000
GROUP SALES (212) 870-7447

TAXI DIRECTIONS:
63rd St. (bet Broadway & Amsterdam Ave.)

PARKING
Lincoln Center Underground Park & Lock
enter on 65th St.
(bet. Amsterdam Ave. & Broadway)
GMC, 2000 Broadway, enter on 68th St.
(bet. Broadway & Columbus Ave.)
BUS
M5, M7, M10, M11, M66, M104
SUBWAYS
1, 9 to 66th St. & Broadway

Nearby restaurants rated by
SEATS

FIROELLO'S ROMAN CAFÉ, 1 900 Broadway 595-5330
THE SALOON, 1920 Broadway 874-1500
LINCOLN TAVERN, 51 W. 64th St. 721-8271
COCO OPERA, 58 W. 65th St. 873-3700
SHUN LEE WEST, 43 W. 65th St. 595-8895
ORLOFF'S DELI & RESTAURANT, 2 Lincoln Sq. 799-4000
GRAND TIER at METROPOLITAN OPERA HOUSE, 799-3400
JOHN'S PIZZERIA, 48 W. 65th St. 721-7001

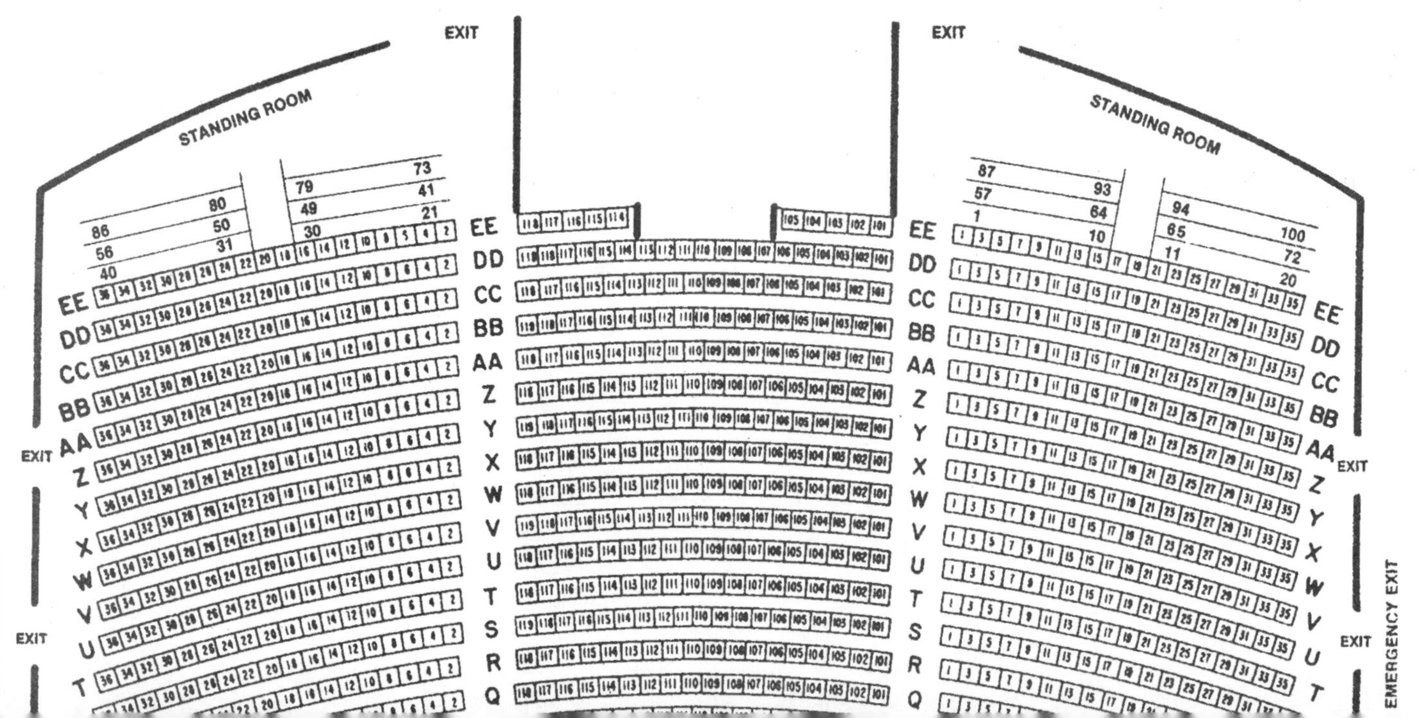
METROPOLITAN OPERA
EXIT
EXIT
STANDING ROOM
STANDING ROOM
EXIT
EXIT
EXIT
EXIT
CORRIDOR TO EME
EMERGENCY EXIT

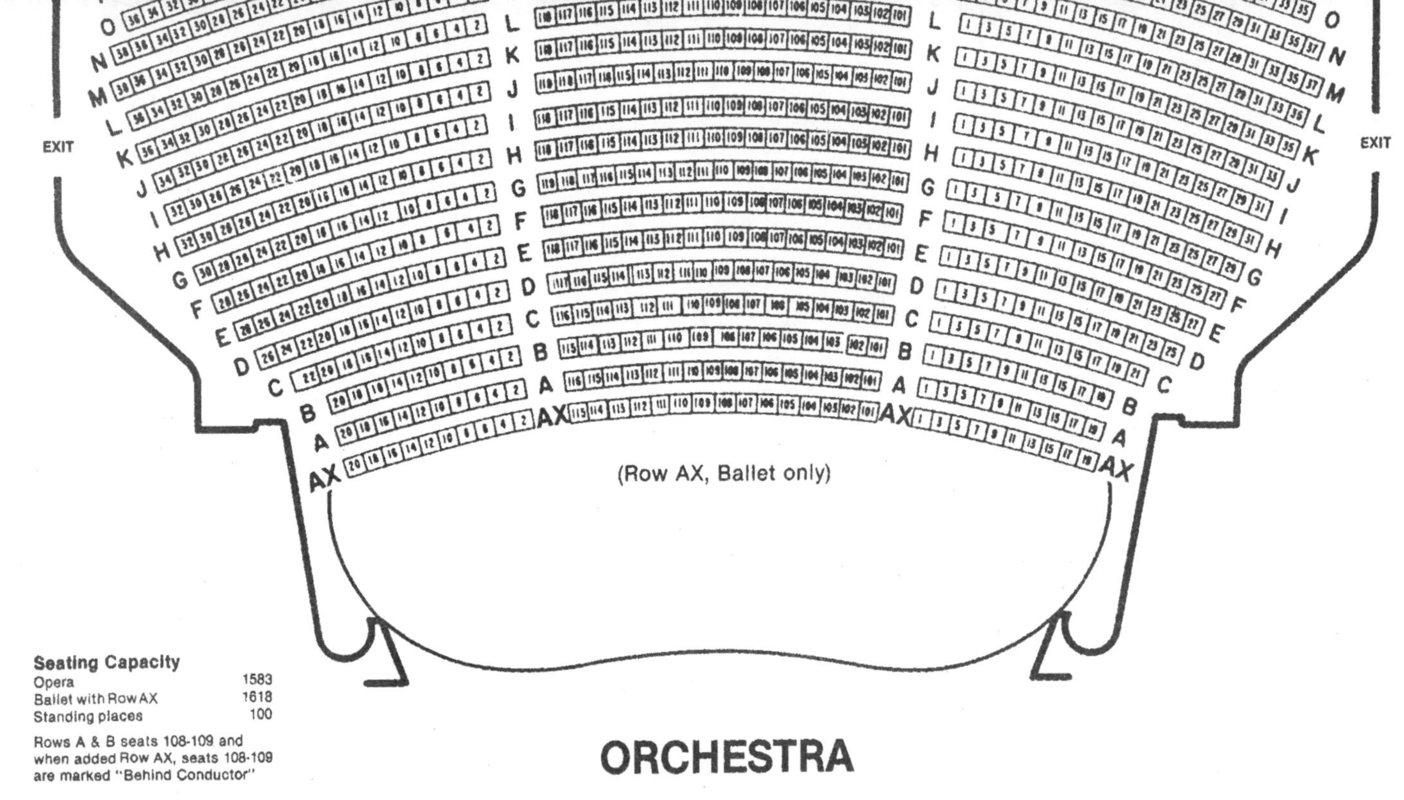
EXIT
EXIT
(Row AX, Ballet only)
ORCHESTRA
Seating Capacity
Opera 1583
Ballet with Row AX 1618
Standing places 100
Rows A & B seats 108-109 and when added Row AX, seats 108-109 are marked "Behind Conductor"

METROPOLITAN OPERA

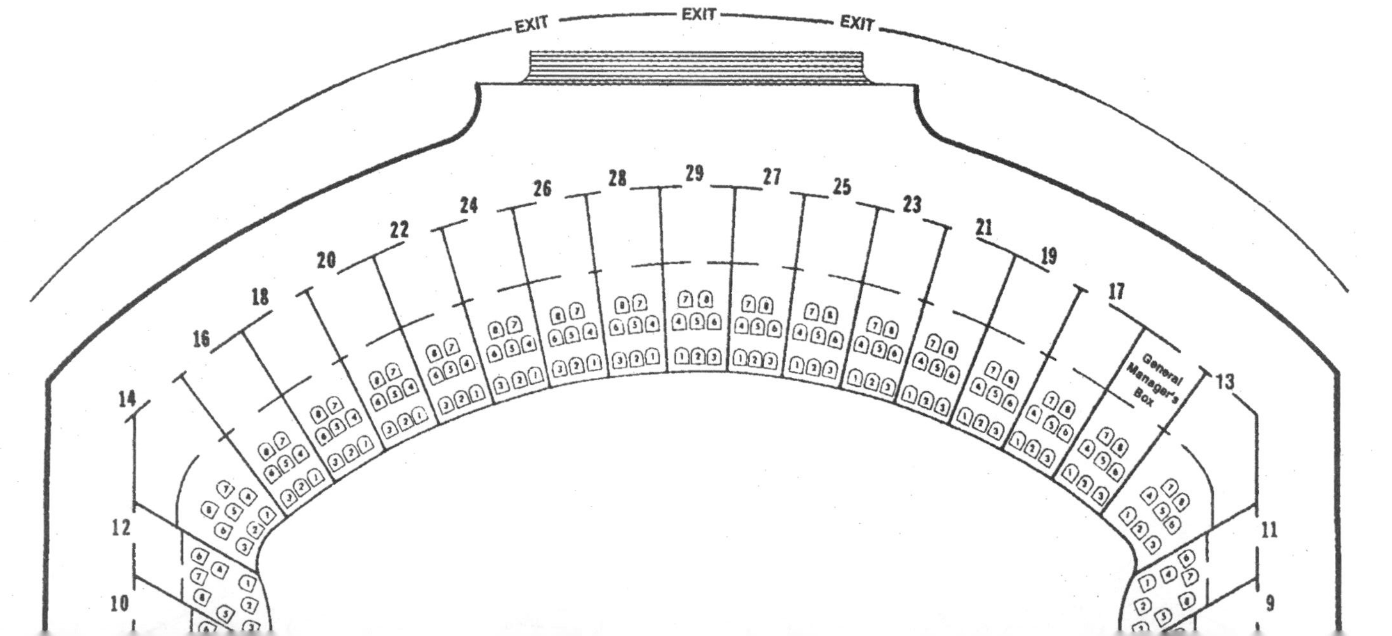

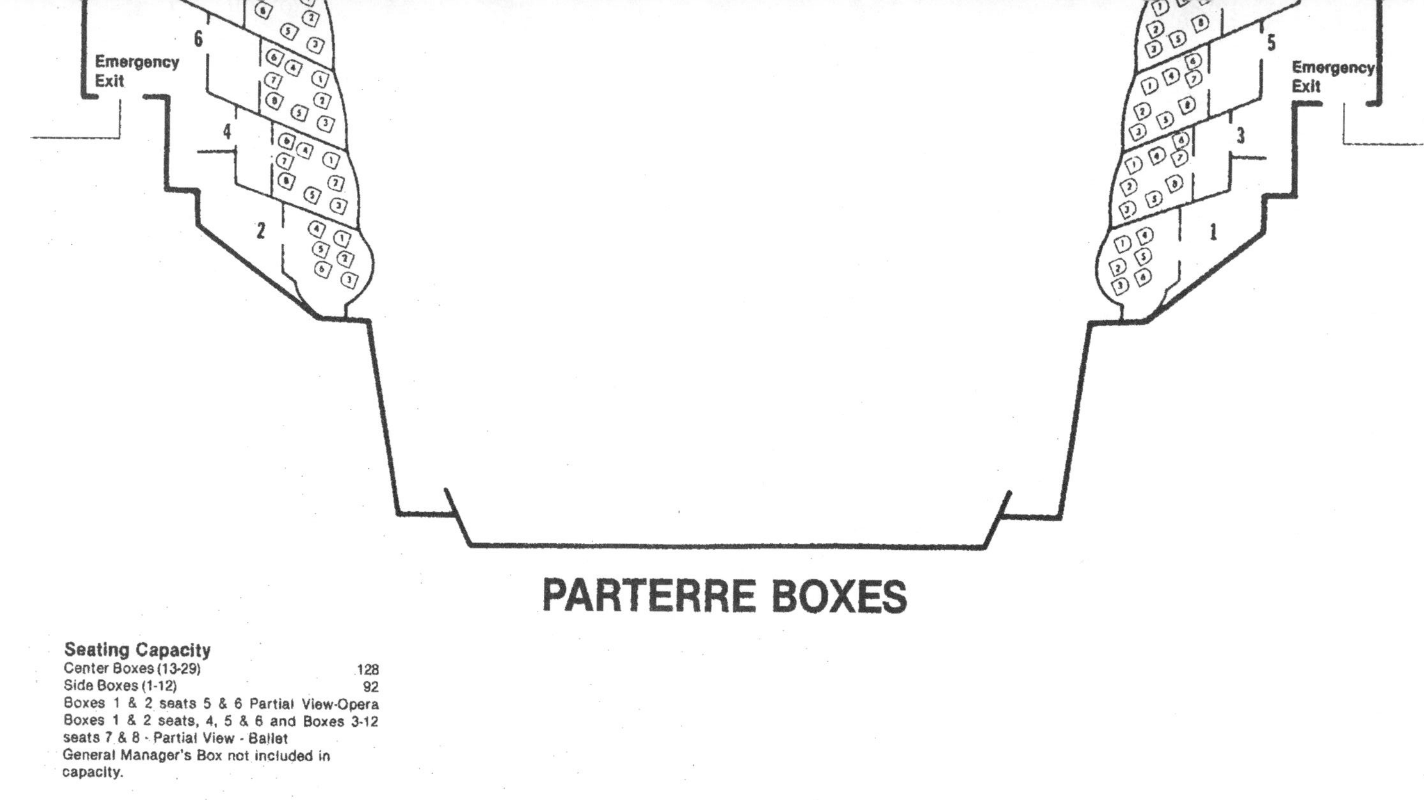

Seating Capacity

Center Boxes (13-29)	128
Side Boxes (1-12)	92

Boxes 1 & 2 seats 5 & 6 Partial View-Opera
Boxes 1 & 2 seats, 4, 5 & 6 and Boxes 3-12 seats 7 & 8 - Partial View - Ballet
General Manager's Box not included in capacity.

METROPOLITAN OPERA

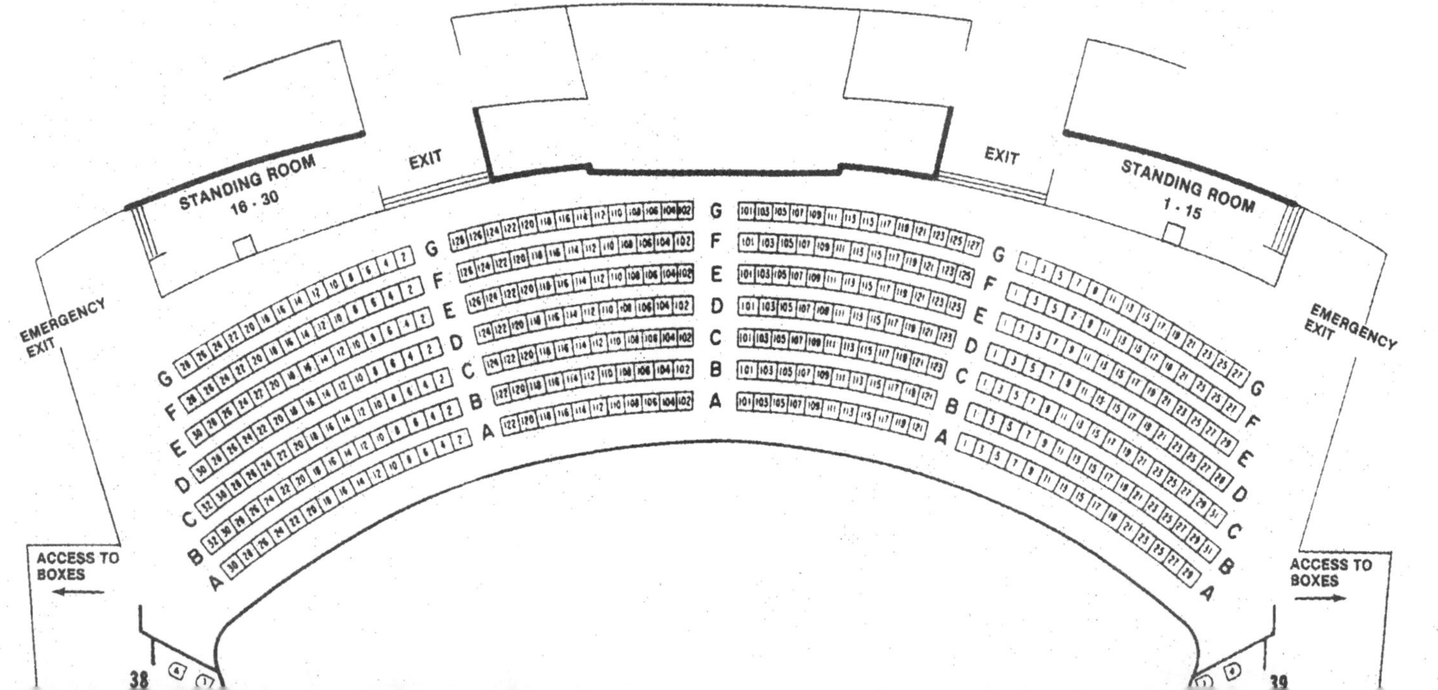

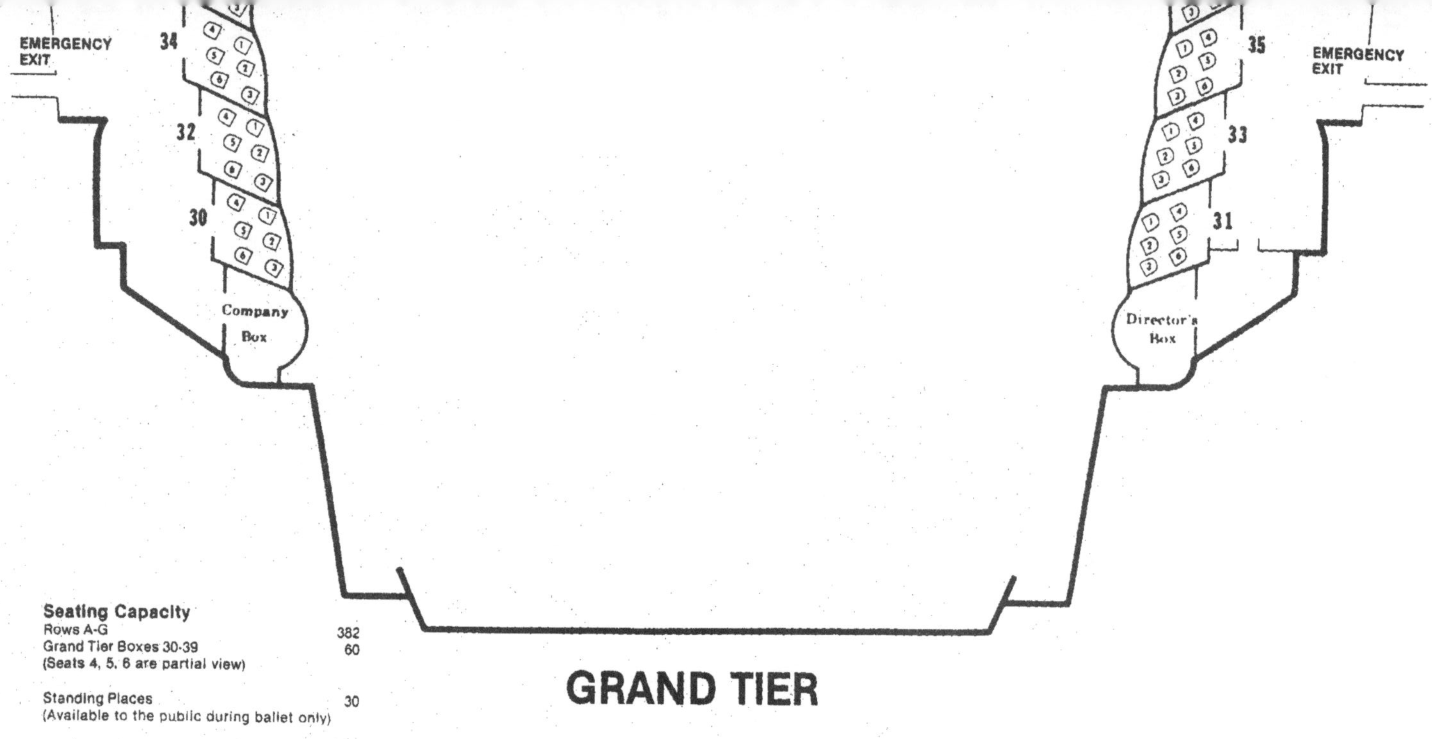

Seating Capacity

Rows A-G	382
Grand Tier Boxes 30-39	60
(Seats 4, 5, 6 are partial view)	
Standing Places	30
(Available to the public during ballet only)	

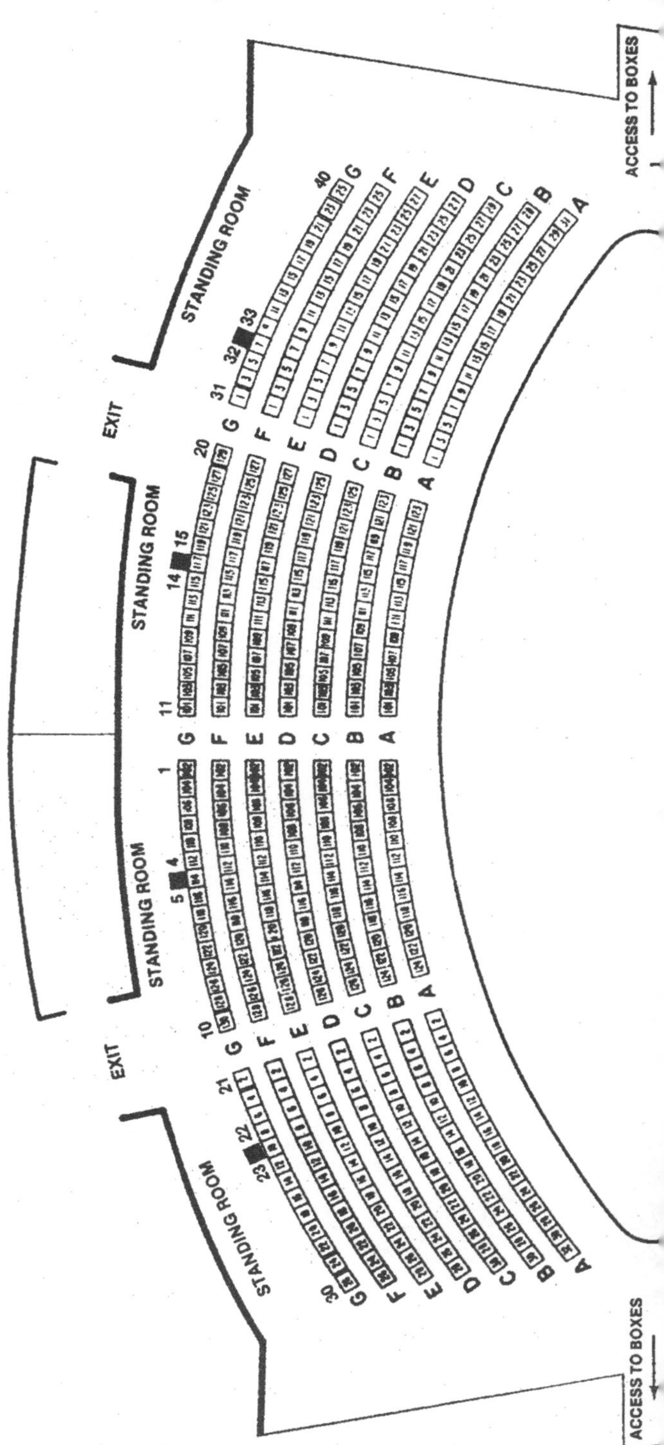
METROPOLITAN OPERA
STANDING ROOM
EXIT
STANDING ROOM
STANDING ROOM
EXIT
STANDING ROOM
ACCESS TO BOXES
ACCESS TO BOXES

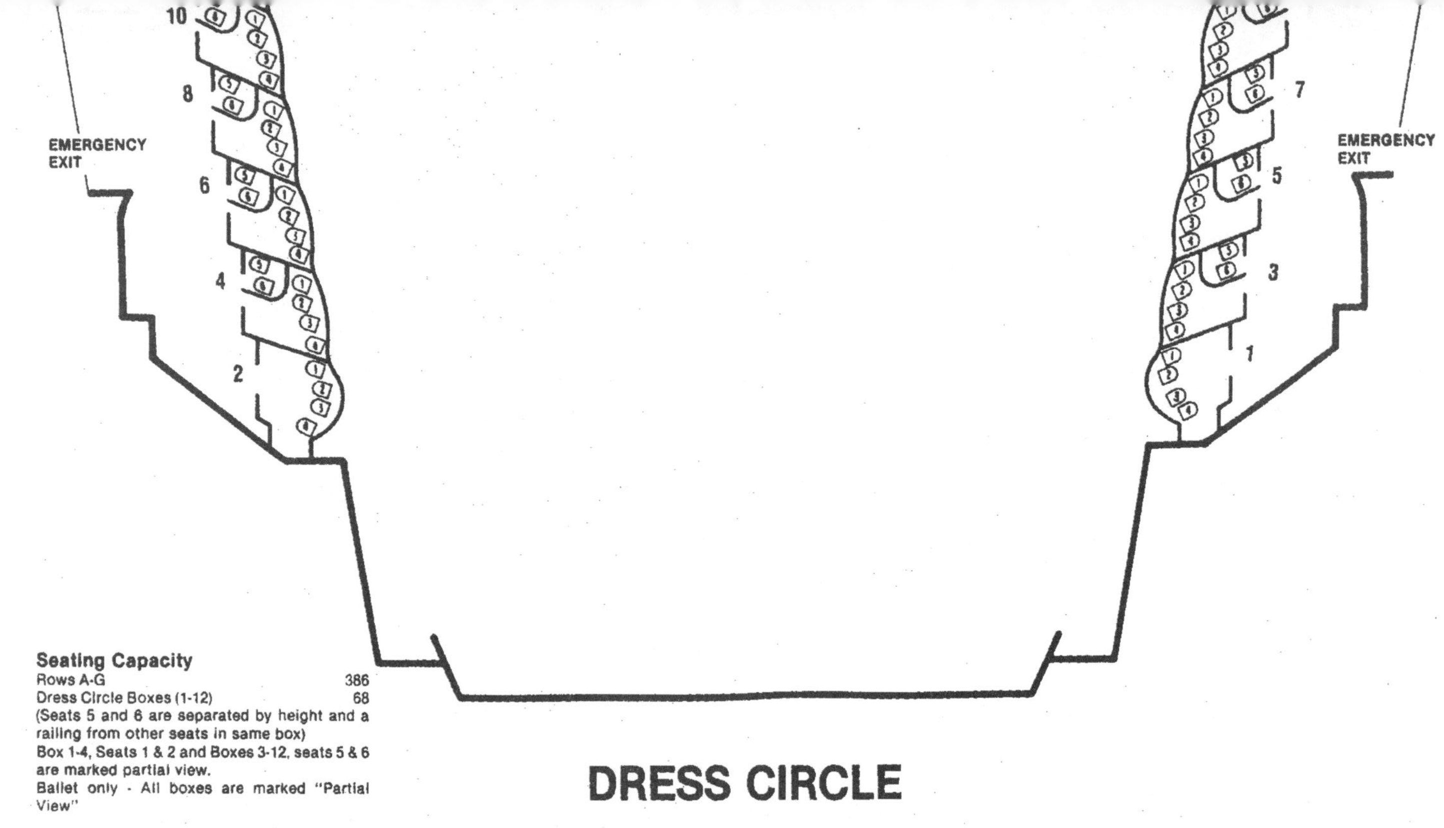

Seating Capacity

Rows A-G	386
Dress Circle Boxes (1-12)	68

(Seats 5 and 6 are separated by height and a railing from other seats in same box)

Box 1-4, Seats 1 & 2 and Boxes 3-12, seats 5 & 6 are marked partial view.

Ballet only - All boxes are marked "Partial View"

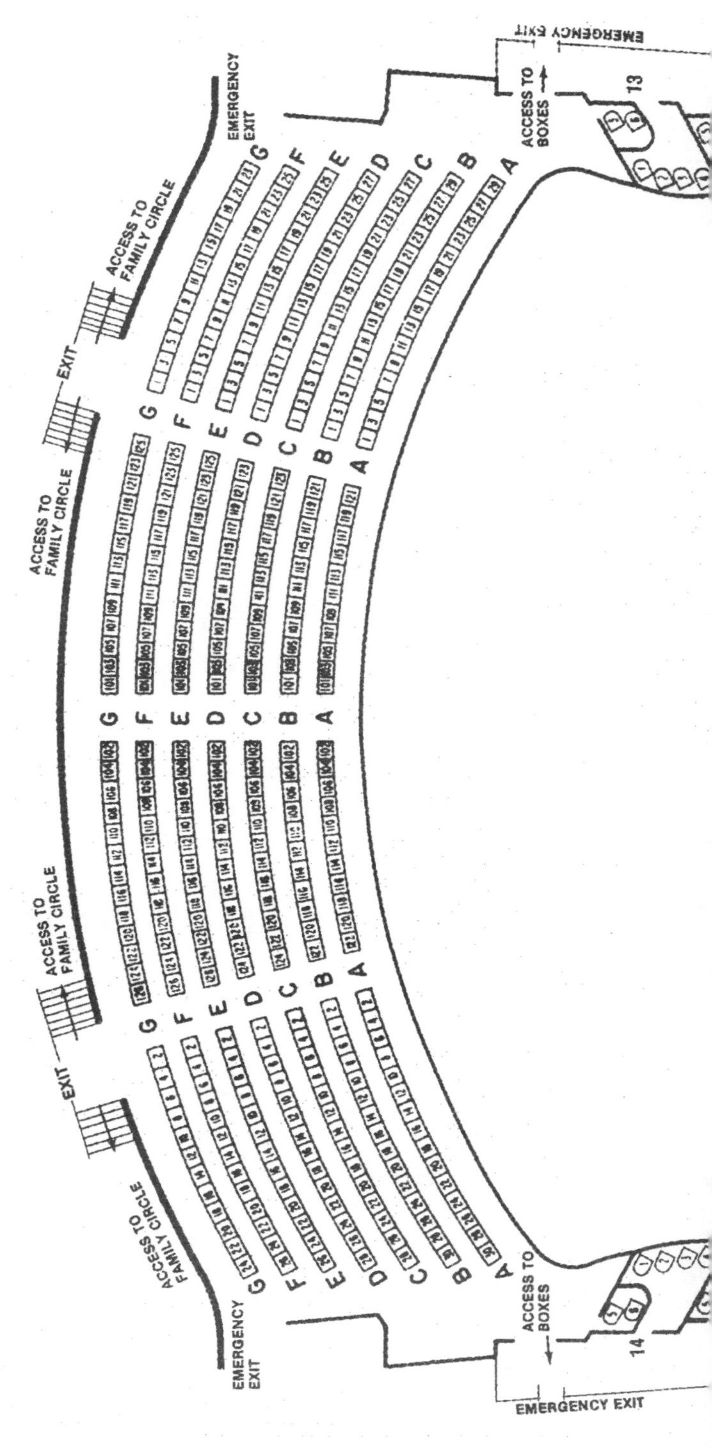
METROPOLITAN OPERA
ACCESS TO FAMILY CIRCLE
EXIT
ACCESS TO FAMILY CIRCLE
ACCESS TO FAMILY CIRCLE
EXIT
ACCESS TO FAMILY CIRCLE
EMERGENCY EXIT
EMERGENCY EXIT
ACCESS TO BOXES
ACCESS TO BOXES
EMERGENCY EXIT
EMERGENCY EXIT
13
14
A
B
C
D
E
F
G

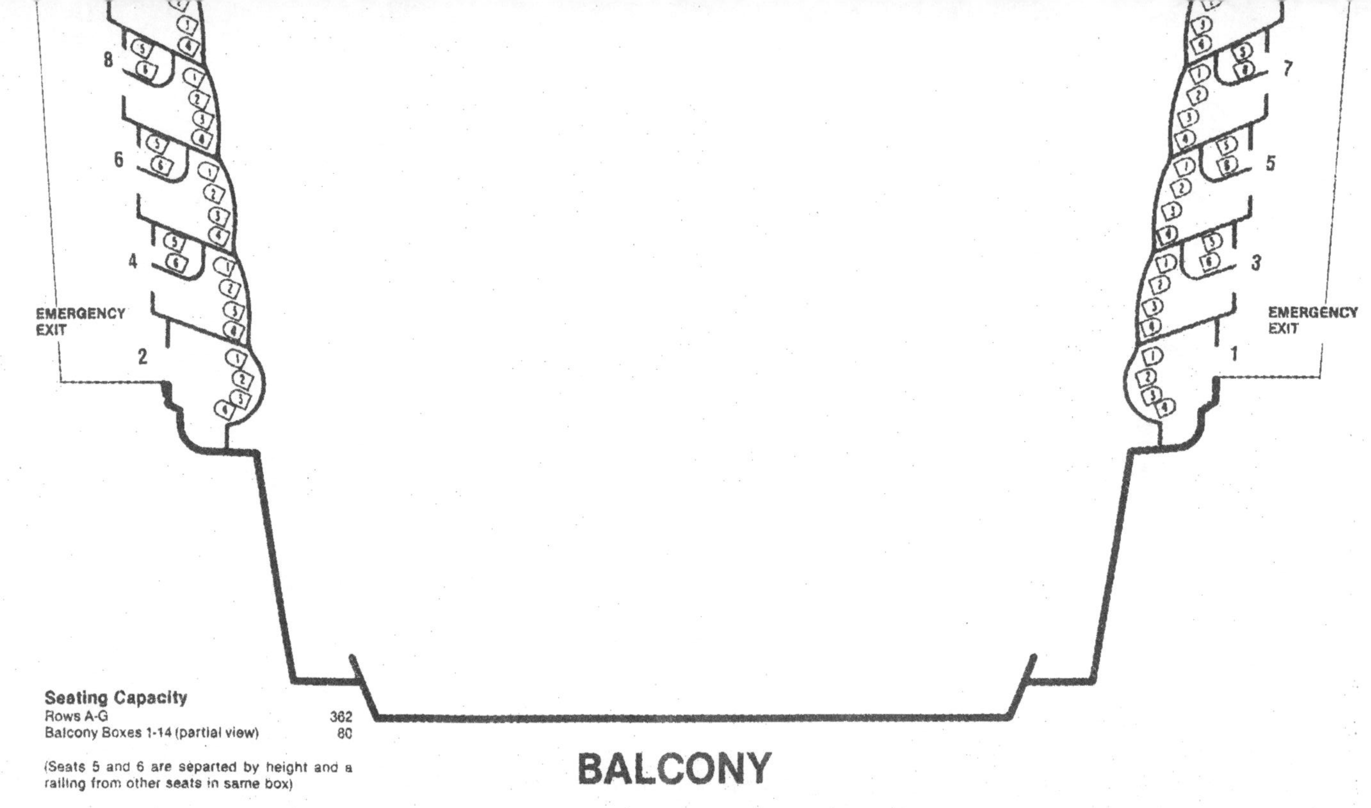

Seating Capacity

Rows A-G	362
Balcony Boxes 1-14 (partial view)	80

(Seats 5 and 6 are separted by height and a railing from other seats in same box)

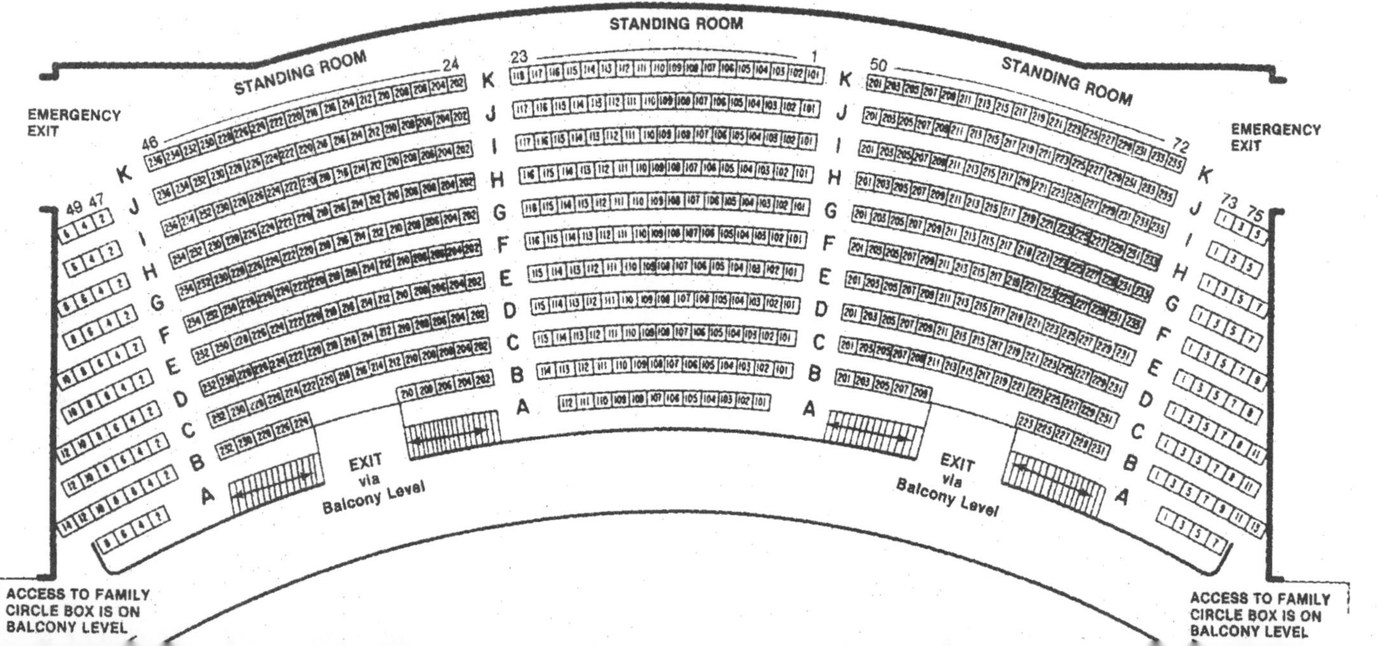
METROPOLITAN OPERA
STANDING ROOM
STANDING ROOM
STANDING ROOM
EMERGENCY EXIT
EMERGENCY EXIT
EXIT via Balcony Level
EXIT via Balcony Level
ACCESS TO FAMILY CIRCLE BOX IS ON BALCONY LEVEL
ACCESS TO FAMILY CIRCLE BOX IS ON BALCONY LEVEL

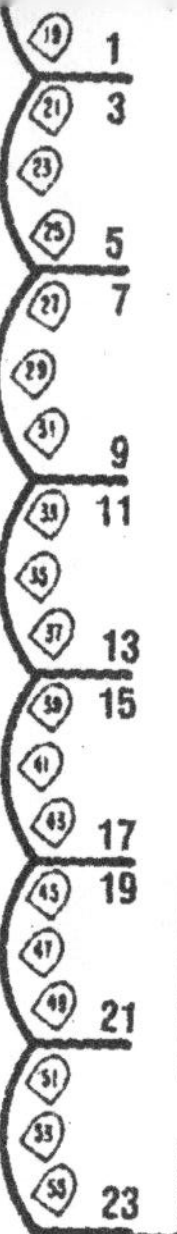

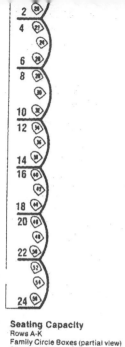

FAMILY CIRCLE

Seating Capacity

Rows A-K	591
Family Circle Boxes (partial view)	42
Standing Places	75

Score Desks 1-24 available only through the Metropolitan Opera Guild Education Department, for the blind, visually impaired and music students. Totally obstructed view.

LINCOLN CENTER

150 West 65th Street, New York, NY 10023

MITZI E. NEWHOUSE THEATRE

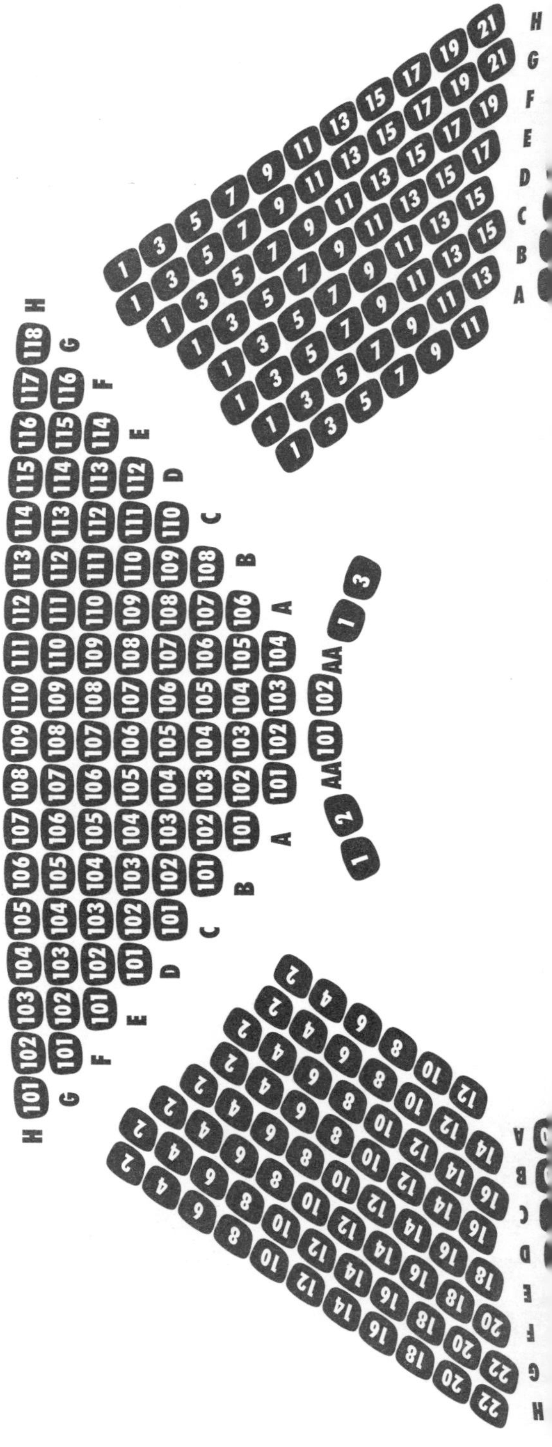

$50.00

TELECHARGE (212) 239-6200

TAXI DIRECTIONS:
65th St. Eastbound
(bet. Broadway & Amsterdam Ave.)

PARKING
Lincoln Center Underground Park & Lock,
enter on 65th St.
(bet. Amsterdam Ave. & Broadway)
GMC, 2000 Broadway,
enter on 68th St.
(bet. Broadway & Columbus Ave.)

BUS
M5, M7, M10, M11, M66, M104

SUBWAYS
1,9, to 66th St. & Broadway

Nearby restaurants rated by
SEATS

FIORELLO'S ROMAN CAFE, 1900 Broadway 595-5330
JOHN'S PIZZERIA, 48 W. 65th St. 721-7001
THE SALOON, 1920 Broadway 874-1500
LINCOLN TAVERN, 51 W. 64th St. 721-8271
COCO OPERA, 58 W. 65th St. 873-3700
SHUN LEE WEST, 43 W. 65th St. 595-8895
ORLOFF'S DELI & RESTAURANT, 2 Lincoln Square 799-4000

LINCOLN CENTER

20 Lincoln Center, New York, NY 10023

NEW YORK STATE THEATER

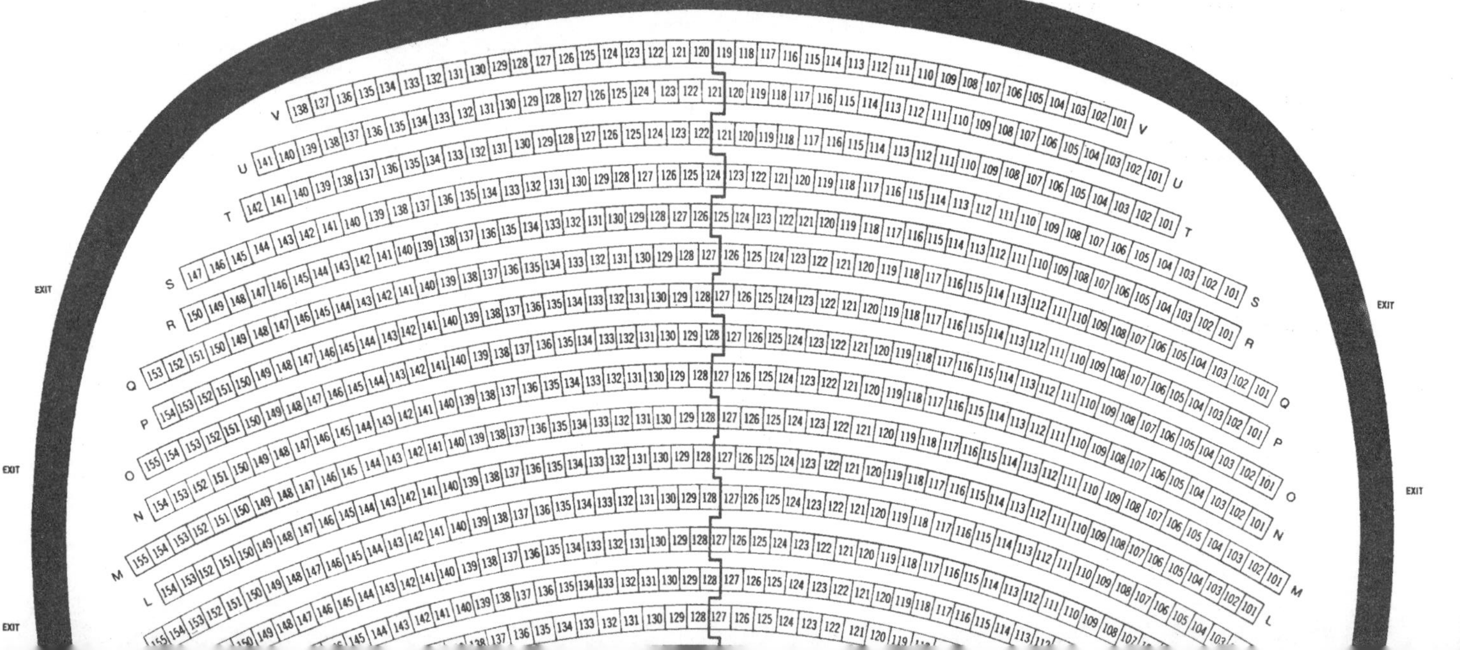

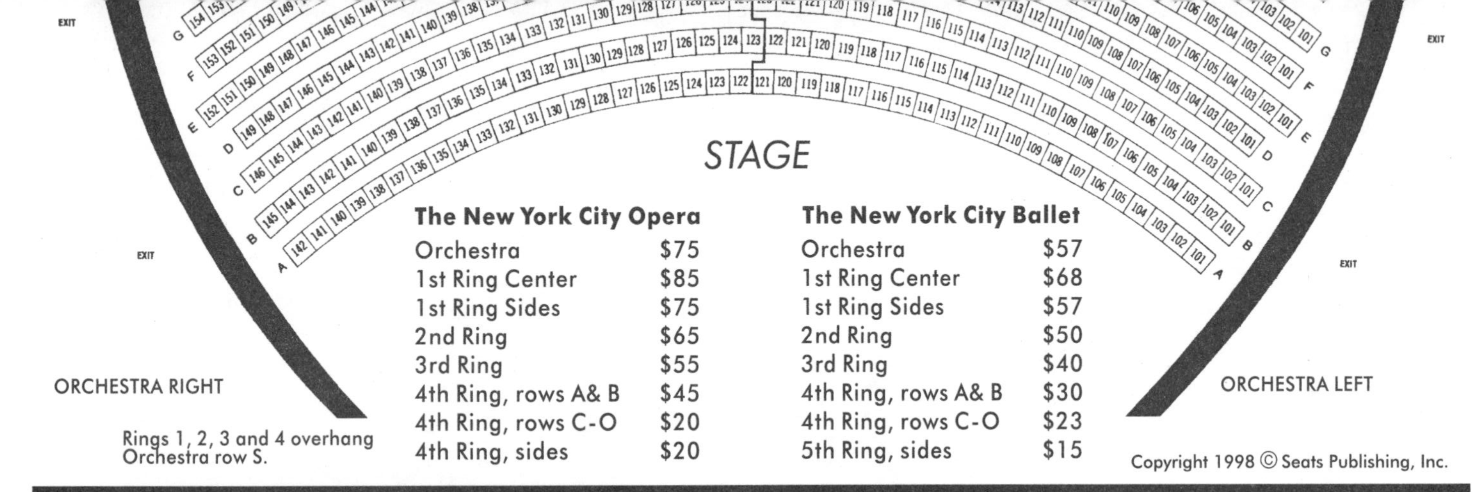

Rings 1, 2, 3 and 4 overhang Orchestra row S.

The New York City Opera	
Orchestra	$75
1st Ring Center	$85
1st Ring Sides	$75
2nd Ring	$65
3rd Ring	$55
4th Ring, rows A& B	$45
4th Ring, rows C-O	$20
4th Ring, sides	$20

The New York City Ballet	
Orchestra	$57
1st Ring Center	$68
1st Ring Sides	$57
2nd Ring	$50
3rd Ring	$40
4th Ring, rows A& B	$30
4th Ring, rows C-O	$23
5th Ring, sides	$15

TICKETMASTER (212) 307-4100
NYC OPERA GROUP SALES 870-5618
NYC BALLET GROUP SALES 870-5660
SUBSCRIPTIONS (212) 496-0600

TAXI DIRECTIONS:
63rd St. (bet. Columbus & Amsterdam Ave.)

ON-LINE:
New York City Opera: www.NYCO.org
New York City Ballet: www.nycballet.com

PARKING
Lincoln Center Underground Park & Lock enter on 65th St. (bet. Amsterdam Ave. & Broadway)
GMC, 2000 Broadway, enter on 68th St. (bet. Broadway & Columbus Ave.)
BUS
M5, M7, M10, M11, M66, M104
SUBWAYS
1, 9 to 66th St. & Broadway

Nearby restaurants rated by
SEATS

FIROELLO'S ROMAN CAFÉ, 1900 Broadway 595-5330
PICHOLINE, 35 W 64th St. 724-8585
LINCOLN TAVERN, 51 W 64th St. 721-8271
COCO OPERA, 58 W 65th St. 873-3700
SHUN LEE WEST, 43 W 65th St. 595-8895
ORLOFF'S DELI & RESTAURANT, 2 Lincoln Sq. 799-4000

NEW YOR

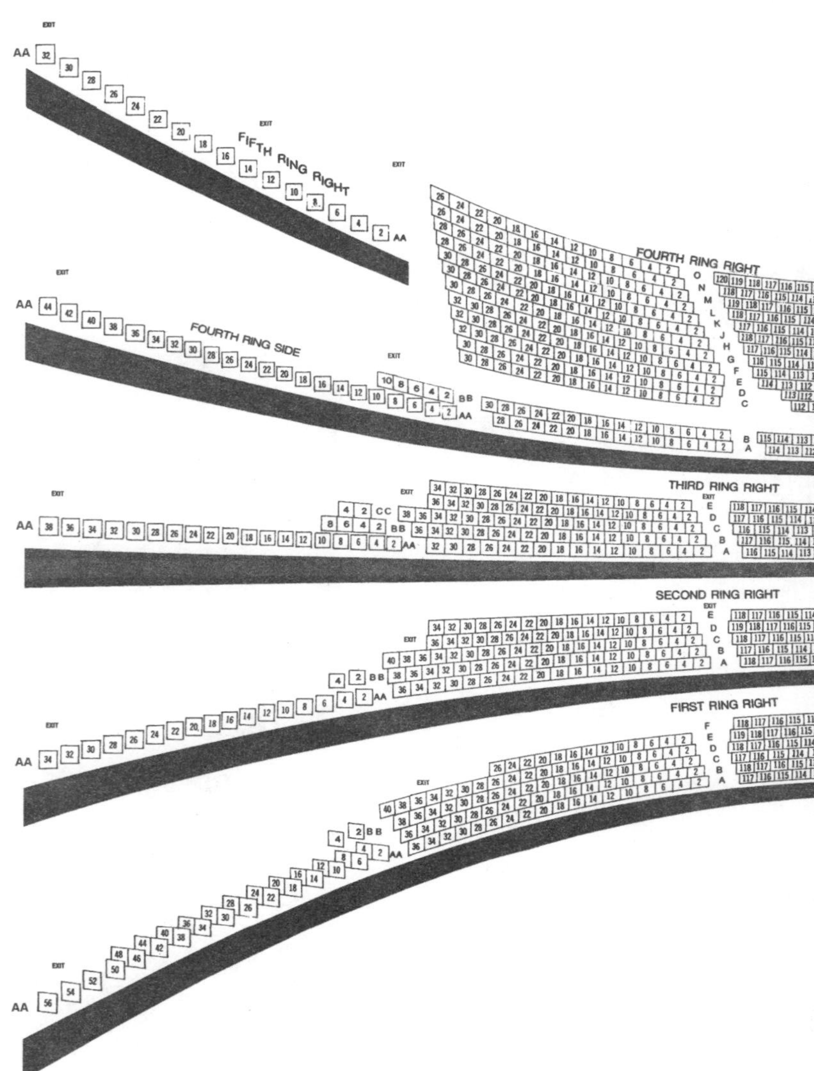
FIFTH RING RIGHT
FOURTH RING RIGHT
FOURTH RING SIDE
THIRD RING RIGHT
SECOND RING RIGHT
FIRST RING RIGHT
EXIT

ATE THEATER

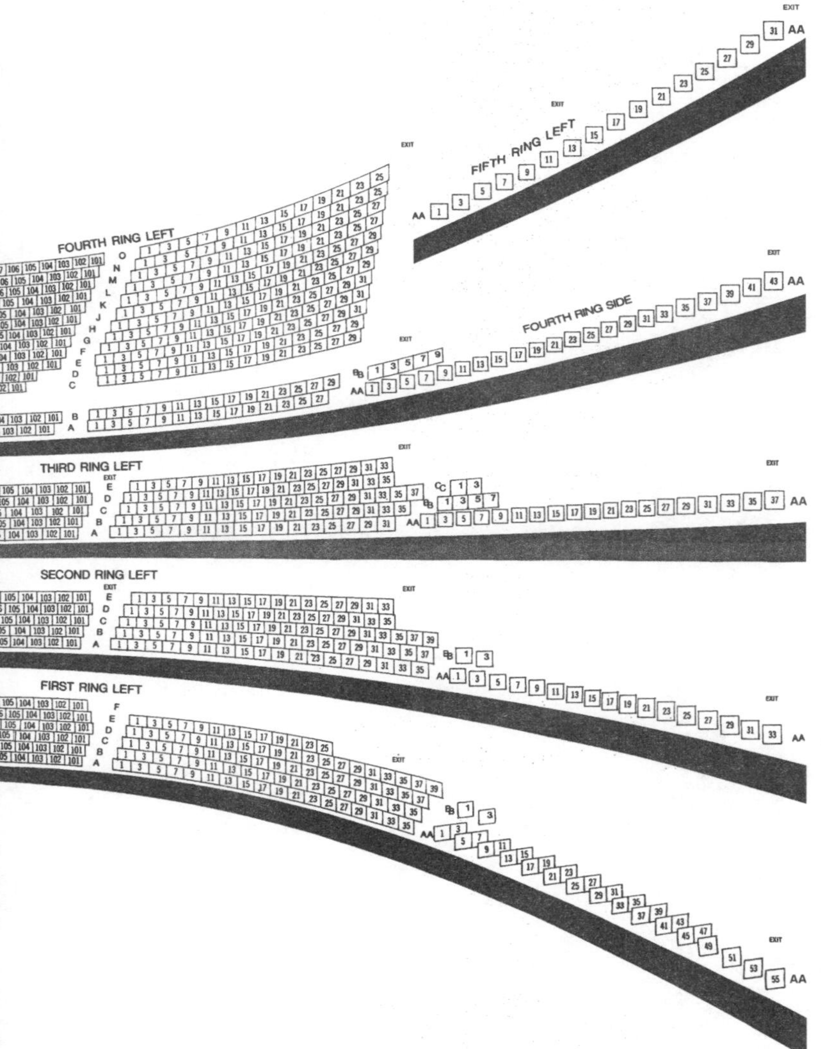
FIFTH RING LEFT
FOURTH RING LEFT
FOURTH RING SIDE
THIRD RING LEFT
SECOND RING LEFT
FIRST RING LEFT
EXIT

LINCOLN CENTER

150 West 65th Street, New York, NY 10023

VIVIAN BEAUMONT THEATRE

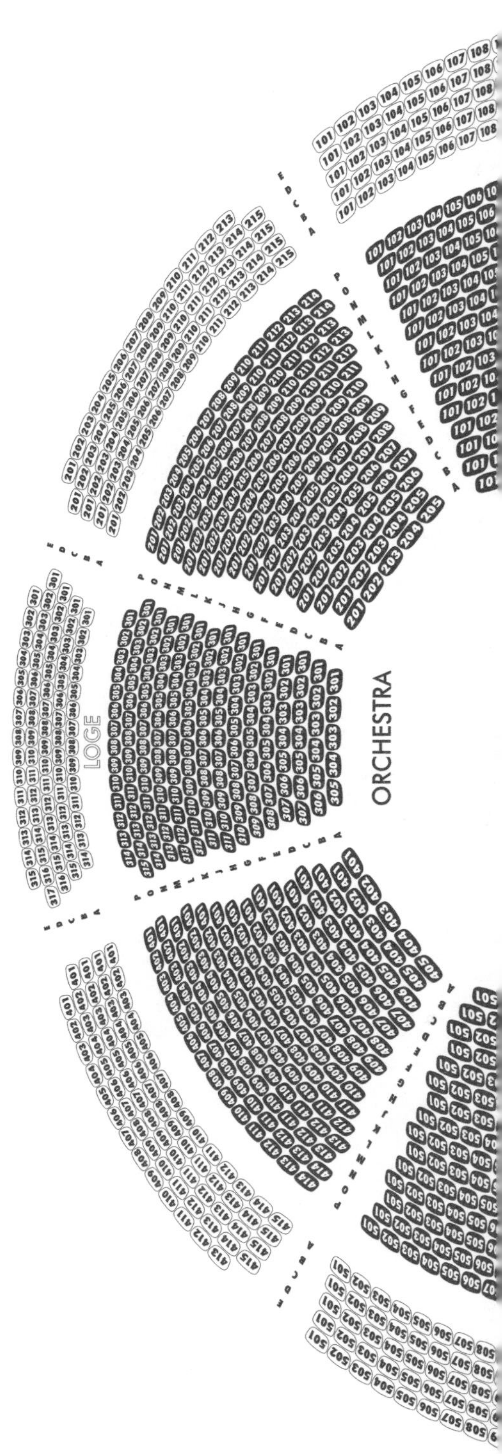

$55.00

$40.00

Hearing devices available

TELECHARGE (212) 239-6200

TAXI DIRECTIONS:
65th St. Eastbound
(bet. Broadway & Amsterdam Ave.)

PARKING
Lincoln Center Underground Park & Lock,
enter on 65th St.
(bet. Amsterdam Ave & Broadway)
GMC, 2000 Broadway,
enter on 68th St.
(bet. Broadway & Columbus Ave.)
BUS
M5, M7, M10, M11, M66, M104
SUBWAYS
1,9, to 66th St. & Broadway

Nearby restaurants rated by
SEATS

FIORELLO'S ROMAN CAFE, 1900 Broadway 595-5330
THE SALOON, 1920 Broadway 874-1500
LINCOLN TAVERN, 51 W. 64th St. 721-8271
COCO OPERA, 58 W. 65th St. 873-3700
SHUN LEE WEST, 43 W. 65th St. 595-8895
ORLOFF'S DELI & RESTAURANT, 2 Lincoln Square, 799-4000

MERKIN CONCERT HALL

Abraham Goodman House, 129 West 67th Street, New York, NY 10023

BALCONY

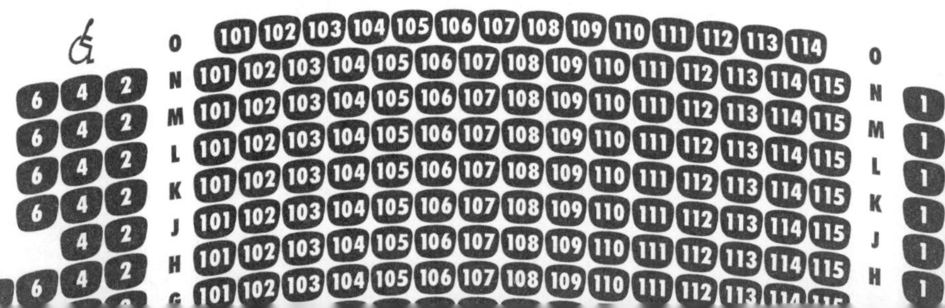

STAGE

Balcony row AA overhangs
Orchestra row K

All Seats One Price

TICKETS (212) 501-3330

TAXI DIRECTIONS:
67th St.Westbound
(bet. Broadway & Amsterdam Ave.)

PARKING
GMC, 2000 Broadway
68th St. & Columbus
BUS
M5, M7, M11, M66, M104
SUBWAYS
1, 9 to 66th St. & Broadway

Nearby restaurants rated by
SEATS

CAFFE LA FENICE, 2014 Broadway 579-1337
FEDERICO'S, 1981 Broadway 873-4210
OLLIE'S, 1991 Broadway 595-8181
PICHOLINE, 35 W. 64th St. 724-8585
ORLOFF'S DELI & RESTAURANT, 2 Lincoln Square, 799-4000
GRAND TIER AT METROPOLITAN OPERA HOUSE, 799-3400

RADIO CITY MUSIC HALL

1260 Avenue of the Americas, New York, NY 10020

THIRD MEZZANINE

SECOND MEZZANINE

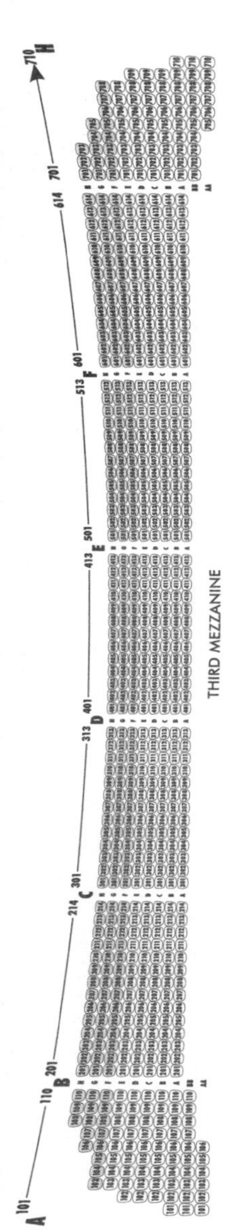

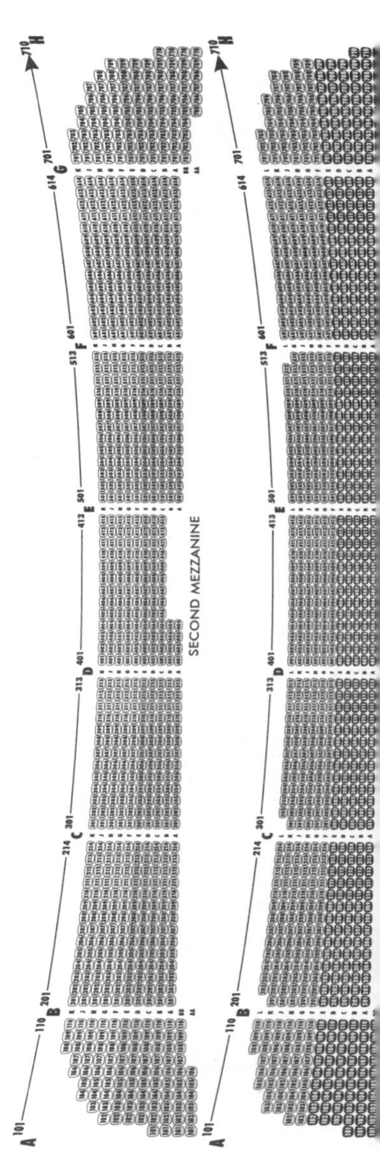

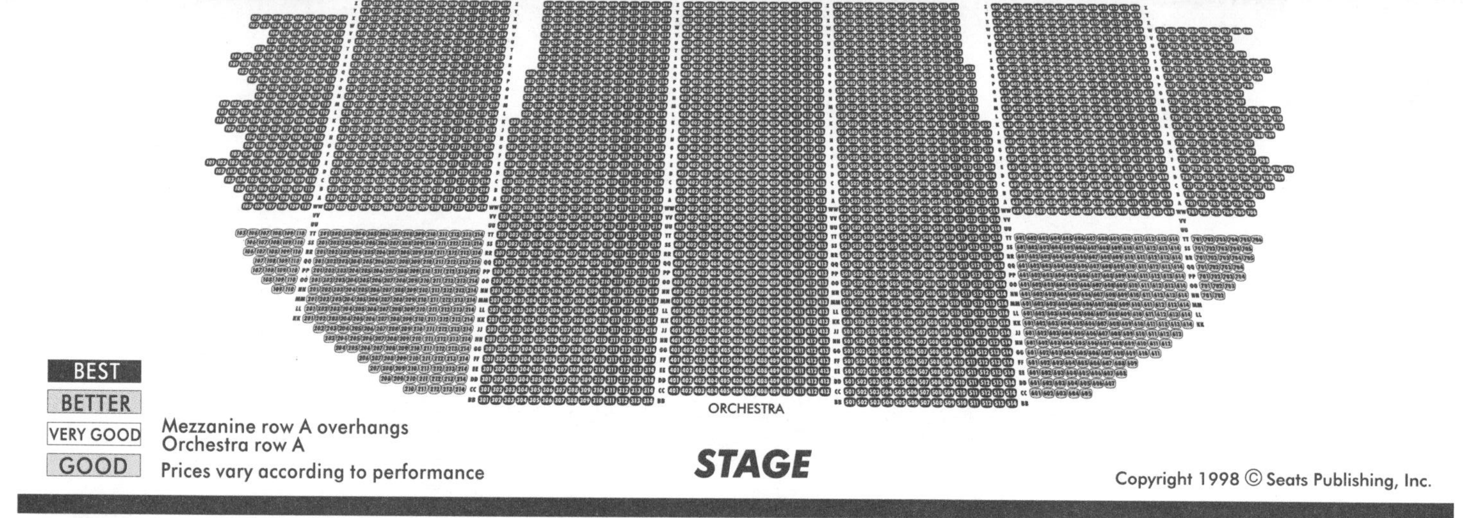

Mezzanine row A overhangs Orchestra row A

Prices vary according to performance

TICKETMASTER (212) 307-7171
INFORMATION (212) 247-4777

PARKING
Kinney System,
155 W.48th St. (bet 6th & 7th Aves.)
159 W. 53rd St. (bet 6th & 7th Aves.)
GMC, 218 W. 50th St. (bet Broadway & 8th Ave.)

BUS
M1,M2,M3,M4,M5,M6,M7,M18,M27,M30,M31,M50,Q32

SUBWAYS
B,D,F,Q to 50th St. & 6th Ave. Rockefeller Center
1,9 to 50th St. & Broadway N,R to 49th St. & 7th Ave.
6 to 51st St. & Lexington Ave. E to 53rd St. & Lexington Ave.

TAXI DIRECTIONS:
6th Ave. Northbound at
50th St. Eastbound

Nearby restaurants rated by
SEATS
SHAAN, 57 W. 48th St. 977-8400
CITE, 120 W. 51st St. 956-7100
FASHION CAFE, 51 Rockefeller Plaza 765-3131

RADIO CITY MUSIC HALL

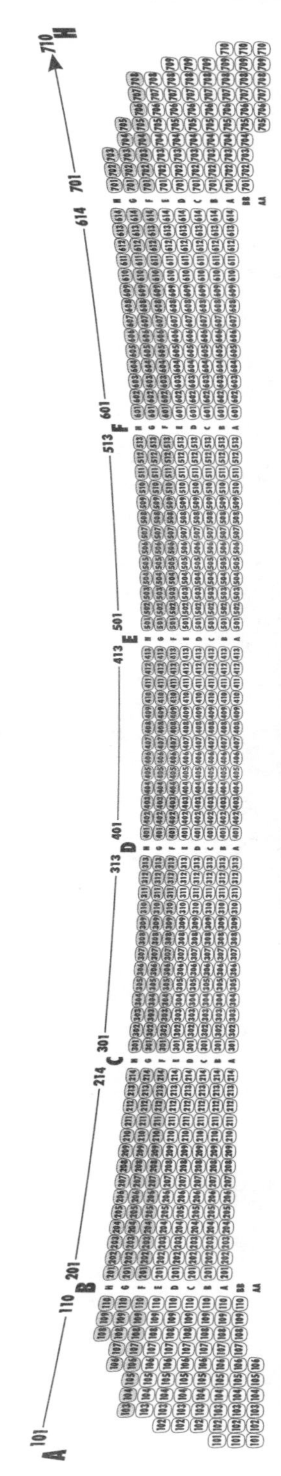

THIRD MEZZANINE

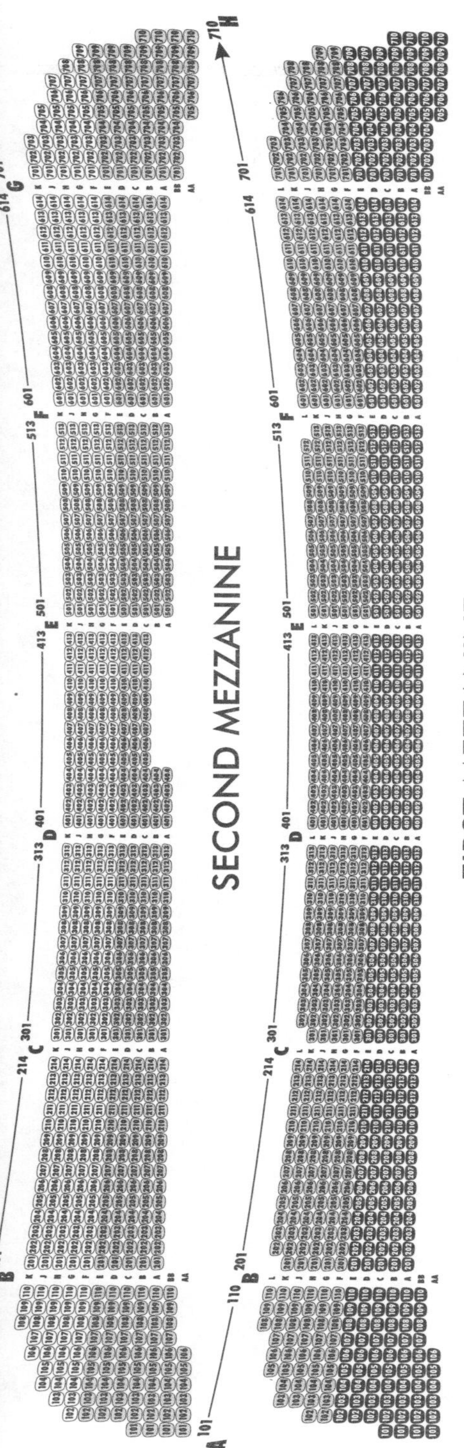
SECOND MEZZANINE
FIRST MEZZANINE

RADIO CITY MUSIC HALL

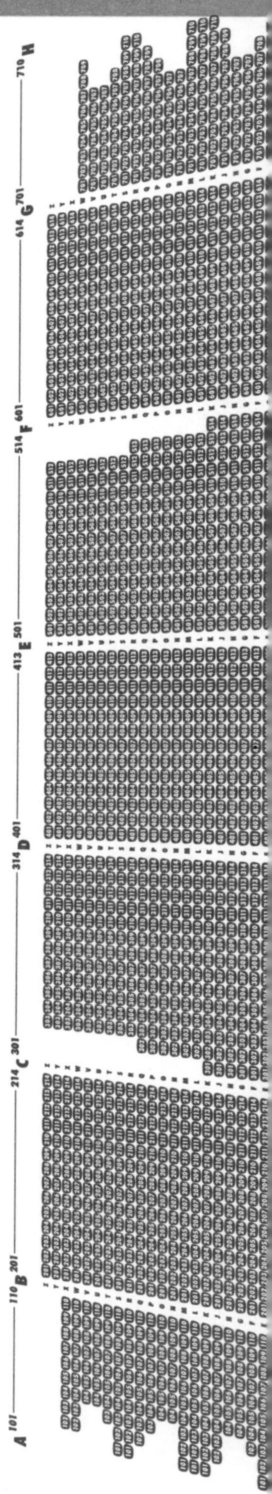

ORCHESTRA
STAGE

RYDZESKI HALL

East Islip High School, Islip Terrace, NY 11752

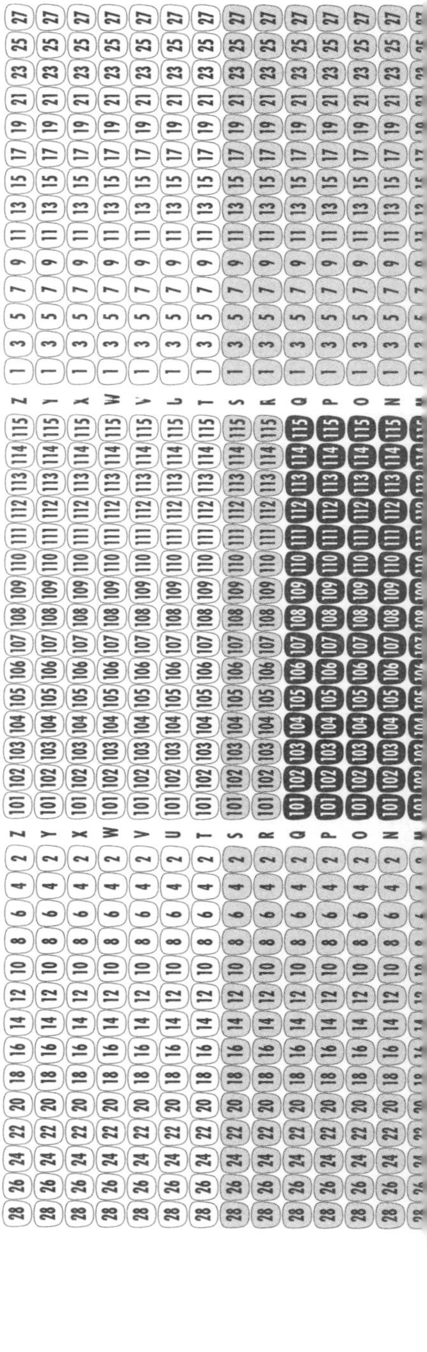

28	26	24	22	20	18	16	14	12	10	8	6	4	2	Z	101	102	103	104	105	106	107	108	109	110	111	112	113	114	115	Z	1	3	5	7	9	11	13	15	17	19	21	23	25	27
28	26	24	22	20	18	16	14	12	10	8	6	4	2	Y	101	102	103	104	105	106	107	108	109	110	111	112	113	114	115	Y	1	3	5	7	9	11	13	15	17	19	21	23	25	27
28	26	24	22	20	18	16	14	12	10	8	6	4	2	X	101	102	103	104	105	106	107	108	109	110	111	112	113	114	115	X	1	3	5	7	9	11	13	15	17	19	21	23	25	27
28	26	24	22	20	18	16	14	12	10	8	6	4	2	W	101	102	103	104	105	106	107	108	109	110	111	112	113	114	115	W	1	3	5	7	9	11	13	15	17	19	21	23	25	27
28	26	24	22	20	18	16	14	12	10	8	6	4	2	V	101	102	103	104	105	106	107	108	109	110	111	112	113	114	115	V	1	3	5	7	9	11	13	15	17	19	21	23	25	27
28	26	24	22	20	18	16	14	12	10	8	6	4	2	U	101	102	103	104	105	106	107	108	109	110	111	112	113	114	115	U	1	3	5	7	9	11	13	15	17	19	21	23	25	27
28	26	24	22	20	18	16	14	12	10	8	6	4	2	T	101	102	103	104	105	106	107	108	109	110	111	112	113	114	115	T	1	3	5	7	9	11	13	15	17	19	21	23	25	27
28	26	24	22	20	18	16	14	12	10	8	6	4	2	S	101	102	103	104	105	106	107	108	109	110	111	112	113	114	115	S	1	3	5	7	9	11	13	15	17	19	21	23	25	27
28	26	24	22	20	18	16	14	12	10	8	6	4	2	R	101	102	103	104	105	106	107	108	109	110	111	112	113	114	115	R	1	3	5	7	9	11	13	15	17	19	21	23	25	27
28	26	24	22	20	18	16	14	12	10	8	6	4	2	Q	101	102	103	104	105	106	107	108	109	110	111	112	113	114	115	Q	1	3	5	7	9	11	13	15	17	19	21	23	25	27
28	26	24	22	20	18	16	14	12	10	8	6	4	2	P	101	102	103	104	105	106	107	108	109	110	111	112	113	114	115	P	1	3	5	7	9	11	13	15	17	19	21	23	25	27
28	26	24	22	20	18	16	14	12	10	8	6	4	2	O	101	102	103	104	105	106	107	108	109	110	111	112	113	114	115	O	1	3	5	7	9	11	13	15	17	19	21	23	25	27
28	26	24	22	20	18	16	14	12	10	8	6	4	2	N	101	102	103	104	105	106	107	108	109	110	111	112	113	114	115	N	1	3	5	7	9	11	13	15	17	19	21	23	25	27
[illegible]	[illegible]	[illegible]	[illegible]	[illegible]	[illegible]	[illegible]	[illegible]	[illegible]	[illegible]	[illegible]	[illegible]	[illegible]	[illegible]	M	[illegible]	[illegible]	[illegible]	[illegible]	[illegible]	[illegible]	[illegible]	[illegible]	[illegible]	[illegible]	[illegible]	[illegible]	[illegible]	[illegible]	[illegible]	M	[illegible]	[illegible]	[illegible]	[illegible]	[illegible]	[illegible]	[illegible]	[illegible]	[illegible]	[illegible]	[illegible]	[illegible]	[illegible]	[illegible]

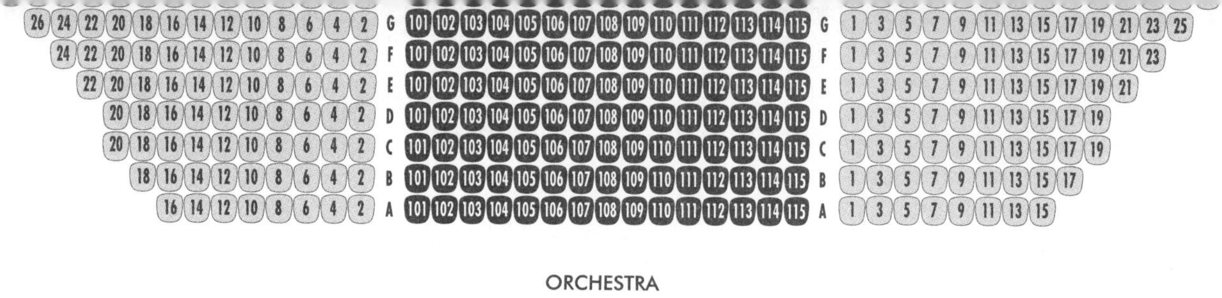

G	26 24 22 20 18 16 14 12 10 8 6 4 2	G	101 102 103 104 105 106 107 108 109 110 111 112 113 114 115	G	1 3 5 7 9 11 13 15 17 19 21 23 25
F	24 22 20 18 16 14 12 10 8 6 4 2	F	101 102 103 104 105 106 107 108 109 110 111 112 113 114 115	F	1 3 5 7 9 11 13 15 17 19 21 23
E	22 20 18 16 14 12 10 8 6 4 2	E	101 102 103 104 105 106 107 108 109 110 111 112 113 114 115	E	1 3 5 7 9 11 13 15 17 19 21
D	20 18 16 14 12 10 8 6 4 2	D	101 102 103 104 105 106 107 108 109 110 111 112 113 114 115	D	1 3 5 7 9 11 13 15 17 19
C	20 18 16 14 12 10 8 6 4 2	C	101 102 103 104 105 106 107 108 109 110 111 112 113 114 115	C	1 3 5 7 9 11 13 15 17 19
B	18 16 14 12 10 8 6 4 2	B	101 102 103 104 105 106 107 108 109 110 111 112 113 114 115	B	1 3 5 7 9 11 13 15 17
A	16 14 12 10 8 6 4 2	A	101 102 103 104 105 106 107 108 109 110 111 112 113 114 115	A	1 3 5 7 9 11 13 15

ORCHESTRA

STAGE

$30.00
$25.00
$19.00

TICKETS: (516) 293-2222

PARKING

Free Parking
Wheelchair Accessible

Nearby restaurants rated by
SEATS

DIRECTIONS:
Long Island Expressway So. to Sagtikos Parkway So. Southern State Parkway E. to Exit 44 (Sunrise Highway/Route 27 W.) First right onto Craig B. Gariepy Ave. 1/2 mile make right onto Redman Ave. School & parking on left

STALLER CENTER FOR THE ARTS

State University of New York, Stony Brook, NY 11794-5425

MAIN STAGE

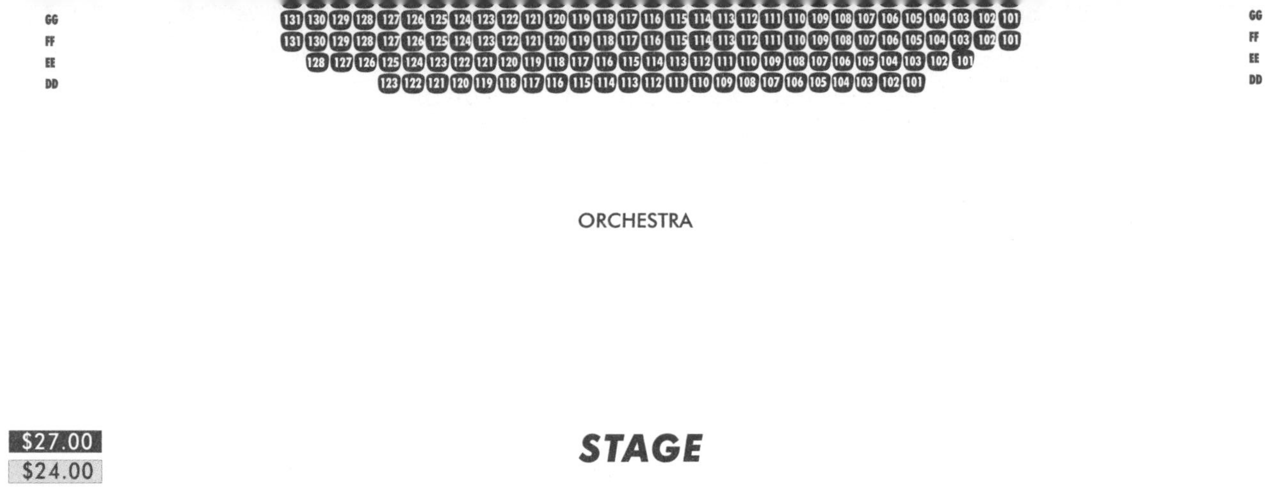

GG 131 130 129 128 127 126 125 124 123 122 121 120 119 118 117 116 115 114 113 112 111 110 109 108 107 106 105 104 103 102 101 GG
FF 131 130 129 128 127 126 125 124 123 122 121 120 119 118 117 116 115 114 113 112 111 110 109 108 107 106 105 104 103 102 101 FF
EE 128 127 126 125 124 123 122 121 120 119 118 117 116 115 114 113 112 111 110 109 108 107 106 105 104 103 102 101 EE
DD 123 122 121 120 119 118 117 116 115 114 113 112 111 110 109 108 107 106 105 104 103 102 101 DD

ORCHESTRA

$27.00
$24.00

STAGE

TICKETS (516)-632-7230

DIRECTIONS:
Long Island Expressway to Exit 62 - Route 97 North (Nicolls Road). Follow Nicolls Road North for 9 miles (cross intersection of 347 - Nesconset Hwy) to the main entrance of the campus.

PARKING
Garage is to the left of the administrative building, no charge on Saturday and Sunday. Metered spots are free after 8 PM
Handicapped parking available

Wheelchair seating available
Hearing devices available

Nearby restaurants rated by
SEATS
EASTERN PAVILION, 750 Route 25A, East Setauket 516- 751-1888
MIRABELLE RESTAURANT, 404 North Country Road, St. James 516-584-5999
MARIO'S ITALIAN KITCHEN, Route 25A, East Setauket 516-751-8663
PENTIMENTO, 93 Main St., Stony Brook 516-689-7755

STALLER CENTER FOR THE ARTS

RECITAL HALL

State University of New York, Stony Brook, NY 11794-5425

N 136 135 134 133 132 131 130 129 128 127 126 125 124 123 122 121 120 119 118 117 116 115 114 113 112 111 110 109 108 107 106 105 104 103 102 N

M 136 135 134 133 132 131 130 129 128 127 126 125 124 123 122 121 120 119 118 117 116 115 114 113 112 111 110 109 108 107 106 105 104 103 102 101 M

L 134 133 132 131 130 129 128 127 126 125 124 123 122 121 120 119 118 117 116 115 114 113 112 111 110 109 108 107 106 105 104 103 102 101 L

K 136 135 134 133 132 131 130 129 128 127 126 125 124 123 122 121 120 119 118 117 116 115 114 113 112 111 110 109 108 107 106 105 104 103 102 K

J 133 132 131 130 129 128 127 126 125 124 123 122 121 120 119 118 117 116 115 114 113 112 111 110 109 108 107 106 105 104 103 102 101 J

H 132 131 130 129 128 127 126 125 124 123 122 121 120 119 118 117 116 115 114 113 112 111 110 109 108 107 106 105 104 103 102 101 H

G 132 131 130 129 128 127 126 125 124 123 122 121 120 119 118 117 116 115 114 113 112 111 110 109 108 107 106 105 104 103 102 G

B 125 124 123 122 121 120 119 118 117 116 115 114 113 112 111 110 109 108 107 106 105 104 103 102 101 B

ORCHESTRA

All Seats One Price

STAGE

TICKETS (516)-632-7230

DIRECTIONS:
Long Island Expressway to Exit 62 - Route 97 North (Nicolls Road). Follow Nicolls Road North for 9 miles (cross intersection of 347 - Nesconset Hwy) to the main entrance of the campus.

PARKING
Garage is to the left of the administrative building, no charge on Saturday and Sunday. Metered spots are free after 8 PM
Handicapped parking available

Wheelchair seating available
Hearing devices available

Nearby restaurants rated by
SEATS
EASTERN PAVILION, 750 Route 25A, East Setauket 516-751-1888
MIRABELLE RESTAURANT, 404 North Country Road, St. James 516-584-5999
MARIO'S ITALIAN KITCHEN, Route 25A, East Setauket 516-751-8663
PENTIMENTO, 93 Main St., Stony Brook 516-689-7755

SYMPHONY SPACE

2537 Broadway, New York, NY 10025-6947

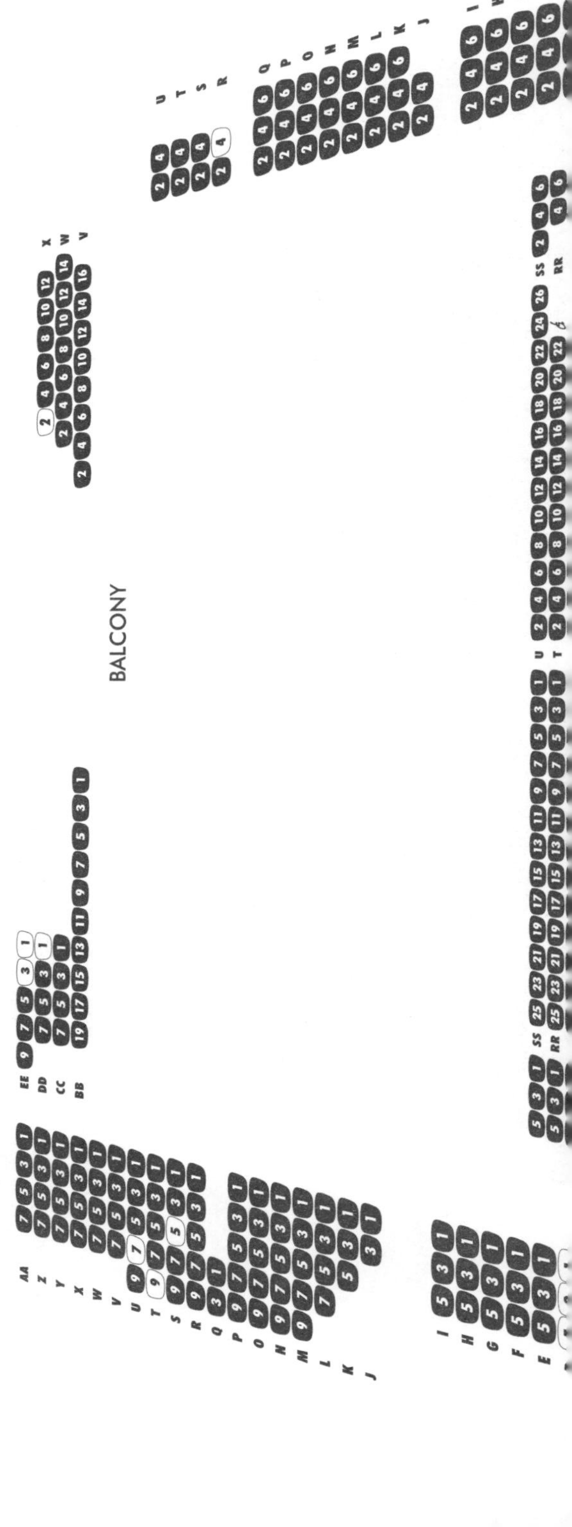

BALCONY

ORCHESTRA

STAGE

Prices vary according to event

RESTRICTED VIEW

TICKETS (212) 864-5400
GROUP SALES (212) 864-1414
MEMBERSHIPS AVAILABLE

TAXI DIRECTIONS:
Broadway, two way at 95th St. Westbound

PARKING
Kinney System, 711 West End Ave. entrance on 95th St.
PAO, 214 W. 95th St. (bet. Broadway & Amsterdam Ave.)

BUS
M104,M96

SUBWAYS
1,2,3,9 to 96th St. & Broadway

Nearby restaurants rated by **SEATS**

CLEOPATRA'S NEEDLE, 2485 Broadway 769-6969
MIMI'S MACARONI, 718 Amsterdam Ave. 866-6311
INDIAN CAFE, 201 W.95th St. 222-1600
INDIA GARDEN, 624 Amsterdam Ave. 787-4530
STRAND DINER, 208 W. 96th St. 865-0500

TILLES CENTER FOR THE PERFORMING ARTS

Long Island University/C.W. Post Campus, Greenvale, NY 11548-0570

MAIN HALL

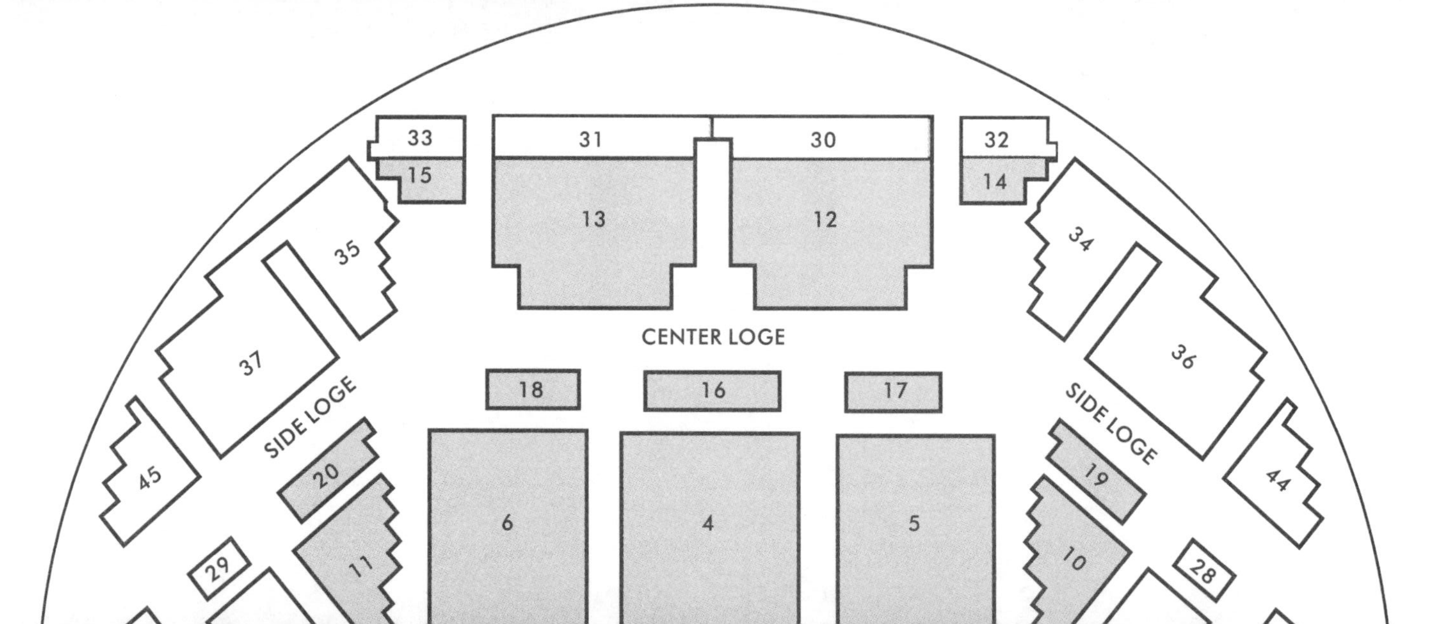

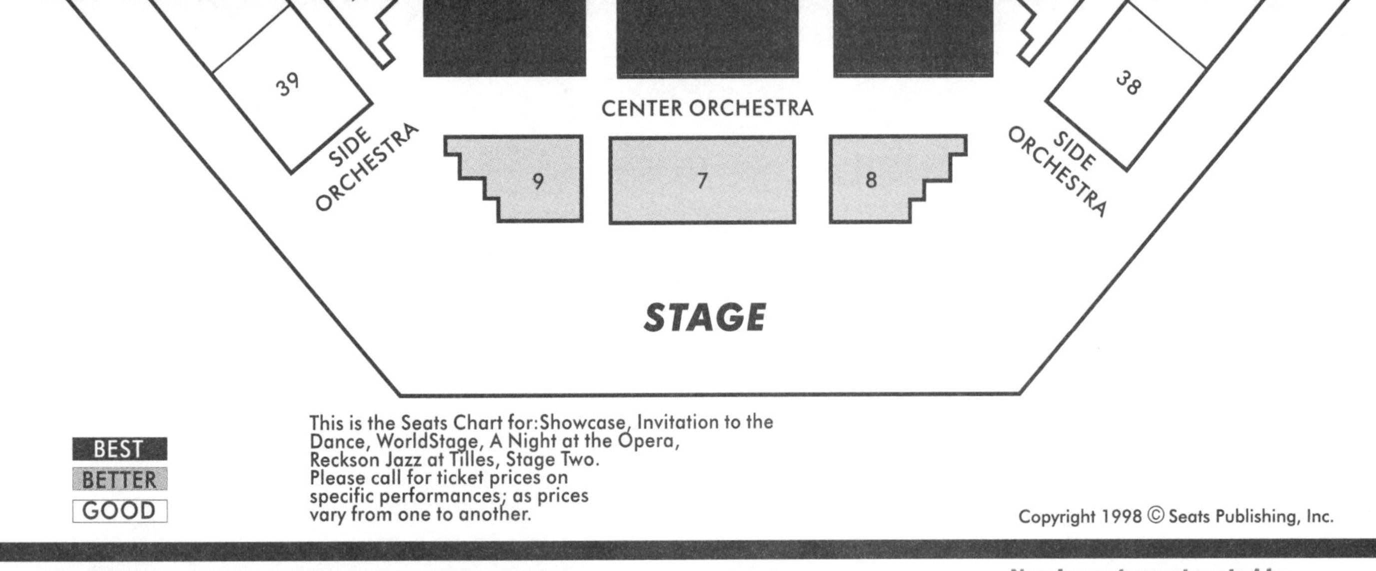

This is the Seats Chart for: Showcase, Invitation to the Dance, WorldStage, A Night at the Opera, Reckson Jazz at Tilles, Stage Two. Please call for ticket prices on specific performances; as prices vary from one to another.

TICKETS (516) 299-3100

DIRECTIONS:
By Car - Long Island Expressway to Exit 39N. Proceed to Northern Boulevard (Route 25A). Turn right onto 25A. C.W. Post is on the right at the fifth traffic light.

PARKING
Free Parking On Premises

BY TRAIN
Long Island Railroad to Great Neck or Hicksville Station. N20 Bus to C.W. Post

Nearby restaurants rated by
SEATS

BEN'S KOSHER DELICATESSEN
149 Wheatley Plaza, Greenvale, N.Y.
CLASSICO ITALIAN RESTAURANT
1042 Northern Boulevard, Roslyn, N.Y.
LA COQUILLE RESTAURANT
1669 Northern Boulevard, Manhasset, N.Y.

TILLES CENTER FOR THE PERFORMING ARTS

Long Island University/C.W. Post Campus, Greenvale, NY 11548-0570

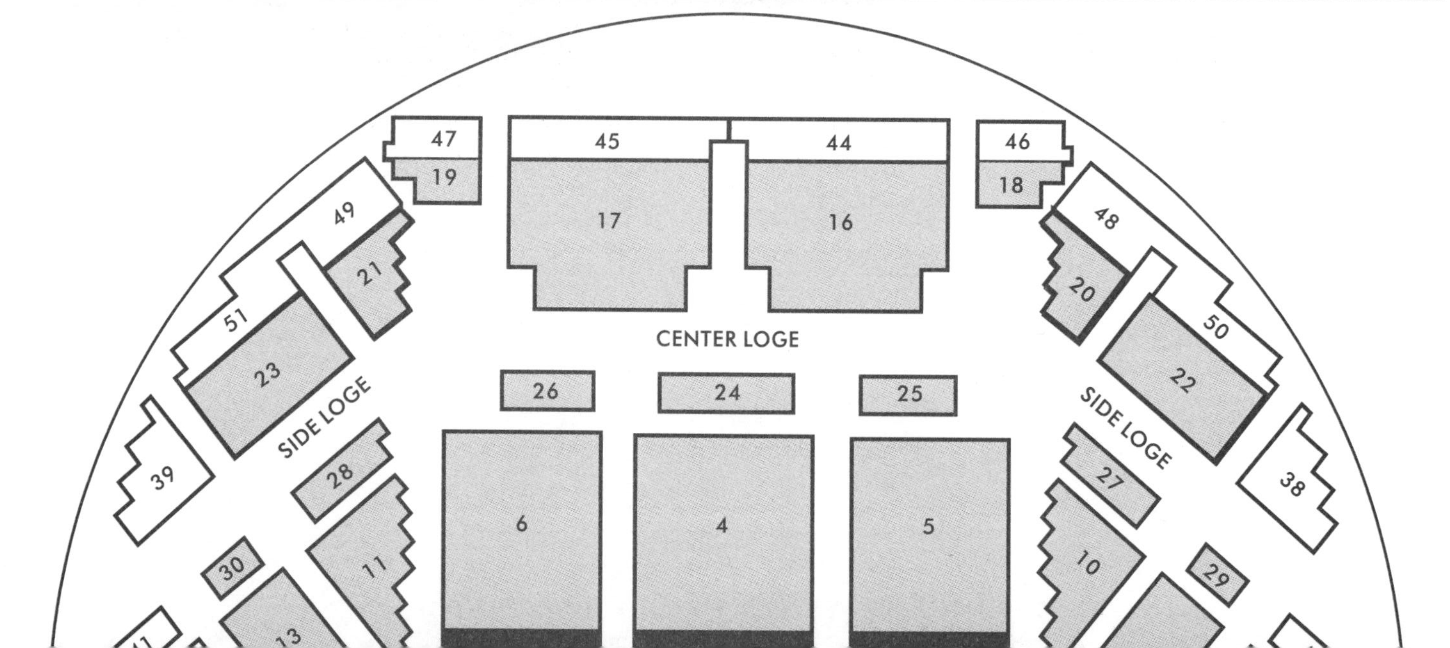

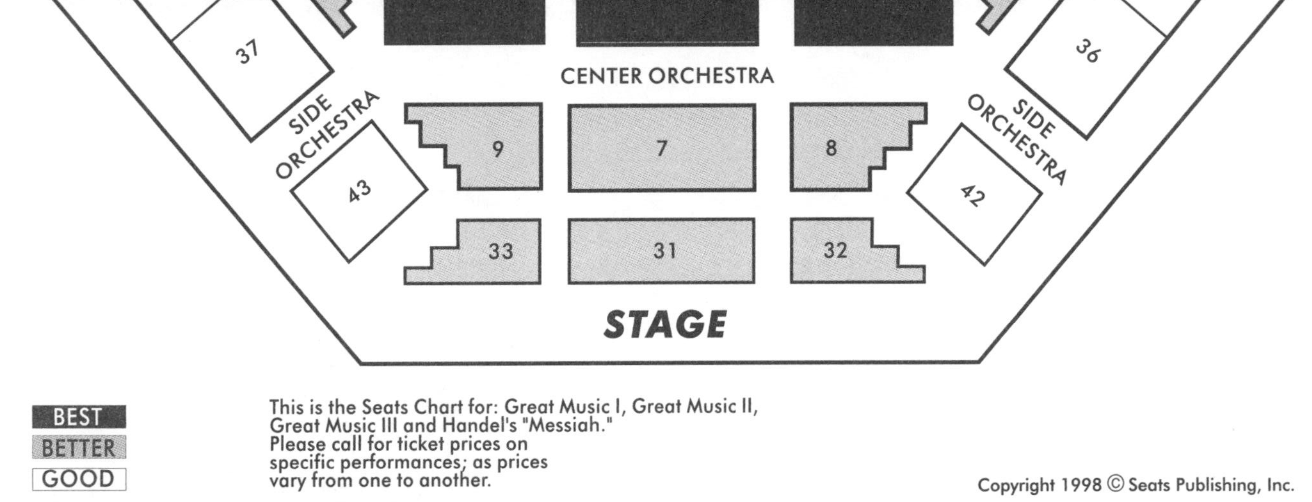

BEST
BETTER
GOOD

This is the Seats Chart for: Great Music I, Great Music II, Great Music III and Handel's "Messiah." Please call for ticket prices on specific performances; as prices vary from one to another.

TICKETS (516) 299-3100

DIRECTIONS:
By Car - Long Island Expressway to Exit 39N. Proceed to Northern Boulevard (Route 25A). Turn right onto 25A. C.W. Post is on the right at the fifth traffic light.

PARKING
Free Parking On Premises

BY TRAIN
Long Island Railroad to Great Neck or Hicksville Station. N20 Bus to C.W. Post

Nearby restaurants rated by
SEATS

BEN'S KOSHER DELICATESSEN
149 Wheatley Plaza, Greenvale, N.Y.
CLASSICO ITALIAN RESTAURANT
1042 Northern Boulevard, Roslyn, N.Y.
LA COQUILLE RESTAURANT
1669 Northern Boulevard, Manhasset, N.Y.

TOWN HALL

123 West 43rd Street, New York, NY 10036

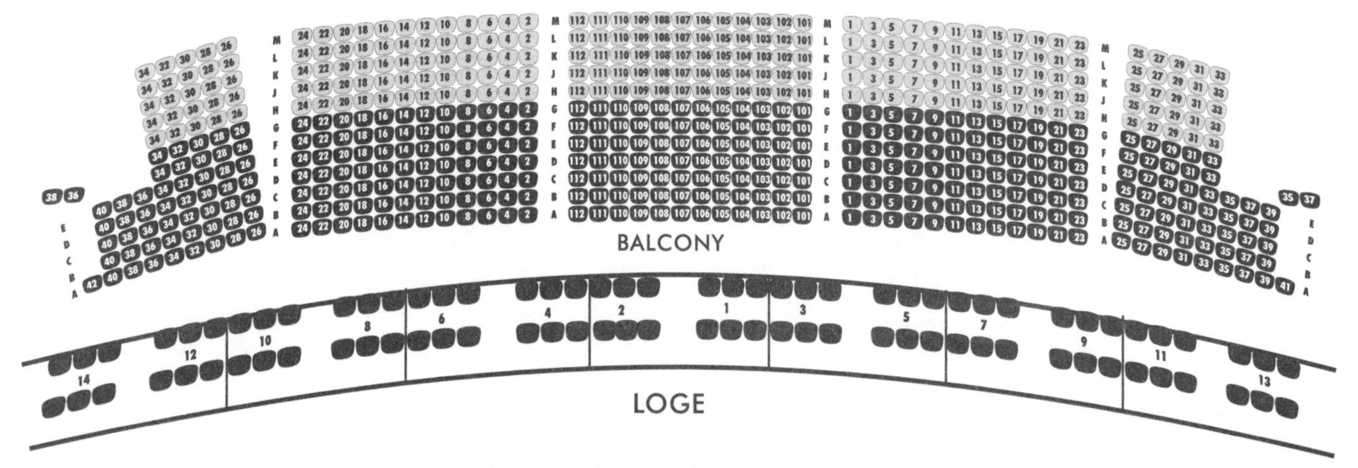

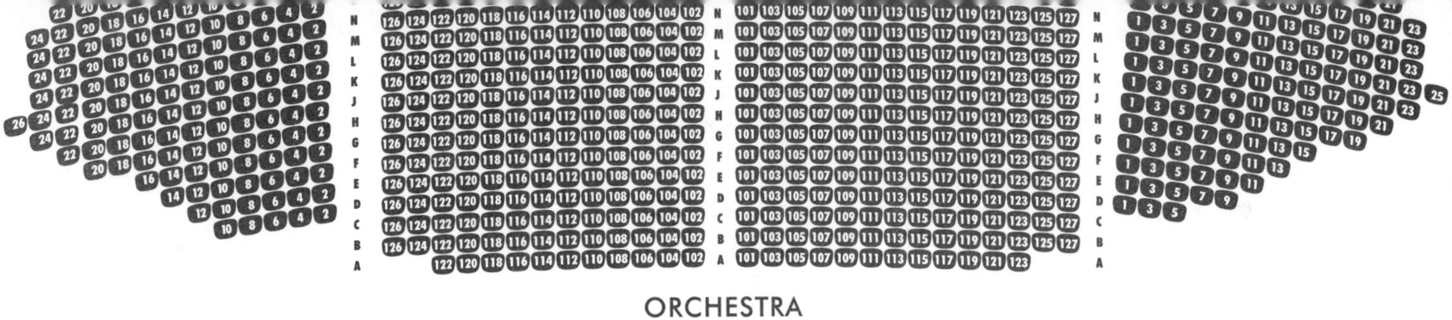

ORCHESTRA

STAGE

Loge begins over row K

Prices vary according to event

TICKETMASTER (212) 307-7171
BOX OFFICE (212) 840-2824

TAXI DIRECTIONS:
43rd St. Westbound
(bet. Broadway & 6th Ave.)

PARKING
Kinney System, 100 W. 44th St.
Meyer, 141-145 W. 43rd St.
BUS
M1, M2, M3, M4, M5, M6, M7,M10
M27, M32, M104
SUBWAYS
B, D, F, Q to 42nd St. & 6th Ave.
1,2,3,N,R,7 to 42nd St. & 7th Ave. Times Square
A, C, E to 42nd St. & 8th Ave. Port Authority
4,5,6, to Grand Central, then Shuttle to Times Square

Nearby restaurants rated by
SEATS
BRYANT PARK GRILL,
20 W. 40th St. 840-6500
ORIGINAL FERRARA PASTRIES,
201 W. 42nd St.398-6064
STARDUST DINE- 0-MAT,
1491 Broadway at 43rd St. 768-3170
MANHATTAN CHILI COMPANY,
1500 Broadway at 43rd St. 730-8666

USTA NATIONAL TENNIS CENTER

Flushing Meadow-Corona Park, Flushing, NY 11368

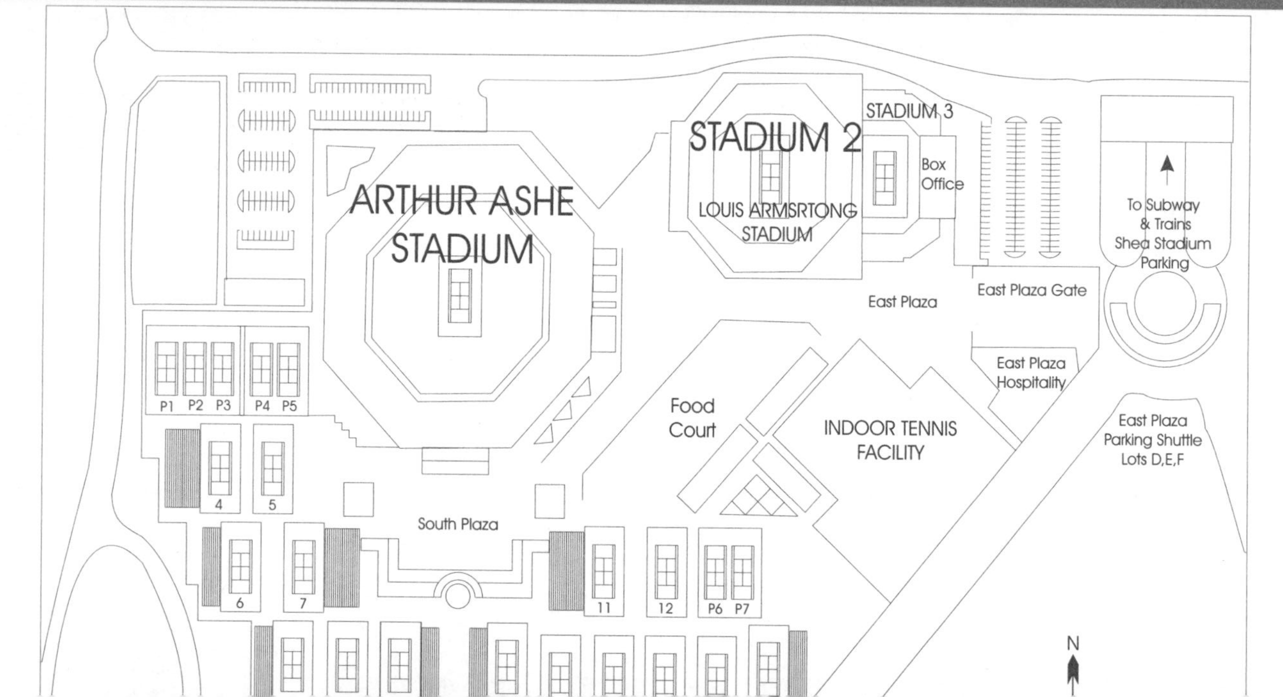

TICKET PRICES

	Monday 8/24 through Friday 8/28		Saturday 8/29 through Monday 8/31		Tuesday 9/1 through Thursday 9/3		Friday 9/4 through Sunday 9/6	Series Price
	DAY	NIGHT	DAY	NIGHT	DAY	NIGHT	DAY	
COURTSIDE PRESTIGE	$256.00	$204.00	$358.00	$204.00	$358.00	$409.00	$613.00	$8,125.00
COURTSIDE PLATINUM	$177.00	$142.00	$248.00	$142.00	$248.00	$279.00	$425.00	$5,625.00
COURTSIDE GOLD	$138.00	$110.00	$193.00	$110.00	$193.00	$217.00	$330.00	$4,375.00
LOGE SILVER	$79.00	$63.00	$110.00	$63.00	$110.00	$122.00	$189.00	$2,500.00
LOGE BRONZE	$59.00	$47.00	$83.00	$47.00	$83.00	$92.00	$142.00	$1,875.00
PROMENADE A-K	$33.00	$26.00	$46.00	$26.00	$46.00	$54.00	$79.00	$1,050.00
PROMENADE L-Z	$28.00	$22.00	$39.00	$22.00	$39.00	$41.00	$66.00	$875.00
GROUNDS ADMISSION	$20.00	n/a	$30.00	n/a	$30.00	n/a	n/a	n/a
STADIUM 2 COURTSIDE	$70.00	n/a	$80.00	n/a	$80.00	n/a	n/a	$600.00

Wheelchair seating is the same price as Promenade A-K

TICKETS (718) 760-6200
(800) OPENTIX

DIRECTIONS: By Car
Take the Triborough Bridge to Grand Central Parkway and take the Shea Stadium exit.

Parking on premises

SUBWAY
Take the IRT #7 Flushing subway from either Times Square or Grand Central to the Shea Stadium/Willets Point Station. The National Tennis Center is about a three minute walk down the ramp from the station.

RAILROAD
The Long Island Railroad/Port Washington branch departs from Penn Station to the USTA National Tennis Center (Shea Stadium/Willets Point Station). Contact the railroad for information (718) 217-5477.

SEATS

ARTHUR ASHE STADIUM at USTA NATIONAL CENTER

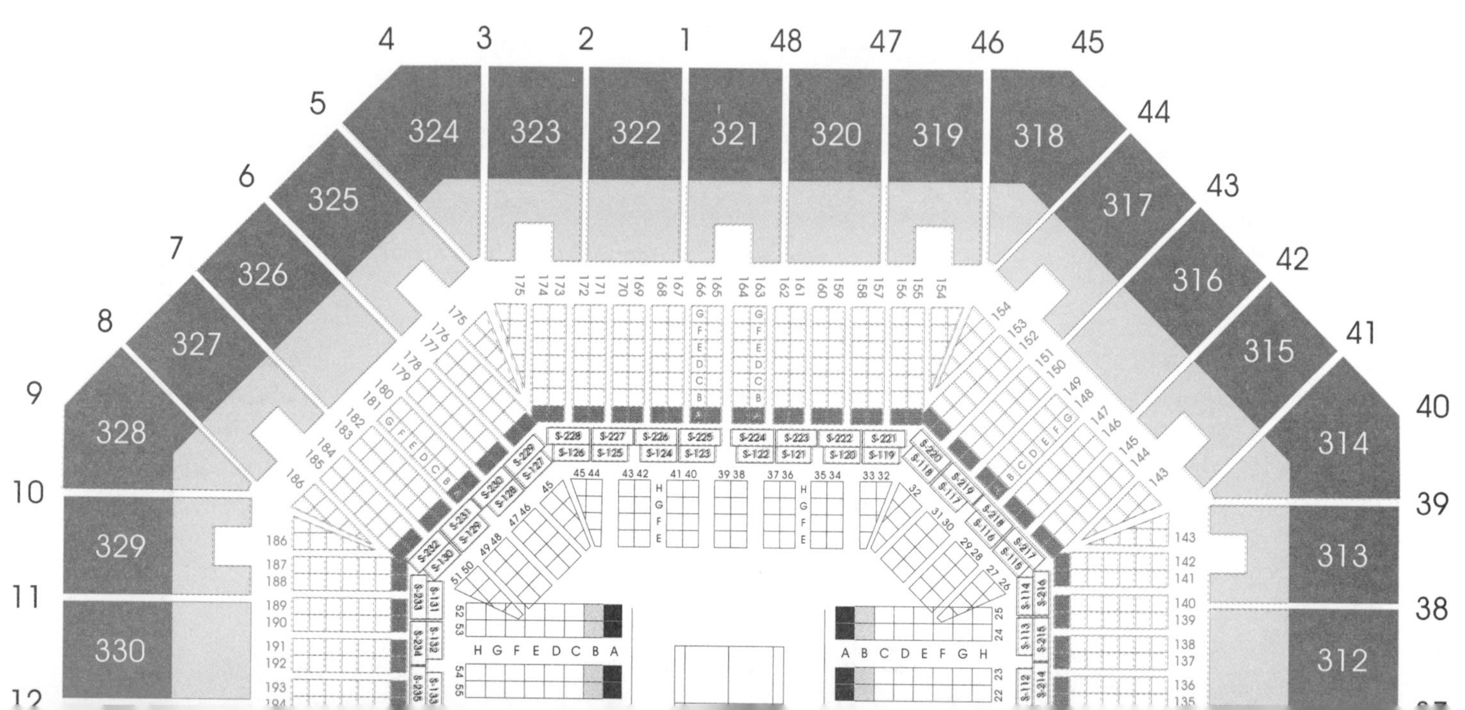

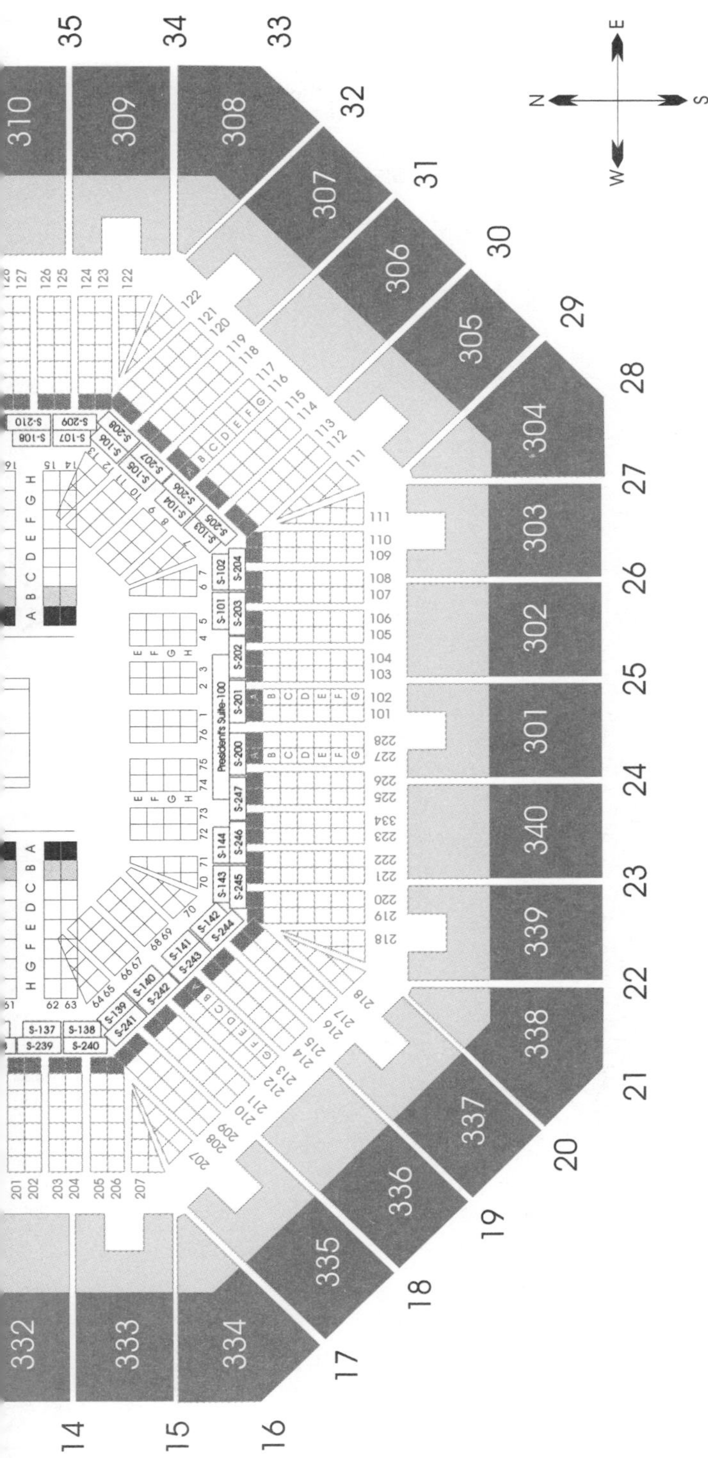

N
E
S
W
310
309
308
307
306
305
304
303
302
301
340
339
338
337
336
335
334
333
332
14
15
16
17
18
19
20
21
22
23
24
25
26
27
28
29
30
31
32
33
34
35
President's Suite-100

MADISON SQUARE GARDEN

4 Penn Plaza, New York, NY 10001

INFORMATION (212) 465-6741, 465-MSG1
GROUP SALES (212) 465-6080
DISABLED ACCESS TICKETS (212) 465-6034
Accessible to all persons with disabilities.

NEW YORK KNICKS INFORMATION (212) 465-JUMP

NEW YORK RANGERS INFORMATION (212) 808-NYRS

SURF THE WEB WITH MADISON SQUARE GARDEN NETWORK

Garden Box Office, all Ticketmaster outlets or by calling Ticketmaster to charge by phone. All tickets purchased through the Madison Square Garden Box Office or Ticketmaster are subject to a Facility Surcharge of $1.00. Ticketmaster purchases are subject to a service charge.

TICKETMASTER
(212) 307-7171
(201) 507-8900
(516) 888-9000
(914) 454-3388
(203) 624-0033

PARKING
Kinney System, 314 W. 34th St.(between 8th & 9th Ave.)
Kinney System, 324 W. 34th St. (between 8th & 9th Ave.)
Kinney System, 313 W. 33rd St.(between 8th & 9th Ave.)

BUS
M4, M6, M7, M10, M16, M34, Q32

SUBWAY
1, 2, 3, 9 to 34th St. & 7th Ave. Penn Station
A, C, E to 34th St. & 8th Ave.
B, D, F, Q, N, R to 34th St. & 6th Ave.

TAXI
7th Ave. Southbound (between 31st & 33rd Sts.)

Nearby restaurants rated by
SEATS

RESTAURANTS INSIDE THE GARDEN:

CLUB BAR & GRILL (for club seat holders)
PLAY BY PLAY

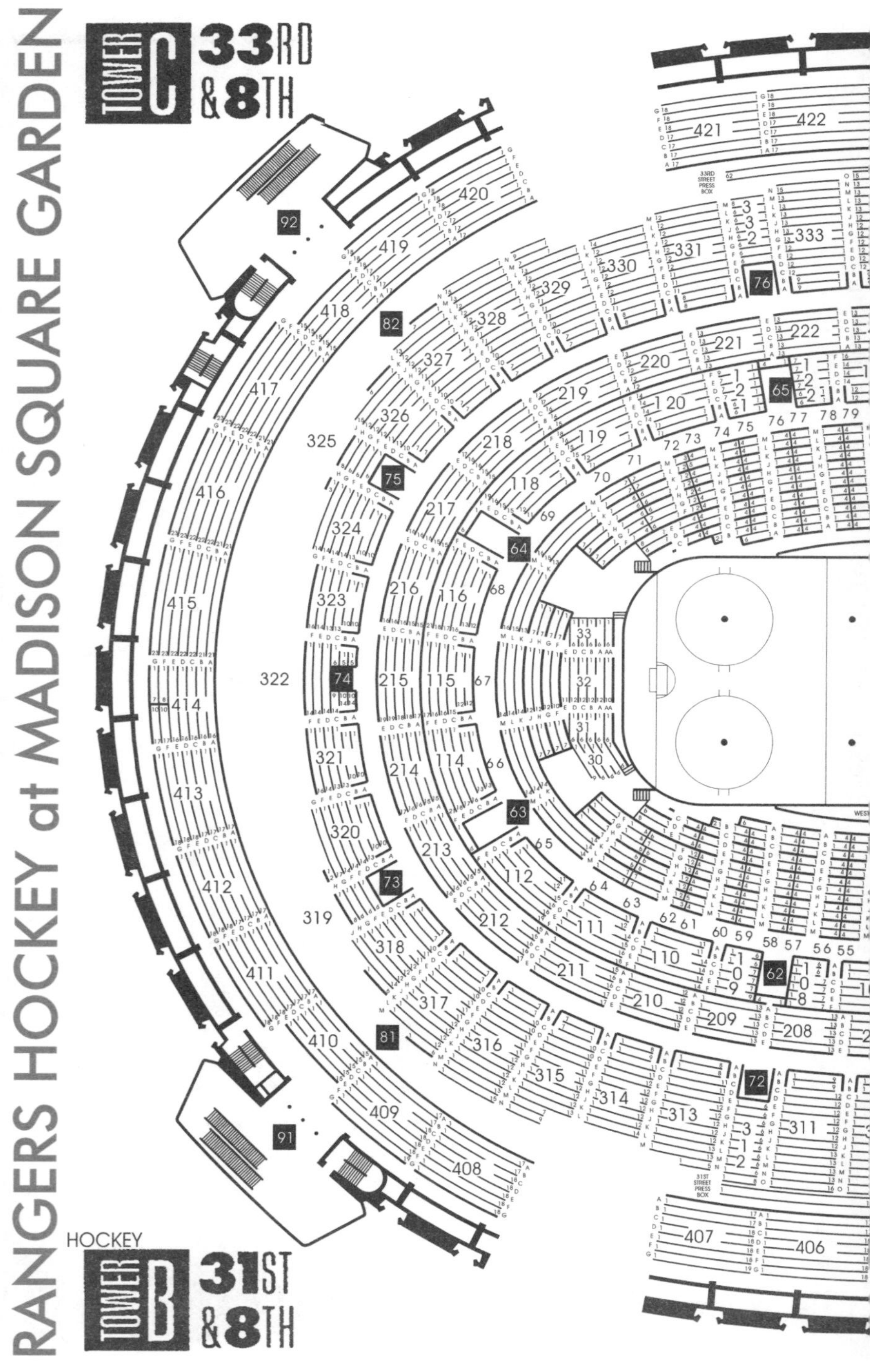
RANGERS HOCKEY at MADISON SQUARE GARDEN
TOWER C
33RD & 8TH
HOCKEY
TOWER B
31ST & 8TH
33RD STREET PRESS BOX
31ST STREET PRESS BOX

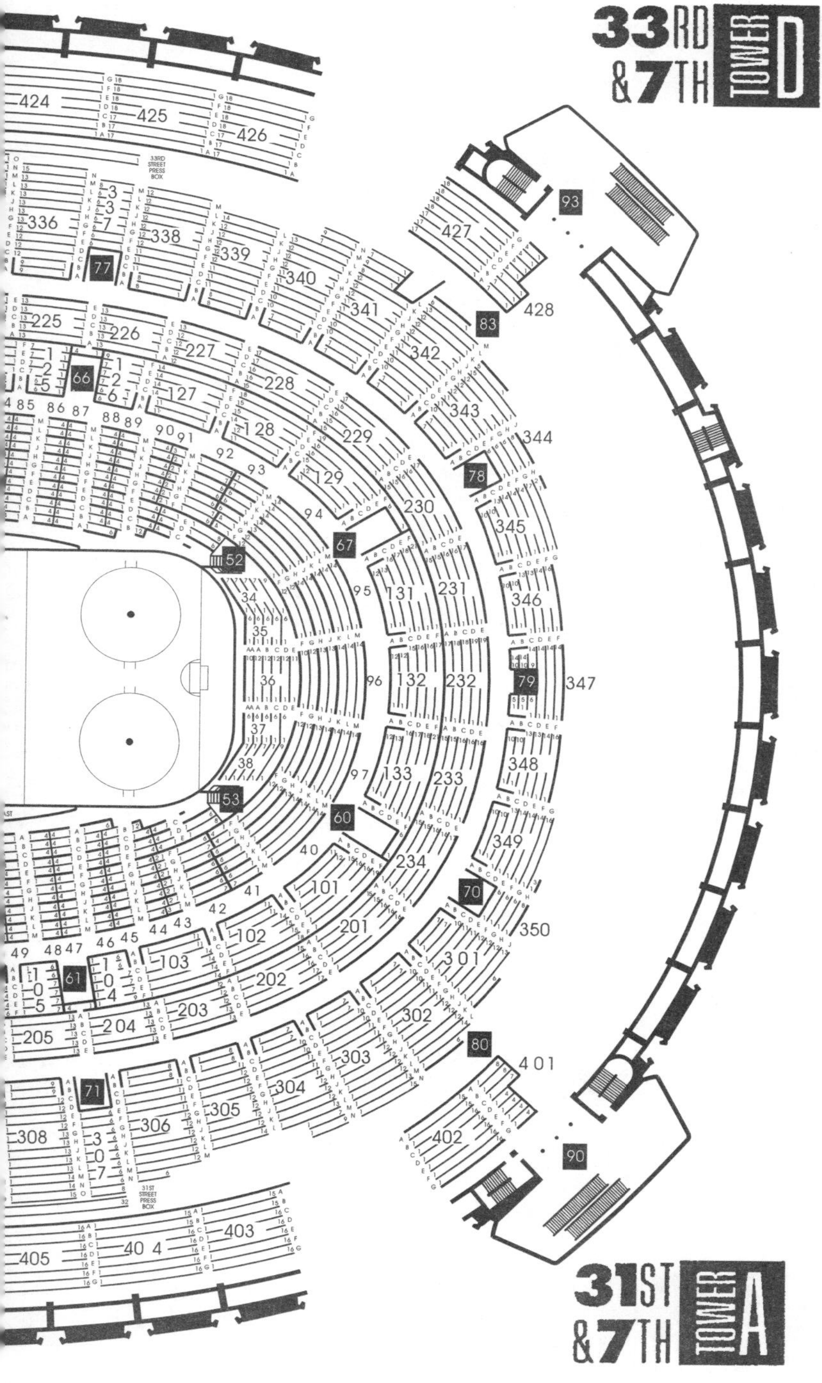
33RD
&7TH
TOWER
D
33RD STREET PRESS BOX
424
425
426
427
428
336
338
339
340
341
342
343
344
345
346
347
348
349
350
225
226
227
228
229
230
231
232
233
234
127
128
129
131
132
133
101
102
103
201
202
203
204
205
301
302
303
304
305
306
308
401
402
403
404
405
31ST STREET PRESS BOX
31ST
&7TH
TOWER
A

KNICKS BASKETBALL AT MADISON SQUARE GARDEN

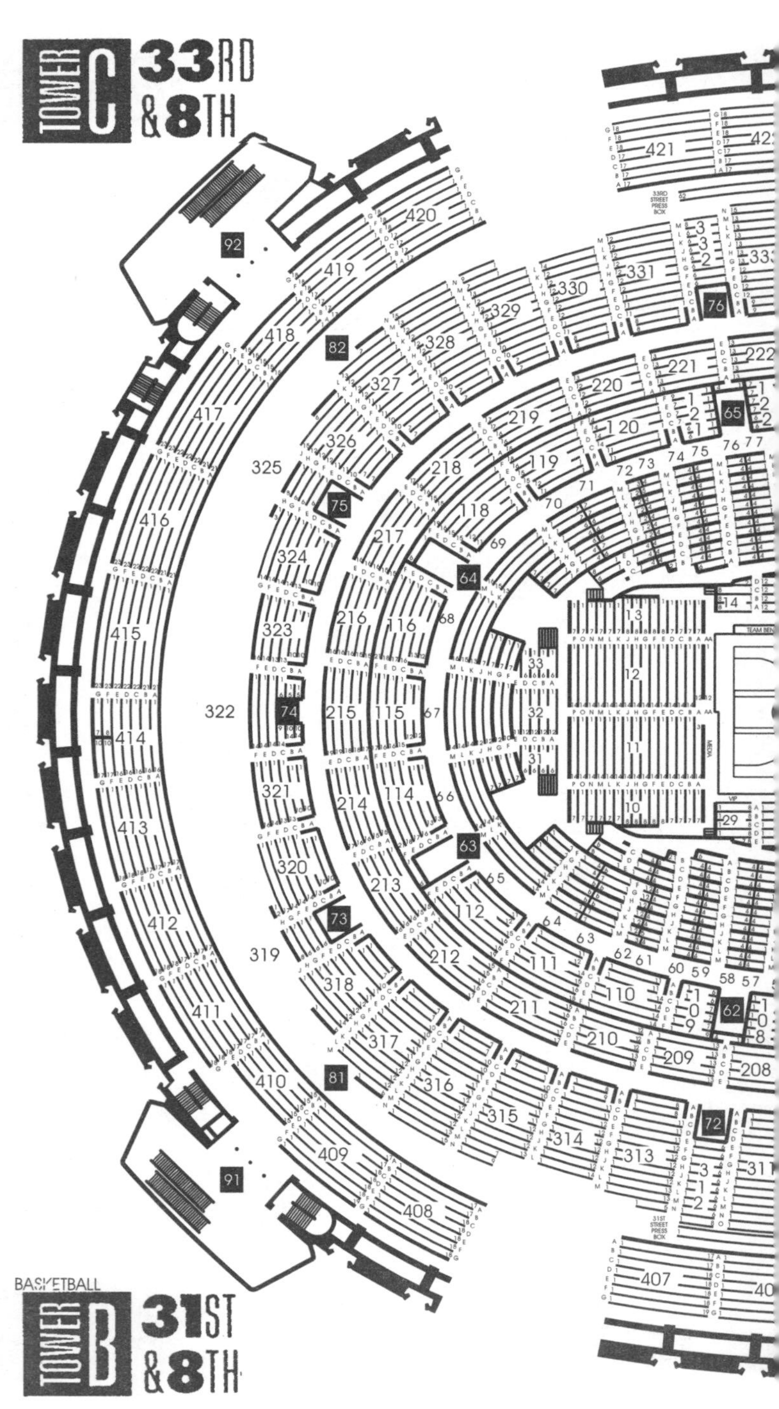

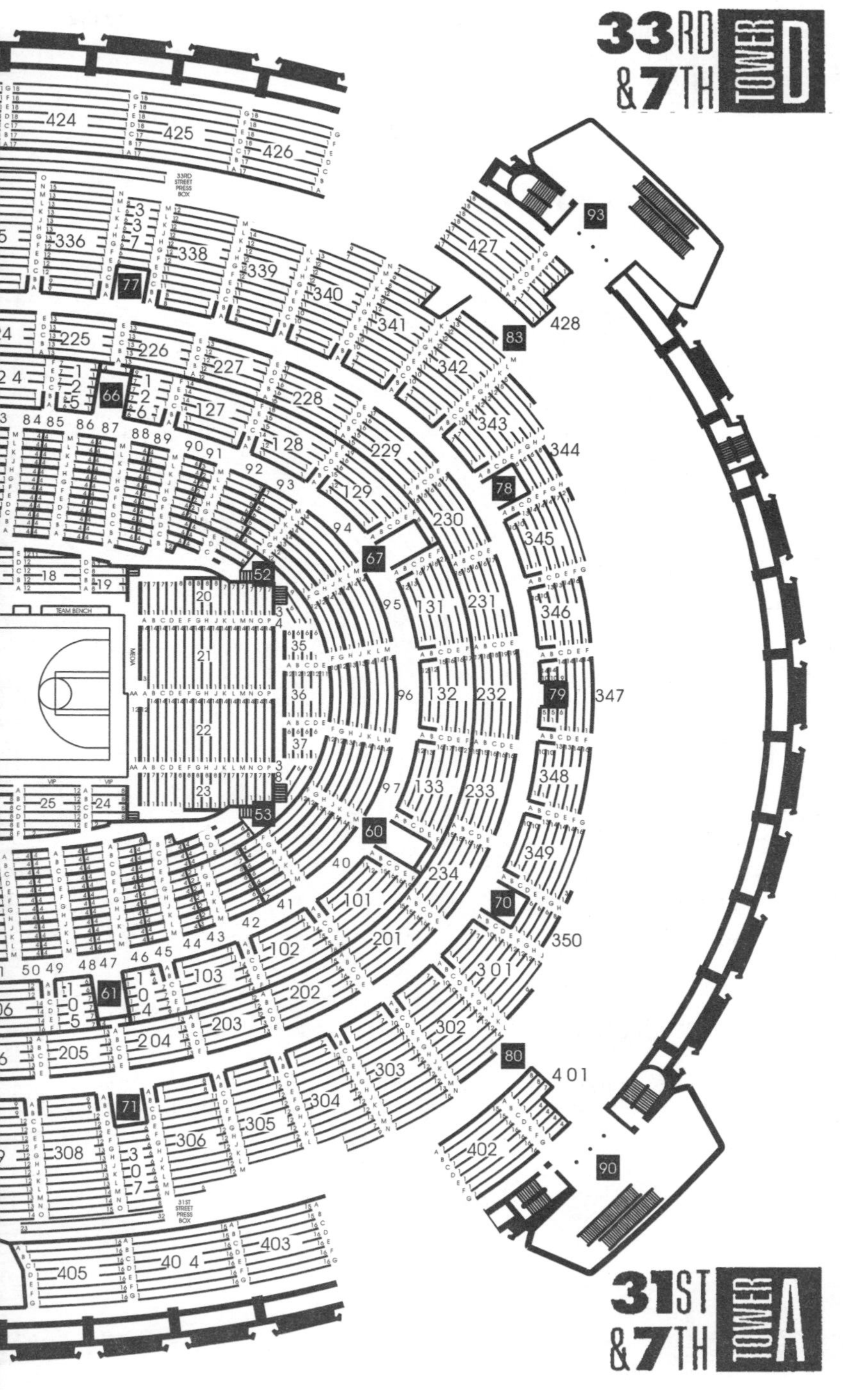
33RD & 7TH TOWER D
31ST & 7TH TOWER A
33RD STREET PRESS BOX
31ST STREET PRESS BOX
TEAM BENCH
MEDIA
VIP
VIP

BOXING IN STADIUM (Madison Square Garden)

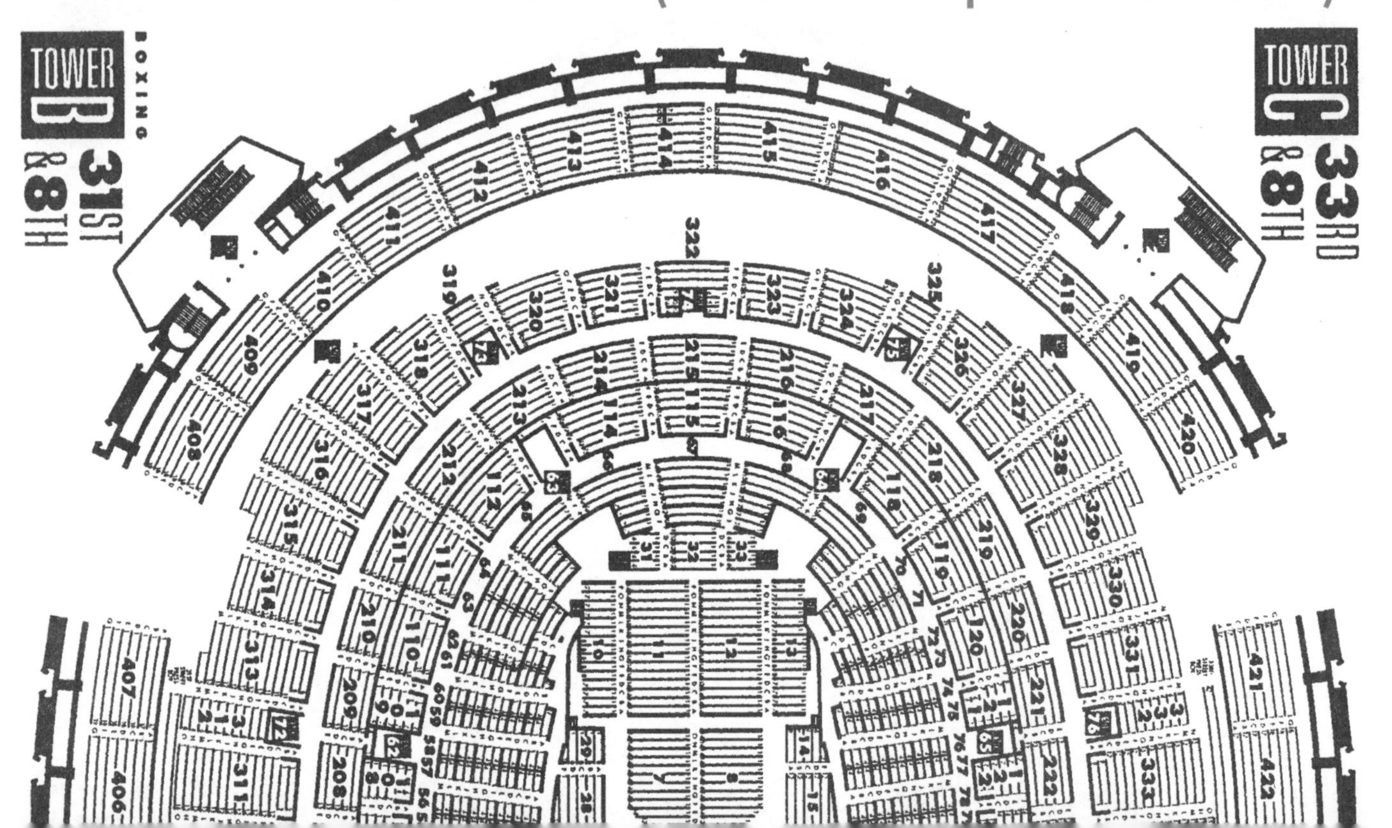

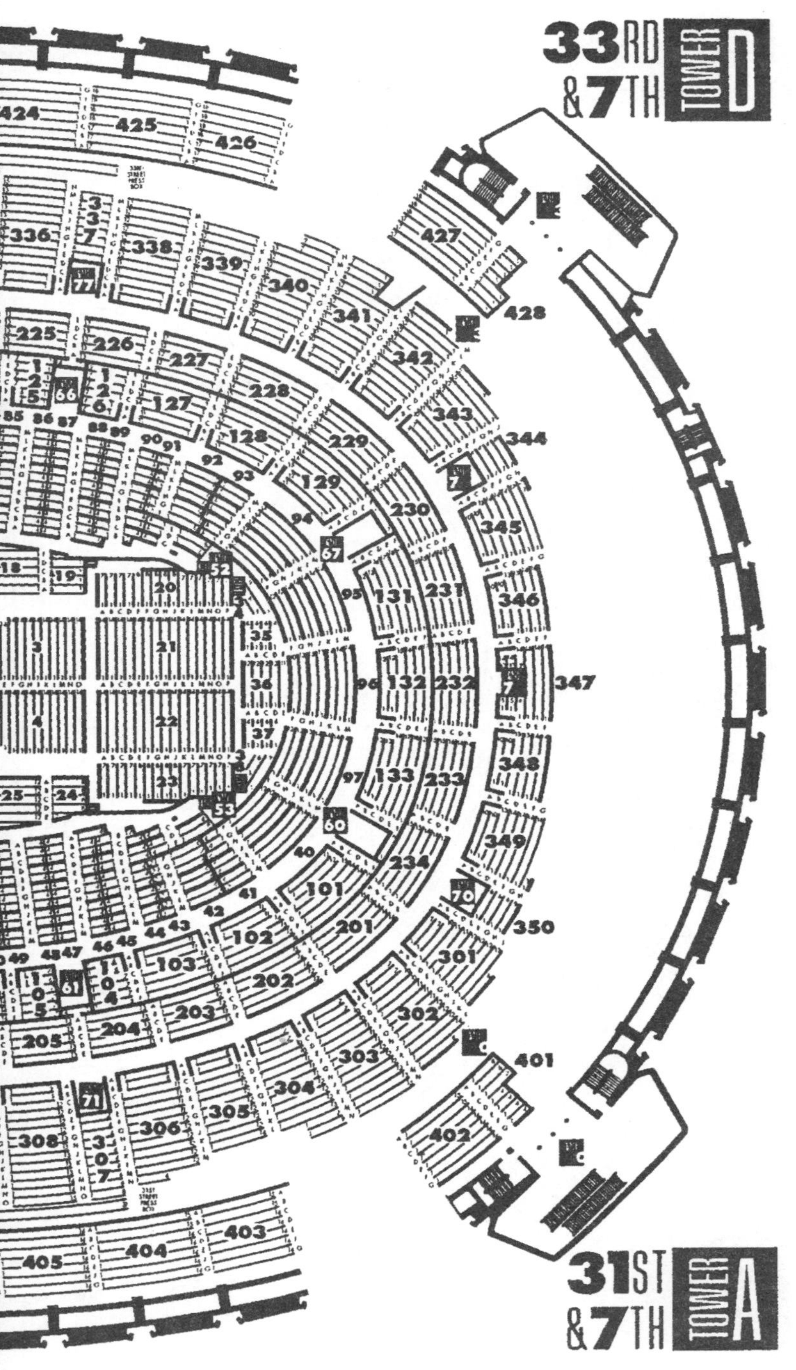
33RD
&7TH
TOWER D
31ST
&7TH
TOWER A

CONCERT IN STADIUM (Madison Square Garden)

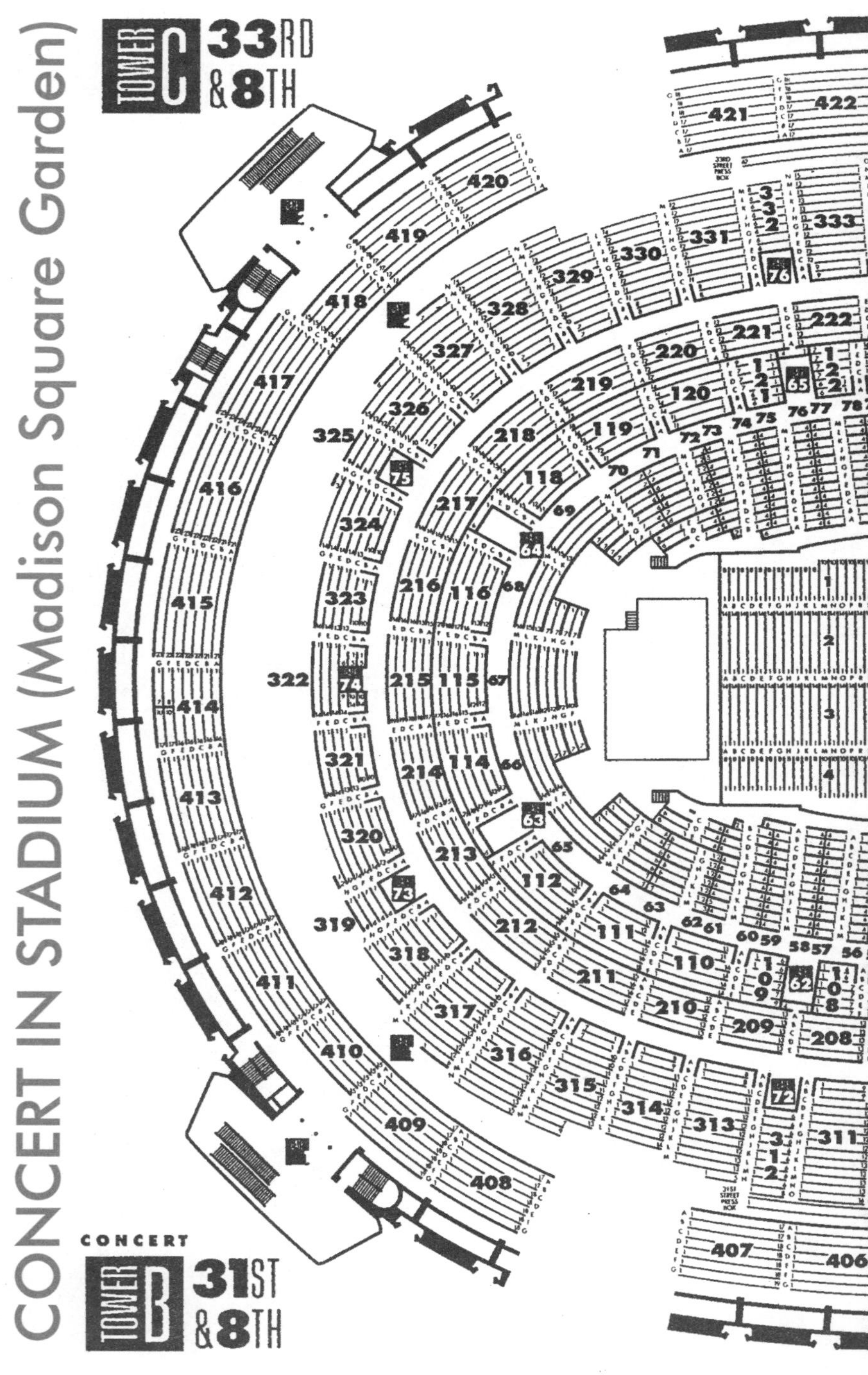

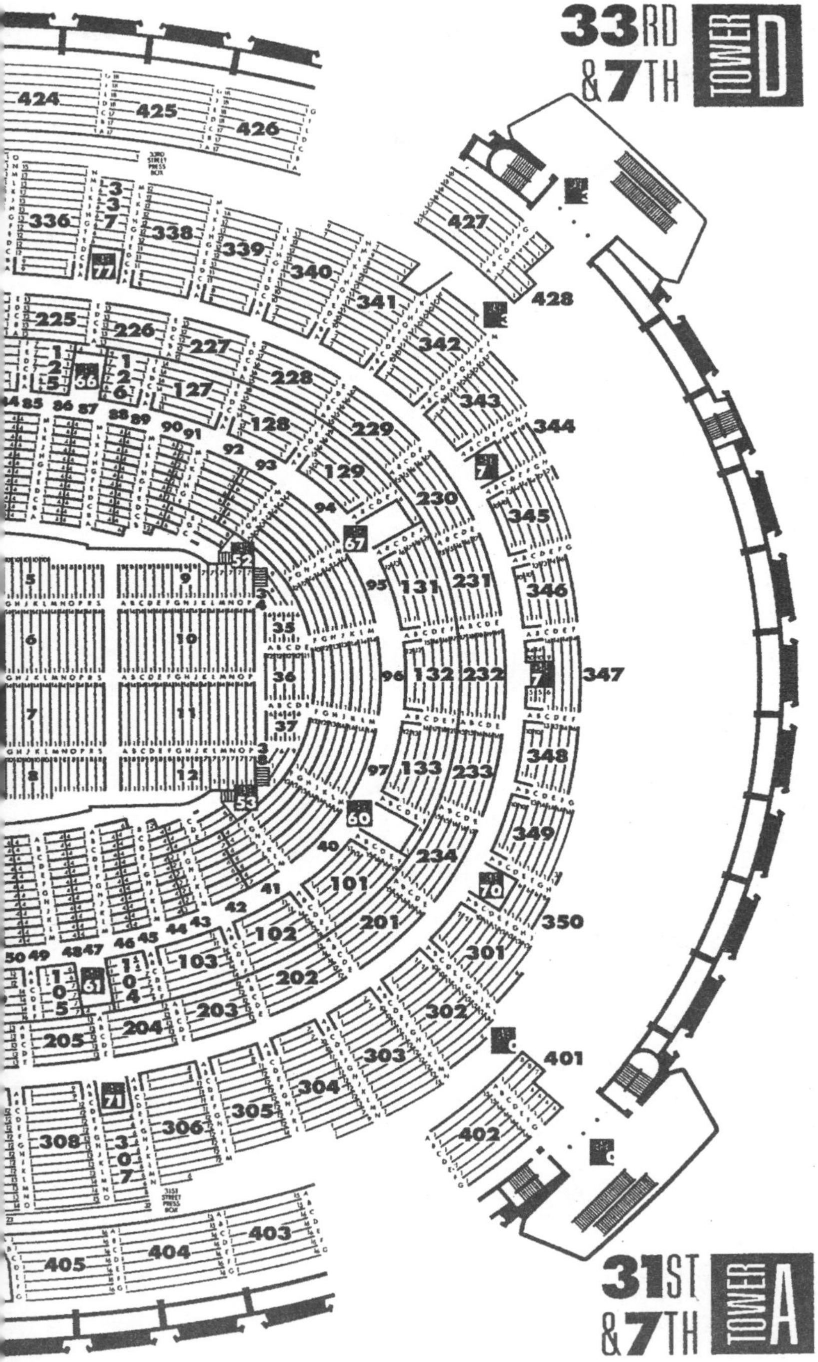
33RD
&7TH
TOWER
D
424
425
426
33RD STREET PRESS BOX
336
337
338
339
340
341
342
343
344
345
346
347
348
349
350
427
428
225
226
227
228
229
230
231
232
233
234
125
126
127
128
129
131
132
133
85
86
87
88
89
90
91
92
93
94
95
96
97
5
6
7
8
9
10
11
12
35
36
37
40
41
42
43
44
45
46
47
48
49
50
101
102
103
104
105
201
202
203
204
205
301
302
303
304
305
306
307
308
401
402
403
404
405
31ST STREET PRESS BOX
31ST
&7TH
TOWER
A

THEATRE at MADISON SQUARE GARDEN

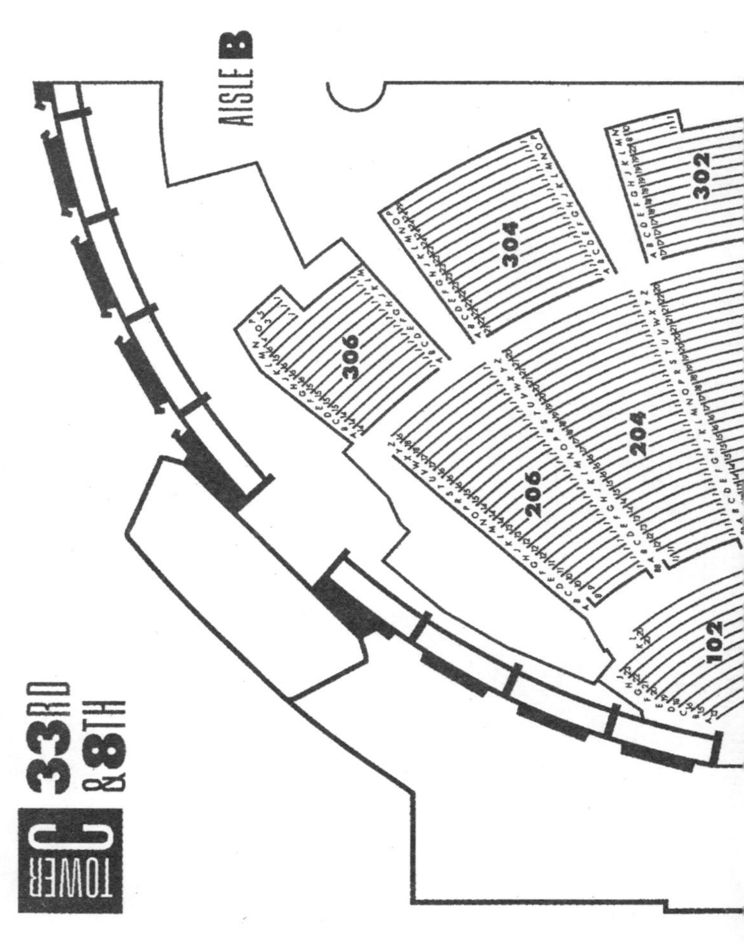

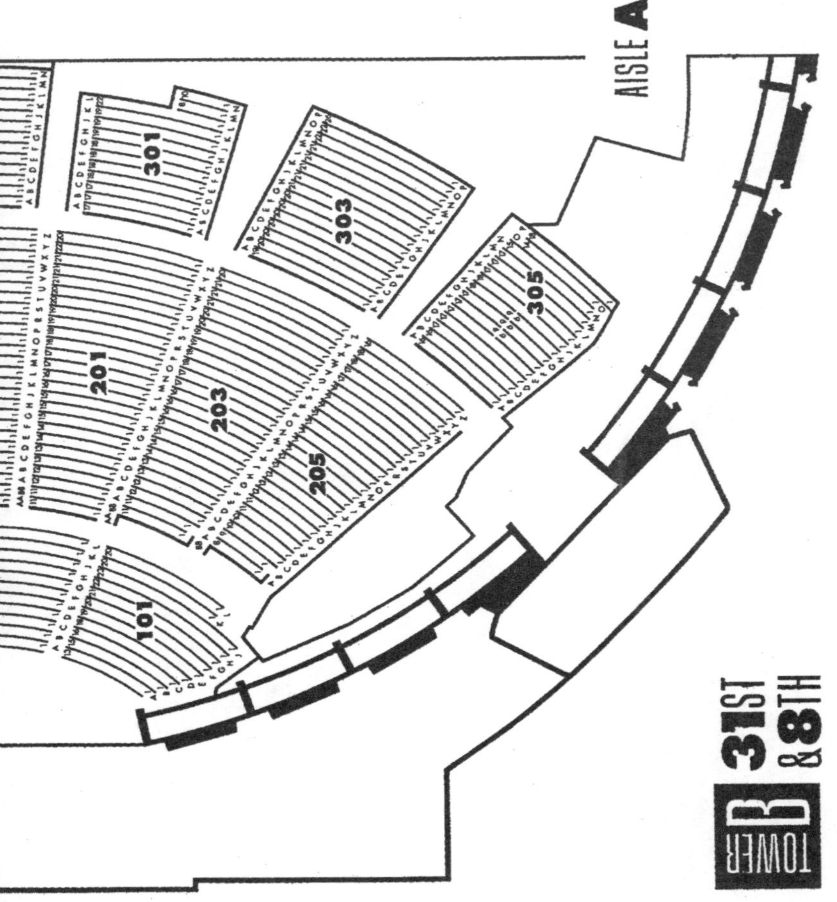
AISLE A
301
303
305
201
203
205
101
TOWER B
31ST
& 8TH

MEADOWLANDS SPORTS COMPLEX

50 Route 120, East Rutherford, NJ 07073

GIANTS STADIUM

GIANTS Season tickets (201) 935-8111

JETS Season tickets (516) 560-8200

METROSTARS Season tickets (800) 330-4666
http://www.metrostars.com

CONTINENTAL AIRLINES ARENA

NETS Season tickets (201) 935-8888

DEVILS Season tickets (201) 935-6050

RED DOGS

Season tickets (201) 507-1303
www.NJFOOTBALL.com

LOCATION:

East Rutherford, Bergen County, New Jersey. Giants Stadium is bounded by Route 120, the Continental Airlines Arena and the New Jersey Turnpike on the east, Route 3 on the south, Berry's Creek and Route 17 on the west and Paterson Plank Road on the north.

-4 miles west of Lincoln Tunnel
-8 miles from George Washington Bridge
-12 miles from Newark International Airport
-Accessible to New Jersey Turnpike, Interstate 80, Routes 3, 17, 120

TICKETMASTER (201) 507-8900
(609) 520-8383
(212) 307-7171
(516) 888-9000
(914) 454-3388
(203) 624-0033

PARKING
Handicap parking and accessibility
Parking on the premises

General information to order tickets for the handicapped or Group Sales (201) 935-3900

Nearby restaurants rated by **SEATS**

INSTANT REPLAY, 185 Rt. 17 South, East Rutherford (201) 935-5057
RIVER BARGE CAFÉ, End of Paterson Plank Rd.(East), Carlstadt (201) 531-0700
SONOMA GRILL, 64 Hoboken Road, E. Rutherford (201) 507-8989
STEVE'S SIZZLING STEAKS, Rt. 17 South, Carlstadt (201) 438-9677

GIANTS and JETS FOOTBALL at GIANTS STADIUM

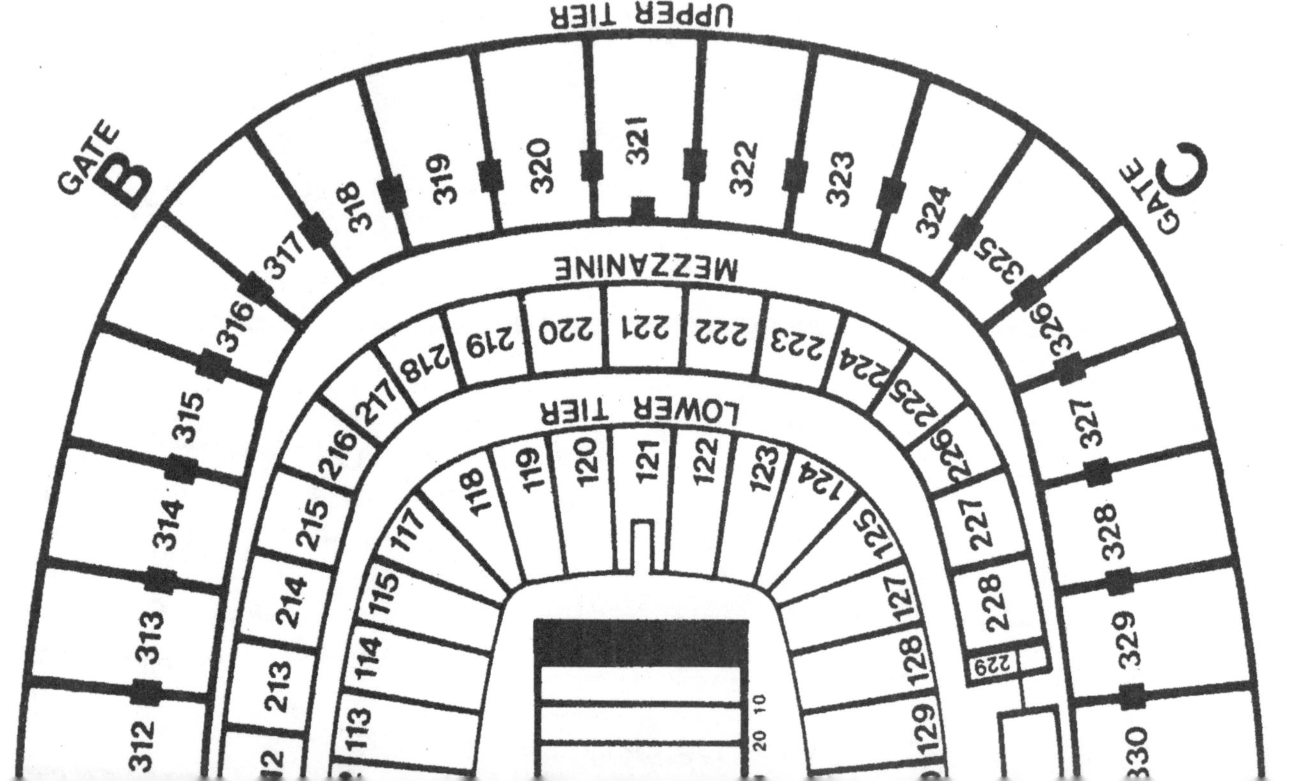

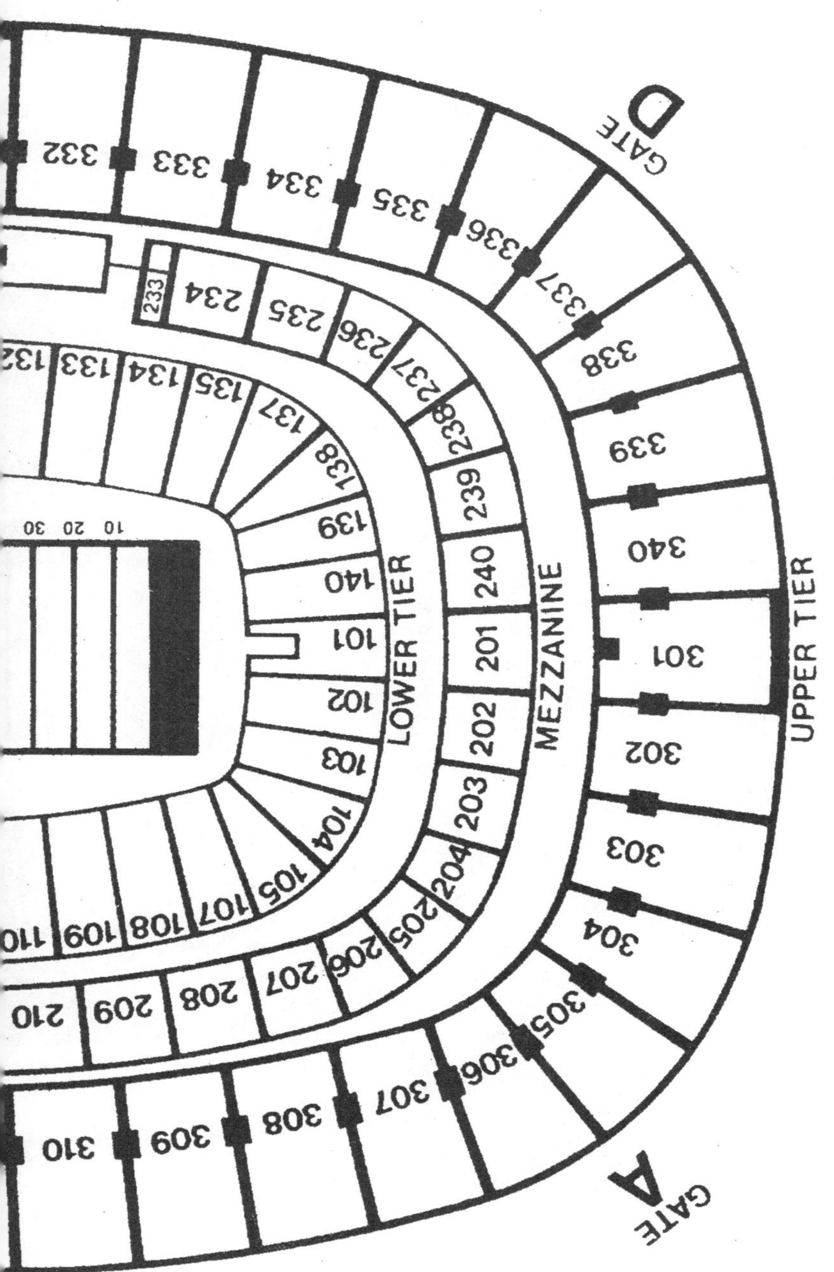
GATE D
GATE A
UPPER TIER
MEZZANINE
LOWER TIER
332
333
334
335
336
337
338
339
340
301
302
303
304
305
306
307
308
309
310
233
234
235
236
237
238
239
240
201
202
203
204
205
206
207
208
209
210
132
133
134
135
137
138
139
140
101
102
103
104
105
107
108
109
110
10 20 30

METROSTARS at GIANTS STADIUM

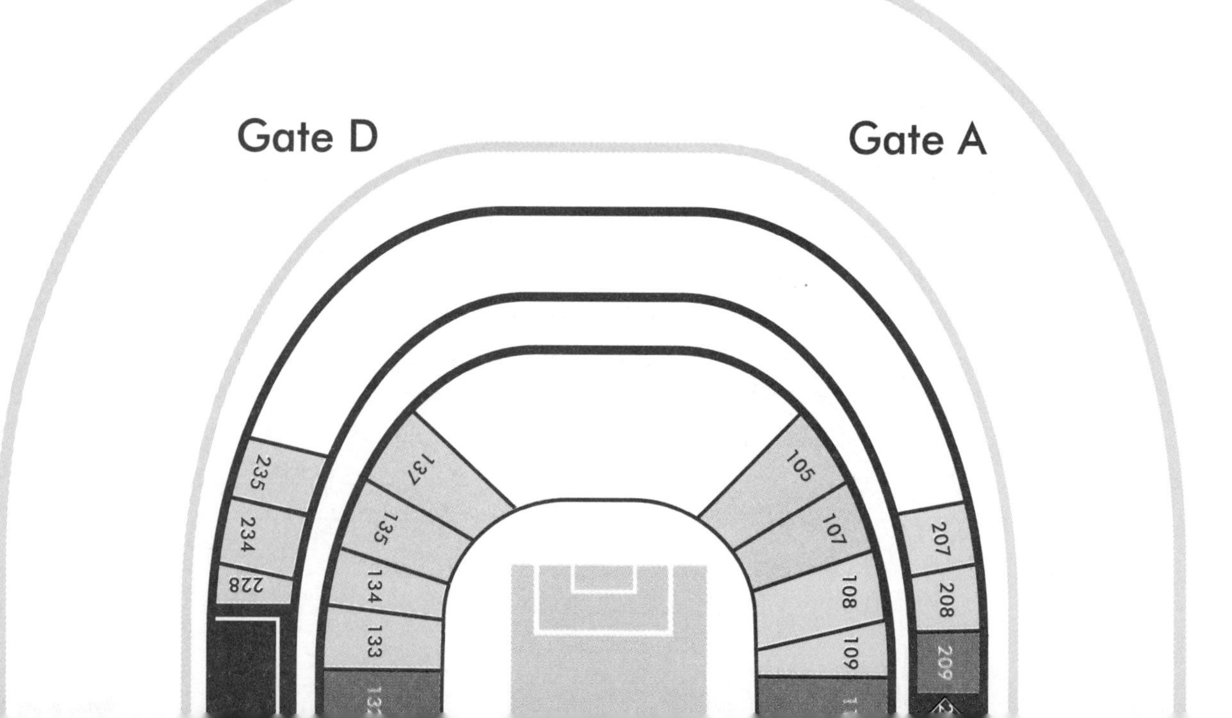

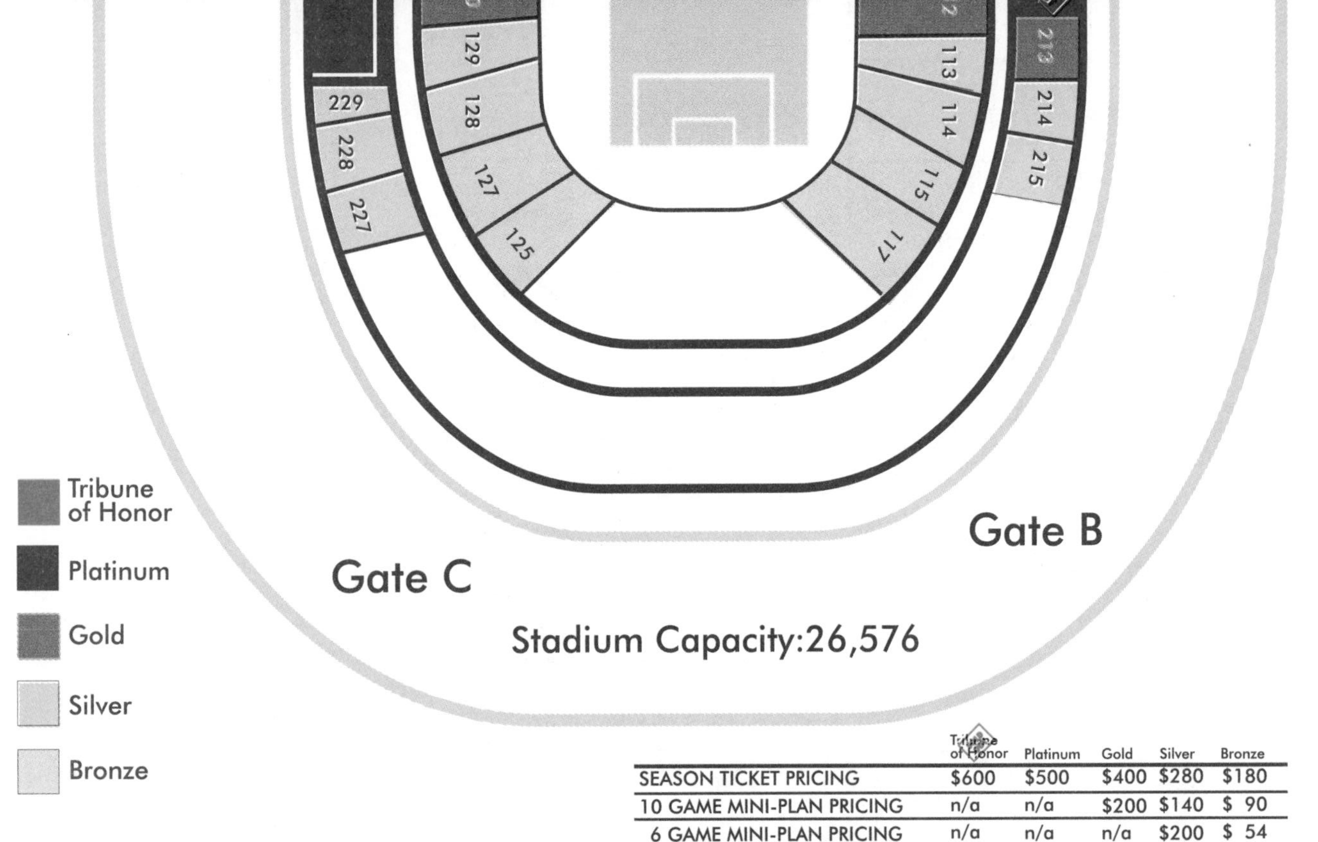

	Tribune of Honor	Platinum	Gold	Silver	Bronze
SEASON TICKET PRICING	$600	$500	$400	$280	$180
10 GAME MINI-PLAN PRICING	n/a	n/a	$200	$140	$ 90
6 GAME MINI-PLAN PRICING	n/a	n/a	n/a	$200	$ 54

NETS BASKETBALL at CONTINENTAL AIRLINES ARENA

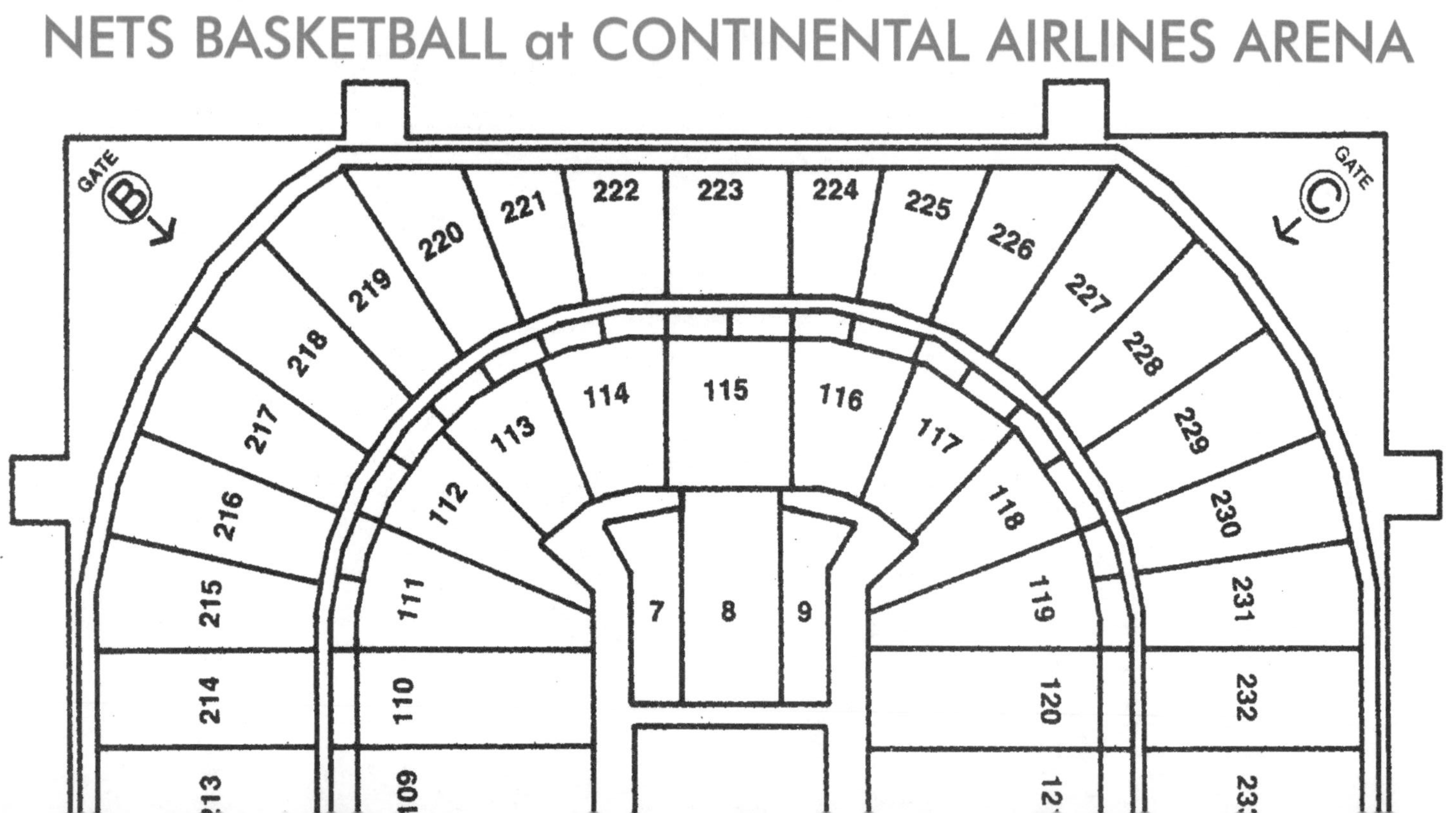

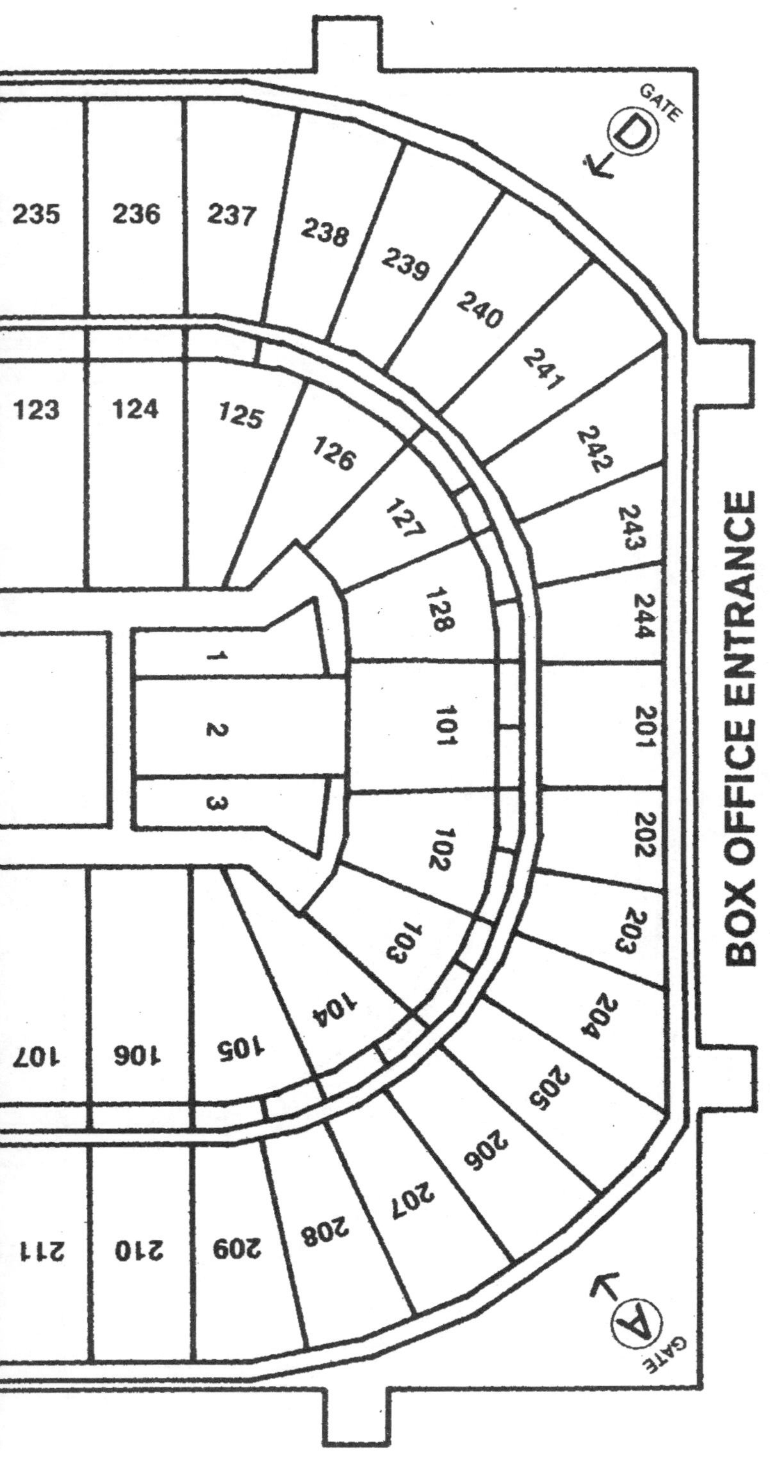
GATE D
235
236
237
238
239
240
241
242
243
244
123
124
125
126
127
128
1
2
3
101
102
103
104
105
106
107
201
202
203
204
205
206
207
208
209
210
211
BOX OFFICE ENTRANCE
GATE A

DEVILS HOCKEY at CONTINETAL AIRLINES ARENA

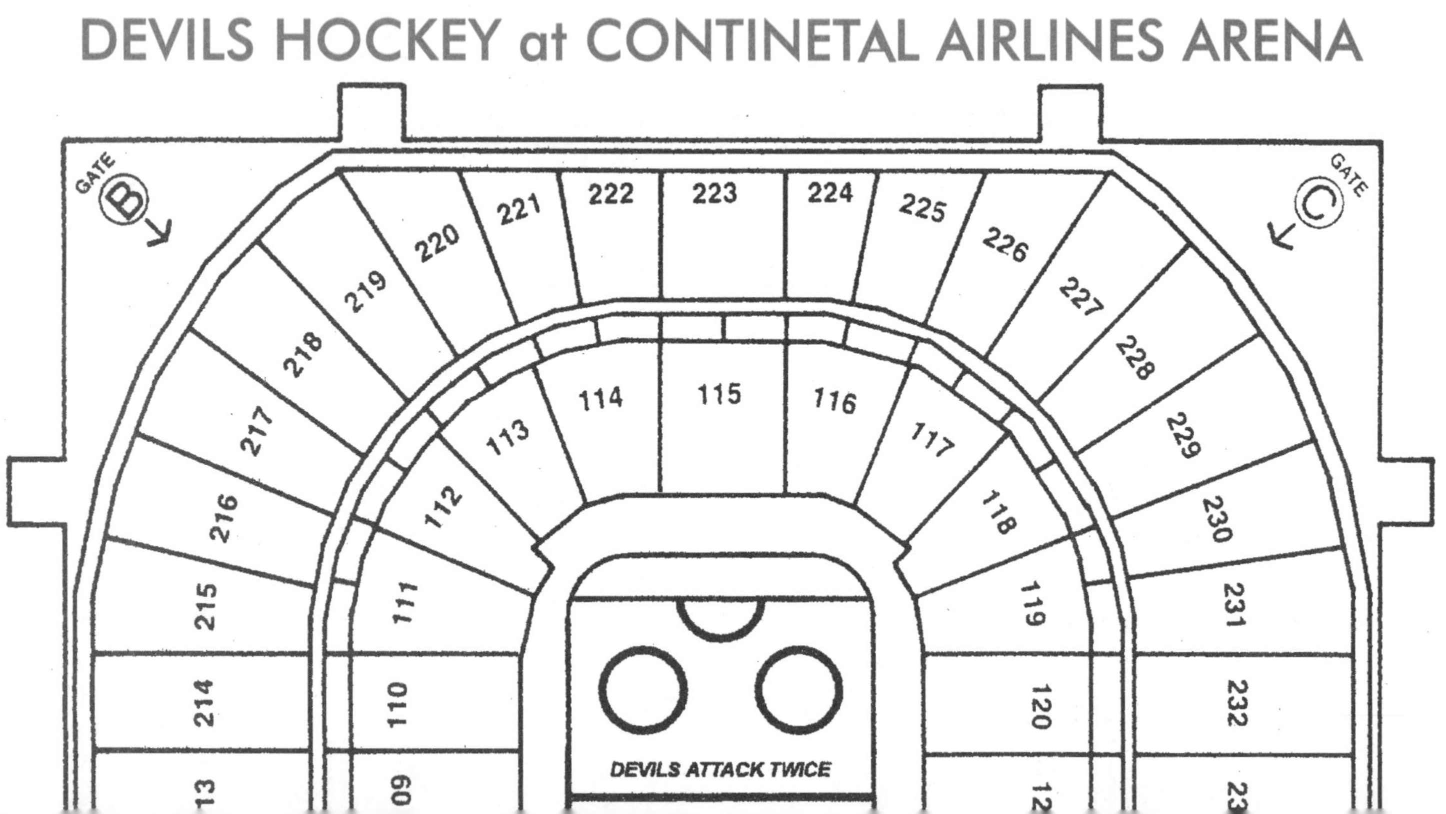

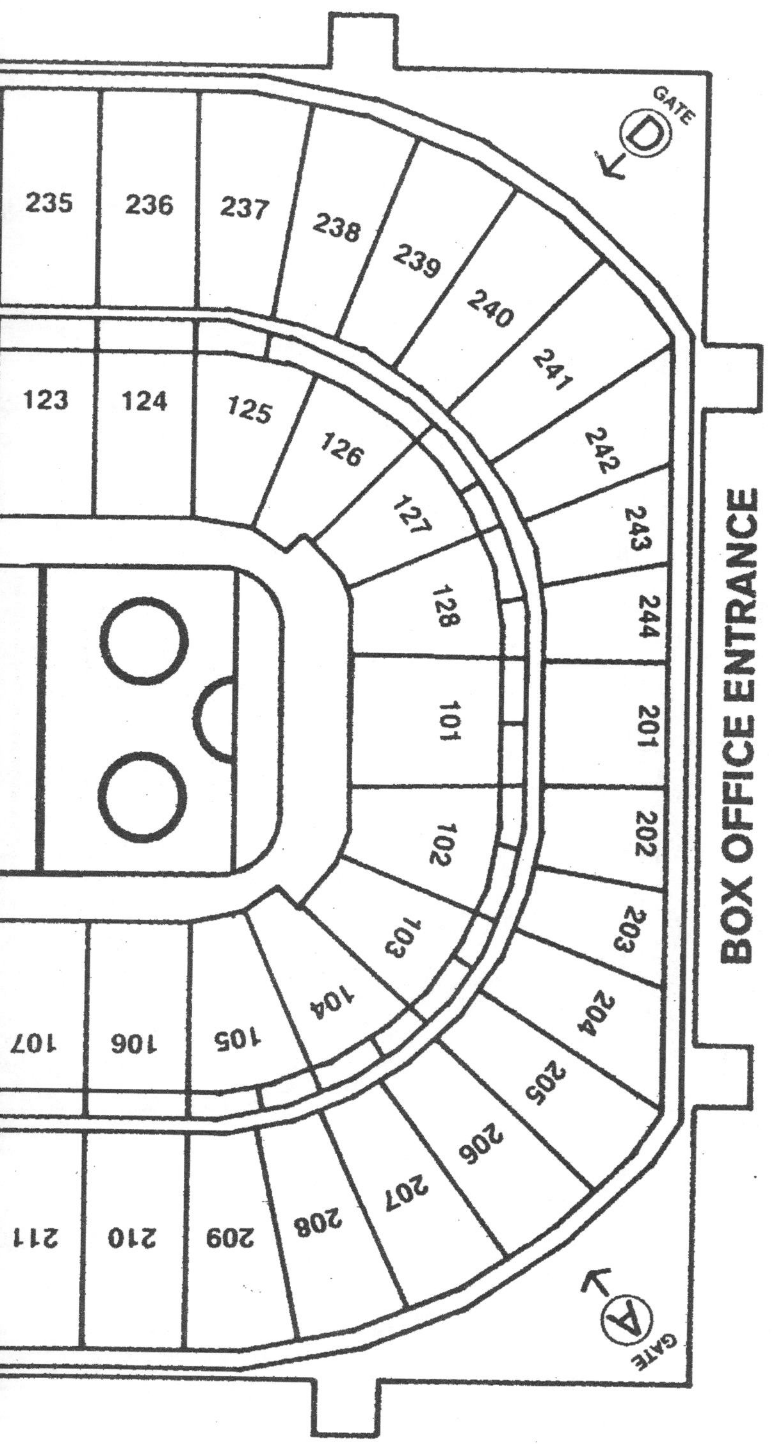
GATE
D
235
236
237
238
239
240
241
242
243
244
201
202
203
204
205
206
207
208
209
210
211
123
124
125
126
127
128
101
102
103
104
105
106
107
BOX OFFICE ENTRANCE
GATE
A

CONCERT at CONTINENTAL AIRLINES ARENA

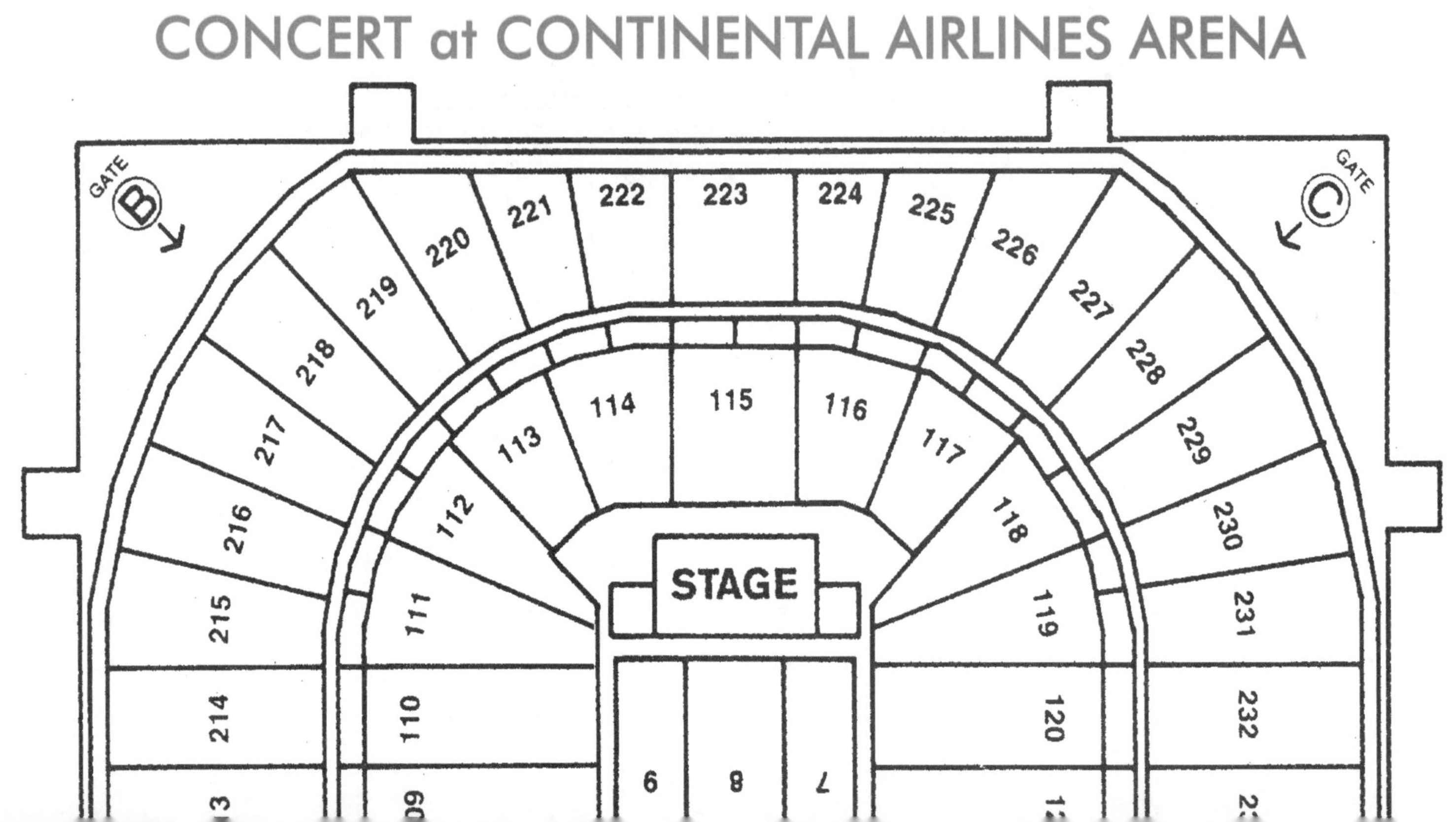

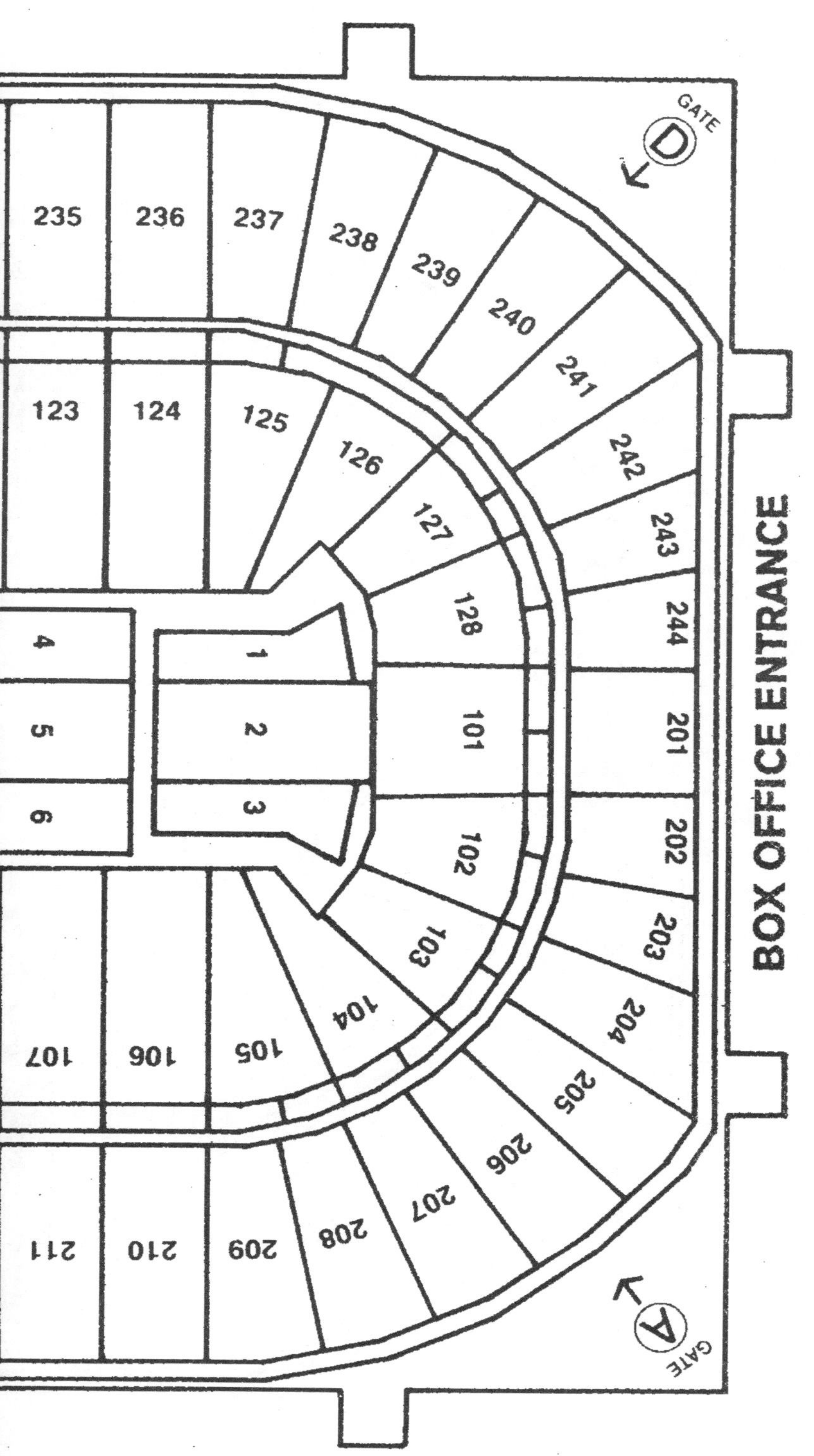
GATE
D
GATE
A
BOX OFFICE ENTRANCE
235
236
237
238
239
240
241
242
243
244
201
202
203
204
205
206
207
208
209
210
211
123
124
125
126
127
128
101
102
103
104
105
106
107
1
2
3
4
5
6

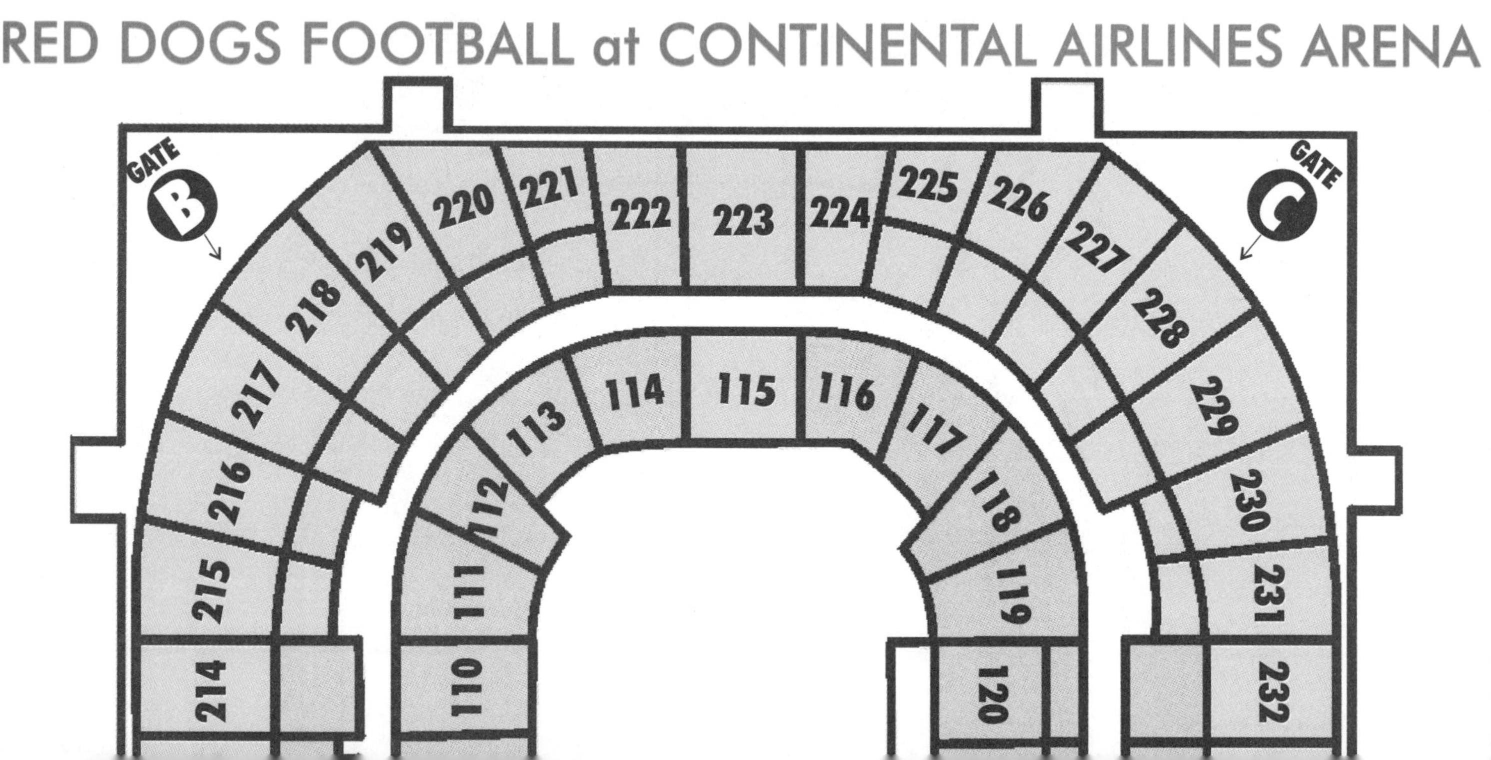
RED DOGS FOOTBALL at CONTINENTAL AIRLINES ARENA
GATE B
GATE C
214
215
216
217
218
219
220
221
222
223
224
225
226
227
228
229
230
231
232
110
111
112
113
114
115
116
117
118
119
120

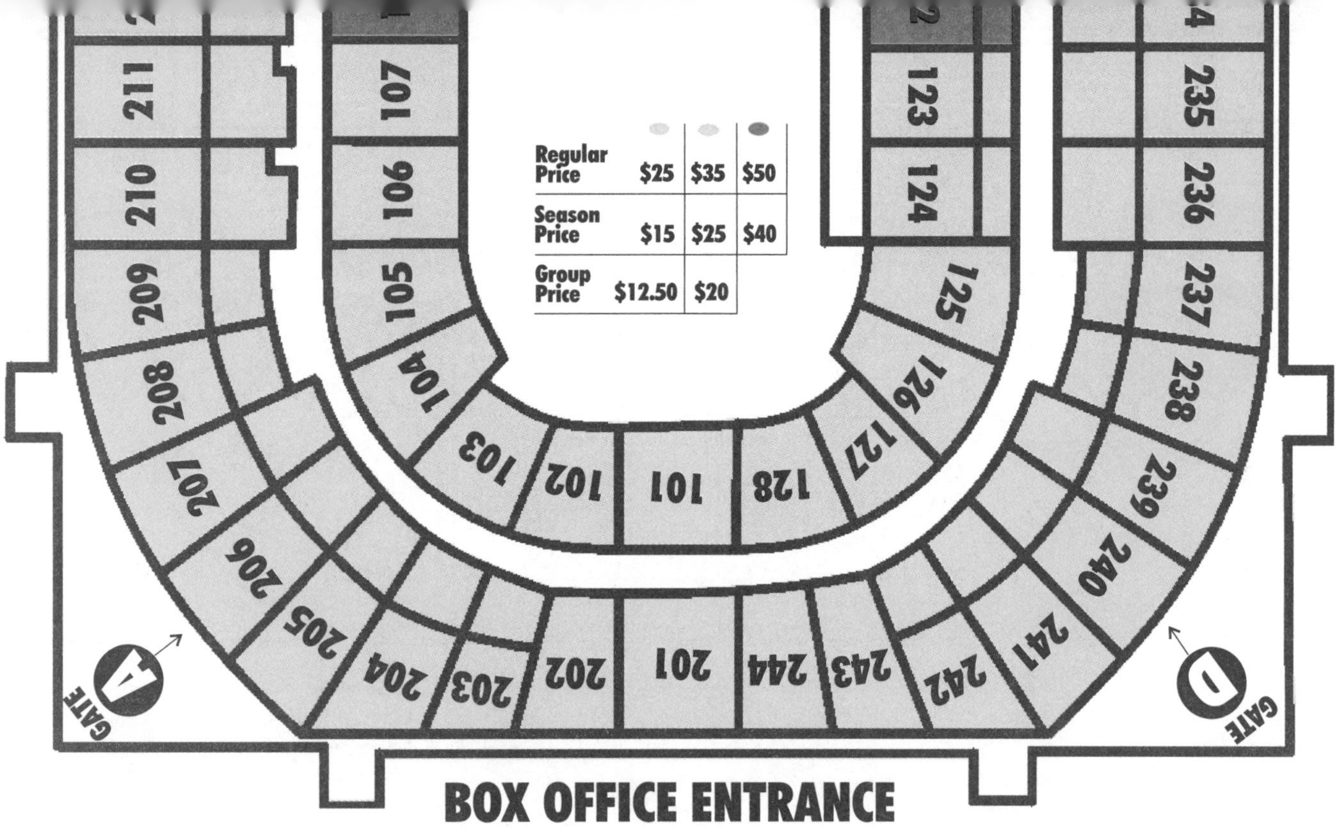
211
210
209
208
207
206
205
204
203
202
201
244
243
242
241
240
239
238
237
236
235
107
106
105
104
103
102
101
128
127
126
125
124
123
GATE A
GATE D
BOX OFFICE ENTRANCE

Regular Price	$25	$35	$50
Season Price	$15	$25	$40
Group Price	$12.50	$20	

NASSAU VETERANS MEMORIAL COLISEUM

1255 Hempstead Turnpike, Uniondale, NY 11553-1200

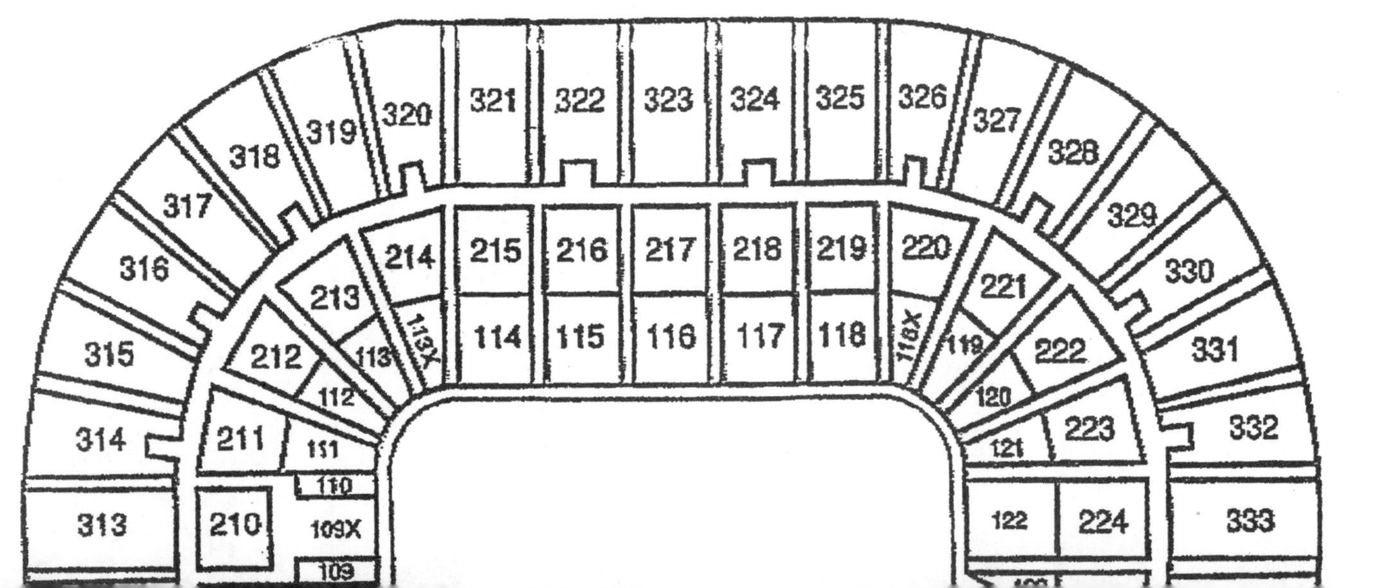

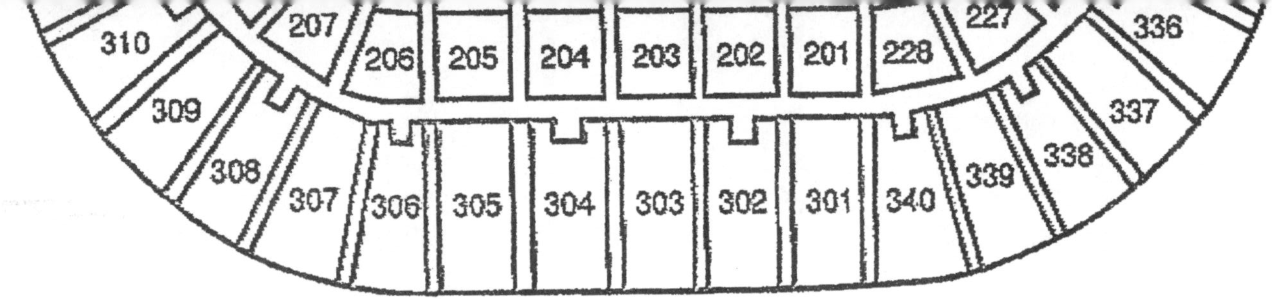

INFORMATION (516) 794-9300
TICKETMASTER (212) 307-7171
TICKETMASTER (516) 888-9000

DIRECTIONS:
Midtown tunnel to Long Island Expressway (495) East to Exit 38, Northern State Parkway to Exit 31A (Meadowbrook Parkway South) to exit M4, Nassau Coliseum

PARKING
On premises $4.75
♿ Handicap seating and parking

Nearby restaurants rated by
SEATS
MONTEREY JACK'S, (516) 538-7881
BOGARTS, 1002 HEMPSTEAD TURNPIKE (516) 486-9464

SHEA STADIUM

123-01 Roosevelt Avenue, Flushing, NY 11368

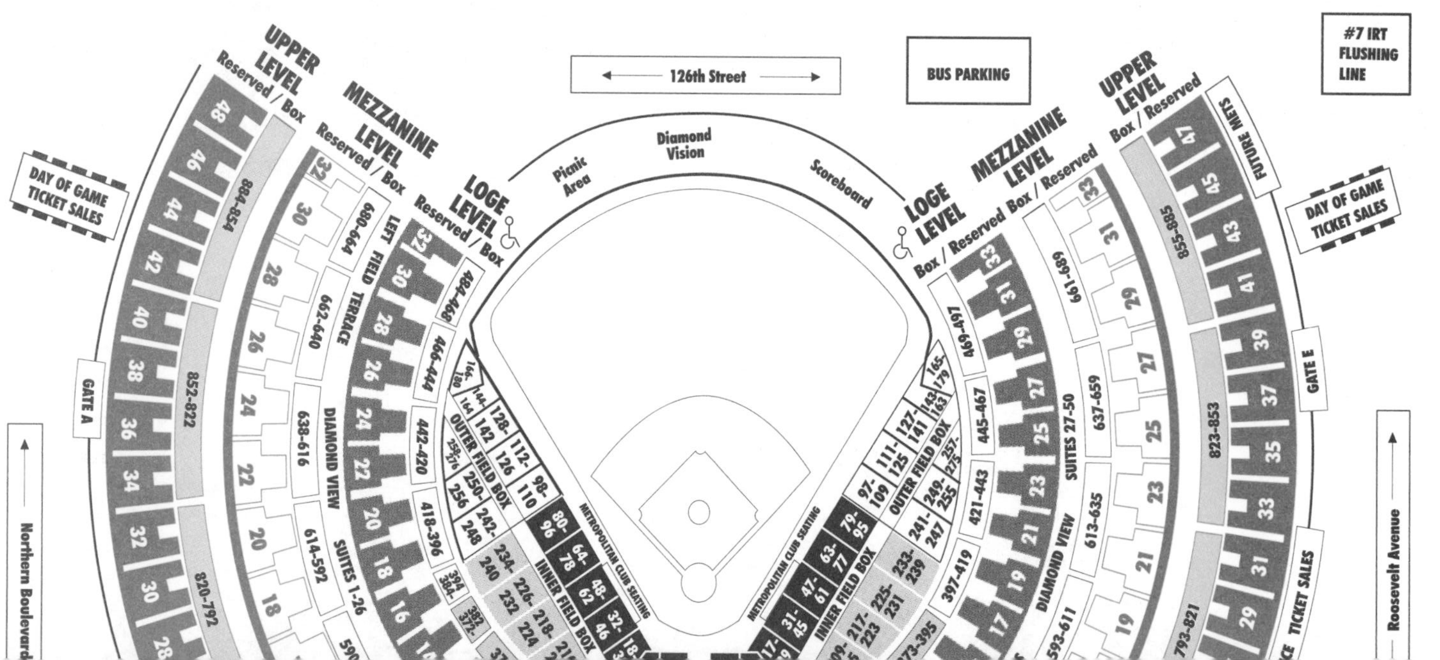

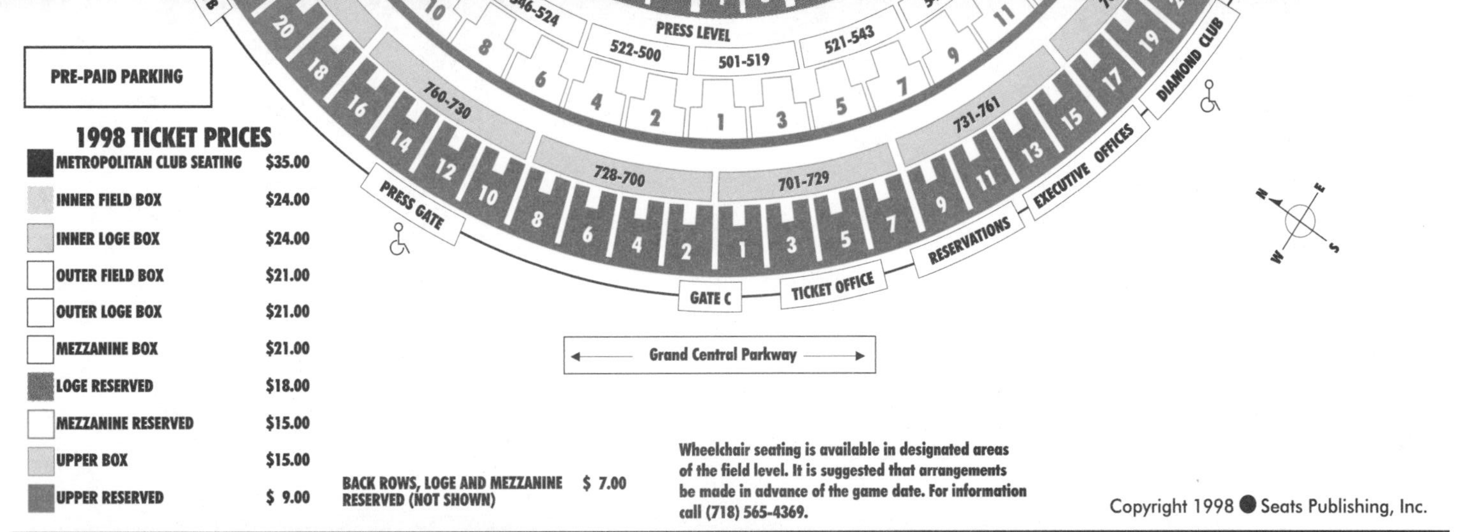

1998 TICKET PRICES

METROPOLITAN CLUB SEATING	$35.00
INNER FIELD BOX	$24.00
INNER LOGE BOX	$24.00
OUTER FIELD BOX	$21.00
OUTER LOGE BOX	$21.00
MEZZANINE BOX	$21.00
LOGE RESERVED	$18.00
MEZZANINE RESERVED	$15.00
UPPER BOX	$15.00
UPPER RESERVED	$ 9.00
BACK ROWS, LOGE AND MEZZANINE RESERVED (NOT SHOWN)	$ 7.00

Wheelchair seating is available in designated areas of the field level. It is suggested that arrangements be made in advance of the game date. For information call (718) 565-4369.

TICKETS (718) 507-8499

PARKING
Free at the commuter lot.
SUBWAYS
7 to Willets Point/Shea Stadium

SEATS

DIRECTIONS
Triborough Bridge to Grand Central Parkway, or Queens Midtown Tunnel to Long Island Expressway to either Van Wyck Expressway (N) or Grand Central Parkway (W) to Shea Stadium

Tickets can be purchased at METS CLUBHOUSE SHOPS
Manhattan: 575 Fifth Ave./47th St. (212) 986-4887
Long Island: Roosevelt Field Mall/Garden City (718) 507-8499
New Jersey: Menlo Park Mall/Edison (908) 548-1955

YANKEE STADIUM

161st Street & River Avenue, Bronx, NY 10451

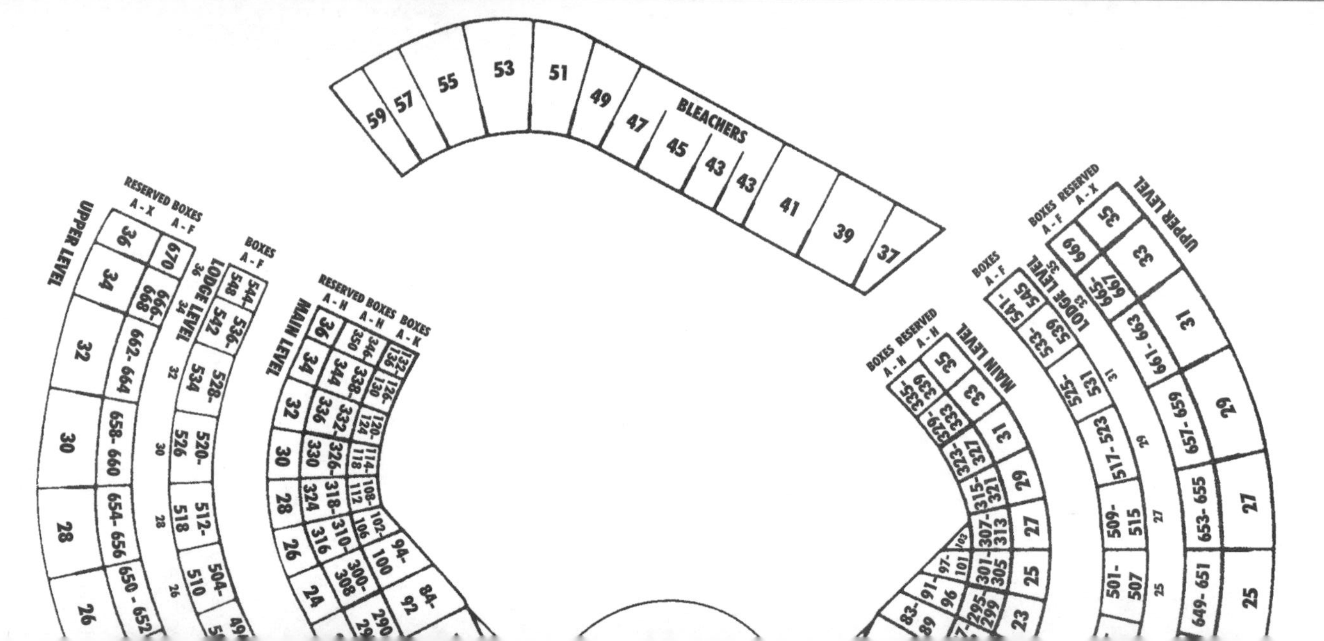

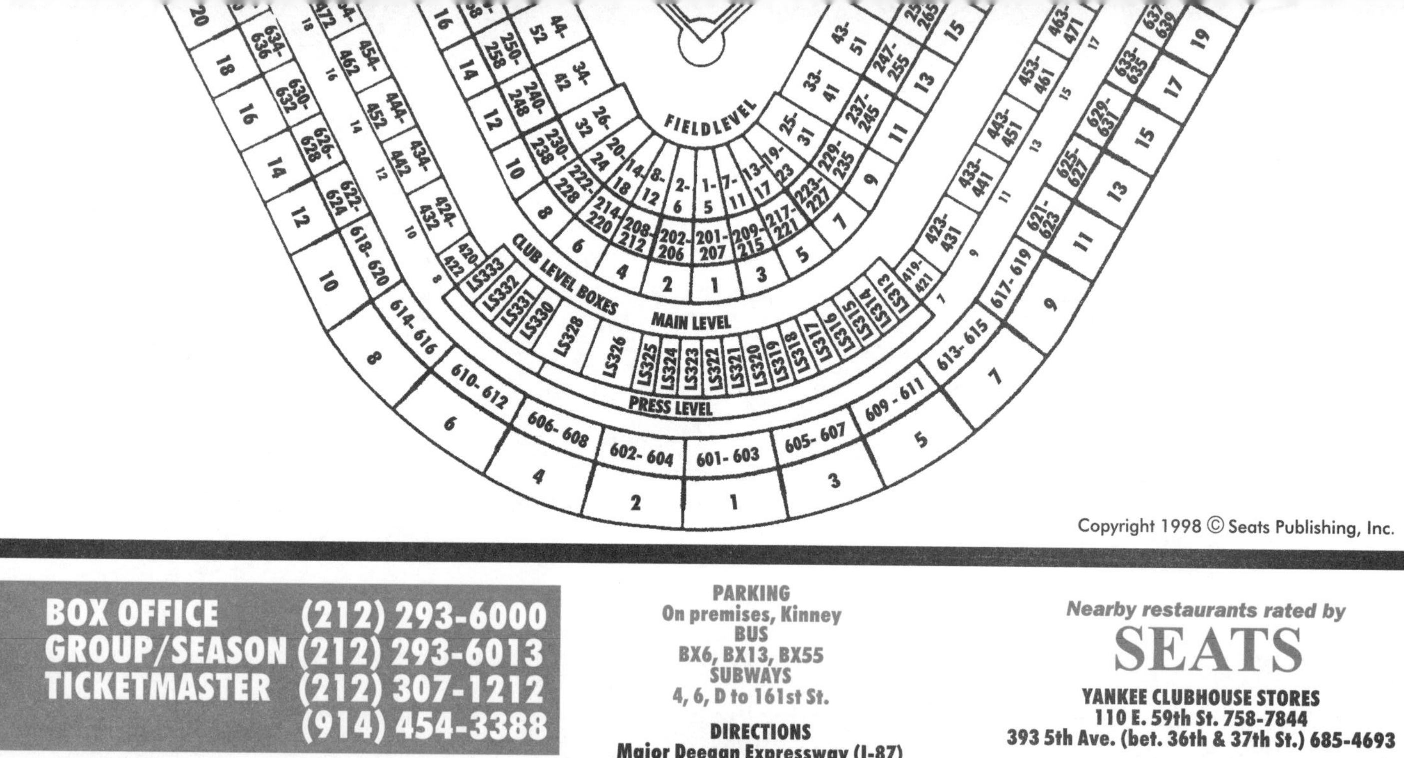

BOX OFFICE	**(212) 293-6000**
GROUP/SEASON	**(212) 293-6013**
TICKETMASTER	**(212) 307-1212**
	(914) 454-3388

PARKING
On premises, Kinney
BUS
BX6, BX13, BX55
SUBWAYS
4, 6, D to 161st St.

DIRECTIONS
Major Deegan Expressway (I-87)
Northbound use exits 149-155th St.
Southbound use exit at 161st St.

Nearby restaurants rated by
SEATS

YANKEE CLUBHOUSE STORES
110 E. 59th St. 758-7844
393 5th Ave. (bet. 36th & 37th St.) 685-4693

BARDAVON 1869 OPERA HOUSE

35 Market Street, Poughkeepsie, NY 12601

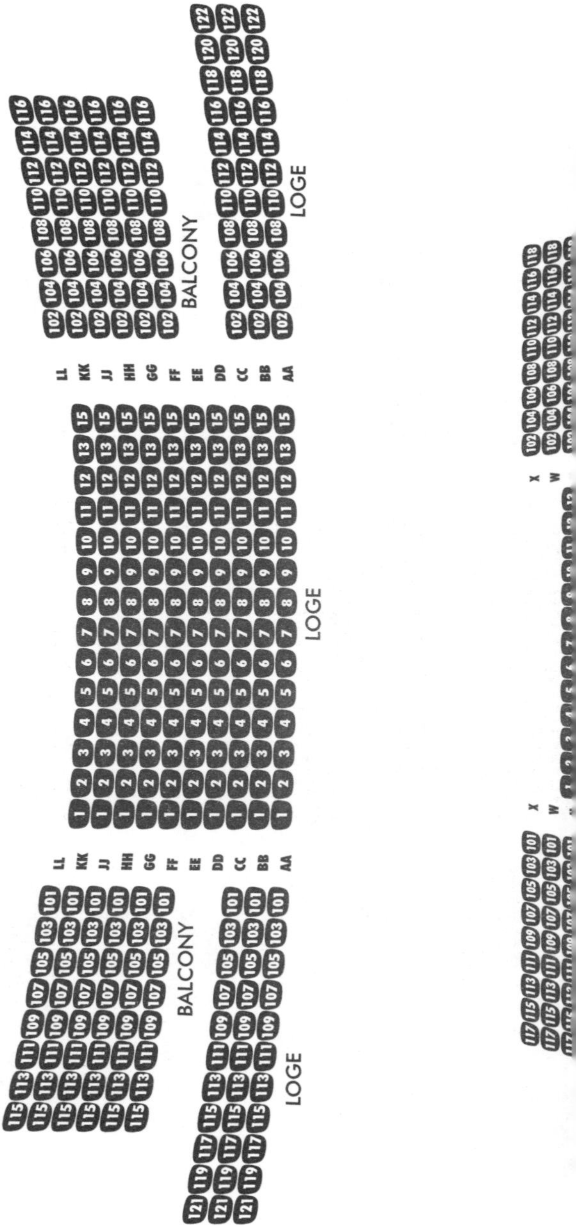

BALCONY

LOGE

LOGE

BALCONY

LOGE

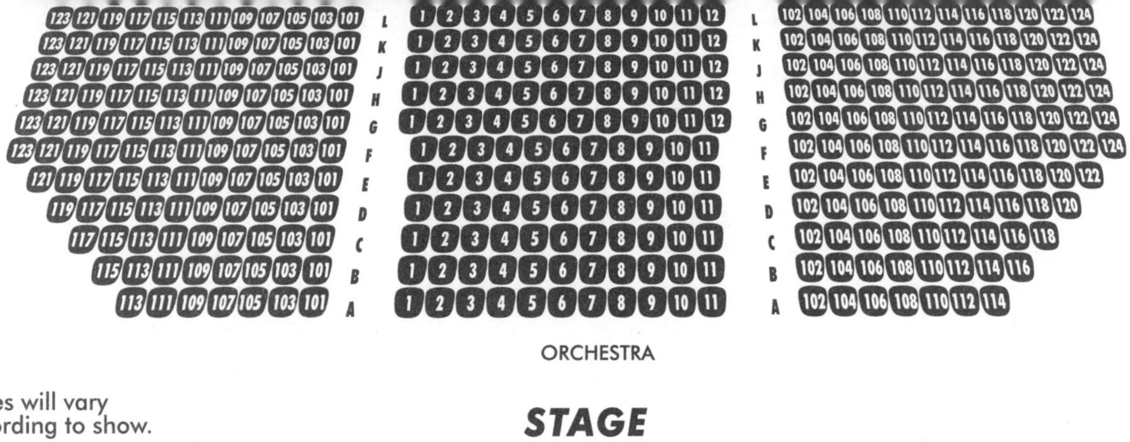

Row	Left	Row	Center	Row	Right
L	123 121 119 117 115 113 111 109 107 105 103 101	L	1 2 3 4 5 6 7 8 9 10 11 12	L	102 104 106 108 110 112 114 116 118 120 122 124
K	123 121 119 117 115 113 111 109 107 105 103 101	K	1 2 3 4 5 6 7 8 9 10 11 12	K	102 104 106 108 110 112 114 116 118 120 122 124
J	123 121 119 117 115 113 111 109 107 105 103 101	J	1 2 3 4 5 6 7 8 9 10 11 12	J	102 104 106 108 110 112 114 116 118 120 122 124
H	123 121 119 117 115 113 111 109 107 105 103 101	H	1 2 3 4 5 6 7 8 9 10 11 12	H	102 104 106 108 110 112 114 116 118 120 122 124
G	123 121 119 117 115 113 111 109 107 105 103 101	G	1 2 3 4 5 6 7 8 9 10 11 12	G	102 104 106 108 110 112 114 116 118 120 122 124
F	123 121 119 117 115 113 111 109 107 105 103 101	F	1 2 3 4 5 6 7 8 9 10 11	F	102 104 106 108 110 112 114 116 118 120 122 124
E	121 119 117 115 113 111 109 107 105 103 101	E	1 2 3 4 5 6 7 8 9 10 11	E	102 104 106 108 110 112 114 116 118 120 122
D	119 117 115 113 111 109 107 105 103 101	D	1 2 3 4 5 6 7 8 9 10 11	D	102 104 106 108 110 112 114 116 118 120
C	117 115 113 111 109 107 105 103 101	C	1 2 3 4 5 6 7 8 9 10 11	C	102 104 106 108 110 112 114 116 118
B	115 113 111 109 107 105 103 101	B	1 2 3 4 5 6 7 8 9 10 11	B	102 104 106 108 110 112 114 116
A	113 111 109 107 105 103 101	A	1 2 3 4 5 6 7 8 9 10 11	A	102 104 106 108 110 112 114

ORCHESTRA

Prices will vary according to show.

STAGE

BOX OFFICE (914) 473-2072

DIRECTIONS:
Taconic Pkwy to Poughkeepsie. Theatre is located in center of downtown Poughkeepsie. N.Y. State Thruway to New Paltz exit. Follow signs to Mid-Hudson Bridge. Over bridge to Market St. From New England take Rte 44-55 into city.

PARKING
Behind theatre at Cannon St. is a public parking lot

TRAIN
Metro North about 1 hr. 45 min. from Grand Central Station, N.Y.
1 hr. 20 min. from Albany
1hr. 30 min. from Penn Station
5 minute taxi ride to theatre

Nearby restaurants rated by
SEATS

MOHONK MOUNTAIN HOUSE, 914-256-2056
MARINER'S HARBOR INN, 914-876-1331
JIMMY CAGNEY'S STAGE SHOP RESTAURANT, 914-868-1042
MILANESE ITALIAN RESTAURANT, 914-471-9533
RIVER STATION, 914-452-9207

Poughkeepsie is also home to the Culinary Arts Institue and its graduates have made the area a culinary delight. Call the CIA at 914-471-6608 well in advance for reservations in one of their 5 restaurants.

EMELIN THEATRE

Library Lane, Mamaroneck, New York 10543

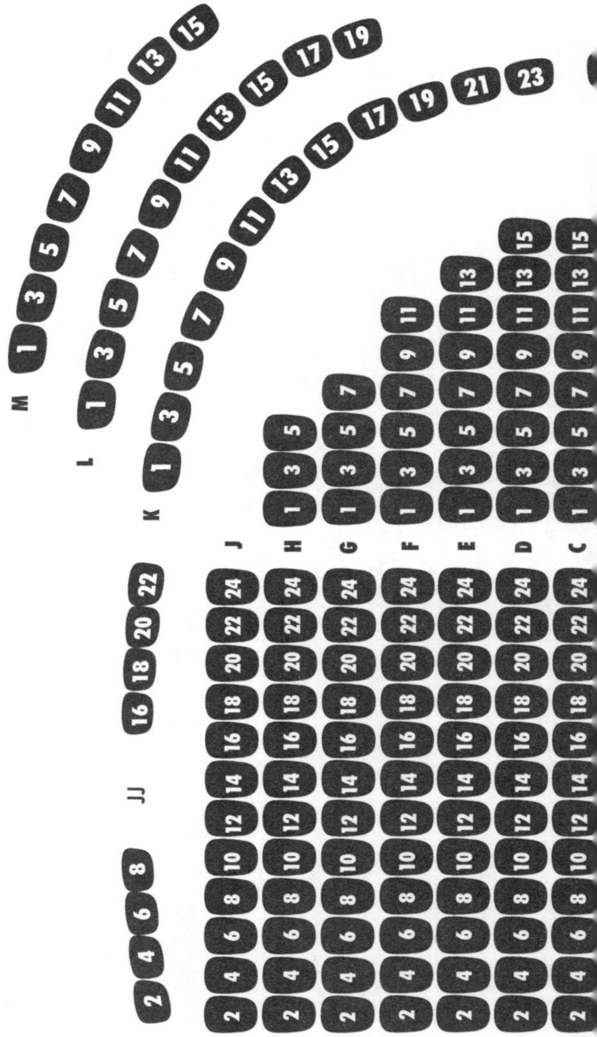

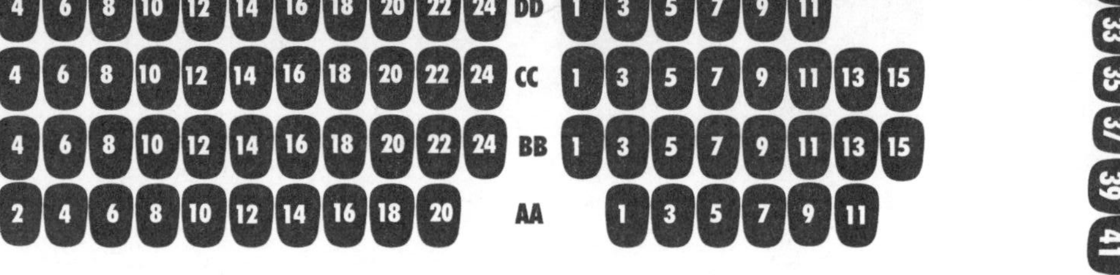

All Seats One Price

THEATRE (914) 698-0098

Directions:

From Hutchinson River Pkwy - Exit 23 S (Mamaroneck Ave. South)Take Mamaroneck Ave. through Mamaroncek Village to the very end (Boston Post Rd./US1) Turn Right on Boston Post Road and take immediate next right (Library Lane) Theatre is on right.

From 95 Northbound (from Manhattan) - Exit 18A (Fenimore Rd.) Turn right at bottom of ramp onto Fenimore Road. Go straight to end (intersection of Boston Post Rd./US1) Turn left on Boston Post Rd. Take 2nd left (Library Lane) Theatre is on right.

From 95 Southbound (from Connecticut) - Exit 18A (Mamaroneck Ave.) follow directions as from Hutchinson.

PARKING
Emelin Theatre Parking Lot
Prospect Avenue Municipal Garage
Library Lane Lot
Johnson Avenue
All offer free parking after
6 PM Mon - Sat and all day Sun
BY TRAIN
Metro North New Haven Line to
Mamaroneck Station
(40-45 minutes from Grand Central Station)
For schedules call: 1-800-638-7646
Taxis are available at North Side of Tracks

Nearby restaurants rated by
SEATS

CAFE MOZART
308 Mamaroneck Ave.
914-698-4166
CAFE CHAZ
265 Mamaroneck Ave.
914-381-4354

GOODSPEED OPERA HOUSE

Route 82, East Haddam, Connecticut, 06423

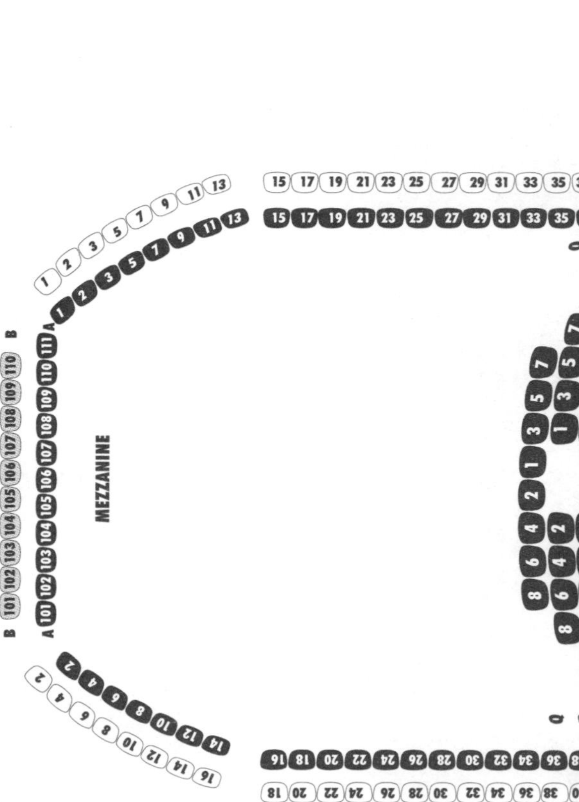

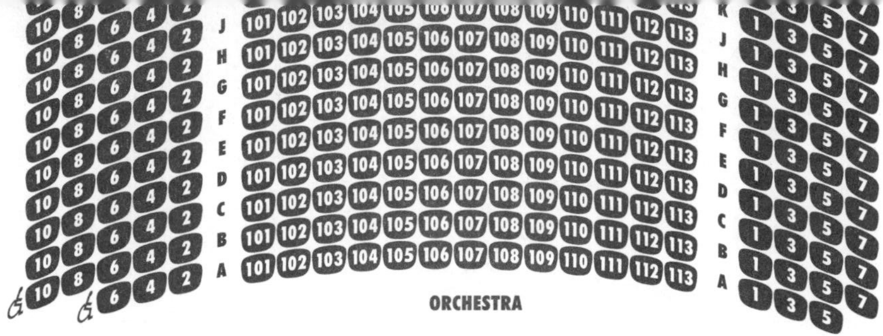

ORCHESTRA

$35.00
$19.00
$19.00 RESTRICTED VIEW

Mezzanine row A overhangs
Orchestra row N

STAGE

THEATRE (860) 873-8668

DIRECTIONS:
North on I-95 to exit 69, follow Route 9 to exit 7, turn left at the end of the ramp, at the first traffic light turn right, the theatre is on the right just over the bridge.

PARKING
Free on Premises

WHEELCHAIR ACCESSIBLE
INFRARED DEVICES AVAILABLE

Nearby restaurants rated by
SEATS

THE GELSTON HOUSE, 8 Main St.East Haddam, CT
(860) 873-1411
CHART HOUSE, 129 W. Main St. Chester, CT
(860) 526-9898

THE NORMA TERRIS THEATRE/GOODSPEED AT CHESTER

North Main Street, Chester, Connecticut 06423

All Seats One Price

STAGE

THEATRE (860) 873-8668

DIRECTIONS:
North on I-95 to exit 69, follow Route 9 to exit 6, turn right onto Route 148, make a left onto North Main Street

PARKING
Free on Premises

WHEELCHAIR ACCESSIBLE
INFRARED DEVICES AVAILABLE

Nearby restaurants rated by SEATS

THE GELSTON HOUSE, 8 Main St.East Haddam, CT
(860) 873-1411
CHART HOUSE, 129 W. Main St. Chester, CT
(860) 526-9898

HARTFORD STAGE COMPANY

50 Church Street, Hartford, Connecticut 06103

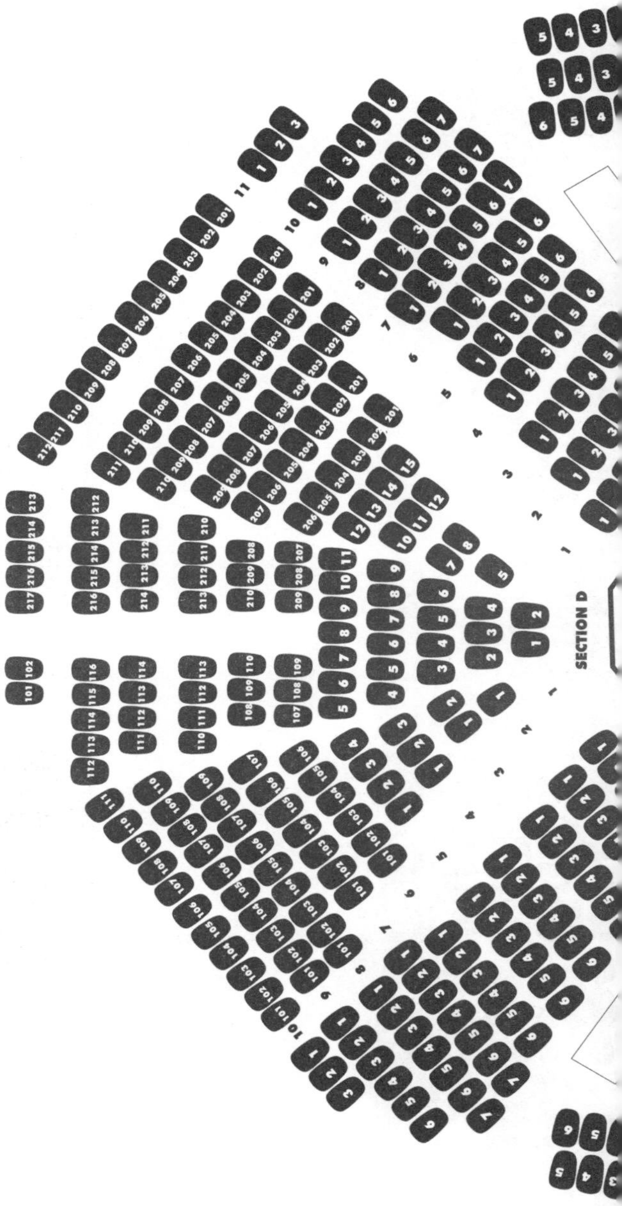

SECTION D

STAGE

SECTION B

SECTION A

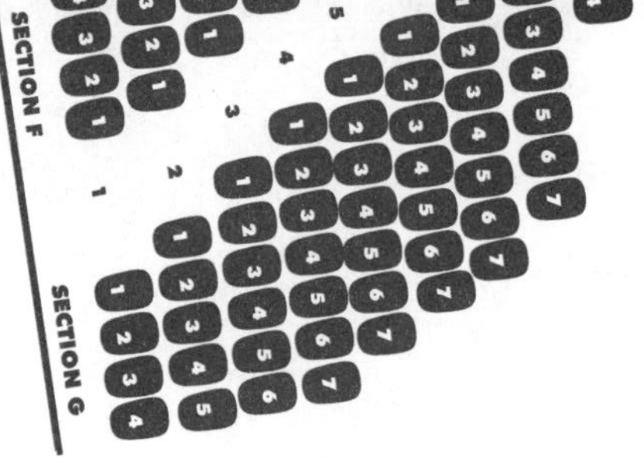

All Seats One Price
Student & Senior Discount

TICKETS (860) 527-5151
GROUP SALES (860) 525-5601

DIRECTIONS:
Henry Hudson Parkway (9A) to Saw Mill River Parkway to I-684 North to I-84 East to Hartford. Take Exit 50 (Main St.). Go to the 2nd traffic light (Main St.) turn right until you reach Church St. Turn right onto Church St.

PARKING
The Mat Garage
The Sheraton Hotel Garage
Civic Center Garage

Nearby restaurants rated by
SEATS
CAFE AT READER'S FEAST, 59 Farmington Ave. (860) 232-3710
CIVIC CAFE AT TRUMBELL, South Trumbell St. (860) 493-7412
MAXS DOWNTOWN, 85 Asylum St. (860) 522-2530

HELEN HAYES PERFORMING ARTS CENTER

117 Main Street, Nyack, NY 10960

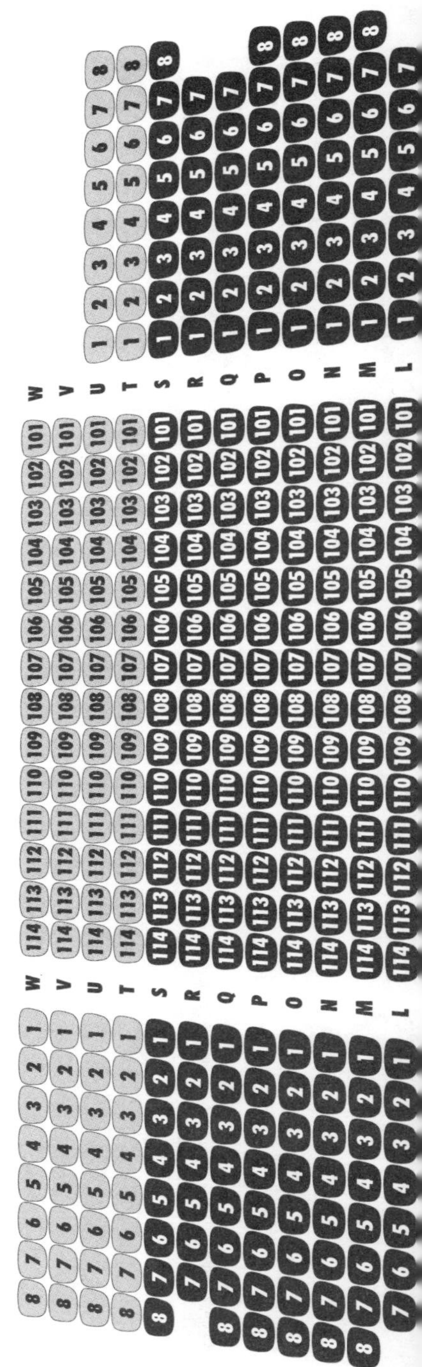

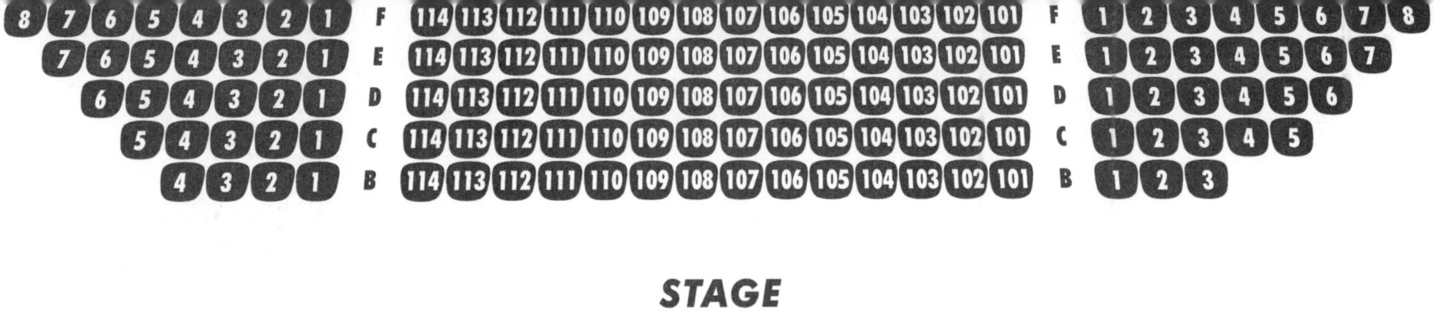

Row	Left	Center	Right
F	8 7 6 5 4 3 2 1	114 113 112 111 110 109 108 107 106 105 104 103 102 101	1 2 3 4 5 6 7 8
E	7 6 5 4 3 2 1	114 113 112 111 110 109 108 107 106 105 104 103 102 101	1 2 3 4 5 6 7
D	6 5 4 3 2 1	114 113 112 111 110 109 108 107 106 105 104 103 102 101	1 2 3 4 5 6
C	5 4 3 2 1	114 113 112 111 110 109 108 107 106 105 104 103 102 101	1 2 3 4 5
B	4 3 2 1	114 113 112 111 110 109 108 107 106 105 104 103 102 101	1 2 3

STAGE

$26.00
$22.00

Senior & student
rates available

TELECHARGE (800) 233-3123
TICKETS (914) 358-6333
CHARGE BY FAX (914) 358-5630

Directions:
New York State Thruway north to the Tappan Zee Bridge, take Exit 11 to Midland Ave. turn right onto Main St.

PARKING
Metered parking on the streets, money required before 6PM except Sundays
Free street parking after 6PM and all day Sunday

♿ **Wheelchair accessible.**
Infrared devices available.

Nearby restaurants rated by
SEATS

RIVER CLUB, 11 Burd St.
914-358-0220
SOUTHERN COMFORT, 7 Main St.
914-353-1775
ICHI RIKI, 110 Main St.
914-358-7977

McCARTER THEATRE

91 University Place, Princeton, NJ 08540

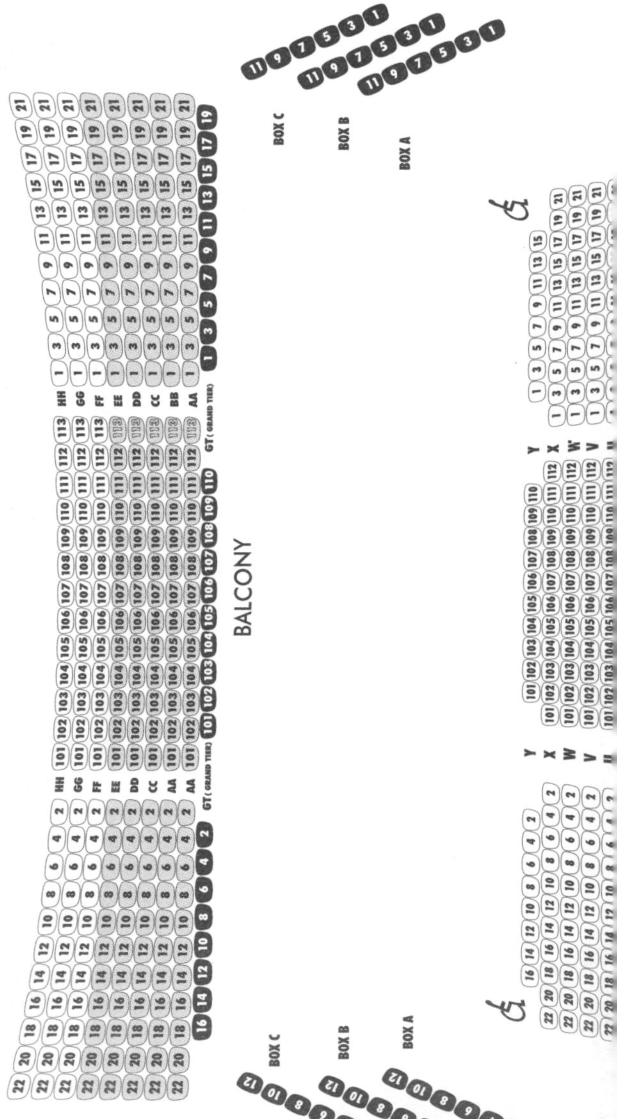

HH GG FF EE DD CC AA AA

GT (GRAND TIER)

HH GG FF EE DD CC BB AA

GT (GRAND TIER)

BALCONY

BOX C BOX B BOX A

BOX C BOX B BOX A

Y X W V U

Y X W' V U

BEST
BETTER
GOOD

Prices may vary according to show

BOX OFFICE (609) 683-8000
HEARING IMPAIRIED (609) 252-0915
EMERGENCY # FOR BABY SITTERS (609) 683-9100

DIRECTIONS:
NJ Turnpike South to Exit 9. Go through toll booth on right. Take the first hard right to New Brunswick, Route 18. Stay in right lane. Go past the turnoff to Northbound Route 1. Exit to the right where the sign says US 1 South to Trenton. About 18 miles South, Route 1 dips down underneath the train tracks. Take the next right onto Alexander Road. At the second traffice light turn right onto University Place. McCarter is on your left.

PARKING
Metered
Parking in front of theatre on first come, first served basis with handicap sticker.

AVAILABLE
Assisted listening devices and large print programs

Nearby restaurants rated by
SEATS

THE ALCHEMIST & BARRISTER, 28 Witherspoon St., 609-924-5555
CAFE NICOLE, Novotel Hotel, 100 Independence Way, 609-520-1200
KAREN'S CHINESE RESTAURANT, 36 Witherspoon St., 609-683-1968
LAHIERE'S, 11 Witherspoon St., 609-921-2798
THE RUSTY SCUPPER, 378 Alexander Rd., 609-921-3279

NEW BRUNSWICK CULTURAL CENTER

CROSSROADS THEATRE

7 Livingston Street, New Brunswick, NJ 08901

All Seats One Price

TICKETS (732) 249-5560
GROUP SALES (732) 249-5581 Ext. 17

DIRECTIONS:
From New Jersey Turnpike: To exit 9. Bear right out of the toll booth onto Route 18 North into New Brunswick and take the New Street exit. At the traffic light, turn right onto Livingston Avenue. The Playhouse is halfway down the block on the left side of the street.

PARKING
Free street parking after 5:00 P.M.
Handicap seating & parking

Nearby restaurants rated by
SEATS
STAGE LEFT: AN AMERICAN CAFE, 5 Livingston Ave.
(732) 828-4444
RIVER CLUB, 85 Church St.
(732) 545-6110
OLD MAN RAFFERTY'S, 106 Albany St.
(732) 846-6153

NEW BRUNSWICK CULTURAL CENTER

GEORGE STREET PLAYHOUSE

9 Livingston Ave, New Brunswick, NJ 08901

All Seats One Price

TICKETS (732) 246-7717
GROUP SALES (732) 846-2895 Ext.134

DIRECTIONS:
From the New Jersey Turnpike: To exit 9. Bear right out of the toll booth onto Route 18 North into New Brunswick and take the New St. exit. At the traffic light, turn right onto Livingston Ave. The Playhouse is halfway down the block on the left side of the street.

PARKING
Free street parking after 5:00pm

Wheelchair parking and seating available
Infrared devices available

Nearby restaurants rated by
SEATS

RIVER CLUB, 85 Church St. New Brunswick, NJ (732) 545-6110
OLD MAN RAFFERTY'S, 106 Albany St. New Bruswick, NJ (732) 846-6153
STAGE LEFT: AN AMERICAN CAFE, 5 Livingston Ave. New Brunswick, NJ (732) 828-4444

NYS THEATRE INSTITUTE

Russell Sage College , Troy, NY 12180

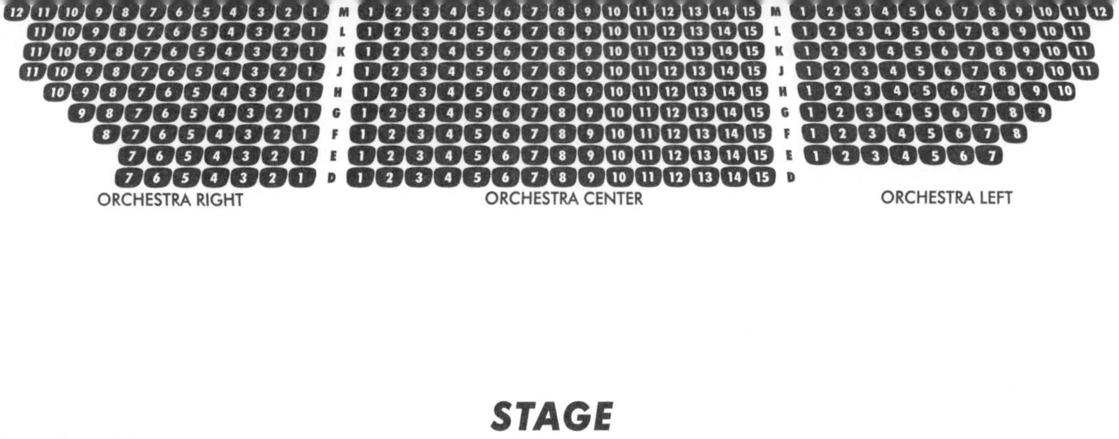

Row	Orchestra Right	Orchestra Center	Orchestra Left
M	12 11 10 9 8 7 6 5 4 3 2 1	1 2 3 4 5 6 7 8 9 10 11 12 13 14 15	1 2 3 4 5 6 7 8 9 10 11 12
L	11 10 9 8 7 6 5 4 3 2 1	1 2 3 4 5 6 7 8 9 10 11 12 13 14 15	1 2 3 4 5 6 7 8 9 10 11
K	11 10 9 8 7 6 5 4 3 2 1	1 2 3 4 5 6 7 8 9 10 11 12 13 14 15	1 2 3 4 5 6 7 8 9 10 11
J	11 10 9 8 7 6 5 4 3 2 1	1 2 3 4 5 6 7 8 9 10 11 12 13 14 15	1 2 3 4 5 6 7 8 9 10 11
H	10 9 8 7 6 5 4 3 2 1	1 2 3 4 5 6 7 8 9 10 11 12 13 14 15	1 2 3 4 5 6 7 8 9 10
G	9 8 7 6 5 4 3 2 1	1 2 3 4 5 6 7 8 9 10 11 12 13 14 15	1 2 3 4 5 6 7 8 9
F	8 7 6 5 4 3 2 1	1 2 3 4 5 6 7 8 9 10 11 12 13 14 15	1 2 3 4 5 6 7 8
E	7 6 5 4 3 2 1	1 2 3 4 5 6 7 8 9 10 11 12 13 14 15	1 2 3 4 5 6 7
D	7 6 5 4 3 2 1	1 2 3 4 5 6 7 8 9 10 11 12 13 14 15	

ORCHESTRA RIGHT ORCHESTRA CENTER ORCHESTRA LEFT

STAGE

All Seats One Price

TICKETS (518) 274-3256

Directions:
New York State Thruway, I-87 north to Exit 23.
1-787 north to Exit 23rd Street/Watervliet/Green Island, left to Watervliet. At 3rd traffic light, left onto 2nd Ave. (Route 32). Next light, left onto Route 2 East. Take Front St. Exit (at end of ramp, rear of theatre is on left corner, entrance through gateway midblock): parking lots on left.

Wheelchair seating available
Large print programs
Williams Assistive-Listening Devices available

Nearby restaurants rated by
SEATS
LO PORTO RISTORANTE CAFFE, 85 Fourth St. (518) 273-8546
ALLEGRO CAFÉ, 33 Second St. (518) 271-1942
THE ITALIA RESTAURANT, 24 Fourth St. (518) 273-8773
CAPEHOUSE, 254 Broadway (518) 274-0167

PAPER MILL PLAYHOUSE

Brookside Drive, Millburn, NJ 07041

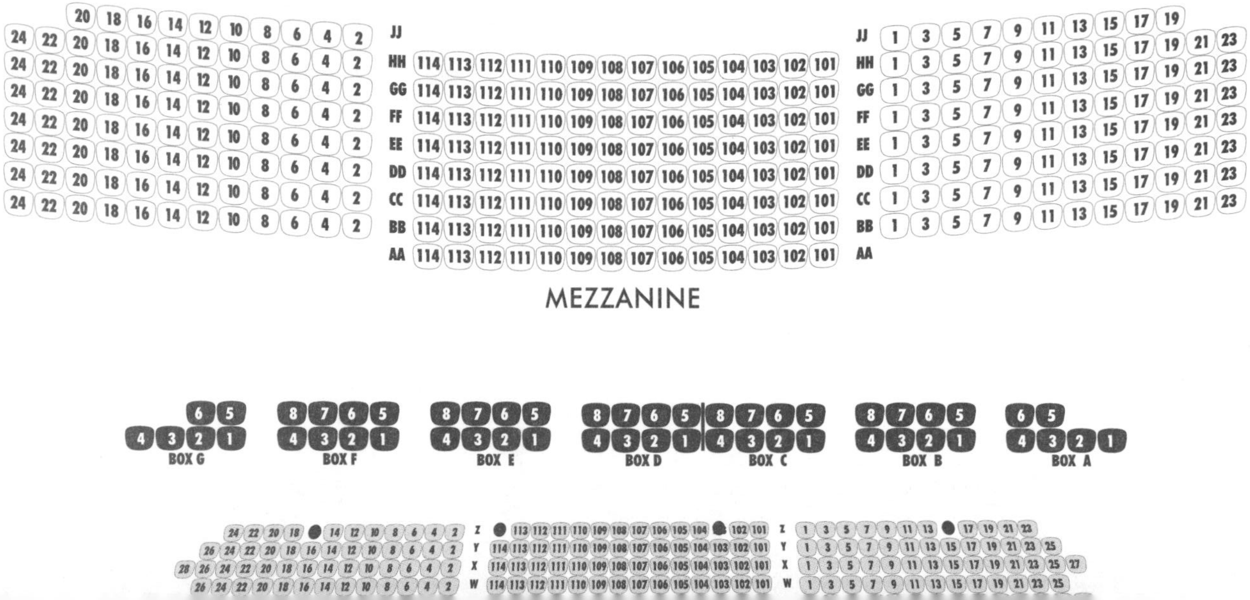

MEZZANINE

BOX A

BOX B

BOX C

BOX D

BOX E

BOX F

BOX G

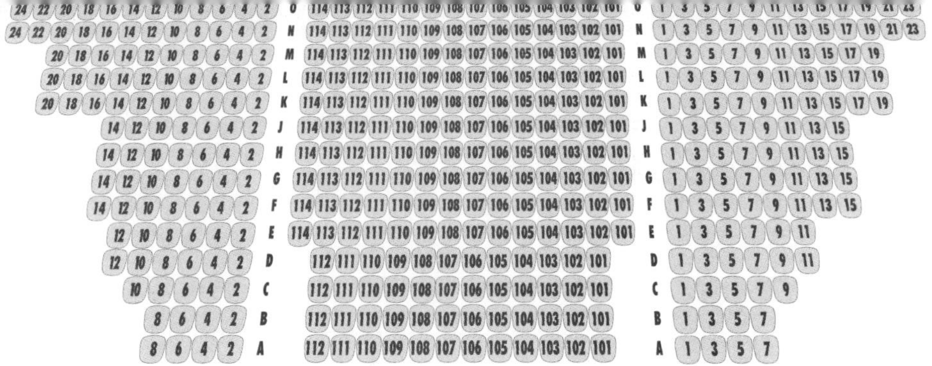

Row	Left	Row	Center	Row	Right
O	24 22 20 18 16 14 12 10 8 6 4 2	O	114 113 112 111 110 109 108 107 106 105 104 103 102 101	O	1 3 5 7 9 11 13 15 17 19 21 23
N	24 22 20 18 16 14 12 10 8 6 4 2	N	114 113 112 111 110 109 108 107 106 105 104 103 102 101	N	1 3 5 7 9 11 13 15 17 19 21 23
M	20 18 16 14 12 10 8 6 4 2	M	114 113 112 111 110 109 108 107 106 105 104 103 102 101	M	1 3 5 7 9 11 13 15 17 19
L	20 18 16 14 12 10 8 6 4 2	L	114 113 112 111 110 109 108 107 106 105 104 103 102 101	L	1 3 5 7 9 11 13 15 17 19
K	20 18 16 14 12 10 8 6 4 2	K	114 113 112 111 110 109 108 107 106 105 104 103 102 101	K	1 3 5 7 9 11 13 15 17 19
J	14 12 10 8 6 4 2	J	114 113 112 111 110 109 108 107 106 105 104 103 102 101	J	1 3 5 7 9 11 13 15
H	14 12 10 8 6 4 2	H	114 113 112 111 110 109 108 107 106 105 104 103 102 101	H	1 3 5 7 9 11 13 15
G	14 12 10 8 6 4 2	G	114 113 112 111 110 109 108 107 106 105 104 103 102 101	G	1 3 5 7 9 11 13 15
F	14 12 10 8 6 4 2	F	114 113 112 111 110 109 108 107 106 105 104 103 102 101	F	1 3 5 7 9 11 13 15
E	12 10 8 6 4 2	E	114 113 112 111 110 109 108 107 106 105 104 103 102 101	E	1 3 5 7 9 11
D	12 10 8 6 4 2	D	112 111 110 109 108 107 106 105 104 103 102 101	D	1 3 5 7 9 11
C	10 8 6 4 2	C	112 111 110 109 108 107 106 105 104 103 102 101	C	1 3 5 7 9
B	8 6 4 2	B	112 111 110 109 108 107 106 105 104 103 102 101	B	1 3 5 7
A	8 6 4 2	A	112 111 110 109 108 107 106 105 104 103 102 101	A	1 3 5 7

ORCHESTRA

$48.00
$46.00
$39.00

STAGE

THEATRE (201) 376-4343
GROUP SALES (201) 379-3636 EXT. 2438

DIRECTIONS:
New Jersey Turnpike South to Exit 14. Take 1-78 West local lanes to Exit 50B for Millburn. Follow exit ramp on Vauxhall Road to its end at Millburn Ave. and make a left on Millburn Ave. to Main St. Turn right on Main St. and then take the immediate right under the rairoad bridge onto Brookside Drive.

PARKING
Limited on site parking
Designated handicapped parking spaces available
Nearby municipal parking lot

Nearby restaurants rated by
SEATS

CAFE MAIN, 42 Main St. (973) 467-2222
CHARLIE BROWN'S STEAKHOUSE, 35 Main St. (973) 376-1724
40 MAIN STREET RESTAURANT, 40 Main St. (973) 376-4444
SERGIO'S, 343 Millburn Ave. (973) 379-7020

PARAMOUNT CENTER FOR THE ARTS

1008 Brown Street, Peekskill NY 10566

REAR MEZZANINE

MEZZANINE

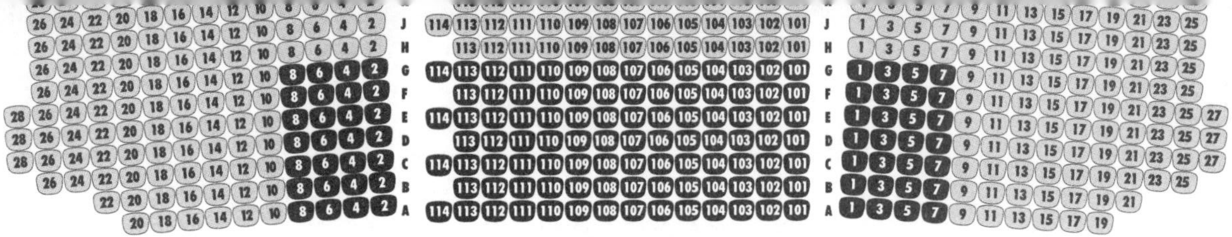

ORCHESTRA

BEST

GOOD

Prices may vary according to show

STAGE

THEATRE (914) 739-2333 AND (914) 739-2447

DIRECTIONS:
Via Taconic State Pkwy North to Route 202/Yorktown Heights exit. At traffic light at end of ramp, make a left on Route 202 West. Follow Route 202 West to Peekskill. At bottom of hill (past the Beach Shopping Center sign) turn right onto Broad St. Make first left onto Brown St. Paramount is 2 blocks on right.

PARKING

Municipal parking next door. Free parking at night and on weekends

Nearby restaurants rated by

SEATS

CRYSTAL BAY SEAFOOD & CO., 5 John Walsh Blvd. (914) 737-8332
THE REEF, Annsville Circle, Cortland Manor, (914) 737-4959
MARKET PLACE, 26-28 N. Division St. (914) 739-6380
CONNOLLY'S BAR & GRILL, 970 Main St. (914) 737-9702

THE PERFORMING ARTS CENTER

CONCERT HALL

Purchase College, State University of New, York M.P.O. Box 140, Purchase, New York 10577-0140

BALCONY

GRAND TIER

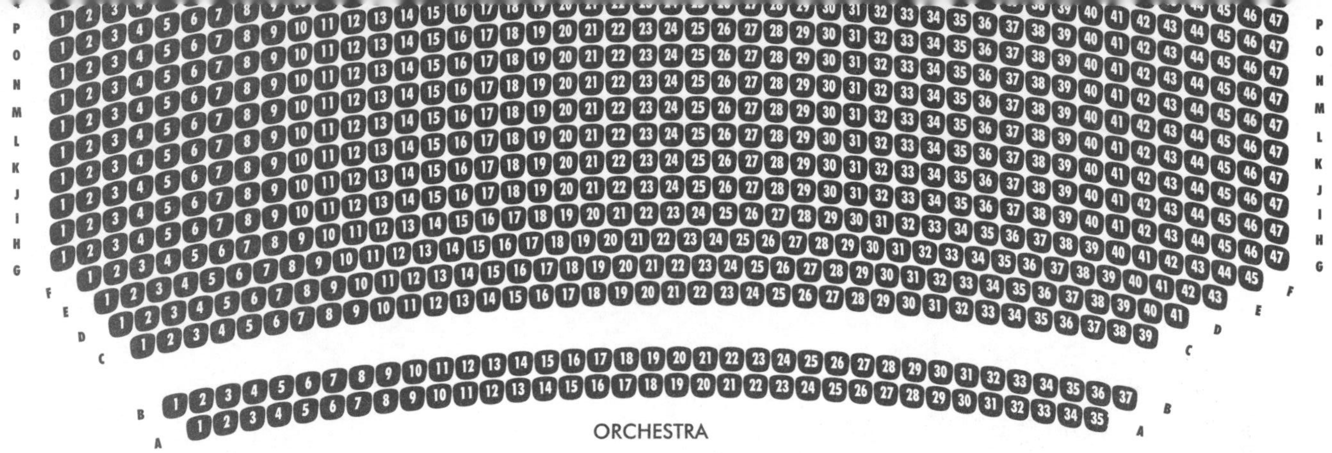

ORCHESTRA

All Seats One Price

STAGE

INFORMATION (914) 251-6200
TICKET MASTER (212) 307-7171
GROUP SALES (914) 251-6192

DIRECTIONS
From Manhattan,
Hutchinson River Parkway
North to Exit 28, Lincoln Avenue.
Turn left onto Lincoln Avenue
1 mile to Anderson Hall Road.
Turn right. Campus is on the left.

PARKING
Free parking on premises.

Nearby restaurants rated by
SEATS
CORNER STONE CAFÉ IN MAIN LOBBY

THE PERFORMING ARTS CENTER

PEPSICO THEATRE

Purchase College, State University of New York, Purchase, NY 10577-0140

Left	Row	Center	Row	Right
28 26 24 22 20 18 16 14 12 10 8 6 4 2	U	101 102 103 104 105 106 107 108 109 110 111 112 113	U	1 3 5 7 9 11 13 15 17 19 21 23 25 27
28 26 24 22 20 18 16 14 12 10 8 6 4 2	T	101 102 103 104 105 106 107 108 109 110 111 112 113	T	1 3 5 7 9 11 13 15 17 19 21 23 25 27
26 24 22 20 18 16 14 12 10 8 6 4 2	S	101 102 103 104 105 106 107 108 109 110 111 112 113	S	1 3 5 7 9 11 13 15 17 19 21 23 25
26 24 22 20 18 16 14 12 10 8 6 4 2	R	101 102 103 104 105 106 107 108 109 110 111 112 113	R	1 3 5 7 9 11 13 15 17 19 21 23 25
24 22 20 18 16 14 12 10 8 6 4 2	Q	101 102 103 104 105 106 107 108 109 110 111 112 113	Q	1 3 5 7 9 11 13 15 17 19 21 23

BALCONY

Left	Row	Center	Row	Right
24 22 20 18 16 14 12 10 8 6 4 2	P	101 102 103 104 105 106 107 108 109 110 111 112 113	P	1 3 5 7 9 11 13 15 17 19 21 23
24 22 20 18 16 14 12 10 8 6 4 2	O	101 102 103 104 105 106 107 108 109 110 111 112 113	O	1 3 5 7 9 11 13 15 17 19 21 23
22 20 18 16 14 12 10 8 6 4 2	N	101 102 103 104 105 106 107 108 109 110 111 112 113	N	1 3 5 7 9 11 13 15 17 19 21
22 20 18 16 14 12 10 8 6 4 2	M	101 102 103 104 105 106 107 108 109 110 111 112 113	M	1 3 5 7 9 11 13 15 17 19 21
20 18 16 14 12 10 8 6 4 2	L	101 102 103 104 105 106 107 108 109 110 111 112 113	L	1 3 5 7 9 11 13 15 17 19

Left	Row	Center	Row	Right
14 12 10 8 6 4 2	E	101 102 103 104 105 106 107 108 109 110 111 112 113	E	1 3 5 7 9 11 13
12 10 8 6 4 2	D	101 102 103 104 105 106 107 108 109 110 111 112 113	D	1 3 5 7 9 11
10 8 6 4 2	C	101 102 103 104 105 106 107 108 109 110 111 112 113	C	1 3 5 7 9
10 8 6 4 2	B	101 102 103 104 105 106 107 108 109 110 111 112 113	B	1 3 5 7 9
8 6 4 2	A	101 102 103 104 105 106 107 108 109 110 111 112 113	A	1 3 5 7
8 6 4 2	BB	101 102 103 104 105 106 107 108 109 110 111 112	BB	1 3 5 7
8 6 4 2	AA	101 102 103 104 105 106 107 108 109 110 111 112	AA	1 3 5 7

ORCHESTRA

STAGE

All Seats One Price

INFORMATION (914) 251-6200
TICKET MASTER (212) 307-7171
GROUP SALES (914) 251-6192

DIRECTIONS
From Manhattan,
Hutchinson River Parkway
North to Exit 28, Lincoln Avenue.
Turn left onto Lincoln Avenue
1 mile to Anderson Hill Road.
Turn right. Campus is on the left.

PARKING
Free parking on premises.

Nearby restaurants rated by
SEATS
CORNER STONE CAFÉ IN MAIN LOBBY

THE PERFORMING ARTS CENTER

Purchase College, State University of New York, M.P.O. Box 140, Purchase, NY 10577-0140

RECITAL HALL

BB 2 4 6 8 10 12 14 — 13 11 9 7 5 3 1 BB

AA 2 4 6 8 10 12 14 — 13 11 9 7 5 3 1 AA

S 1 2 3 4 5 6 7 8 9 10 11 12 13 14 15 16 17 18 19 20 21 22 23 24 25 26 27 28 29 30 S

R 1 2 3 4 5 6 7 8 9 10 11 12 13 14 15 16 17 18 19 20 21 22 23 24 25 26 27 28 29 30 R

Q 1 2 3 4 5 6 7 8 9 10 11 12 13 14 15 16 17 18 19 20 21 22 23 24 25 26 27 28 29 30 Q

P 1 2 3 4 5 6 7 8 9 10 11 12 13 14 15 16 17 18 19 20 21 22 23 24 25 26 27 28 29 30 P

O 1 2 3 4 5 6 7 8 9 10 11 12 13 14 15 16 17 18 19 20 21 22 23 24 25 26 27 28 29 30 O

N 1 2 3 4 5 6 7 8 9 10 11 12 13 14 15 16 17 18 19 20 21 22 23 24 25 26 27 28 29 30 N

M 1 2 3 4 5 6 7 8 9 10 11 12 13 14 15 16 17 18 19 20 21 22 23 24 25 26 27 28 29 30 M

H	1	2	3	4	5	6	7	8	9	10	11	12	13	14	15	16	17	18	19	20	21	22	23	24	25	26	27	28	29	30	H
G	1	2	3	4	5	6	7	8	9	10	11	12	13	14	15	16	17	18	19	20	21	22	23	24	25	26	27	28	29	30	G
F	1	2	3	4	5	6	7	8	9	10	11	12	13	14	15	16	17	18	19	20	21	22	23	24	25	26	27	28	29	30	F
E	1	2	3	4	5	6	7	8	9	10	11	12	13	14	15	16	17	18	19	20	21	22	23	24	25	26	27	28	29	30	E
D	1	2	3	4	5	6	7	8	9	10	11	12	13	14	15	16	17	18	19	20	21	22	23	24	25	26	27	28	29	30	D

STAGE

All Seats One Price

INFORMATION (914) 251-6200
TICKET MASTER (212) 307-7171
GROUP SALES (914) 251-6192

DIRECTIONS
From Manhattan,
Hutchinson River Parkway
North to Exit 28, Lincoln Avenue.
Turn left onto Lincoln Avenue
1 mile to Anderson Hall Road.
Turn right. Campus is on the left.

PARKING
Free parking on premises.

Nearby restaurants rated by
SEATS
CORNER STONE CAFÉ IN MAIN LOBBY

SARATOGA PERFORMING ARTS CENTER

Saratoga Springs, NY 12866-0826

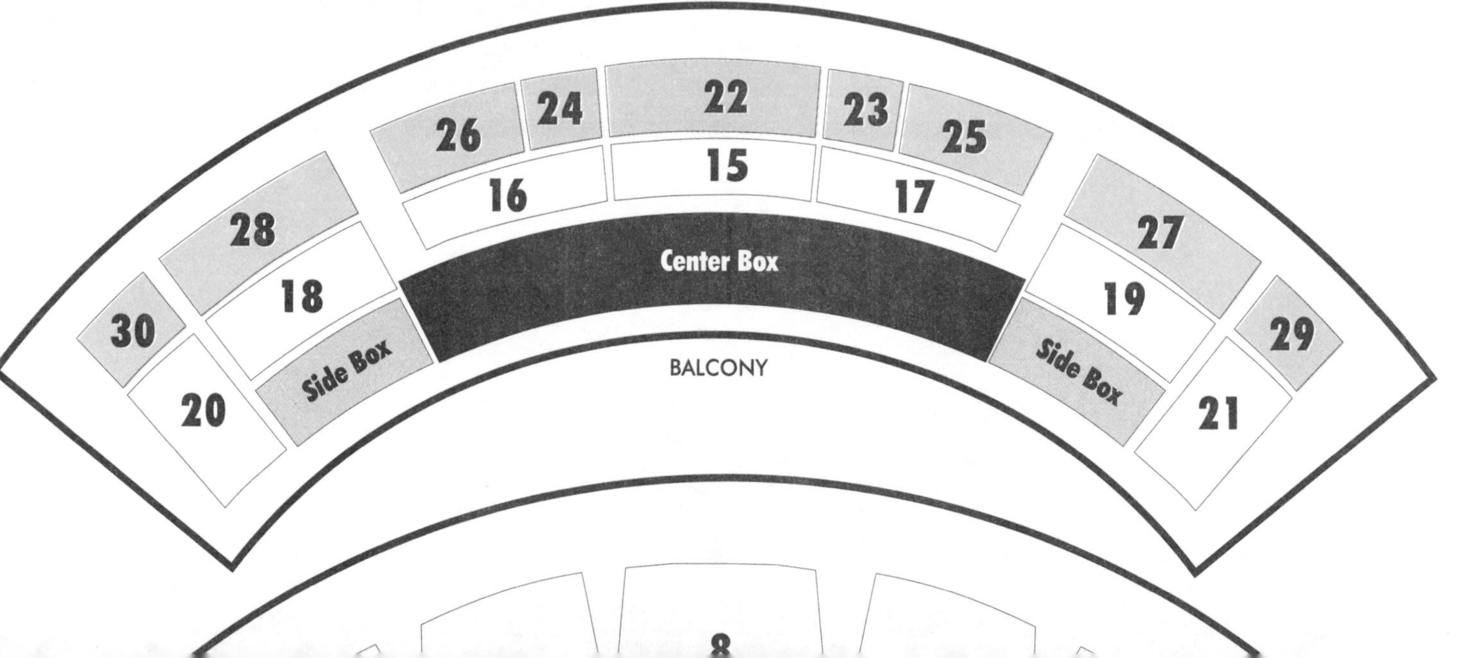

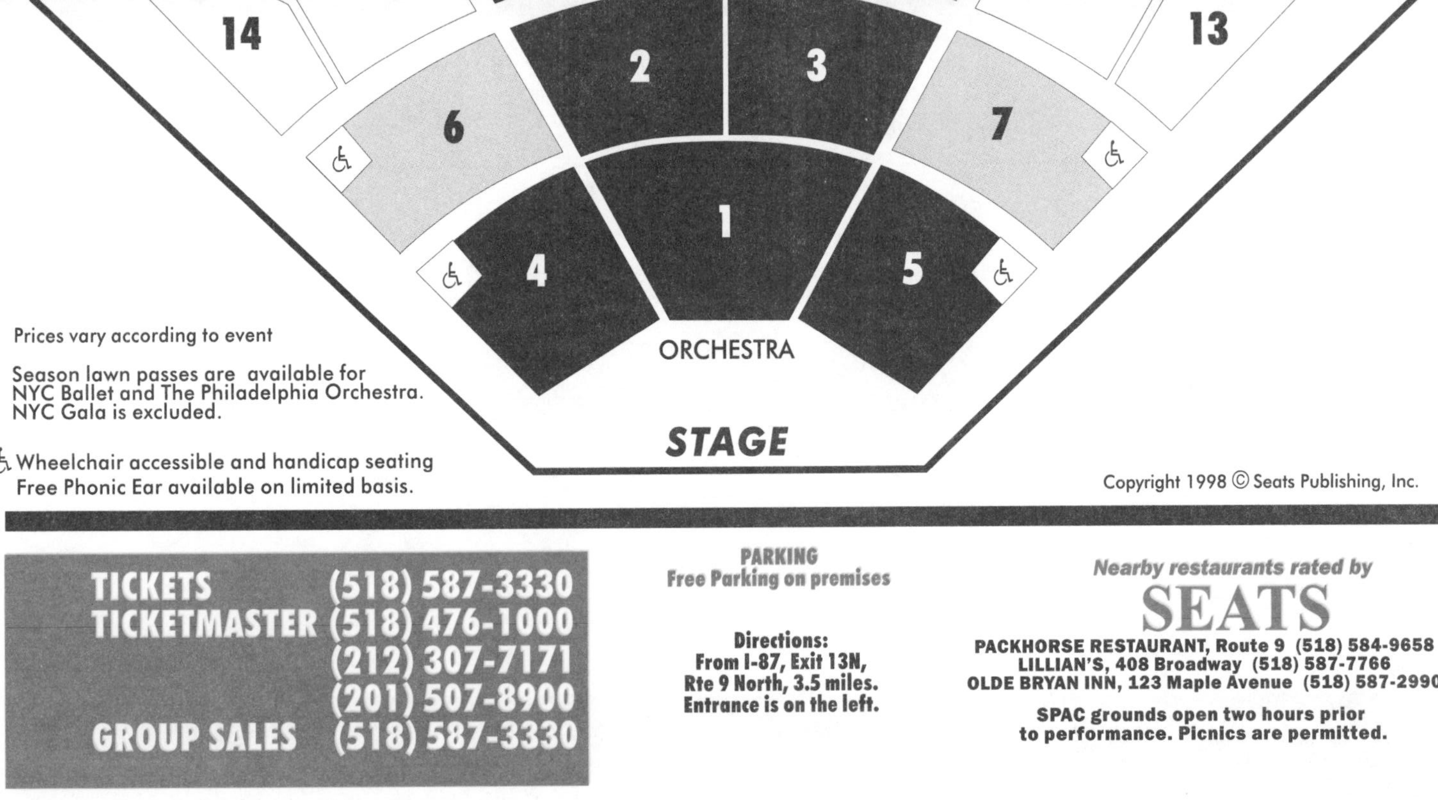
14
13
2
3
6
7
1
4
5
ORCHESTRA
STAGE
Prices vary according to event
Season lawn passes are available for NYC Ballet and The Philadelphia Orchestra. NYC Gala is excluded.
Wheelchair accessible and handicap seating
Free Phonic Ear available on limited basis.
Copyright 1998 © Seats Publishing, Inc.
TICKETS (518) 587-3330
TICKETMASTER (518) 476-1000
(212) 307-7171
(201) 507-8900
GROUP SALES (518) 587-3330
PARKING
Free Parking on premises
Directions:
From I-87, Exit 13N,
Rte 9 North, 3.5 miles.
Entrance is on the left.
Nearby restaurants rated by
SEATS
PACKHORSE RESTAURANT, Route 9 (518) 584-9658
LILLIAN'S, 408 Broadway (518) 587-7766
OLDE BRYAN INN, 123 Maple Avenue (518) 587-2990
SPAC grounds open two hours prior
to performance. Picnics are permitted.

WESTCHESTER BROADWAY THEATRE

1 Broadway Plaza, Elmsford, NY 10523

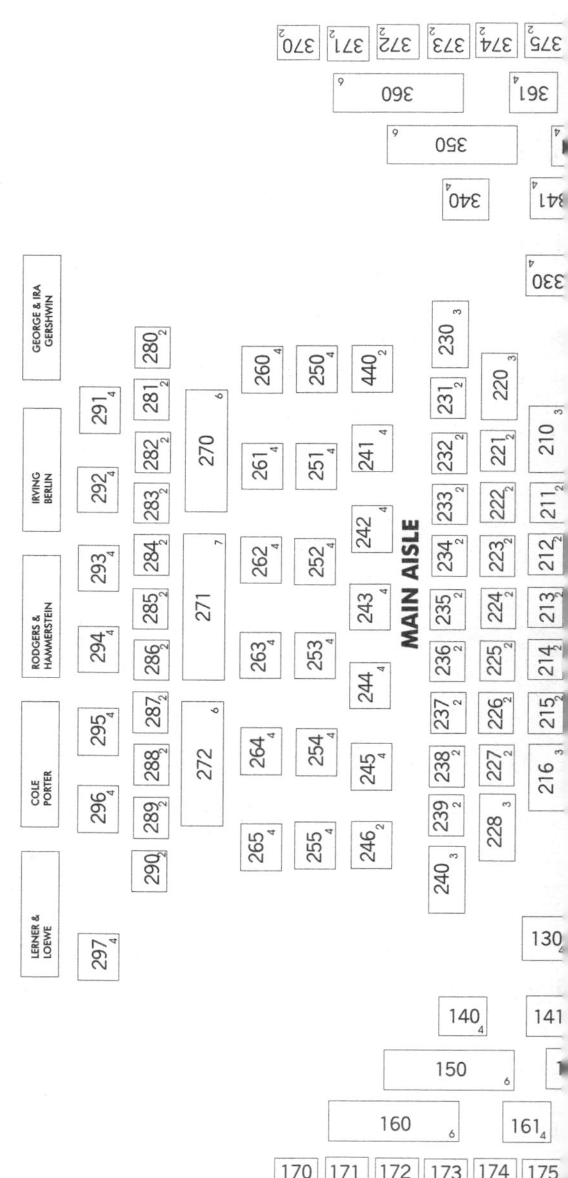

STAGE

Ticket prices for dinner and a show range between $45.00 and $65.00, plus tax. Luxury boxes accomodate private parties of 6 to 22 people. Enhanced menu featured.

Subscriptions available

TICKETS (914) 592-2222
GROUP SALES (914) 592-2225
LUXURY BOX RESERVATIONS (914) 592-8730
INTERNET: http://www.broadwaytheatre.com

DIRECTIONS:
Take Henry Hudson Parkway or Route 87 North to Saw Mill Parkway North to Exit 23 (Eastview). Make a right onto 100C (end of ramp) and go through Landmark Building. Bear left at fork and go up hill to first traffic light. Make a right onto Clearbrook Rd. Theatre is first road on right.

PARKING
Parking is free around the building

THEATRE IS WHEELCHAIR ACCESSIBLE; PLEASE MENTION IF NEEDED

CIDER MILL PLAYHOUSE

2 South Nanticoke Avenue, Endicott, NY 13760

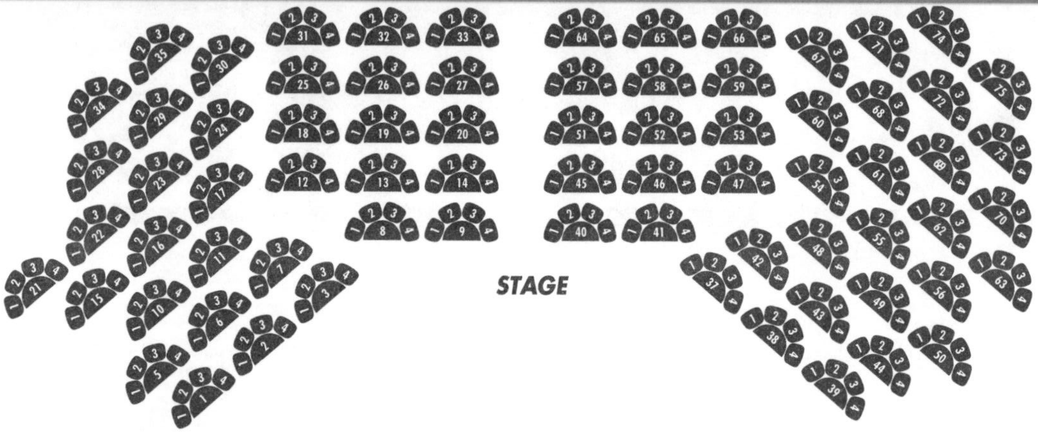

STAGE

TICKET PRICES $15.00 to $22.00
Senior Citizens and Student Discounts

THEATRE (607) 748-7363
(or visit the box office)

PARKING

Free on premises

Nearby restaurants rated by
SEATS

ORANDO'S, 107 W. Main St. 607-757-9276
ticket holders receive a discount

DIRECTIONS:
George Washington Bridge to Route 4 West to Route 17W to

CUT CAREFULLY FROM BOOK

SEATS
THEATRE CASH
SAVE
$5.00
NO CASH VALUE
O'FLAHERTY'S
ALE HOUSE
334 W.46th St.
N.Y., N.Y. 10036
212-246-8928
* WITH THIS COUPON
SEE BACK FOR DETAILS
$5.00 PER PERSON
PER DINNER OF OVER
$25.00 OR MORE

SEATS
THEATRE CASH
SAVE
$5.00
NO CASH VALUE
DANNY'S GRAND
SEA PALACE
348 W. 46th
N.Y., N.Y. 10036
212-265-8130
* WITH THIS COUPON
SEE BACK FOR DETAILS
$5.00 PER PERSON
PER DINNER OF OVER
$25.00 OR MORE

SEATS
THEATRE CASH
SAVE
$5.00
NO CASH VALUE
CIRO
813 8th Ave.
N.Y., N.Y. 10019
212-307-5484
* WITH THIS COUPON
SEE BACK FOR DETAILS
$5.00 PER PERSON
PER DINNER OF OVER
$25.00 OR MORE

SEATS
THEATRE CASH
SAVE
$5.00
NO CASH VALUE
MESKEREM
468 W. 47th St.
N.Y., N.Y. 10036
212-664-0520
* WITH THIS COUPON
SEE BACK FOR DETAILS
$5.00 PER PERSON
PER DINNER OF OVER
$25.00 OR MORE

SEATS
THEATRE CASH
SAVE
$5.00
NO CASH VALUE
MESKEREM II
682 11th Ave.
N.Y., N.Y. 10036
212-541-7858
* WITH THIS COUPON
SEE BACK FOR DETAILS
$5.00 PER PERSON
PER DINNER OF OVER
$25.00 OR MORE

COUPONS

THE FIRST TIME YOU USE THIS COUPON YOU WILL HAVE RECOVERED YOUR ENTIRE INVESTMENT IN SEATS!

*ONE TIME USE ONLY
USE FOR UP TO 4 PEOPLE

PLEASE PRESENT TO SERVER BEFORE ORDERING

THE FIRST TIME YOU USE THIS COUPON YOU WILL HAVE RECOVERED YOUR ENTIRE INVESTMENT IN SEATS!

*ONE TIME USE ONLY
USE FOR UP TO 4 PEOPLE

PLEASE PRESENT TO SERVER BEFORE ORDERING

THE FIRST TIME YOU USE THIS COUPON YOU WILL HAVE RECOVERED YOUR ENTIRE INVESTMENT IN SEATS!

*ONE TIME USE ONLY
USE FOR UP TO 4 PEOPLE

PLEASE PRESENT TO SERVER BEFORE ORDERING

THE FIRST TIME YOU USE THIS COUPON YOU WILL HAVE RECOVERED YOUR ENTIRE INVESTMENT IN SEATS!

*ONE TIME USE ONLY
USE FOR UP TO 4 PEOPLE

PLEASE PRESENT TO SERVER BEFORE ORDERING

THE FIRST TIME YOU USE THIS COUPON YOU WILL HAVE RECOVERED YOUR ENTIRE INVESTMENT IN SEATS!

*ONE TIME USE ONLY
USE FOR UP TO 4 PEOPLE

PLEASE PRESENT TO SERVER BEFORE ORDERING

CUT CAREFULLY FROM BOOK

$5
SEATS
THEATRE CASH
SAVE
$5.00
NO CASH VALUE
SHAAN
57 W. 48th St.
N.Y., N.Y. 10220
212-977-8400
* WITH THIS COUPON
SEE BACK FOR DETAILS
$5.00 PER PERSON
PER DINNER OF OVER
$25.00 OR MORE

$5
SEATS
THEATRE CASH
SAVE
$5.00
NO CASH VALUE
TURKISH CUISINE
631 9th Ave.
N.Y., N.Y. 10036
212-397-9650
* WITH THIS COUPON
SEE BACK FOR DETAILS
$5.00 PER PERSON
PER DINNER OF OVER
$25.00 OR MORE

$5
SEATS
THEATRE CASH
SAVE
$5.00
NO CASH VALUE
LA PRIMAVERA
234 W. 48th St.
N.Y., N.Y. 10019
212-586-2797
* WITH THIS COUPON
SEE BACK FOR DETAILS
$5.00 PER PERSON
PER DINNER OF OVER
$25.00 OR MORE

$5
SEATS
THEATRE CASH
SAVE
$5.00
NO CASH VALUE
STARDUST
DINE-O-MAT
1491 BROADWAY
N.Y., N.Y. 10036
212-768-3170
* WITH THIS COUPON
SEE BACK FOR DETAILS
$5.00 PER PERSON
PER DINNER OF OVER
$25.00 OR MORE

$5
SEATS
THEATRE CASH
SAVE
$5.00
NO CASH VALUE
BROADWAY JOE
STEAK HOUSE
315 W. 46th St.
N.Y., N.Y. 10036
212-246-6513
* WITH THIS COUPON
SEE BACK FOR DETAILS
$5.00 PER PERSON
PER DINNER OF OVER
$25.00 OR MORE

COUPONS

COUPONS

THE FIRST TIME YOU USE THIS COUPON YOU WILL HAVE RECOVERED YOUR ENTIRE INVESTMENT IN SEATS!

*ONE TIME USE ONLY
USE FOR UP TO 4 PEOPLE

PLEASE PRESENT TO SERVER BEFORE ORDERING

THE FIRST TIME YOU USE THIS COUPON YOU WILL HAVE RECOVERED YOUR ENTIRE INVESTMENT IN SEATS!

*ONE TIME USE ONLY
USE FOR UP TO 4 PEOPLE

PLEASE PRESENT TO SERVER BEFORE ORDERING

THE FIRST TIME YOU USE THIS COUPON YOU WILL HAVE RECOVERED YOUR ENTIRE INVESTMENT IN SEATS!

*ONE TIME USE ONLY
USE FOR UP TO 4 PEOPLE

PLEASE PRESENT TO SERVER BEFORE ORDERING

THE FIRST TIME YOU USE THIS COUPON YOU WILL HAVE RECOVERED YOUR ENTIRE INVESTMENT IN SEATS!

*ONE TIME USE ONLY
USE FOR UP TO 4 PEOPLE

PLEASE PRESENT TO SERVER BEFORE ORDERING

THE FIRST TIME YOU USE THIS COUPON YOU WILL HAVE RECOVERED YOUR ENTIRE INVESTMENT IN SEATS!

*ONE TIME USE ONLY
USE FOR UP TO 4 PEOPLE

PLEASE PRESENT TO SERVER BEFORE ORDERING

CUT CAREFULLY FROM BOOK

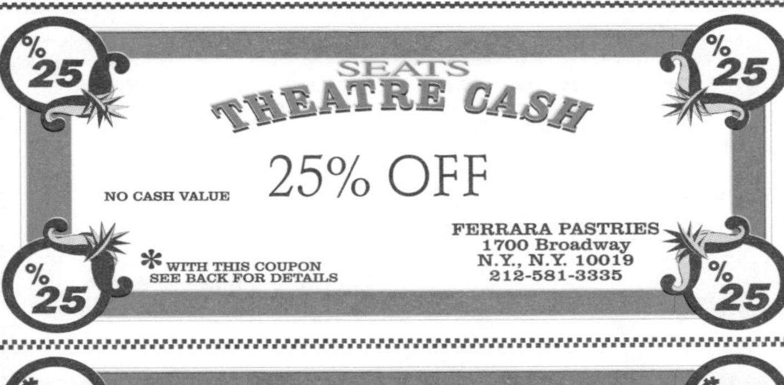

COUPONS

COUPONS

THE FIRST TIME YOU USE THIS COUPON YOU WILL HAVE RECOVERED YOUR ENTIRE INVESTMENT IN SEATS!

*ONE TIME USE ONLY
USE FOR UP TO 4 PEOPLE

PLEASE PRESENT TO SERVER BEFORE ORDERING

THE FIRST TIME YOU USE THIS COUPON YOU WILL HAVE RECOVERED YOUR ENTIRE INVESTMENT IN SEATS!

*ONE TIME USE ONLY
USE FOR UP TO 4 PEOPLE

PLEASE PRESENT TO SERVER BEFORE ORDERING

THE FIRST TIME YOU USE THIS COUPON YOU WILL HAVE RECOVERED YOUR ENTIRE INVESTMENT IN SEATS!

*ONE TIME USE ONLY
USE FOR UP TO 4 PEOPLE

PLEASE PRESENT TO SERVER BEFORE ORDERING

THE FIRST TIME YOU USE THIS COUPON YOU WILL HAVE RECOVERED YOUR ENTIRE INVESTMENT IN SEATS!

*ONE TIME USE ONLY
USE FOR UP TO 4 PEOPLE

PLEASE PRESENT TO SERVER BEFORE ORDERING

THE FIRST TIME YOU USE THIS COUPON YOU WILL HAVE RECOVERED YOUR ENTIRE INVESTMENT IN SEATS!

*ONE TIME USE ONLY
USE FOR UP TO 4 PEOPLE

PLEASE PRESENT TO SERVER BEFORE ORDERING